TOWARDS A NEW
ETHNOHISTORY

TOWARDS A NEW ETHNOHISTORY

COMMUNITY-ENGAGED SCHOLARSHIP
AMONG THE PEOPLE OF THE RIVER

Edited by Keith Thor Carlson
John Sutton Lutz
David M. Schaepe
Naxaxalhts'i (Albert "Sonny" McHalsie)

UNIVERSITY OF MANITOBA PRESS

Towards a New Ethnohistory: Community-Engaged
Scholarship among the People of the River
© The Authors 2018

22   21   20   19   18   1   2   3   4   5

University of Manitoba Press
Winnipeg, Manitoba, Canada
Treaty 1 Territory
uofmpress.ca

Cataloguing data available from Library and Archives Canada
ISBN 978-0-88755-817-7 (PAPER)
ISBN 978-0-88755-549-7 (PDF)
ISBN 978-0-88755-547-3 (EPUB)

Cover design by Kirk Warren
Interior design by Karen Armstrong
Cover image: (top) photo by Tenille Campbell, Sweetmoon Photography;
(bottom) photo by Gary Feighan.
Map design by Weldon Hiebert, with information licensed under the
Open Government Licence – Canada; shaded relief courtesy
NASA/JPL-Caltech.

Printed in Canada

The University of Manitoba Press acknowledges the financial support for
its publication program provided by the Government of Canada through
the Canada Book Fund, the Canada Council for the Arts, the Manitoba
Department of Sport, Culture, and Heritage, the Manitoba Arts Council,
and the Manitoba Book Publishing Tax Credit.

Funded by the Government of Canada | Canadä

DEDICATION

We dedicate this collection to Xwiyolemtel (Grand Chief Clarence Pennier) for his leadership in encouraging collaboration and partnerships between academics and the Stó:lō communities, and to Tia Halstad, librarian/archivist at the Stó:lō Research and Resource Management Centre, for her remarkable generosity, expertise, spirit, and energy, and to Dianne and Kevin Gardner, the most stalwart of all the home-stay hosts, for their extraordinary support and hospitality.

CONTENTS

PROLOGUE

NAXAXALHTS'I (ALBERT "SONNY" McHALSIE)

There are certain kinds of work we can (and should) do ourselves, and then there are the sorts of work where we have to humble ourselves and reach out and ask other respected people to do the work for us. That is an ancient and deeply held tradition in Stó:lō society. When one of our Stó:lō families hosts a potlatch feast to transfer a hereditary name across generations we always hire a speaker from another family to conduct the ceremony (work) and to be the voice through which the family communicates its history. When a loved one passes away, the people who conduct the funeral ceremony, and those who dig the grave, have to come from outside the family. It's also like this when we clean our cemeteries. As communities, we work together each year to clear away the brush and grass that's grown up, but we can't clean our own family members' individual graves. That history is too close too us. It's too strong. We need someone else to be in-between. These traditions show that there is important work that we need our friends and allies to do with us and sometimes for us. I see the work that Keith and John and the students do with us through the Ethnohistory Field School as fitting into this tradition. We have history and we live and communicate that history every day through our ceremonies and our oral traditions. But there are times when it is appropriate to have someone you trust communicate aspects of that history to others on your behalf. Doing it this way allows us to humble ourselves, and it enables others to see that the historical interpretation has passed through another set of eyes and ears. I understand that's what they call "peer review" in the Xwelítem (non-Native) world.

It is in that spirit that I can say just how amazing it is to see this collection completed, and even more amazing to think that people are going to be able to read the words of our Stó:lō elders, past and present, directly within the text of the various chapters. When the Ethnohistory Field School started in 1998 I was very pleased to see that the students were as interested in reading the old archival documents and listening to the tapes of oral histories recorded in the past as they were in conducting their own interviews with living elders. Ethnohistory Field School students have now added dozens and dozens of new original oral history interviews to the Stó:lō Nation archives, helping to create a repository of traditional knowledge that will be consulted by Stó:lō and non-Stó:lō people alike well into the future. That, in itself, is a great achievement and contribution.

But these young ethnohistorians have done much more than simply record and document Stó:lō history. By working on research projects that have been identified by Stó:lō community members they have helped to find answers to historical questions that are priorities for Stó:lō people and families. And by bringing their academic training to these subjects they have provided us with interpretations that link Stó:lō history to broader Indigenous histories. As I understand it, they bring insights to their study of the Stó:lō past from their readings of scholarship pertaining to other Indigenous communities, and in turn, their research into Stó:lō history can be used to help others who are seeking answers to similar question about other Indigenous communities' histories. That is a great thing because it respects the distinctness of Stó:lō culture and history while revealing things about that past that are common to Indigenous people everywhere.

One thing that the authors of these essays have done that really shows the way scholarship has been changing since I first started doing heritage research with non-Natives in the mid-1980s is build long-term relationships with elders and community members. There was a time when many students and professors would show up in our communities with their own research objectives and projects, do their summer fieldwork and then disappear. I remember elders telling me how much they resented the researchers who came to interview them and then were never heard from again. After these students from Victoria and Saskatoon have completed their research projects it would be easy for them to simply walk away. But they don't. The Ethnohistory Field School emphasizes long-term relationships. It is built upon older existing partnerships with the professors Keith Carlson and John Lutz. They have been working with us since the early 1990s and the elders know them and trust them. The way it works with the Ethonohistory Field School is that we identify the projects we want done, then we open the doors for the faculty and their students, and we know we can rely on them to keep coming back in a respectful way. The former students who have contributed to this collection of essays have come back multiple times, presenting their findings at our bi-annual "People of the River Conference," for example, where they get feedback from community members and from our staff at our Stó:lō Research and Resource Management Centre. Many of the students have been inspired to dig even deeper and in the end expanded their original field school papers into full graduate theses and publications.

One thing I always encourage the field school students to think about is the fullness of our culture and history. Years ago Chief Lester Ned of Sumas told me and the other researchers in the old Aboriginal rights and title department at the Stó:lō Tribal Council, "tell us what we need to hear, not what we want to hear." I have always remembered this, just like I have always remembered the way that Skwah elder Rosaleen George explained that it is important for us to share our knowledge with others—as she said, "If I don't share what I know, how are my grandchildren going to learn?" Knowledge and wisdom are gifts that elders have to share with others. Chawathil elder Tillie Gutierrez said that it is a sin if you do not take care of things that belong to you—things like fishing sites that are passed down within families. Knowledge is like that too. It is passed down within families and within communities, and the elders want to share that knowledge. But sharing means that both sides get something. The Ethnohistory Field School shares back at the end of each class by hosting a real potlatch feast where they acknowledge the elders with gifts. And they share back by coming to visit our elders long after the field school is over. And they share back by being careful in their research and in publishing things about our history that help other non-Natives come to learn about us and to respect and appreciate us. And they also help our community members come to better understand settler society and the history of colonialism, and that is important. So those are ways to share back, and by doing good quality research that does not just sugar-coat our history they are respecting us. The essays in this collection do that.

The things in our culture that interest me the most are our sxwōxwi-yám. These are the stories about X̱exá:ls, the three brothers and sister who were the children of Red-headed Woodpecker and Black Bear. They were the transformers, and our elders explain that they "made the world right." I am really pleased to see that several of the essays in this collection focus on sxwōxwiyám stories. And I am glad that these stories are being historicized.

One of the other new projects that I am currently working on with Keith Carlson is looking at how residential schools and colonialism have caused some of the old sx̱wōx̱wiyám that were shared by elders more than a century ago to sort of disappear. Some of the earliest recorded sx̱wōx̱wiyám are not talked about or even remembered today. And sometimes today some people in our own communities have different ideas about our sx̱wōx̱wiyám. Some of them sort of mix them up with Christian stories, and some of them sort of mix them up with pan-Indian stories. But the sx̱wōx̱wiyám are grounded right here in S'ólh Téméxw (our land), and they explain who we are and why we are the way we are. I am really glad to see that some of the essays in this collection discuss this subject.

Working with my fellow editors, Keith Carlson, John Lutz, and Dave Schaepe, has been rewarding. We all learn from each other, and that sort of respect and sharing is what we have seen happen with the students of the Ethnohistory Field School as well. They work together and they support each other. That is what we all need to move forward in this country. I like the idea behind the recently completed Truth and Reconciliation Commission. The field-school is helping to reveal the truth, and bit by bit, elder by elder and student by student, the field school is helping to create the respectful relationships that will build genuine and meaningful reconciliation in Canada. We can see that things are changing, they are getting better. But there are still hurdles to jump. Stó:lō women are among the missing and murdered Indigenous women of Canada; Stó:lō lands continue to be alienated without our consent as we struggle to negotiate a treaty with the federal and provincial governments; Stó:lō salmon continue to return to our rivers in dangerously low and still diminishing numbers after running the gauntlet of industrial fisheries in the oceans; Stó:lō youth continue to struggle with addictions and with lower than acceptable education levels, as well as with lower than acceptable employment levels; and Stó:lō families continue to struggle with the legacies of residential schools and the Sixties Scoop.

But there are signs that things are changing for the better, and I am hopeful for the future. And I think the essays in this collection, and the respectful research relationships that they are built upon, are helping contribute to a better future with understanding and respect between Stó:lō and non-Indigenous people—a future where my grandchildren and my children's children's grandchildren will hopefully be able to exercise their right to fish at our family's hereditary sites on the Fraser River, will speak our Halq̓eméylem language, will participate in the winter dance and other Stó:lō ceremonies, will have a university education, will have good jobs, will not suffer from racism, will have Xwelitem (non-Indigenous) friends, and will eventually be able to say that they are not only proud to be Stó:lō, but also proud to be Canadian. Getting to that point will take a lot of work. Some of that work we Indigenous people can do, and must do, ourselves. But some of that work can be done, and should be done, in partnership with our friends and allies.

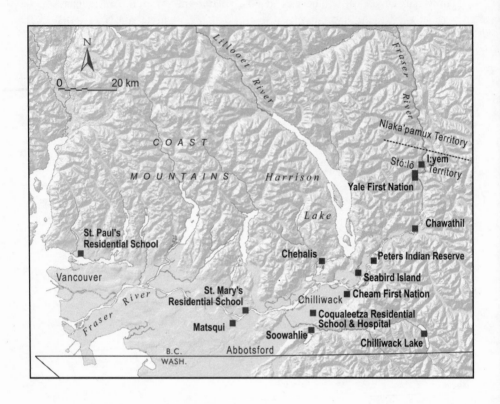

Decolonizing Ethnohistory

KEITH THOR CARLSON, JOHN SUTTON LUTZ,
AND DAVID SCHAEPE

> *To know your history is to be smelalh—that's "worthy." If you don't know your history (if you've lost it or forgotten it), well, then you are stexem—and that's "worthless."*
>
> — Stó:lō elder, Rosaleen George, May 1995

It was unusual for a witness to return to the longhouse floor after he and the other three designated witnesses had spoken, and so no one knew what to expect. Siyémches, Frank Malloway, Grand Chief of the Stó:lō Nation and the hereditary leader of the Chilliwack tribe from the Yakweakwioose First Nation, had already addressed the hundred or so Stó:lō people and non-Indigenous visitors sitting on the tiered benches that lined the walls of the earth-floor Coqualeetza longhouse in Chilliwack, British Columbia. Had there been a breach of protocol? What would bring this respected septuagenarian back to the floor of this feast, in his own breach of protocol?

Siyémches had been one of the twenty or so dignitaries asked at the start of the potlatch that warm May evening in 2017 to be formal witnesses to the work that was to be done. Each of the witnesses had their hands shaken by four of the ten Ethnohistory Field School students, each of whom included a few dollars in quarters with each handshake. Siyémches was one of only four expressly invited to respond publicly to the work at the end of the feast.

The audience had come as guests to witness a team of non-Indigenous faculty and mostly non-Indigenous history graduate students from the universities of Victoria and Saskatchewan host a potlatch—a thank-you feast. While this was the tenth time in twenty years that the Ethnohistory Field School students had spent a month immersed and imbedded in the Stó:lō community

Xwelixweltel (Grand Chief Steven Point) serving as speaker at Ethnohistory Field School "Thank You" Potlatch feast, 2015. Photo courtesy of Tenille Campbell.

conducting original research on topics that the Stó:lō had themselves identified as important and meaningful, it was the first potlatch feast this year's cohort had attended, let alone hosted, and so they were understandably anxious. Certainly they feared making a protocol mistake and accidentally offending or insulting the Stó:lō. The students and their two faculty advisors had worked hard to follow the appropriate traditions. Hosting a feast to publicly present personalized gifts to those elders and other knowledge keepers who had shared aspects of their knowledge and wisdom was in accord with Stó:lō traditions and had been suggested by elders in the community. Like Stó:lō families doing such work, they fed the guests, hired a trained Stó:lō speaker to serve as master of ceremonies, commissioned Stó:lō drummers, and called witnesses. Partway through the ceremony, and just before the students and faculty presented their gifts to elders, the speaker announced that there was additional work that needed to be done that night—work that had been set in motion two years earlier at the previous field school potlatch by Xwelixweltel, Stó:lō Grand Chief and former Lieutenant Governor of British Columbia, Steven Point. In 2015, Xwelixweltel had stood on the same longhouse floor and suggested that in recognition of the long, respectful partnership between the universities and the Stó:lō community, the Ethnohistory Field School should be given a Xwelméxw (Indigenous) name. The name given at this feast, two years later, was Xwelalámsthóxes—"he/

she who is called to witness." All those in attendance were asked to repeat the name four times so that it would settle into their minds and become familiar to their tongues.

The students were worried about violating the customs and protocols and they also had a deeper worry. They worried that in trying to host a potlatch they would be appropriating and thereby colonizing Stó:lō cultural traditions. So, when Siyémches, Chief Frank Malloway, rose the second time and held up his hand and asked, "Can I have another five minutes? I have something more I want to say," they feared the worst.

What Chief Malloway said took much longer than five minutes, and it moved listeners to tears. It also inspired a great many of the other Stó:lō present to rise and share additional reflections. Chief Malloway said he wanted to address his comments to those community members who might not be as familiar as he was with academics so that they could appreciate what it was that was different about the way the field school students were doing research. Over the past three decades Chief Malloway had been interviewed by dozens of students and faculty from a range of disciplines and universities. But these Ethnohistory Field School students and their faculty mentors were different, he said. They were part of a long-term relationship that was based upon respect and, importantly, trust. He had come to know the faculty and so could trust them to ensure that the students' work was respectful, and he could additionally trust the staff at the Stó:lō Research and Resouce Management Centre who hosted and facilitated the field school to provide the support and guidance required to make certain that the research and the analysis was always done in a good way that was driven by Stó:lō interests.

Elder Mary Malloway spoke soon after her husband Frank. For her what was distinctive and most important about the Ethnohistory Field School was the role the students and faculty were playing in helping the Stó:lō community transcend the pain and hurt of colonialism. She detailed examples of the harm that non-Indigenous people and culture had caused her community over the past two centuries, but she ended by emphasizing that she wanted the students not to feel guilty, and to know that their work was actually a type of healing, and that it was appreciated. Soon after, Elder Gerald George of the Skwah First Nation stood and said that he deeply appreciated the Ethnohistory Field School not only because the research done by the students and faculty helped Stó:lō people to both share their knowledge of the past and to learn new things about their past, but because of the trust he had in the faculty and students and Stó:lō research office staff. The Ethnohistory Field School, he explained, brought community together and helped move Indigenous people and settler society closer to that day when "things would be ok."

Many others spoke along similar lines, sharing painful stories about their residential school experiences and then acknowledging how good it made them feel that non-Stó:lō student researchers showed such sincere desire to learn both Indigenous history and colonial history. Toward the end of the evening a young man who had been one of the invited drummers rose to his feet. He began by acknowledging that he had been reluctant to attend a potlatch that was being hosted by non–First Nations people, but now that he was there and had heard about the research the students had done and had listened to the elders speak of how they valued it, he felt changed. In all his life, he explained, he had never heard elders open up and share the way they had done that night. And he said he now realized that part of the process of fixing the pain of colonial history was going to involve working with, and sharing with, people who were part of settler society.

The reflections shared by Stó:lō people at that potlatch illuminate the complexities and the responsibilities associated with doing ethnohistory in the twenty-first century, and they emphasize the centrality of long-term trustful relationships to any methodology that could lay claim to being genuinely decolonizing. If an earlier generation of ethnohistorians were principally concerned with navigating between the Scylla (rock) of anthropology and the Charybdis (hard place) of history,[1] today's cohort of scholars, represented in part by those profiled in this collection, recognize that the greater challenge (and opportunity) lies in finding appropriate ways to heed the call of Indigenous leaders who are giving fresh voice to the ancient principle of *nihil de nobis, sine nobis* (nothing about us without us). Ethnohistorians such as those whose essays are presented below recognize the necessity of working "with," rather than merely "for," the people whose history and culture they study. And they apreciate that success will require working "in" Indigenous communities and "with" Indigenous people rather than merely "on" Indigenous topics. This "New Ethnohistory" appears in a variety of forms, but each requires sustained conversations over prolonged periods of time. It is dependent upon maintaining respectful and trusting relationships built over years upon a foundation of attentiveness and responsiveness. It is constructed through an investment of emotional labour that requires outside researchers to spend the vast majority of their time in Indigenous communities not conducting interviews but in demonstrating their commitment to being helpful.

Trust and familiarity allow for people on either side of the relationship to rebuild on those occasions where things might have slipped, and in so doing, expand and enrich the complex responsibilities and privileges associated with long-term partnerships. The scholarship in this collection is a product of such relationships.

These essays are important contributions to the larger field of ethnohistory because they demonstrate many features of the new directions in the field, because of the fascinating history and culture of the Stó:lō themselves, and because the Stó:lō have experienced the ethnohistorical evolution of anthropology and history since Franz Boas first worked in their territory in 1884. The Northwest Coast of North America has been a particularly fertile ground for new ideas in anthropology, history, and ethnohistory, and the Stó:lō have been both a part of that inspiration and at the forefront of the New Ethnohistory.[2] As the name bestowed upon the field school implies, ethnohistorians are being asked to conduct their research in ways that reflect the protocols and philosophical outlooks of Indigenous communities themselves. In this collection we invite you to join us in "witnessing" a new body of decolonized ethnohistory that is anchored within the Indigenous communities of the lower Fraser River watershed.

An Introduction to the Stó:lō

The Stó:lō, literally "River People," are the Indigenous inhabitants of the lower Fraser River watershed located in what is now known as southwest British Columbia (with territory that stretches into parts of northwest Washington). While archaeological evidence shows continuous occupation for over 9,000 years, Stó:lō knowledge keepers explain that their ancestors have occupied the region since time immemorial. They share legendary stories (sxwōxwiyám) that describe the ancient arrival of sky-born heroes who, along with others who were earth-born, became the genealogical founders of the various Stó:lō tribes. In those early days, elders explain, the world was chaotic and dangerous. People and animals regularly transformed their shape, wicked or misguided Indian doctors played malevolent and sometimes harmful tricks on others, and food was not consistently available.

Into this world came Xexá:ls, the three sons and one daughter of Red-headed Woodpecker and Black Bear. They possessed remarkable transformative powers that became even greater after an epic journey to the sun. After riding with the sun to the sunset, Xexá:ls travelled eastward back to the Fraser River and its tributaries, and as they passed through the various tribal territories they transformed the unpredictable and frightening landscape into the stable world we recognize today. Their transformative feats included changing certain "Indian doctors" into stone, making a particularly generous man into the remarkably useful red cedar tree, arranging for the salmon runs to be consistent and predictable, and transforming a kindly mother into the highest mountain peak in the region so that she could always watch over the Stó:lō people and the salmon. (For more on the X̱exá:ls stories see the essay by Adar Charlton in this volume.)

There are no fewer than twenty-nine First Nations located along the Fraser River and its tributaries downriver of the rapids in the lower Fraser River canyon that demarcate the Stó:lō and their Coast Salish neighbours' territories from Interior Salish territories. Formerly there were many more settlements, but introduced diseases (such as smallpox, tuberculosis, and alcoholism), coupled with nineteenth-century colonial government policies that sought to transform fishers and hunters into European-style farmers, caused many villages to be abandoned. While all share a common language and culture, some of these communities (especially those on the eastern and northern territorial extremities such as Musqueam, Tsawwassen, Semiahmoo, Coquitlam, Katzie, Chehalis, Yale, and Union Bar) are inclined to emphasize their local tribal identity over their Stó:lō affiliation. Some tribes consist of a single First Nation (such as Chehalis on the Harrison River and Matsqui in the Abbotsford region). Other tribes (such as the Chilliwack and the Pilalt) are made up of multiple First Nations. In total there are roughly sixteen different Stó:lō tribal communities, each with varying degrees of formal and informal political and economic association and independence. Eight First Nations have come together to form the Stó:lō Tribal Council (Shxw'ōwhámél, Seabird, Cheam, Chawathil, KwawKwawApilt, Scowlitz, Soowahlie, and Kwantlen). Similarly, eleven First Nations make up the Stó:lō Nation (Aitchelitz, Leq'á:mel, Matsqui, Skawahlook, Skowkale, Shxwha:y, Squiala, Sumas, Tzeachten, Yakweakwioose, and Popkum). Membership in each of these larger groups is somewhat fluid, and each member First Nation receives slightly different services and programs from the central tribal agencies. Over the past forty years the Stó:lō Tribal Council and the Stó:lō Nation have twice merged and twice divided, and indeed, despite certain differences in political objectives and leadership style, cooperation between the two remains common.

When Simon Fraser, the first European to set foot on Stó:lō lands, travelled in 1808 down the river that now bears his name, he encountered a culture that just twenty-six years earlier had been devastated by a smallpox epidemic.

Stó:lō society in the early nineteenth century was primarily built upon complex extended family kinship networks. Wealth was equated with food resources, access to which fluctuated with seasons and according to microclimatic niches that ranged from saltwater estuaries, through riverine meadows, and temperate rainforests, to subalpine mountains. Stó:lō society was divided between a relatively small hereditary elite, a large group of commoners, and a small but significant slave class. The most valuable forms of property and wealth were the Fraser Canyon fishing sites that were typically regulated by elite males who inherited them through either their mother's or father's line. After smallpox, the next significant external challenge to Stó:lō society came with the arrival of Hudson's Bay Company traders at Fort Langley in 1827. Profound contestation over the land and resources and governance did not occur, however, until the sudden influx of over 30,000, mostly American, gold miners who arrived along the Fraser River corridor in the spring of 1858—still the largest single influx of immigrants in British Columbia history. After this point, Stó:lō people were no longer encountering sporadic events of colonial contestation. Rather, to borrow from Patrick Wolfe, they were confronted by the sustained structures of settler colonialism—a particular expression of colonialism characterized by the arrival of permanent settlers who sought to displace Indigenous people from their lands in order to exploit Indigenous resources.[3] In the immediate wake of the miners came settler-colonial land speculators and a host of government regulatory schemes, including the Indian reserve system, residential schools, and the banning of their central cultural activities, the potlatch and the sacred winterdance.

The Stó:lō and the Evolution of the "Old Ethnohistory"

In this essay we describe the elements of the New Ethnohistory, but it is important to know what sets it apart from what went before. Ethnohistory as a field of intellectual enquiry has a long pedigree. Ethnohistory's formal origins are often associated with the advent of the journal *Ethnohistory* in 1954, which in turn was an academic response to the pragmatic challenge posed to U.S.-based scholars by the American Indian Claims Commission.[4] The practice of ethnohistory, however, predates the Commission's work. Felix Braun identifies anthropologists as the first to reach out across disciplinary lines and Franz Boas as among the initial leaders in this regard. Significantly, some of Boas's earliest fieldwork was conducted among the Stó:lō (in 1884), and then, as has been well documented, Boas went on to inspire and train an entire cadre of scholars whose works collectively distinguished North American anthropology not only from what went before, but from what was being taught and practised in Britain and elsewhere.

What is less well known is that Boas's early work among the Coast Salish launched an intellectual pathway within anthropology that significantly shaped the development of ethnohistorical enquiry. Moreover, some of the most significant works of twentieth-century ethnohistory have been conducted by scholars either trained directly by Boas at Columbia University, or subsequently by one of his students. Many of these works have been, in some way, connected to the Stó:lō and their neighbours.

Central to Boas's approach was the notion that the particulars of local history shaped culture. However, while Boas's "historical particularism" alerted him to the importance of tracking historical change, his desire to recover and understand cultures in their "pure" forms (i.e., before they were affected by colonial cultures) blinded him to paying serious attention to the importance and agency of post-contact changes sparked by Indigenous people's engagement with settler colonialism and modernity.[5] It would be another two academic generations before anthropologists working in the Pacific Northwest began seriously contemplating the significance of externally inspired and directed cultural change.

The first and arguably the most intellectually influential of this new generation was Helen Codere, a doctoral student of one of Boas's students, Ruth Benedict, of Columbia University.[6] The Winnipeg-born Codere was interested in assessing the dynamic way Indigenous cultures changed in the face of colonialism. Fresh from a summer of fieldwork among the Stó:lō under the direction of anthropologist Marian Smith in 1945,[7] Codere moved northward with her doctoral research to examine the combined impact of increased wealth (associated with the fur trade) and Britain's willingness to use gunboats to curtail inter-community Indigenous violence on the Kwakwaka'wakw potlatch. In light of these developments, she argued, certain West Coast Indigenous people began "fighting with property" rather than with weapons.[8]

Joyce Wike, a fellow Columbia University doctoral student from the Department of Political Science, conducted ethnohistorical research that complemented Codere's work. Her remarkable 1951 PhD dissertation, "The Effect of the Maritime Fur Trade on Northwest Coast Indian Society,"[9] was the first clear articulation of what came to be known as the "enrichment thesis." Wike recognized that Northwest Coast Indigenous people had remarkable political acumen and economic agency, and therefore took advantage of opportunities presented by the introduction of new technologies (such as iron knives, guns, powder, and shot). These adaptations, she noted, worked to enrich and enhance previous cultural forms causing, among other things, a surge in the carving of what we now call totem poles.

Wike's thesis was embraced by Wilson Duff, the creative young curator at what is now the Royal British Columbia Museum, who carried an MA in anthropology from the University of Washington where he had studied under Erna Gunther (another of Boas's students).[10] Significantly, Duff's formative graduate ethnographic fieldwork work had been conducted among the Stó:lō over the summers of 1949 and 1950.[11] The archival research that Duff used to complement his ethnographic study of the Stó:lō inspired him to dig more deeply and simultaneously to cast his net more broadly to better appreciate the expressions of colonial-induced cultural change in the nineteenth century. A few years later he published his still influential study of the effects of settler colonialism on the Indigenous people of British Columbia: *The Indian History of British Columbia: The Impact of the Whiteman*. Not only was this the first book-length publication on western Canadian Indigenous history to apply ethnohistorical methods, but it broke additional new ground in issuing a challenge to other anthropologists to historicize their scholarship and to redirect their academic activities towards helping advance the political and social goals of Indigenous people—an aspect of ethnohistorical scholarship that remains strong to this day.[12]

Working among the Coast Salish in a similar vein to Duff was another of Erna Gunther's University of Washington graduate students, Wayne Suttles. Suttles's intellectually robust (and still underappreciated) 1950 essay, "The Early Diffusion of the Potato Among the Coast Salish," drove home the argument that cultural innovation and change was best regarded within the context of cultural continuity. He understood that continuity and change need not be regarded as exclusive of one another, and that even seemingly innocuous post-contact innovations (in this case the introduction of a source of food starch) could play transformative roles in Indigenous history without making that history a merely colonial tale.[13] What was most insightful about Suttles's work was that he recognized that cultural change was not necessarily a unidirectional process; that externally induced innovation was always tempered by the forces of internally valued and deeply imbedded cultural continuity. Four years later, in 1954, Suttles followed up with a seminal study examining the more complex factors that had led to "Post-contact Change Among the Lummi Indians."[14]

During the same decade, University of Oregon–based professor of anthropology Homer Barnett produced his remarkable book-length ethnohistorical study of spiritual and cultural syncretism within Coast Salish history, *Indian Shakers in Puget Sound*.[15] This work made explicit the extent to which Coast Salish societies could change and adapt while remaining fundamentally and distinctly Coast Salish. Suttles's and Barnett's efforts to dismantle the change-versus-continuity binary anticipated by more than thirty years Marshall Sahlin's more fully developed thesis of the "structure of the conjuncture," in which he advanced a full theoretical interpretation of cultural change that accounted for both change within continuity and for continuity within change.[16] Aletta Biersack subsequently characterized the real-world implications of this approach within ironic terms—that is, contrary to popular perceptions and many scholarly expectations, the outcome of globalization had not been a world in which the "Indigenous other" had disappeared, but rather a world in which Indigenous people have found new ways to be different.[17]

Nevertheless, if anthropologists were at the forefront in early Northwest Coast ethnohistory, it would be unfair to suggest that historians were not also contributing in important ways. Certainly, it was historian Robin Fisher's 1977 monograph, *Contact and Conflict: Indian-European Relations in British Columbia*, that did the archival heavy lifting to put historical flesh on the ethnographic bones of Wike's and Duff's enrichment thesis. But long before this, F.W. Howay, who first became acquainted with Coast Salish people in the 1880s,[18] had developed a passion for maritime fur trade history and the history of colonial British Columbia. Howay's intellectual curiosity evolved into a desire to understand the way Indigenous people negotiated modernity within the context of settler colonialism. Struck by the demise of Coast Salish weaving in his own lifetime, for instance, Howay published "The Dog's Hair Blankets of the Coast Salish" (1918), and then, intrigued by the ongoing contestations between Native people and settler society, he penned "Indian Attacks Upon Maritime Traders of the North-west Coast, 1785–1805" (1925), and, finally, a study that opened the door to investigations into the significance of cultural change triggered by the introduction of Western technologies in his essay "The First Use of Sail by the Indians of the Northwest Coast" (1941).[19]

And Howay was not alone. Throughout the 1930s and 1940s, Great War veteran and Vancouver City archivist Major James S. Matthews conducted numerous lengthy interviews with Coast Salish people in the vicinity of Vancouver, British Columbia, to document not merely their traditional lifeways, but also the history of the impact of non-Native urbanization and industrialization of their homelands. Matthews's interview notes remain accessible (and oft consulted) in manuscript form to this day.[20]

These path-breaking anthropologists and historians laid a foundation upon which today's ethnohistorians working in the Coast Salish world build their analysis.

The Stó:lō Role in the New Ethnohistory

From the late 1960s to today, the Stó:lō have taken the lead in both doing their own ethnohistories and in hiring, or in other ways partnering with, others to work with them on projects they have selected and directed themselves. The closure of the federal-run Indian Hospital (and former tuberculosis sanatorium) on the former grounds of the Coqualeetza Indian Residential School in 1969 coincided with growing movement among Stó:lō leaders to take control of the education system for First Nations children and a recognition that fluent speakers of their language would be lost in a generation. In 1969, nine of the Stó:lō bands joined together in the Coqualeetza Education Society with the goal of turning the buildings and lands into a cultural education centre.

Initially frustrated in their efforts to acquire the hospital lands, the group pushed ahead and in 1971 were among the first Indigenous groups in Canada to receive multi-year funding to start oral history and language projects. The Skulkayn Heritage Project hired Stó:lō community researchers such as Steven Point, Bob Hall, Matilda "Tillie" Gutierrez, and Mark Point to collect oral history and language lessons from fluent elders. The project transformed into the Stalo Heritage Project and eventually into the Coqualeetza Education Training Centre (see the essay by Ella Bedard, this volume.)

Accordingly, the Coqualeetza Education Training Centre's (CETC) archival collection became one of the best and most extensive community-controlled Indigenous cultural heritage resources in Canada. Years before Linda Tuhiwai Smith's groundbreaking book on Indigenous research methodologies and its suggestion of the importance of community control of research, by the mid-1980s the CETC was hiring academic staff to assist them in undertaking research directed towards language documentation and revitalization, as well as elementary school cultural-awareness curriculum. Among the researchers were linguist Brent Galloway and archivist/historian Rueben Ware. Galloway's classified word list, transcriptions of legendary stories, and Halq'eméylem dictionary have proven invaluable cultural and historical resources to a host of subsequent researchers. Publications that emerged from Coqualeetza, such as Ware's 1983 book, *Five Issues, Five Battlegrounds: An Introduction to the History of Indian Fishing in British Columbia 1850–1930*, were models of what could be achieved when ethnohistorical methods were applied by community intellectuals and scholars working cooperatively.[21]

By the 1990s the research activity at cultural centres like Coqualeetza was being complemented by research facilitated through more overtly political Coast Salish organizations such as the Stó:lō Tribal Council and Stó:lō Nation Canada—both of which were situated alongside the CETC on the former Methodist residential school/Indian Hospital grounds in Chilliwack. Here staff anthropologists and historians worked on projects designed by tribal leadership that were explicitly linked to the more than two dozen Stó:lō First Nation communities' social, economic, educational, and political aspirations. These inherently collaborative research projects were being deeply informed by Coast Salish ways of knowing. By 1996, Chief Clarence Pennier of the Scowlitz First Nation, in his capacity as director of the Aboriginal rights and title department, oversaw the activities of staff working in the fields of cultural anthropology, archaeology, environmental management, and ethnohistory. Where in 1990 Pennier had a staff of just two, by 1996 he had twenty-six employees. Parallel growth was likewise happening within both the Stó:lō Nation's departments of education and community development under the leadership of Chief Joe Hall from Tzeachten. By 1997, the Stó:lō Nation had more than 220 people on their payroll working in fields as diverse as archaeology, community nursing, and child welfare, and each department was involved in multiple partnerships with a variety of different academic institutions as well as with various federal and provincial government agencies.

The Stó:lō again took a leadership role in writing and presenting their history with the 1997 publication of a collection of essays titled *You Are Asked to Witness: The Stó:lō in Canada's Pacific Coast History*.[22] The book was edited by staff historian Keith Carlson and authored by Stó:lō Nation staff with support from allied faculty from several universities. This work took inspiration from a new stream of scholarship, led in the Canadian context by Julie Cruikshank, Paul Tennant, and R. Cole Harris. They coupled these scholars' methods and insights with Stó:lō-specific new oral history and archival research. Along with its accompanying teacher's guide, *You Are Asked to Witness* was formally approved by the provincial ministry of education and then immediately adopted into high schools throughout the British Columbia lower mainland. The following year, Keith Carlson and Stó:lō cultural advisor Albert "Sonny" McHalsie followed up with the publication of *"I am Stó:lō!": Katherine Explores Her Heritage*,[23] an illustrated book introducing grade four students to the ongoing relevance of historical traditions among contemporary Stó:lō families, and the personal struggles and successes that individual Stó:lō families face in transferring cultural traditions across generations.[24]

By the time the Stó:lō Tribal Council and Stó:lō Nation Canada united to collectively enter into the new British Columbia treaty process in 1994,[25] carefully conducted research to advance political goals, inspired by curriculum and public education opportunities and informed by the postcolonial turn in scholarship, had become the norm at the Stó:lō offices. Efforts to document Stó:lō historical land use and traditional knowledge, for example, could be more effectively and holistically done by acknowledging and documenting the impacts that settler colonialism had on Stó:lō resources and the way those resources were accessed and managed over time. Together, staff archaeologists, anthropologists, historians, archivists, ethnobotanists, environmental scientists, and others working with Stó:lō knowledge keepers and cultural leaders were producing a vast body of "grey literature"—technical reports composed for specific purposes that, unfortunately, receive limited exposure. To give these records a wider audience, staff suggested to the leadership that much of the research would be well suited to being compiled and edited into a coherent historical atlas.

The result was the 2001 publication of the multi-award-winning *A Stó:lō-Coast Salish Historical Atlas*[26]—a work of ethnohistory and historical geography built from the ground up that sought to provide Stó:lō community members with a depiction of history and a geography that reflected their ways of knowing, and that could assist in resource management. It also served as a cross-cultural communication tool that would help the several million non-Indigenous people living in Stó:lō territory better appreciate Stó:lō culture, history, and their relationship to the land and water resources of their territory. The atlas (which sat atop the British Columbia best-sellers list for many months) aspired to unsettle settler Canadians by challenging them to recognize that both the geography they thought they understood and the history they thought they had created were in fact contested. The *Stó:lō Atlas* inspired other Indigenous communities across North America to undertake work on similar projects. A decade after its publication, Ned Blackhawk, Shoshone scholar and Yale University history professor, described the *Stó:lō Atlas* as "a monumental cartographic survey ... that unlike any other cartographic study ... illustrates the myriad ties that bind Native and non-Native peoples together in the increasingly tactile mosaic of British Columbia history."[27]

The Stó:lō have also taken a lead in representing themselves and their history to a wider public. In 1994, Stó:lō Education Director Gwen Point and Teresa Carlson opened Shxwt'a:selhawtxw (The House of Long Ago and Today)—essentially the Stó:lō people's own history and culture museum—on the Coqualeetza grounds to complement a longhouse built in 1983 by the CETC for public educational purposes. The Stó:lō also collaborated in the running of a cultural centre focused on a group of chiefs that the transformers X̱exá:ls had turned to rock at X̱á:ytem, formerly called Hatzic Rock, after their staff archaeologist, Gordon Mohs, led a campaign to prevent its destruction by developers. In 2011, Stó:lō Nation and the Stó:lō Research and Resource Management Centre opened an exhibit at the Reach Gallery Museum in Abbotsford showcasing the history of another person transformed by X̱exá:ls, and in 2012 published the book about it, *Man Turned to Stone: T'xwelátse*. In 2005, many community members also participated in the creation of *The Lynching of Louis Sam*, a documentary film based on the true story of a lynching of a Stó:lō boy in Canada by an American mob, researched by Keith Carlson.[28] In 2007, Bruce G. Miller edited a collection of essays that contained several chapters on Stó:lō topics, including one by Sonny McHalsie which included the phrase that ultimately became the title of the volume *Be of Good Mind: Essays on the Coast Salish*.[29] The Stó:lō likewise collaborated with the Simon Fraser University Museum of Archaeology and Ethnography on the Virtual Museum of Canada exhibit, *A Journey into Time Immemorial* (2009). This in turn was part of what inspired the Sq'éwlets First Nation and David Schaepe (and the team at the Stó:lō Research and Resource Management Centre) to collaborate in the production of the interactive web resource *Sq'éwlets: A Stó:lō-Coast Salish Community in the Fraser River Valley* (2017). A complementary physical exhibit of the same name was hosted by the Reach Gallery in Abbotsford, British Columbia.[30] The Stó:lō Research and Resource Management Centre is also a key founding partner in a collaborative digital holdings venture of twenty-seven British Columbia and international museums known as the Reciprocal Research Network, started in 2010.[31]

It was in the 1980s and 1990s milieu of creative, applied, community-engaged scholarship that several universities began collaborating with the Stó:lō to offer archaeology and anthropology field schools. Unlike the social science field schools of an earlier generation, the research questions that drove these courses were primarily identified by the Stó:lō communities themselves, or at a minimum were approved and authorized by the Stó:lō after extensive consultation. With endorsement from the Stó:lō political leadership, staff archaeologist Gordon Mohs and then later David Schaepe invited faculty from Simon Fraser University, the University of British Columbia, and the

University of California, Los Angeles, among other universities, to come to Stó:lō territory to conduct research that would answer questions the Stó:lō deemed important and that would help advance their political agendas. Asking elders and other Stó:lō knowledge keepers to identify research projects and to set research priorities for the archaeology and anthropology students participating in the field schools provided not only a powerful Indigenous focus to the work, but also helped the students come to appreciate just how meaningful their research could be for Indigenous people. Certainly, this was the case for the anthropology MA students from the University of British Columbia who, under the faculty mentorship of Bruce Miller, arrived annually for over a decade to live in Frank Malloway's longhouse for a month while working on individual projects that not infrequently expanded to become master's theses and even published articles. To the extent that these collaborations also often resulted in participating faculty and graduate students producing peer-reviewed scholarly publications that could stand up in court if need be, the Stó:lō doubly benefited from the partnerships.[32]

Stó:lō Ethnohistory Field School

In 1997, Keith Carlson, the staff historian at the Stó:lō Nation office, approached Chief Clarence "Kat" Pennier and asked if he would be willing to authorize an experiment: invite historians and history graduate students to come to live and conduct community-led research among the Stó:lō on topics members of the Stó:lō community had identified as important. Similar to an anthropology field school, but on topics that were historical in nature, this research would highlight the assessment of change over time and enrich archival analysis with oral history methods and postcolonial theoretical insights. Pennier approved.

Other Stó:lō staff at that time, including the cultural adviser Sonny McHalsie, archaeologist David Schaepe, and archivist David Smith, talked with community members to generate a list of more than twenty potential ethnohistorical topics that would be beneficial to the community and to the ongoing research within the rights and title department. Drawing on an existing trust relationship, John Lutz, at the University of Victoria's history department, was invited to be the faculty supervisor, and he in turn ultimately arranged for half a dozen students to embark on Canada's first Ethnohistory Field School. The University of Victoria additionally provided funding to the Stó:lō Nation to release Carlson from some of his regular duties so he could serve as co-instructor for the course.

Over the two decades that the Ethnohistory Field School has been operating, the model has been adapted to enhance the student experience and the benefits to the Stó:lō community, but the framework has remained essentially the same throughout. The course operates within a long-term history of trust and reciprocity. The class is offered roughly every second year. Students spend four weeks in the field. For the first week they attend daily seminars where they read and discuss an array of ethnohistorical scholarship. During this week, they are orientating themselves to their surroundings, acquiring methodological skills and theoretical perspectives, and working to define the parameters of their individual research projects. They spend their evenings and nights during the first week billeted with Stó:lō families in the various communities and in this way acquire first-hand understandings of Stó:lō social life while building relationships that will facilitate their research. At the end of the first week, students move to the Coqualeetza site in Chilliwack—the former residential school and tuberculosis hospital site and now the administrative headquarters of the Stó:lō Nation—where they live communally, sharing meals and sleeping on wooden benches around open-pit fires inside a dirt-floor cedar longhouse. Thanks to the enormous generosity of the Stó:lō communities, throughout the remainder of the month the students are frequently invited to attend and, as appropriate, sometimes participate in First Salmon feasts, ancestral burning ceremonies, spiritual cleansing ceremonies, naming potlatches, cedar bark harvesting, salmon fishing, spring berry picking, and other cultural activities.

Striving to make the entire ethnohistorical research and learning process as reflective of Stó:lō ways of knowing as possible, the field school adopts Stó:lō protocols and integrates them into the pedagogical procedures. Early on, Stó:lō knowledge keepers such as Haytaluc (a.k.a. Ray Silver of Sumas) and Swolsiya (a.k.a. Alan Gutierrez of Chawathil) had suggested to the faculty that they follow Stó:lō traditions when thanking the elders who taught them. Instead of paying honoraria, they proposed the students and faculty host a formal potlatch feast at the end of the field school. There a trained Stó:lō "speaker" could "call witnesses" and gifts could be distributed to elders and others who had assisted the students in their research in a culturally appropriate way. The generosity shown towards, and the faith expressed in, the faculty and students by the elders who encouraged them to host a potlatch might be thought of as the Stó:lō community reaching out to help build not only cross-cultural competencies but also a degree of Indigenous cultural capacity within the academic community. In hosting a potlatch feast, calling witnesses, and giving gifts, the university representatives are not simply replacing one form of paying honoraria with another. Rather, to use a phrase that is increasingly common in academic circles, but not always well defined, they are taking steps to indigenize the way academic research and analysis is conducted, constructed, and communicated.

Importantly, such capacity building and cross-cultural enrichment is a two-way street. At the very first Ethnohistory Field School in 1998, Stó:lō Grand Chief Clarence "Kat" Pennier told the students that, in additional to whatever else they might be, they were first and foremost ambassadors of the academic world. As such they had a responsibility to represent and model all that was best about academic traditions and scholarly approaches so as to help inspire Stó:lō youth to become post-secondary students and researchers themselves. Chief Pennier regarded the field school as holding the potential to help contribute to building a future where the Stó:lō would have the capacity to lead and conduct their own research in all areas of interest to them. And, indeed, today there is a new generation of Stó:lō researchers working for their community in a wide range of fields.

The Ethnohistory Field School has always embraced opportunities to engage with the Stó:lō community. Increasingly, youth and other community members accompany field school students on visits with Stó:lō elders and cultural experts to storied sites to learn the teachings associated with such places; Stó:lō youth and field school students and faculty together embrace the opportunities that emerge from being invited to participate in camp life at hereditary Stó:lō salmon and sturgeon fishing sites; and youth from the families who billet the students in their homes during the first week of the field school regularly invite the students to attend and participate in sport and cultural activities in the evenings and weekends. Each of these represents an opportunity for non-Stó:lō field school students to learn about Indigenous history with Indigenous people, just as it presents an opportunity for Stó:lō youth and community members to learn about academic research methods and motivations from university students. To leverage these opportunities even further, at the 2013 Ethnohistory Field School potlatch, the provosts of the University of Saskatchewan and the University of Victoria both committed to further enriching and nurturing the relationship with the Stó:lō by providing funding for student scholarships and other initiatives that would build capacity within the Stó:lō community.

Change and adaptation are necessarily a part of the field school. Over the years political and administrative changes at the Stó:lō office saw the Stó:lō Aboriginal rights and title office that originally hosted the field school transformed into the Stó:lō Research and Resource Management Centre. David

Schaepe now serves as director, and Sonny McHalsie holds the position of historian and cultural adviser. Together McHalsie and Schaepe work with archivist Tia Halstad (who replaced David Smith) and the various Stó:lō communities to generate student topics and to facilitate the infrastructure needs of the field school while providing important daily cultural guidance and logistical direction. Each student's field school term paper eventually finds its way to the Stó:lō archives, along with digital copies of any oral history interviews. These reports and associated digitized oral evidence contribute to the Stó:lō Nation's growing archival resources and help build capacity as the Stó:lō engage in ongoing negotiations with federal and provincial authorities over the management and governance of the people and resources of their traditional territory.

Students consistently say that they work harder in the field school than in any other course. Individual students have described their field school experience as "life-altering," and "the best academic experience I've ever had." Certainly, their term papers stand out among graduate essays for their innovativeness, methodological sophistication, and depth of intellectual insight. Since its inception in 1998, field school students have created more than seventy field reports for the Stó:lō, and more than a dozen PhD or MA theses have been generated from the field school work (see www.ethnohist.ca). At this date, five field school alumni have gone on to secure professorial positions of their own where the methodologies and insights derived from their field school experience shape their, and their own students', research and pedagogies.[33] In 2016, the field school won a special award from the Society for Applied Anthropology for its pioneering partnership work, its advancement of applied anthropology, and its longevity.

Additional Stó:lō Contributions

In addition to being pioneers in undertaking community-based historical research, in hiring non-Indigenous professionals like historians, archaeologists, and archivists to work on Stó:lō research agendas, in publishing innovative books, and in hosting field schools, Stó:lō scholars themselves have made a contribution to the New Ethnohistory.

Dr. Jo-ann Archibald from the Soowhalie community recently retired after a long tenure as associate dean for Indigenous education at the University of British Columbia. Her scholarship has directly contributed to the field through her writings about storywork as a methodology. In her book and articles she has emphasized attentiveness to Indigenous pedagogy, and in particular to the cultural practices around storytelling, as a key to understanding Stó:lō and other Indigenous worldviews.[34]

Dr. Wenona Victor is a member of the Skowkale community and an assistant professor in the Indigenous Studies Department at the University of the Fraser Valley. With a PhD in criminology from Simon Fraser University, her research focuses on finding solutions to pressing problems facing the Stó:lō community and especially Stó:lō youth. One of her initiatives aims at reducing youth suicide rates by helping young people reconnect to the land through an engagement with ancient legendary sx̱wōx̱wiyám stories.

After retiring from the Faculty of Education at Simon Fraser University, Dr. Ethel Gardner transitioned into the role of Simon Fraser University elder in residence. A member of the Skwah community in Chilliwack, her research has focused on Halq'eméylem language programs with the aim of promoting language revival. Her research examined the relationship between language, identity, land, and spirituality, and as such, history has been a central interest of hers.

Renowned Stó:lō author and Indigenous rights activist Lee Maracle has made historical themes central elements in many of her novels and artistic works. Her first major work of non-fiction, *Bobbi Lee: Indian Rebel*, revealed for Canadian readers not only the legacy of settler colonialism but the resilience of Indigenous women in the face of adversity.

Dr. Albert "Sonny" McHalsie, from the Shxw'ōwhámél First Nation, has also joined the scholarly conversation. In addition to his contributions to the *Stó:lō Atlas* and the book *"I am Stó:lō!": Katherine Explores Her Heritage*, he has published an essay that describes the holism of Stó:lō ways of knowing and engaging the world, a characterization of a Stó:lō epistemology that treats spiritual knowledge obtained through teachings and personal revelations as important as the knowledge gained through observation, personal experience, and scholarly research.[35] Sonny has been the cultural advisor and staff historian with the Stó:lō Research and Resource Management Centre since its inception and worked previously with Stó:lō Nation.

The New Ethnohistory

The Stó:lō have been a focus of innovations in anthropology, ethnography, and ethnohistory since the 1880s and at the bow edge of ethnohistory since the 1970s. More recently, they have been leaders in many of the elements that make up the New Ethnohistory.

There is no single methodology that encompasses the "New Ethnohistory" but rather there are a series of complementary approaches that together can be said to make a break with the past and lay a foundation for new directions in the field. In turn, these approaches draw on related developments including a growing literature on Indigenous ways of knowing and decolonizing research methods, a new postcolonial literature on settler colonialism, and the growing importance of community-engaged scholarship and community-university partnerships.

The origins of the New Ethnohistory are as diverse as is the set of practices that characterize this hybrid offspring of social-scientific anthropological investigation and humanistic historical enquiry. And, to the extent that the New Ethnohistory aspires not simply to mix disciplinary methods and approaches, but rather to transcend them in order to create something new that is more than the sum of its parts, the New Ethnohistory is explicitly seeking to be transdisciplinary in ways that are similar to those that Winona Wheeler, president of the Native American and Indigenous Studies Association in 2015, has described as central to the cognate field of Indigenous studies.[36]

The past decades have also seen ethnohistory adapting and correcting its course in response to critiques from Indigenous scholars who recognized the multiple ways in which Western scholarship has contributed to the colonization of Indigenous lands, resources, bodies, and minds. Vine Deloria's *Custer Died for Your Sins* was among the earliest Indigenous-authored works to garner such attention from academics, but there were other, more reflective, works such as Georges Sioui's *For An Amerindian Autohistory* and Donald Fixico's and Angela Cavender Wilson's (Waziyatawin) chapters in *Rethinking American Indian History*.[37] In the end, no scholar in the field could escape the heat of the critical evaluations of history and anthropology that came from Indigenous thinkers such as Howard Adams, Taiaiake Alfred, Harold Cardinal, Philip Deloria, Donald Fixico, George Erasmus, George Manuel, Leroy Little Bear, Maria Campbell, Tomson Highway, Sean Wilson, Jo-ann Archibald, and Winona Wheeler. Non-Indigenous academics were put on notice that the audience for ethnohistory was no longer merely other scholars and the courts, but the communities about whom they were writing and with whom they should be collaborating.

Indigenous participation, creation, permission, and direction in research on Indigenous communities is one of the main manifestations of the New Ethnohistory, and the Stó:lō, as described above, have been international leaders in this area since the 1970s. The Stó:lō have also been highlighting and understanding the narrative and cognitive structures of stories from Indigenous perspectives—what Raymond Fogelson has referred to as "ethno-ethnohistory"[38]—for decades. Fogelson has encouraged ethnohistorians, with their partners and collaborators, to step into a world that does not necessarily "make sense" to them and do their best to see how it is ordered according to the rules of others. Raymond DeMallie, another leader in this field, strives to understand Indigenous cultures and histories from within their own languages and worldview.[39] One way the New Ethnohistory accomplishes this is by embracing what Dennis Tedlock and Dell Hymes have termed the ethnopoetics of Indigenous stories.[40] Thus, the New Ethnohistory seeks not only to depict the sounds of Indigenous poetic voices, but to view Indigenous society and history through Indigenous ways of organizing knowledge and memory, including poetry, voice, song, ritual, and dance.

The acknowledgement that there are completely coherent parallel historiographies in different cultures that have different origins, different cultural roles, prioritize time differently, and have sometimes incommensurable means of verification may be thought of as deconstructive cultural relativism. As Marshall Sahlins noted, "relativism is the simple prescription that, in order to be intelligible, other peoples' practices and ideals must be placed in their own context, thus understood as positional values in a field of their own cultural relationships, rather than appropriated in the intellectual judgement of our own categories."[41] From this starting point, the role of ethnohistory is finding and interpreting (rather than assuming) what is relevant for the culture under consideration.

Getting to a point where Indigenous ways of knowing can inform academic ways of understanding, however, is not easy. The New Ethnohistory learned much from heated exchanges between Marshall Sahlins and Gananath Obeyesekere, for example, when they argued over how Hawaiian people of the late eighteenth century understood British explorer James Cook. The central issue of their debate ostensibly was whether or not Western scholars could genuinely understand Indigenous cultures and epistemologies, but with the passing of time, the larger lesson seems to have been just how intellectually and ethically misguided it is for *anyone* to try to represent Indigenous cultural perspectives and historical experiences until those community members meaningfully contribute to the analysis.[42]

The New Ethnohistory can be thought of as incorporating the study of Indigenous historical consciousness—that is to say, how Indigenous people in the past thought about and understood their history, and how such understandings have, or have not, changed over time as each new generation acquired information and insights that could be used to complement (or sometimes supplement and even revise) the understandings of their ancestors. The study of historical consciousness owes its primary debt of gratitude to Peter Sexias and Sam Wineburg, whose work, when read in concert with Mark Salber's and Gordon Schochet's revisionist scholarship on "tradition," has invigorated ethnohistory. In combination, their work allows ethnohistory to break free of the conundrum created by Eric Haubsbaum and Terence Ranger that led many to dismiss all traditions as "invented" and therefore illegitimate, inauthentic, and unworthy of serious study.[43]

Keith Carlson's long relationship with the Stó:lō has enabled him to make some of the most innovative contributions in the study of Indigenous historiography. In his article on the 1906 visit of a Coast Salish delegation to meet the King of England, Carlson posits an understanding of Stó:lō–Coast Salish historiography that explains the delegation's subsequent account of meeting with the King, which is at odds with earlier academic accounts. In his article on early contact stories among the Stó:lō, likewise, Carlson describes how the Stó:lō differentiate good from bad history and how history revealed through dreams can be accepted as a highly credible account of the past.[44]

A fundamental contribution to the rebalancing of ethnohistory offered by the new scholarship is that it does not ask that we treat Indigenous and folk (or other non-scholarly stories) as factual, but rather that we recognize that Western historic sources (both primary and secondary) are themselves stories and need to be treated as such. In other words, as John Lutz has argued, we need to treat the interpretations of the observer and the observed as "equally mythohistorical."[45] Moreover, if, as University of British Columbia anthropologist (and one-time co-supervisor of the Stó:lō–UBC Anthropology Field School) Julie Cruikshank has so persuasively argued, Indigenous stories have a social life, the same must be true of the non-Indigenous tales.[46] Perhaps more to the point, we also need to examine them as a single field. Treating the interaction coherently means putting both parties under the same ethnohistorical lens, posing the same questions to the different sources about the relationship of myth to history, and then finding the interpretive lenses that are best suited to bringing insights.[47]

Concerned as it is with understanding the consequences of modernity and the multi-faceted expressions of colonialism on distinct Indigenous communities, the New Ethnohistory is often, of necessity, theoretical. So-called "postcolonial" scholarship, initially developed in the mid-to-late twentieth century to better understand the history of former British and French colonies in India and Algeria, not only more lucidly revealed the ongoing exploitative economic consequences of colonialism into the supposed postcolonial era of national independence, but did so with an eye towards creating scholarship that could be used to directly combat colonialism itself—what has come to be known as "critical theory."

Drawing on the insights offered by postcolonial studies, both Patrick Wolfe and Lorenzo Varacini theorized the implications of the distinction between "settler colonialism" (as characterized by North American, Australian, and New Zealand colonialism) and classic "conquest colonialism" (as occurred in most parts of Asia and Africa controlled by the British and French). The key difference, Wolfe determined, was that settler colonialism remains an ongoing form of colonization faced by Indigenous people who confront a settler society that, within a few generations, came to regard itself and its descendants as collectively inheriting Indigenous people's lands and resources.[48] Thus, much of the New Ethnohistory is predicated on the recognition that both the Canadian and American governments are settler-colonial regimes. Coming to understand the intricacies of how colonialism was deployed and the implications of this deployment for Indigenous people is accomplished more readily through the application of decolonizing methodologies such as those that are central to the New Ethnohistory.

On the Northwest Coast it was Michael Harkin, in particular, who worked to bring the perspective of literary theory scholars like Mikhail Bakhtin and the discourse analysis of Michel Foucault to ethnohistory. The dialogism in Bakhtin's work was later amplified by Lutz in his examination of the history of Indigenous wage labour and the emergence of hybrid "moditional" economies (part *mod*ern and part trad*itional*). Lutz invites us to practise Bakhtin's "exotopic trick" to surmount the double challenge of how to become enough of an "insider" to have a partial understanding of the other and enough of an "outsider" to have a partial understanding of one's own side of the dialogue. This place, which Bakhtin refers to as "exotopy," requires an acute awareness of one's positioning in one culture (be it ethnic or academic) to engage in effective conversation with another.[49]

The New Ethnohistory therefore necessarily embraces notions like hybridity; seeks to deconstruct discourse for what it reveals about colonial and patriarchal exploitation; is comfortable finding and critiquing power relationships of various kinds—including those within Indigenous society; recognizes that cultural change (even colonial-induced cultural change) need

not be unidirectional; embraces the tensions between tradition and innovation; and does not need to be reminded that non-Native newcomers are not
always the most important thing in Indigenous society and history. Indeed,
as Keith Carlson notes in his study of the history of Stó:lō collective identity,
"once history is resituated so that Aboriginal people can be appreciated not
only as minor players on the stage of Indian-white relations but as leading
characters in plays that they increasingly co-author if not compose outright
themselves, interesting images of the dynamics within Indigenous society
emerge."[50] Collectively, the work of Carlson and David Schaepe, director of
the Stó:lō Research and Resource Management Centre, highlight a Stó:lō
history that dates back centuries before the arrival of Europeans and that
persists throughout the colonial period. Thus, ethnohistory today asks us to
explore the full history of Indigenous people, not just their story in Western
and colonial history.[51]

Carlson and Alexandra Harmon have independently used the complexities of the Coast Salish people of the Pacific Northwest to highlight another
element of the New Ethnohistory: attention to the evolution and shifting
nature of identity among Indigenous people both before and after contact with
Europeans. As Harmon points out, the identities of settler and Indian were
in constant flux in Puget Sound in the nineteenth and twentieth centuries.
Carlson shows that there was no stable "Stó:lō" identity at any point in time but
rather that collective identity and affiliations were constantly being remade as
the people of the Lower Fraser River adapted to emerging situations in ways
that were consciously informed by precedents left by their ancestors (see also
the essay by Amanda Fehr, this volume). Lutz, Penelope Edmonds, and Renisa
Mawani have all pointed to how settler colonialism has used shifting racial
identities as a tool of displacement,[52] while Carlson and Harmon examine
the often innovative Indigenous responses to settler colonialism as played out
within multiple Indigenous histories.[53]

Almost since its origin, ethnohistory has been interdisciplinary, encompass-
ing archaeology, ethnology, history, and linguistics. The New Ethnohistory has
additionally drawn on a range of skill sets from disciplines as diverse as cultural
studies, law, statistical analyses, and of course Indigenous studies to work with
partners—often Indigenous partners—to discern which are the correct and
appropriate tools for a given ethnohistorical situation and then to use them to
engage empathetically in deep and humble(ing) conversations. The objective
is to better understand the history of the people with whom we research from
their own perspective so they can be heard, seen, and understood on their own

terms and not merely in relation to colonial identities and forces. This richer, expanded ethnohistory is characteristic of the essays here, and indeed, we are opening up that definition further to include literary criticism and other classically humanist approaches.[54] As part of the reflexivity of the new scholarship, authors have become increasingly aware of their analytical tools and more willing to foreground their theoretical and methodological influences.[55]

The faculty and students who have worked with the Stó:lō have been inspired by many of the principles that define Indigenous studies, such as those articulated by legal theorists Robert Williams (Lumbee) and John Borrows (Anishinabec) who have each taken as a starting point that Indigenous rights are derived from Indigenous people's prior occupation of, and special relationship to, particular lands and resources.[56] Indigenous rights, seen from this perspective, are unlike any other rights in Canada or the United States in that they are *sui generis* and as such neither derived from, nor bestowed by, the nation state.

The intellectual power and social/political potential of postmodern, postcolonial, and subaltern critiques have revealed that, despite individual scholars' efforts to the contrary, the disciplines of anthropology and history had been closely tied to colonialist projects—actually facilitating them in the case of anthropology and systematically justifying them in the case of history.[57] As a consequence, as Māori scholar Linda Tuhiwai Smith pointed out in her 1999 path-breaking book, *Decolonizing Methodologies: Research and Indigenous People*, the word *research* "is probably one of the dirtiest words in the indigenous world's vocabulary." Smith challenged Indigenous people to assert themselves and assume authority and authorship over research that involved and impacted them. She also pointed out ways in which non-Indigenous scholars could reimagine their scholarship to enable them to participate respectfully and supportively in the decolonizing agenda. Smith's book has been joined since then by other examples of Indigenous research practice. Indigenously driven research coupled with methodologies and analysis that emphasized partnerships and the co-creation of knowledge offer an avenue for extricating history and anthropology from their colonial complicity.[58]

Although analytically sophisticated, the New Ethnohistory is also very much grounded in interpersonal, on-the-ground relationships. That is to say, the New Ethnohistory requires its practicioners to make a point of visiting Indigenous people outside the context of scheduled interviews, playing cards, helping set up for bingo, helping cook at feasts, splitting wood, participating in gathering and harvesting activities, running errands, providing rides to stores and to the doctor or dentist, conducting micro research projects to help answer questions emerging from within a family, attending ceremonies, and in inviting Indigenous people to visit them at their own homes and institutions outside of the Indigenous community, etc....

To help ensure its usefulness and meaningfulness, the New Ethnohistory aspires to the best practices in community-engaged scholarship (CES). Deeply influenced by Ernest Boyer's and Eugene Rice's work, spearheaded through the Carnegie and the Kellogg Foundations in the 1990s, it recognizes that community *outreach* is not the same thing as community *engagement*. Outreach involves scholars reaching out to communities to provide them with the benefits of their research, but does not necessarily mean that the community was meaningfully involved in identifying the research as a priority, let alone in the planning and conducting of the research and subsequent analysis or interpretation. The New Ethnohistory recognizes that to qualify as truly community-engaged, scholarship must be not only of benefit for communities and of high academic quality, but it must also be genuinely collaborative and cooperative.[59] Such relationships are built upon a web of cultural expectations and social obligations that ultimately transcend the actions and the person-alities of any one researcher. For the Field School, for example, consistent, returning faculty provide the linking relationships and offer successive cohorts of students with introductions to elders and community members, and these students in turn develop their own relationships that remain connected to and are inevitably informed by the earlier ongoing relationship that the faculty and earlier cohorts of students have sustained. Importantly, such multi-faceted relationships, if nurtured, are robust enough to survive the occasional misstep or mistake.

In summary, best practice in the New Ethnohistory we have been describing includes some or all of the following:

- It is an expression of community-engaged scholarship where the research is co-designed and co-executed with communities so that the scholarship can be genuinely co-created by communities in partnership with scholars (faculty and students).

- It is a relationship that requires time to build, time to do, and time to share the results.

- It places emphasis on a methodology of sustained conversa-tion where scholars return to communities and engage in conversations with the same people over the course of years and, often, multiple research projects.

- The scholarship created is both meaningful to and accessible to the community being researched.

- It is reflexive in that the authors are aware of their subjectivity and positionality.

- It brings the culture of the researchers and the community into a single field, breaking down the barriers between the researcher and the researched.

- It embraces the notion that historiographies are culturally bound, and as intercultural research, New Ethnohistory requires understandings of other historiographical approaches.

- It is interdisciplinary, and aspires to transdisciplinarity, so that it can better answer questions and provide insights.

- It is analytical, informed by appropriate methodologies and theoretical insights.

- It is complex, realizing that identities change over time and are built within relationships, rejecting received racial or ethnic categorization, and romantic simplifications of complex societies.

- It embraces the opportunities for research, dissemination, and sharing presented by new media tools and arts-based cultural practices.

The New Ethnohistory in Practice

This volume presents a selection of the Stó:lō Ethnohistory Field School research that best reflect the promise of the New Ethnohistory. With funding from the University of Saskatchewan's Provost's Office, we hosted a symposium in March 2015, where most of the authors had the opportunity to workshop their chapters. We also invited a few of the students from the May 2015 field school to join the project.

Adar Charlton's chapter, "Kinship Obligations to the Environment: Interpreting Stó:lō X̱exá:ls Stories of the Fraser Canyon," brings a literary scholar's eye to the ethnohistorical enterprise. Responding to a request from Grand Chief Clarence Pennier, Charlton's study originally waded into the discursive landscape where stories of X̱exá:ls—the Transformers—reside to try and tease out some of the lessons they offer to contemporary Stó:lō about ecological responsibility. What Charlton found, however, was that attempting to reduce the rich multiplicity of interpretations and teachings of the stories of these sites into codified and singular didactic environmental lessons became almost impossibly problematic because the stories cannot be taken out of their anchored context in the canyon landscape. Her study illuminates an ecology of real and fictive kinship ties between stories, their tellers, and the transformation sites that are written into the landscape. Rather than providing didactic lessons, she helps illuminate the ways that the X̱exá:ls stories of the canyon serve as continual reminders of the familial obligations Stó:lō people have to the land—which is itself populated by ancestors who were transformed into the trees, animals, fish, and landscape features by X̱exá:ls.

If Charlton's paper provides a broad framework for viewing Stó:lō kinship and place-based knowledge, Amanda Fehr's essay, "Relationships: A Study of Memory, Change, and Identity at a Place Called I:yem," helps us appreciate the way individuals connect to a particular location within the Fraser Canyon—a site called I:yem, originally identified as a topic with great community currency by Sonny McHalsie. Fehr investigates the multiple ways I:yem has been understood by different people over time, for the site is a disputed location, simultaneously associated with salmon fishing and wind drying, the early Native rights movement, environmental change brought about by industrial developments, and a graveyard where ancestral spirits reside. It is also the site where, in 1938, Stó:lō people concerned that their fishing rights and ancestors might be forgotten or overlooked in a rapidly changing world erected a concrete memorial cross.[60] Fehr examines the functioning of memory around I:yem to reveal the way relationships are built between people and places, and how these relationships change over time. Indeed, the I:yem memorial, located four kilometres north of Yale, British Columbia, represents the first time that the name "Stalo" was publicly used "in print" by the people of the Fraser River Valley and Canyon to describe themselves. This is significant, as the nature of what it means to be, and who should be considered, Stó:lō continues to be contested today. Incorporating interviews with Stó:lō elders and community members, this essay is an attempt to trace the themes of memory and changing understandings of place, and the implications of I:yem for Indigenous claims.

In a related way, Katya MacDonald's contribution to this collection, "Crossing Paths: Knowing and Navigating Routes of Access to Stó:lō Fishing Sites," examines that same canyon landscape through the lens of Stó:lō people's concerns over compromises to their rights to access salmon due to various restrictions that government and corporate bodies have imposed. MacDonald's focus goes beyond an analysis of the physical, administrative, and legal issues associated with accessing the salmon fishery to examine the broader intellectual, social, and hereditary cultural matters pertaining to "access" in a much larger sense. Access to the fishery, she argues, involves matters that are sometimes in conflict with and always affecting one another. MacDonald's study stretches to encompass such culturally nuanced and historically contested matters as intellectual and social access to the protocols and ideas of tradition; access to the political knowledge necessary to circumvent, discuss, or adapt to government restrictions; and, above all, access to collective and individual histories and the arguments for identities that accompany them.

Anastasia Tataryn's examination of the changing role of hereditary names among the Stó:lō in recent decades helps explain some of the ambiguity and contestation associated with the ownership of fishing sites described in MacDonald's chapter. Tataryn argues that a deeper understanding of Indigenous identity emerges as one comes to appreciate the role of ancestral names in Stó:lō society and the colonial pressures that have challenged the transference of names and associated rights over time. Ancestral names remain a tangible manifestation of a Stó:lō person's connection not only to ancestors but to future generations. Her analysis uses names to reveal a deep, multi-layered understanding of history and, through that history, identity. Tataryn notes that individuals who carry ancestral names, and more widely those who participate in naming ceremonies, play a significant role in rekindling ethical and moral teachings. Importantly, ancestral names reinforce an individual's accountability to their family and community.

Kathryn McKay is also interested in the ways that Stó:lō people connect with their ancestors to build family and community, but her study approaches this through an examination of the historical treatment of ancestral remains and contemporary cultural heritage policy development at the Stó:lō Nation. Recognizing that the treatment of human remains is a controversial topic in many First Nations communities, her essay, "Caring for the Dead: Diversity and Commonality Among the Stó:lō," reveals just how dynamic tradition can be. McKay compares the attitudes and beliefs of contemporary Stó:lō elders and cultural workers with descriptions of cultural practices derived from archaeological, ethnographic, and historical information. Her work, motivated by a case involving the Royal Canadian Mounted Police and the recovery of "found human remains" being dealt with by the Stó:lō Nation's archaeologist

(Schaepe) and cultural advisor (McHalsie) in 2000, provided practical information on Stó:lō protocols involving the care of ancestral remains. The results of her work helped inform Schaepe and McHalsie's development of elements of the Stó:lō Heritage Policy Manual, adopted by the Stó:lō Nation Chiefs Council in 2003. Significantly, McKay links her analysis to discussions of the ongoing relationship between the living and the dead, and to the preservation of cultural heritage in the twenty-first century.

Examining Stó:lō views of traditional foods, Lesley Wiebe provides voices—or "talk"—about the value of "non-Western" foods in contemporary Stó:lō society to explore Stó:lō peoples' perceptions of twentieth-century changes in their dietary practices. Stó:lō people's discussion of the historic shift from a "traditional" to "store-bought" diet reveals attitudes towards cross-cultural exchange within the context of colonial power relationships. Stó:lō elders and community members emphasized the nutritional and even spiritual superiority of Indigenous vs. "store-bought" foods. In some cases, however, certain "Western" foods have been acceptably used in traditional contexts. The fluidity and multiplex nature of such "talk" about food defies academics' previous attempts to characterize this twentieth-century transition as either wholly a scenario of decline or a testament to the "power" of Stó:lō traditional knowledge. The discourse surrounding traditional as opposed to "store-bought" foods among the Stó:lō comprises a set of historical understandings in continual dialogue with the present. Wiebe's focus on food provides a common ground that elucidates cultural differences as well as historical power plays.

History and culture are likewise the focus of Ella Bedard's chapter in this collection. Bedard provides a history of the efforts by Stó:lō women and men in the early 1970s to not only research Stó:lō history and culture, but to exercise control over the process and results of that research. The Skulkayn Heritage Project, later called the Stalo Heritage Project was, in some ways, a beneficiary of the shift in government funding priorities following the universal condemnation of the federal government's 1969 White Paper.[61] Indeed, the Skulkayn/ Stalo Heritage Project (initiated in 1971) was one of the first Indigenous-run cultural education projects to receive funding from the British Columbia government. For the Stó:lō people who spearheaded the initiative, the idea that heritage research and cultural revival were essential to the protection of Indigenous rights was a given. Indeed, the pan-Indian discourse of cultural rejuvenation served to galvanize Stó:lō people in defence of their rights and title. Bedard reveals that, to the organizers and workers of the Skulkayn/Stalo History Project, the goal of facilitating intergenerational cultural transference was regarded as requiring the reclamation of authority over knowledge. Shared efforts to further these goals served to foster a meaningful, historically based sense of collective Stó:lō identity rooted in the region's landscape.

Cultural change and innovation is also the theme, albeit in a different direction, of Christopher Marsh's essay. Marsh takes inspiration not only from Stó:lō mixed martial artists (MMA) like Darwin Douglas, but also from Philip Deloria's remarkable book, *Indians in Unexpected Places*.[62] Marsh was invited by Douglas to research the history of his community's engagement in boxing—the "manly art of self defence," as expressed in the Marquis of Queensberry rules. His chapter, "Totem Tigers and Salish Sluggers: A History of Boxing in Stó:lō Territory, 1912–1985," reveals the centrality of sports to Stó:lō people, and especially to young Stó:lō men, who found in boxing an arena where they could compete with and against non-Indigenous people in a manner that reinforced pride in their own cultural traditions. And, as the retired boxers that Marsh interviewed explained, being a good boxer not only gave one status and prestige within Stó:lō society, it also enabled one to contest many of the negative stereotypes non-Indigenous people applied to Stó:lō people in the mid-twentieth century.

Colin Osmond's study of logging in Stó:lō history and historical consciousness likewise tells the story of a largely overlooked aspect of Indigenous history: Stó:lō men's participation in the logging industry. His chapter, "'I was born a logger': Stó:lō Identities Forged in the Forest," examines the way retired Stó:lō loggers remember their careers as highball fallers and chokermen in the forest industry. He also interrogates the way these men associated their employment in this hypermasculine industry as providing them with a means of escaping aspects of the racism directed at most Coast Salish people in the mid-twentieth century. In part a reaction to some earlier scholarship that depicted West Coast Indigenous men as reluctant and largely transient loggers who participated in the clear cutting of forests despite their inherently environmentalist opposition to the commodification of trees, Osmond gives voice to Stó:lō loggers who tell a story that is much more complicated and nuanced, and that ultimately helps depict the complex humanity associated with Indigenous identity in the modern era.

Wrapping up this collection is an essay by Noah Miller that speaks to the way micronarratives and macronarratives challenge one another not only within scholarship, but within the context of Indigenous historical consciousness. His thoughtful argument in "'They're Always Looking for the Bad Stuff': Rediscovering the Stories of Coqualeetza Indian Hospital with Fresh Eyes and

Ears" is that ethnohistory can provide a balance to some of the more ideologi-cally driven postcolonial studies that worked to portray cultural binaries even as they worked to break down earlier stereotypes. In responding to Chief Frank Malloway's critique of the assumptions that underlay the perspectives of some of the academics who have interviewed him in the past, Miller reveals the benefits of careful listening as a methodology, particularly as a means to allow the listener to attend to the submerged voices that sometimes run contrary to those highlighted in academic discourse. In Miller's article, federally run seg-regated Indian tuberculosis hospitals cease to be mere tools of colonialism for the simple reason that they were spaces where Indigenous people lived portions of their complex lives. As such, while there is no denying that they were sites of oppression, they were also, to Stó:lō people, sites where they went to get well, sites where they sometimes met caring doctors and nurses, sites where they gave birth, sites where they met other Indigenous people from throughout the province and built lasting friendships and alliances, and therefore complicated sites that tell an important part of their history.

At the end of this volume readers will find a short, crisply worded afterword by University of Alberta Indigenous studies scholar Adam Gaudry. Adam is at the forefront of efforts within Canadian universities to shift not only the location of learning away from the university campus and onto the land of First Nation and Metis communities, but to do so in ways that meaningfully build capacity within those communities. With Elaine Alexie and a team of community-based knowledge keepers from the Teetl'it Zheh community, he has recently launched a land-based "bush-camp learning initiative." We invited him to read over the manuscript of this book and to provide us with a reflection on the work that is being accomplished through and with the Stó:lō Ethnohistory Field School. His contribution helps to highlight the major trends, challenges, and opportunities facing scholars and Indigenous communities as they explore new ways to partner into the future.

Collectively, the New Ethnohistory depicted in these essays speaks to intimate local Stó:lō concerns, but in ways that illuminate larger intellectual and social issues. We started this essay with a quote from the late Stó:lō elder Rosaleen George highlighting the importance of historical knowledge to Stó:lō people's sense of place, identity, and belonging. Those who know their history, Rosaleen explained, have worth. They know where they come from, they know who they come from, and through that knowledge they secure their position within their family and their broader community. In helping co-create new forms and expressions of historical knowledge in partnership with Stó:lō community members, the new ethnohistorians featured in this collection are helping Stó:lō knowledge keepers secure an anchor that their descendants will be able to use—an anchor located somewhere in the waters between the rock of ancestral tradition and the hard place of settler colonialism.

Notes

1   Homer's *The Odyssey* describes Scylla and Charybdis, two sea monsters situated on opposite sides of the Strait of Messina between Sicily and Italy posing an inescapable threat to passing sailors. Scylla lived in a rock and ate sailors, but avoiding her meant being sucked up in the whirlpool created by Charybdis and vice versa. The Stó:lō have their own version: in heading into the Fraser Canyon fishery they have to avoid S'ch'e:il, wife of X̱éylx̱elemòs, who manifests as a whirlpool, and X̱éylx̱elemòs himself, a medicine man who was transformed into a giant rock, also known as Lady Franklin Rock. Sebastian Felix Braun argues it remains commonplace for too many anthropologists and historians to "distrust the use of the other's methodologies and, therefore, often appropriate it in such a way as to eliminate any potential threat. This leaves them comfortably grounded in disciplinary perspectives but also eliminates the valuable contributions to and critiques of these perspectives. It prevents an engagement of alternative narratives on their own terms." See Sebastian Felix Braun, ed., *Transforming Ethnohistories: Narrative, Meaning, and Community* (Norman: University of Oklahoma Press, 2013), 5.

2   Marie Mauzé, Michael E. Harkin, and Sergei Kan, eds., *Coming to Shore: Northwest Coast Ethnology, Traditions, and Visions* (Lincoln, NE: University of Nebraska Press, 2004).

3   See Patrick Wolfe, "Settler Colonialism and the Elimination of the Native," *Journal of Genocidal Research*, 8, no. 4 (December 2006): 387–409.

4   See, for example, Helen Hornbeck Tanner, "In the Arena: An Expert Witness View of the Indian Claims Commission," in *Beyond Red Power: American Indian Politics and Activism since 1900*, eds. Daniel M. Cobb and Loretta Fowler (Santa Fe: SAR Press, 2007), 178–200; and Michael Harkin, "Ethnohistory's Ethnohistory: Creating a Discipline from the Ground Up," *Social Science History*, 34, no. 2 (Summer 2010): 113–28.

5   Patrick Wolfe, *Settler Colonialism and the Transformation of Anthropology: The Politics and Poetics of an Ethnographic Event* (New York: Cassell, 1999); Lorenzo Varacini, *Settler Colonialism: A Theoretical Overview* (New York: Palgrave Macmillan, 2010).

6   Benedict studied under Boas at Columbia, graduating with a PhD in 1923.

7   Smith had likewise been a graduate student of Benedict's at Columbia, receiving her PhD in 1938. She went on to become president of the American Ethnological Society.

8   Helen Codere, *Fighting with Property: A Study of Kwakiutl Potlatching and Warfare, 1792–1930* (1950; repr., Seattle: University of Washington Press, 1966). This gloss sums up a major shift but the Kwakwaka'wakw had also competed with each other through the potlatch before the arrival of Europeans.

9   Joyce A. Wike, "The Effect of the Maritime Fur Trade on Northwest Coast Indian Society" (PhD diss., Columbia University, 1951).

10 Gunther received her MA in anthropology from Columbia University in 1920, having been mentored by Franz Boas.

11 Duff's MA thesis was subsequently published as Wilson Duff, *The Upper Stalo Indians of the Fraser Valley, British Columbia*, Anthropology in British Columbia. Memoir No. 1 (Victoria: British Columbia Provincial Museum, 1952).

12 Wilson Duff, *The Indian History of British Columbia: The Impact of the Whiteman*, Anthropology in British Columbia Memoir No. 5 (Victoria: Royal British Columbia Museum, 1964). Notably, Wike tempered some of her earlier arguments in a 1958 article, "Problems in Fur Trade Analysis: The Northwest Coast," *American Anthropologist* 60 (1958): 86–101. While the "enrichment thesis" has largely been superseded, it started serious engagement with Indigenous cultural responses to colonialism.

13 Wayne Suttles, "The Early Diffusion of the Potato among the Coast Salish," *Southwestern Journal of Anthropology*, 7, no. 3 (Autumn, 1951): 272–88.

14 Wayne Suttles, "Post-contact Change Among the Lummi Indians," *British Columbia Historical Quarterly*, 18, no. 1–2 (Jan–April 1954): 29–102.

15 Homer Barnett, *Indian Shakers: A Messianic Cult of the Pacific Northwest* (Carbondale: Southern Illinois University Press, 1957).

16 Marshall Sahlins, *Islands of History* (Chicago: University of Chicago Press, 1985).

17 Aletta Biersack, "Introduction," in *Clio In Oceania: Toward a Historical Anthropology*, ed. Aletta Biersack (Washington, DC: Smithsonian Institution Press, 1990), 14.

18 Howay became acquainted with the Coast Salish while working as a schoolteacher and living adjacent to the Tsawwassen and Semiahmoo communities near the mouth of the Fraser River.

19 F.W. Howay, "The Dog's Hair Blankets of the Coast Salish," *Western Historical Quarterly* 9 (April 1918): 83–92; F.W. Howay, "Indian Attacks Upon Maritime Traders of the North-west Coast, 1785–1805," *Canadian Historical Review* 6, no. 4 (1925): 287–309; F.W. Howay, "The First Use of Sail by the Indians of the Northwest Coast," *American Neptune*, 1 (October 1941): 374–80.

20 All of the notes from Major Matthews's interviews have now been transcribed and made available as digital files on the City of Vancouver Archives website: http://former.vancouver.ca/ctyclerk/archives/digitized/EarlyVan/index.htm. See also Daphne Sleigh, *The Man Who Saved Vancouver: Major James Skitt Matthews* (Vancouver: Heritage House, 2008).

21 Reuben M. Ware, *Five Issues, Five Battlegrounds: An Introduction to the History of Indian Fishing in British Columbia, 1850–1930* (Sardis, BC: Coqualeetza Education Training Centre for the Stó:lō Nation, 1983).

22 Keith Thor Carlson, ed., *You Are Asked to Witness: The Stó:lō in Canada's Pacific Coast History* (Chilliwack, BC: Stó:lō Heritage Trust, 1997).

23 Keith Thor Carlson with Albert "Sonny" McHalsie, *"I Am Stó:lō!": Katherine Explores Her Heritage* (Vancouver: Douglas and McIntyre, 1998).

24 Recently, in 2015, scholars from Linyi University in China worked with Carlson and the Stó:lō to produce a Chinese-language translation of selections from *You Are Asked to Witness*, along with the entirety of *I am Stó:lō*, constituting the first book-length ethnohistorical examination of Canadian Indigenous people available in the Chinese language. Keith Thor Carlson, Sonny McHalsie, and Frank Malloway, 加

拿大太平洋海岸第一民族的历史与文化 [*Canadian Pacific Coast First Nations History and Culture*], translated by Xing Chihong and Zhang Haixia (Saskatoon: Confucius Institute, University of Saskatchewan; Chilliwack, BC: Stó:lō Research and Resource Management Centre, 2015).

25 No treaties had been finalized in Stó:lō territory nor in much of British Columbia. In 1992, the British Columbia and federal governments created the BC Treaty Commission to facilitate the creation of modern treaties.

26 Keith Thor Carlson, David Schaepe, Sonny McHalsie, et al., eds., *A Stó:lō-Coast Salish Historical Atlas* (Vancouver: Douglas and McIntyre/Chilliwack: Stó:lō Heritage Trust, 2001).

27 Ned Blackhawk, "Currents in North American Indian Historiography," *Western Historical Quarterly* 42, no. 3 (Autumn 2011): 323.

28 Wild Zone Productions, *The Lynching of Louis* Sam, directed by David McIlwraith, 2005, based on Keith Thor Carlson, "The Lynching of Louis Sam," *BC Studies*, 109 (Spring 1999): 63–79.

29 Bruce G. Miller, ed. *Be of Good Mind: Essays on the Coast Salish* (Vancouver: University of British Columbia Press, 2007).

30 David M. Schaepe, Natasha Lyons, Kate Kennessy, et al., *Sq'éwlets: A Stó:lō-Coast Salish Community in the Fraser River Valley,* Virtual Museum of Canada, 2017, http://www.digitalsqewlets.ca ; *A Journey into Time Immemorial*, Simon Fraser University Museum, Vancouver, 2009, http://www.sfu.museum/time/en/enter/.

31 Reciprocal Research Network, https://www.rrncommunity.org/.

32 See, for example, Bruce G. Miller, "The 'Really Real' Border and the Divided Salish Community," *BC Studies* 112 (1996–1997): 63–79; Michael J. Kew and Bruce G. Miller, "Locating Aboriginal Governments in the Political Landscape," in *Seeking Sustainability in the Lower Fraser Basin: Issues and Choices* ed. Michael Healey (Vancouver: Institute for Resources and the Environment/Westwater Research, 1999), 47–63; Thomas McIlwraith, "The Problem of Imported Culture: The Construction of Contemporary Stó:lō Identity," *American Indian Culture and Research Journal* 20, no. 4 (1996): 41–70; Dana Lepofsky, Michael Blake, Douglas Brown, et al., "The Archaeology of the Scowlitz Site, SW British Columbia," *Journal of Field Archaeology*, 27, no. 4 (2000); Dana Lepofsky, David Schaepe, Anthony Graesch, et al., "Exploring Stó:lō-Coast Salish Interaction and Identity in Ancient Houses and Settlements in the Fraser Valley, British Columbia," *American Antiquity* 74, no. 4 (2009).

33 Liam Haggarty is on faculty at Mount Royal University, Andrée Boisselle at York University, Jon Clapperton was appointed tenure track faculty at Memorial University, Sarah Nichols at the University of Saskatchewan, and Anastasia Tataryn at University of Liverpool. In addition, Lissa Wadewitz, a post-doctoral fellow with the field school, is on faculty at Linfield College, McMinnville, Oregon.

34 Jo-ann Archibald, *Indigenous Storywork: Educating the Heart, Mind, Body and Spirit* (Vancouver: University of British Columbia Press, 2008), 59–82; Jo-ann Archibald, "An Indigenous Storywork Methodology," in *Handbook of the Arts in Qualitative Research*, ed. J. Gary Knowles and Ardra L. Cole (Sage: Thousand Oaks, 2008), 371–86.

35 Albert "Sonny" McHalsie, "We have to Take Care of Everything That Belongs to Us," in *Be of Good Mind: Essays on the Coast Salish*, ed. Bruce G. Miller (Vancouver: UBC Press, 2007), 82–130. He was awarded an Honourary Doctorate of Laws from the University of Victoria in 2011 in recognition of his scholarship and teaching.

36   Winona Wheeler argued that it is important to conceive of Indigenous studies as
     being transdisciplinary (rather than interdisciplinary as it was often described by
     the previous generation of Native studies scholars). She made this statement during
     her participation in the "Historical Scholarship and Teaching in Canada After the
     TRC" round table discussion at the annual meeting of the Canadian Historical
     Association in Calgary, June, 2016.

37   Vine Deloria Jr., *Custer Died for Your Sins: An Indian Manifesto* (London: Macmillan,
     1969); Georges Sioui, *For an Amerindian Autohistory: An Essay on the Foundations of
     a Social Ethic* (Montreal: McGill-Queen's University Press, 1992); Angela Cavender
     Wilson, "Power of the Spoken Word: Native Oral Traditions in American Indian
     History," and Donald Fixio, "Methodologies in Reconstructing Native American
     History," in *Rethinking American Indian History*, ed. Donald Fixio (Albuquerque:
     University of New Mexico Press, 1997).

38   Ray Fogelson, "The Ethnohistory of Events and Non-events," *Ethnohistory* 36, no.
     2 (1989): 133–48. For an honouring of Fogelson's work, see Sergei Kan and Pauline
     Turner Strong, *New Perspectives on Native North America* (Lincoln, NE: University
     of Nebraska Press, 2006); Ray Folgelson, "Epilogue," in *Transforming Ethnohistories:
     Narrative, Meaning, and Community*, ed. Sebastian Felix Braun (Norman: University
     of Oklahoma Press, 2013), 227–32.

39   Raymond DeMallie, "'These Have No Ears': Narrative and the Ethnohistorical
     Method," *Ethnohistory*, 40, no. 4 (1993): 515–38.

40   Denis Tedlock, *The Spoken Word and the Work of Interpretation* (Philadelphia:
     University of Pennsylvania Press, 1983); Dell H. Hymes, *Now I Know Only So Far:
     Essays in Ethnopoetics* (Lincoln, NE: University of Nebraska Press, 2003).

41   Marshall Sahlins, "Comments," in Robert Borofsky's "Cook, Lono, Obeyeskere, and
     Sahlins: Forum on Theory in Anthropology," *Current Anthropology*, 38, no. 2 (April
     1997): 271.

42   Marshall Sahlins, *Historical Metaphors and Mythical Realities: Structure in the Early
     History of the Sandwich Island Kingdom* (Ann Arbor: University of Michigan Press,
     1981); Gananath Obeyesekere, *The Apotheosis of Captain Cook: European Myth-
     making in the Pacific* (Princeton: Princeton University Press, 1992); Marshall Sahlins,
     How "Natives" Think: About Captain Cook, for Example (Chicago: University of
     Chicago Press, 1995).

43   Peter Seixas, ed., *Theorizing Historical Consciousness* (Toronto: University of
     Toronto Press, 2004); Sam Wineburg, *Historical Thinking and Other Unnatural
     Acts* (Philadelphia: Temple University Press, 2001); Mark Salber Phillips and
     Gordon Schochet, eds., *Questions of Tradition* (Toronto: University of Toronto
     Press, 2004). Hobsbawm famously posited, "'Invented tradition' is taken to mean a
     set of practices, normally governed by overtly or tacitly accepted rules and of a ritual
     or symbolic nature, which seek to inculcate certain values and norms of behaviour
     by repetition, which automatically implies continuity with the past. In fact, where
     possible, they normally attempt to establish continuity with a suitable historic past."
     Eric Hobsbawm and Terence Ranger, eds., *The Invention of Tradition* (Cambridge:
     Cambridge University Press, 1984).

44   Keith Thor Carlson, "Rethinking Dialogue and History: The King's Promise
     and the 1906 Aboriginal Delegation to London," *Native Studies Review*, 16, no. 2
     (2005): 1–38; Keith Thor Carlson, "Reflection on Indigenous History and Memory:
     Reconstructing and Reconsidering Contact," in *Myth and Memory: Stories of*

Indigenous-European Contact, ed. John Sutton Lutz (Vancouver: University of British Columbia Press, 2007), 46–68.

45 John Sutton Lutz, *Makúk: A New History of Aboriginal-White Relations* (Vancouver: UBC Press, 2008), 16.

46 Julie Cruikshank, *The Social Life of Stories: Narrative and Knowledge in the Yukon Territory* (Vancouver: University of British Columbia Press, 1998).

47 See for example John Sutton Lutz, "Myth Understandings; or First Contact, Over and Over Again," in *Myth and Memory,* 1-14.

48 Patrick Wolfe, *Settler Colonialism and the Transformation of Anthropology: The Politics and Poetics of an Ethnographic Event* (New York: Cassell, 1999). More recently, in *Settler Colonialism: A Theoretical Overview* (New York: Palgrave Macmillan, 2010), Lorenzo Varacini has provided settler colonial studies with a theoretical framework. More recently still, Adam Baker has provided an overview of the current state of settler colonialism studies, "Locating Settler Colonialism," *The Journal of Colonialism and Colonial History* 13: no. 3 (Winter 2012).

49 Mikhail Bakhtin, *Questions of Literature and Aesthetics* (Moscow: Russian Progress, 1975); Michael Harkin, *Dialogues of History: Transformations and Change in Heiltsuk Culture, 1790–1920* (Chicago: University of Chicago, 1988); John Sutton Lutz, *Makúk: A New History of Aboriginal-White Relations* (Vancouver: University of British Columbia Press, 2008), 26–7; Michael Harkin, "Ethnohistory's Ethnohistory: Creating a Discipline from the Ground Up," *Social Science History,* 34, no. 2 (Summer 2010).

50 Keith Thor Carlson, *The Power of Place: Aboriginal Identity and Historical Consciousness in the Cauldron of Colonialism* (Toronto: University of Toronto Press, 2010), 29.

51 Carlson, *Power of Place*; David Schaepe, "Pre-colonial Sto:lo-Coast Salish Community Organization: An Archaeological Study" (PhD diss. University of British Columbia, 2009); David Schaepe, "Rock Fortifications: Archaeological Insights Into Pre-contact Warfare and Sociopolitical Organization Among the Stó:lō of the Lower Fraser River Canyon, B.C.," *American Antiquity,* 71, no. 4 (October 2006): 671–705.

52 John Sutton Lutz, "Making 'Indians' in British Columbia: Power, Race and the Importance of Place," In *Power and Place in the North American West,* eds. John Finlay and Richard White (Seattle: University of Washington Press, 1999), 61–86; Penelope Edmonds, *Urbanizing Frontiers: Indigenous Peoples and Settlers in 19th-century Pacific Rim Cities* (Vancouver: University of British Columbia Press, 2010); Renisa Mawani, *Colonial Proximities: Crossracial Encounters and Juridical Truths in British Columbia, 1871–1921* (Vancouver: University of British Columbia Press, 2009).

53 Alexandra Harmon, *Indians in the Making: Ethnic Relations and Indian Identities around Puget Sound* (Berkeley: University of California Press, 1998); Carlson, *Power of Place.*

54 Lutz, *Makúk,* 16.

55 See also the eclectic influences in the essays in Sebastian Felix Braun, ed., *Transforming Ethnohistories: Narrative, Meaning, and Community* (Norman: University of Oklahoma Press, 2013).

56 Robert A. Williams, *Linking Arms Together: American Indian Treaty Visions of Law and Peace, 1600–1800* (New York: Oxford University Press, 1997); John Borrows, *Freedom and Indigenous Constitutionalism* (Toronto: University of Toronto Press, 2016).

57   See, for example, Homi Bhabha, *The Location of Culture* (New York: Routledge, 1994); Aletta Biersack, "History and Theory in Anthropology," in *Clio in Oceania: Toward a Historical Anthropology*, ed. Aletta Biersack (Washington, DC: Smithsonian Institution Press, 1990); John R. Wunder, "Native American History, Ethnohistory, and Context," *Ethnohistory* 54, no. 4 (2007): 591–604; Jill Doerfler, "Recent Works in North American Biography and Ethnography," *Ethnohistory*, 55, no. 2 (2008): 331–4.

58   Linda Tuhiwai Smith, *Decolonizing Methodologies: Research and Indigenous People* (London: Zed Books/Dunedin: University of Otago Press, 1999). More recently, Smith has continued to engage in conversations over Indigenous research methods in her article "Culture Matters in the Knowledge Economy," in *Interrogating Development: Insights from the Margins*, ed. Frédérique Apffel-Marglin, Sanjay Kumar, and Arvind Mishra (New Delhi: Oxford University Press, 2010). See also Margaret Kovach, *Indigenous Methodologies: Characteristics, Conversations, and Context* (Toronto: University of Toronto Press, 2009); Sean Wilson, *Research is Ceremony: Indigenous Research Methods* (Black Point, NS: Fernwood, 2008); Archibald, "An Indigenous Storywork Methodology"; Archibald, *Indigenous Storywork.*

59   Ernest L. Boyer, *Scholarship Reconsidered: Priorities of the Professoriate* (New York: Carnegie Foundation for the Advancement of Teaching, 1990); Ernest L. Boyer, "The Scholarship of Engagement," *Journal of Public Service & Outreach*, 1, no. 1 (1996); R. Eugene Rice, "Ernest Boyer's 'Scholarship of Engagement' in Retrospect," *Journal of Higher Education Outreach and Engagement*, 20, no. 1 (2016).

60   Interestingly, as part of a larger dispute this memorial was destroyed by members of the Yale First Nation in 2012 and then reconstructed by the new Yale First Nation leadership, in collaboration with the Stó:lō Nation and Stó:lō Tribal Council, in 2016.

61   The White Paper was a policy document that proposed eliminating the "Indian Act" and any distinctive status for Indigenous People in Canada.

62   Philip J. Deloria, *Indians in Unexpected Places* (Lawrence, KS: University Press of Kansas, 2004).

1

Kinship Obligations to the Environment: Interpreting Stó:lō X̱exá:ls Stories of the Fraser Canyon

ADAR CHARLTON

The beginning of my field school journey started off, like for many of the students, attempting to negotiate the somewhat awkward position of a cultural outsider assigned to research very culturally significant and sensitive insider knowledge. Grand Chief Clarence "Kat" Pennier of Scowlitz, then director of the Stó:lō Tribal Council, had asked me to document and interpret Stó:lō legends that discuss how to take care of the environment and teach us to be good people. I quickly learned that this was not a straightforward task. Gleaning particular interpretations from stories that have multiple lessons, individual interpretive expressions and iterations, and contextually dependent meanings that require a high degree of listener cultural sensibility was near to impossible for me. Not wanting to fail or disappoint Pennier, I began to think about what I, as a literary scholar, could bring to these texts that would be significant to the community, while not claiming knowledge that I could not possibly and should not have access to. Expanding the disciplinary boundaries of ethnohistorical methodology by applying a literary framework to these stories, I was able to examine the broadly shared knowledge and larger structures of significance contained within them. Ultimately, the stories I look at illuminate the importance of kinship structures and taking care of family, the notion of which extends to include all ancestral entities in the environment.

Following Pennier's initial research topic request, David Schaepe, director of the Stó:lō Research and Resource Management Centre (SRRMC), further refined the topic by recommending that I focus specifically on the X̱exá:ls stories of the Fraser Canyon in order to continue SRRMC's ongoing

Naxaxalhts'i (Sonny McHalsie) at the entrance of the Fraser Canyon, where X̱éylx̱elemòs battled X̱ex̱á:ls. Photo courtesy of John Lutz.

work on Iyoqthet (transformation sites).[1] A few days later, I found myself at one of those transformation sites as part of an orientation to Stó:lō territory offered by Ná:x̱axalhts'i, Albert "Sonny" McHalsie of Shxw'ōwhámél First Nation, historian, and cultural advisor at SRRMC. McHalsie had taken the field school students, myself included, to a spot immediately west of the town of Yale, British Columbia, where the Fraser River exits the Fraser Canyon through a fifty-metre gash in the Coast Range Mountains. In the middle of this narrow gap he pointed out a huge rock, X̱éylx̱elemòs, known by settlers as Lady Franklin Rock. McHalsie told us X̱éylx̱elemòs was an "Indian doctor" whom X̱ex̱á:ls had turned to stone as the result of an epic battle, partly as a punishment for X̱éylx̱elemòs having charged sick people to heal them.

A couple of weeks later, on 28 May 2013, I had the privilege of interviewing McHalsie about the X̱éylx̱elemòs story in Dragon Dynasty, his favourite Chinese restaurant in Chilliwack, British Columbia, with Professor John Lutz (for the full story as told by Sonny McHalsie, see the appendix to this chapter). After reviewing the tape and researching numerous versions of this story that had been recorded by others,[2] I realized how both the content and my interpretation of the story were affected by the setting and context within which it was told.

When in the restaurant, McHalsie had to describe physical places instead of simply pointing to them. He spent significant time explaining in detail the Stó:lō custom of not taking money for spiritual work or not hiring a spiritual worker—something a cultural insider would not need explained. He also knew that I had been asked to research lessons from the Fraser Canyon X̱exá:ls stories. I had a specific purpose to my interview and asked questions pertaining to the context in which the story was typically told and the lessons the story taught. McHalsie mentioned that Matilda "Tillie" Gutierrez was told this story during her puberty rites and sat on the rock where X̱exá:ls sat, but did not know of a general occasion where the story was regularly told. The lessons he mentioned were as follows:

> Well, one for sure about the Indian Doctors, not taking money and not charging, not getting rich.... And then it seems like the whole teaching about xo:lí:s ... that's an example of what could happen if you don't listen or don't do what you're supposed to do.... I don't know, just seems like there's probably some kind of showing connection to people upriver too, because it talks about X̱éylx̱elemòs coming from Spuzzum.... People from X̱elhálh are intermarried with people up there, so it seems like that's a lesson as well, because the Halkomelem word for Thompson people is S'em'omélá and S'em'omélá means like "our grandchildren." ... And then the importance of tunnels is probably in there as well.... What else is it? Not sure why he would have transformed his cane, I don't know what sort of teaching would be from that.[3]

The potential lessons of the X̱éylx̱elemòs story are numerous, but not fixed. McHalsie has dedicated his life to listening, learning, researching, documenting, and telling Stó:lō transformation stories and yet it is clear that when he shares the X̱éylx̱elemòs story he does not prescribe the exact lesson it teaches. He provided informed and educated guesses (viz. it "seems like" particular messages are implied; lessons are "probably in there") but there is room left for multiplicity and personal interpretation. How, then, was I going to direct my research and analysis so that I could reduce this rich multiplicity into a particular environmental lesson? And if I did, how might that change the story and future tellings of the story? How would that lesson be used and to what effect? Each of these questions pertains to what Julie Cruikshank has defined as the social life of stories: the context and intent behind a story's use that ultimately produces its social significance and meaning.[4] What social life was I attempting to create for these stories and what ultimate meaning was I making (up)?

I soon came to realize that seeking out and finding didactic lessons within the transformer stories of the Fraser Canyon is problematic when stories are taken out of the original interpersonal context in which they are shared. Stories are mobilized by tellers for specific purposes, teachings, and causes, and tailored to suit, which makes extracting didactic lessons from records of older tellings a difficult and potentially damaging task. Many anthropological records provide only point-form notes on the major plot points of stories, leaving a sketch of what once was; and more recent interview transcripts, like mine, are usually recorded with the intention of preservation or providing only a reference point for future tellings. Important as it is to preserve stories, codifying their lessons and interpretations requires a specific context and intent that seemed beyond my scope. With these concerns in mind, however, I argue that applying a literary framework to the interpretation of transformer stories of the Fraser Canyon allows for multiplicity and complexity, and in turn the future mobilization of these stories in a variety of contexts. A literary framework also illuminates an ecology of real and fictive kinship ties between stories, their tellers, and the transformation sites. Xexá:ls stories of the canyon act as a continual reminder of the familial obligations Stó:lō people have to the land and their ancestral connection to transformation sites.

I first became aware of some of the drawbacks of seeking to find didactic lessons in the stories of the canyon through an interview I conducted with Chief Clem Seymour of Seabird Island. Seymour was cautious about telling me the particulars of the stories themselves, and instead focused on the role of the stories in teaching how to look after and respect what he described as "the balance" of the canyon.[5] He stressed the importance of learning the stories on the land and not being told what they mean, but finding out what they mean for yourself. People have their own interpretations of the events the stories describe, and those interpretations translate into responsibility to the land. Seymour's understanding of the stories comes from growing up with them and knowing his history. He understands that the stories teach that "what you look after in life, looks after you" and "this is your land, you look after it, because the creator's not going to make any more."[6] He warned me in particular that an understanding of these stories does not come from printed words on paper and to keep in mind that his understanding was that informants usually told anthropologists "what they wanted to hear," hinting at the tenuousness and unreliability of written records.[7]

Seymour's warning takes into account the intent behind telling stories, alluding to one of the difficulties in reviewing anthropological records for didactic lessons. Through the act of recording, most recorded stories are removed from their original contexts and the typical social settings in which they are told. For example, James A. Teit recorded the following transformer tale at Hope from "an old man who could speak some Thompson":

> A Transformer came down the Fraser River from Utā'mqt country. When he arrived at a creek a little west of Spuzzum, he saw a girl washing herself in the water. He asked her what she was doing, and she answered that she was washing herself. He said, "You must die," and transformed her into a rock, which may still be seen in the creek.
>
> A Transformer came to Yale, and there he saw a man smoking. He asked him what he was doing, and he answered that he was smoking. The Transformer said to him, "You must die," and the man answered, "Very well, but do not put me into the water. I want to remain here, so that the people may see me and talk to me, and that I may see them." When he finished speaking, he was transformed into a stone, which may be seen there. It is shaped like a man.[8]

From Teit's account it might appear that the transformer is condemning washing and smoking; however, the lack of causal links in the passage or any context for its telling leaves large gaps in the narrative that problematize any clear message or lesson. Is the didactic lesson to not wash or smoke? In the first transformation, perhaps the transformer is more concerned with the girl's modesty: not necessarily a traditional concern for Stó:lō people, but one that Western settlers placed high value upon. Wilson Duff recorded a similar story from Patrick Charlie of Yale in the summer of 1950 that specifically refers to the girl's pubic region, which potentially corroborates such a lesson of modesty.[9] Maybe the girl was not supposed to bathe in that particular creek or in that particular spot. However, so many years later, without context for why or to whom the stories were told, determining a singular lesson is impossible. In the second transformation, Teit does not elaborate on what type of smoking or the man's purpose for smoking. I assume that at the turn of the twentieth century the story was not promoting healthy lifestyles and the dangers of recreational smoking; however, a contemporary storyteller (or interpreter) might be motivated to use the story for that purpose today. This story may refer to

X̱éylx̱elemòs, because of the location and stone "shaped like a man." The man's request "that I may see them" could be in reference to X̱éylx̱elemòs's third eye. But Teit's account does not provide enough detail to even begin interpreting the same kinds of teachings that McHalsie has been able to offer after years of studying the X̱éylx̱elemòs story. In both transformations, the informant may also have been referring to spiritual practices of cleansing. Above all, the story could be mistranslated, as it is not clear whether the man was communicating to Teit in English or in the Thompson language, Nlaka'pamuctsin, of which the storyteller could only speak "some."[10]

As a countermeasure to misinterpretation, in his study of Haida mythtellers Robert Bringhurst advocates for precise word-for-word transcriptions and translations of myths as more accurate representations of stories. He claims that "all the rest is paraphrase: a fraudulent form of silence."[11] Even though he holds a fairly uncompromising position, Bringhurst is rightfully wary of anthropologists' paraphrasing, because it detaches stories from their contexts, details, literary and artistic qualities, oral performances, and individual tellers. Teit's account may be mistranslated, misinformed, or merely a scant outline of the original story, generating at best slippery interpretations. Anthropological records contain masked complexity, missing links, and gaps that inhibit singular interpretation.

Another concern in extracting didactic lessons from X̱ex̱á:ls stories is the question of how the lessons will be used. The social significance assigned to the stories within the time and context in which they are used will directly affect what lessons emerge. Cruikshank observes that she has "seen written versions of narratives used as a reference point for reanimating social meanings that might otherwise be erased."[12] However, those social meanings are not universal, and the same story and textual reference point can be used for a number of purposes. Cruikshank labels this process "editing in performance," where a teller will tailor performances to suit different audiences. She remarks, "a single story can 'do' several different things."[13] Depending on what a story is "doing," the intended lesson will change.

Recently, stories have been used to compile traditional knowledge in order to create culturally appropriate heritage management and environmental policy. One of the ways the SRRMC has created such policy is to gather statements from community elders, along with other anecdotal accounts, as a basis for overarching principles of heritage management. Schaepe and McHalsie have "codif[ied] Stó:lō cultural teachings, practices, and perspectives in order to provide principles that would function as a foundation for Stó:lō policy and law."[14] They both have conducted integral work for the Stó:lō Nation, proposing and implementing culturally appropriate heritage management plans that uphold Stó:lō values and benefit Stó:lō communities. Such policy development provides a fruitful and beneficial context for interpreting X̱exá:ls stories and other traditional Stó:lō stories; however, the context of contemporary policy reveals only one social meaning of a story that is mobilized at a specific time and for a specific purpose. For instance, the transformer story of Xepa:y told to McHalsie by the late Bertha Peters from Seabird Island tells of a very generous man who is transformed into a cedar tree. For the purposes of policy, someone could be forgiven for taking the story as an indication that clear-cutting cedar trees conflicts with Stó:lō beliefs, because cedar is sacred. However, in his article "We Have to Take Care of Everything That Belongs to Us," McHalsie associates numerous teachings with this story, such as how to use the different parts of the cedar tree, how to harvest the bark and roots, and to say a prayer to Xepa:y, because he is an ancestor.[15] Using stories for policy only deploys one of the multiple teachings and understandings of a story. The teachings taken from a X̱exá:ls story for the purposes of policy can never constitute a universal, singular lesson of that story, but only a particular contemporary social significance.

One of the dangers of attempting to find singular lessons for the creation of policy is the potential erasure of other meanings, interpretations, and social uses of stories. In some cases, this may lead to the erasure of some stories altogether because they do not fit the current context or usage. Cruikshank observes that once original tellers are gone, written records tend to be viewed as data and codified into databases. Unfortunately, stories that do not fit the categories of this data are most likely not to be included in a database, because they "confus[e] rather than confir[m] familiar categories."[16] Cruikshank further points out that stories "are not even really about facts or events; they are about coming to grips with the personal meanings of broadly shared knowledge and converting those meanings to social ends," rendering categorization an inadequate task.[17] Without mobilizing the X̱exá:ls stories of the canyon for an explicit purpose, and particularly as a cultural outsider uninitiated in Stó:lō storytelling practices, I find it more productive to analyze and interpret the stories' "broadly shared knowledge," while still permitting space for personal meaning and multiple social significances.

In order to conduct an analysis of the shared knowledge of X̱exá:ls stories of the canyon, I apply a literary framework, as opposed to an anthropological or historical one. A standard anthropological framework would analyze these stories as cultural production and an historical framework would typically view them as a product of a moment in time, whereas a literary framework seeks to account for individual expression and social significance.[18] Clifford Geertz, in his article "Deep Play: Notes on the Balinese Cockfight," supports a movement away from anthropological analysis towards literary analysis of expressive forms of culture: such a change "shifts the analysis of cultural forms from an endeavor in general parallel to dissecting an organism, diagnosing a symptom, deciphering a code, or ordering a system—the dominant analogies in contemporary anthropology—to one in general parallel with penetrating a literary text."[19] Geertz recognizes the integral role of interpretation in any kind of anthropological study and argues that analysis should sort out "structures of signification," the usual job of a literary critic.[20] Any expressive form, whether it is a cockfight or a transformer story, is a reflection *on* culture rather than a reflection *of* culture. Viewing the X̲exá:ls stories of the canyon as narrative production allows for subjectivity and individual sensibilities, while still maintaining shared cultural knowledge and general teachings, as opposed to essentialized didactic lessons.

Literary interpretation of the X̲exá:ls stories also aligns with certain Stó:lō philosophies of teaching. Crisca Bierwert, in her work *Brushed by Cedar, Living by the River: Coast Salish Figures of Power*, explains that a Stó:lō "teaching delivers . . . a path for an intuitive leap in its direction and a template for thinking in its own way."[21] Stories function in a similar way; they provide a direction of understanding, but ultimately are not prescriptive or didactic. Each story provides only a framework for teaching; it is up to the individual, as Chief Seymour noted, to discover the story's personal meaning and true understanding.[22] Lee Maracle has expressed a similar point of view in her essay "Toward a National Literature: 'A Body of Writing'": "Stó:lō story, poetry, and song express people's spiritual connections to the earth; they embrace the human journey from the past to the present and strive to prepare us for the future in a way that keeps the nation connected to the earth and all living beings without dictating direction or personal conduct."[23] If X̲exá:ls stories of the canyon do not dictate personal conduct, what do they tell us?

While I find it problematic to extract didactic lessons as to exactly "how" to take care of the environment, for the reasons detailed above, I did examine the larger structures of significance in X̲exá:ls stories of the canyon that deliver teachings about the environment and Stó:lō people's relationship to the land. One of the central elements of these transformer stories is their discussion of direct ancestral connections to the land. In many cases Stó:lō families carry the ancestral names of transformation sites.[24] McHalsie mentioned that some ancestral names have been forgotten or lost, but a genealogical study would most likely uncover names similar to those of transformation sites.[25] Charles Hill-Tout documented what is one of the earliest records of a version of the X̱éylx̱elemòs story as told by Captain Paul, his chief informant among the Lillooet tribe, but someone who was also of Stó:lō descent and who had relatives living within Stó:lō villages, in particular Sts'ailes. Interestingly enough, the story outlines ancestral connections that the Lillooet have to X̱éylx̱elemòs, but has quite a different ending than other, later recorded Stó:lō versions:

> The family hereditary names of the group, whom tradition derives from the *ertwa* men, all relate to the mystery powers of the "first man" or to the magic contest he had with the demi-god Qals. It is recorded that when Qals was travelling down the Fraser he stopped at Yale to try his mystery power upon Paul's paternal ancestor whose name was Qailqilmos, which means "great in mystery power," having much the same signification as Qals itself. The contest between the two was very severe, and Qailqilmos was the victor. The trial between them seems to have consisted in taking away each other's strength and vigour. When Qals perceived that he was beaten, he told his adversary to take a measuring stick (*sqelemten*) and measure all the different parts of his body. Qailqilmos did this. Qals then said, "O my grandfather, you are very strong; now make me strong again." Qailqilmos restores him to strength and vigour again, and as they parted Qals bade him thereafter call his children by the names of the different measurements he had taken of his body. One of Paul's names, *sqelemken* "head measure," is a specimen of these names. Other names of this family are *slatctel*, *slatcetluk*, *slatcelat*. These are also called *tel Qals* "Qals names." They signify "power to transform."[26]

Captain Paul's story outlines his ancestral connection to Qailqilmos, but does not make mention of Lady Franklin Rock or any other transformations into stone. Franz Boas collected a similar version of the X̱éylx̱elemòs story in the late 1800s, most likely from Chief George of Sts'ailes, that also omits the transformation and makes mention of X̱éylx̱elemòs as the first man of X̱elhálh:[27] "The QEtlä'tl. Qe'lqElEmas, the first of the QEtlä'tl was very powerful. His people were all river monsters. Once Qäls came to him. The three brothers crossed the river to visit him while their sister stayed on the opposite shore.

They managed to cross the river, which is very dangerous at this spot, without mishap. But when they came to Qe'lqElEmas, he called his people and when Qäls saw the dreadful shapes, he fainted. Qe'lqElEmas took a magic substance out of his basket, sprinkled it over Qäls, and revived him."[28] As the first man of X̱elhálh, X̱éylx̱elemòs is historically significant to that place and to the people who trace their lineage back to that village. In addition, Brent Galloway claims that X̱e'yx̱elema:s is a well-known ancestral name, which illustrates X̱éylx̱elemòs's ancestral connections to descendants who became identified with both the Stó:lō and the Lillooet.[29] More importantly, both versions reveal that X̱éylx̱elemòs is not just a rock, but also an ancestor.

In conjunction with ideas of ancestral connection, Jo-ann Archibald has described transformation sites, and all natural things and beings, as sí:le, or grandparents in Halkomelem, stressing a familial bond even without an explicit link through ancestral names. Bierwert recalls that at a Coqualeetza Elders' meeting in the spring of 1982, Elizabeth Phillips confirmed for Archibald that mountains were sí:le and that another woman commented that "all living things, they are si:le. And the rocks too, even the little rocks. Everything there is si:le, to be respected."[30] Not only does the use of the word sí:le attest to familial connection to transformation sites, but it reinforces the obligation of respect for all living things as family.

In his article "We Have to Take Care of Everything," McHalsie demonstrates that the word shxwelí describes a similar relationship between humans and nature. Shxwelí means spirit or life force and each living thing has shxwelí: "everything has that spirit and everything's connected through that."[31] In a conversation with McHalsie, the late Rosaleen George described shxwelí as follows: "She put her hand on her chest and she said, 'Shxwelí is inside us here.' And she put her hand in front of her and she said, 'Shxwelí is in your parents.' She raised her hand higher and said, 'then your grandparents, your great-grandparents, it's in your great-great-grandparents. It's in the rocks, it's in the trees, it's in the grass, it's in the ground. Shxwelí is everywhere.'"[32] The transformer rocks contain the shxwelí of the ancestors that were transformed, a life force that connects the sites to Stó:lō people. McHalsie adds, "we're connected it to it; we need to take care of that place [transformation sites]."[33] Being connected through shxwelí translates into respect and the responsibility to look after the transformation sites. Schaepe also comments on the role of shxwelí and ancestral connections to transformation sites: "The Stó:lō fundamentally maintain that not only are all 'natural' things alive and animated by a life force (shxwelí) but also that, in many cases, they are *ancestral*; that is, they are linked to the contemporary community through the transformative acts of *Xexá:ls*, the Transformers."[34] The presence of shxwelí is foundational to Xexá:ls stories of the canyon and constitutes a kinship obligation to transformation sites and the canyon itself.

Kinship, I argue, is one of the main broadly shared knowledges and structures of significance in Xexá:ls stories of the canyon, and is a teaching that is carried on and passed down without prescribing specific behaviour or actions. The kinship represented by these stories, however, is an active relationship. Literary scholar Daniel Heath Justice in his work on kinship criticism has defined kinship as "something that's *done* more than something that simply *is*."[35] He views kinship as an active obligation, not a passive tie: a verb instead of a noun. Justice argues that kinship "gives us the best measure of interpretive possibility, as it speaks to the fact that our literatures, like our various peoples, are *alive*."[36] Stories define relationships and in turn provide "an understanding of a common social interdependence within the community, the tribal web of kinship rights and responsibilities that link the People, the land, and the cosmos together in an ongoing and dynamic system of mutually affecting relationships."[37] Kinship criticism is an appropriate literary framework to apply to Stó:lō Xexá:ls stories, because it reinforces the integral role of ancestral connection and shxwelí, acknowledging traditional Stó:lō beliefs as living and active. Kinship exists in familial and ancestral lineages, but also in relation to history, neighbouring tribes, community, power, and features of the landscape. Stó:lō people cannot know the land outside of their relationship to it. In an environmental context, kinship is the obligation Stó:lō people have to take care of the land. Stories are used to actively attend to kinship bonds with the land. The telling helps fulfill the obligation of kinship to the land by establishing a relationship between the listener and the surroundings. Significantly, each of the stories I have identified about the canyon contains a teaching about kinship and with it the obligation to attend to kinship bonds.

Many versions of the canyon stories incorporate personal experiences that attach contemporary significance to transformation sites through time. As Bierwert remarks, many ancestral teachings are combined with recent reports of a place, "link[ing] transformational events of the past with extraordinary events of the present world."[38] Integrating the present into the past reveals historical influence on the contemporary world. A common oral formula used in Xexá:ls canyon stories is "which may still be seen,"[39] "I've seen the rock,"[40] "stone is still there,"[41] etc. This convention reinforces the truth of and physically situates the stories, but also makes reference to the present day, stressing the

continued impact and importance of X̱exá:ls' transformations. Ideally, these
stories are told at the physical transformation sites where the formula adjusts
to "that rock there," more effectively demonstrating the impact of ancient times
on the present. The story establishes a relationship to the past and ancient history for the listener, promoting respect for and ultimately a kinship bond with
that history. The transformer stories teach a Stó:lō person an aspect of his/her
history and, as Seymour expressed, the importance of "knowing your history."[42]

As previously noted in the X̱éylx̱elemòs story, X̱exá:ls stories teach the
importance of kinship to ancestral transformation sites, but they also teach the
importance of kinship to surrounding geographic features and animals. Charlie
told Duff one such story of a whale transformation called Qwél:es, just above
I:yem: "When water is low, can see head of whale in rocks."[43] McHalsie related
this transformation to another one in Harrison Lake of a whale that came up
the lake from the ocean during high water.[44] The whale rock reminds people
that the Fraser River is regarded as an extension of the ocean itself, or perhaps
that the ocean is considered an extension of the mighty Stó:lō river,[45] and of
the kinship and mutually affecting relationship the river has with the ocean and
its animals. The story also potentially reminds people of a time of imbalance;
the whale could be a symbol of the delicate nature of ecological balance. The
whale has spiritual significance in many West Coast tribes[46] and its presence
in Stó:lō territory may be an allusion to cross-tribal relationships as well.

X̱exá:ls stories of the canyon also teach the importance of relationships
within a community, and an individual's responsibility and obligation to his/her
community over personal interests. McHalsie's retelling of the transformation
of a woman and her two children (told to him separately by Elders Agnes Kelly,
Tillie and Alan Gutierrez, and Bailey Douglas) reinforces the value of sharing
and not thinking of oneself above others. During a time of famine a woman
catches a salmon, does not share it with her community, and instead keeps it
for herself and her two children. X̱exá:ls punish them by turning them into
stone on the hillside across from Yale.[47] Out of all the stories in the canyon,
this one seems to have a fairly clear, didactic lesson that promotes sharing, or
at least punishes selfishness; however, the larger structure of significance is the
mindfulness of community well-being that this story communicates as well. At
the centre of this story is the overall obligation of people to their collectives,
be they family, village, or tribe.

Transformer stories of the canyon provide a relational framework for
interacting with power as well. In addition to the teachings McHalsie associates with the X̱éylx̱elemòs story, Bierwert interprets the transformation as a

warning against dangerous power and the potential for power to exist within ourselves and others.[48] She gathers this interpretation from Sweetie Malloway's version of the tale: "As we sit at her fishing place in 1992, Sweetie tells me, 'there used to be an old Indian doctor there, gesturing at the rock. He was killing people with his power. So they put him there, he's in the rock. You can still see him, his eye.'"[49] As McHalsie mentioned, the presence of X̱éylx̱elemòs's eye and the danger of xo:lí:s (literally "twisting up and dying," or to be "bent over backward" or "laid out" as Mrs. August Jim described it in an interview with Oliver Wells in 1962[50]) is a teaching of the consequences of not doing what you are told.[51] While xo:lí:s may seem like a didactic lesson enforced by fierce punishment, I believe that the story also promotes awareness of the dangers of power and the need to respect it. For children perhaps the story teaches, "do what you are told," but for an adult this story seems to convey certain sensibilities in interpersonal relationships. Xo:lí:s potentially teaches a certain amount of humility, asking people to realize their own fallibility against larger powers and to know when to avoid confrontation. Above all, the story teaches people not to abuse power. Each person applies this knowledge in a variety of different situations in their life, but the story establishes a relationship to power and the responsibility to be careful, "warn[ing] us that such danger still lives in the world" and of "the possibility of finding a 'fixing eye' within ourselves as well."[52]

The story of S'ch'e:il,[53] X̱éylx̱elemòs's sister, also establishes a relationship to power, in this case the power and force of the river. Bob Joe told this story to both Duff in 1950 and Wells in 1964, and described the whirlpool as the Indian doctor's wife. To Duff he explained: "While waiting, saw woman across, this man's wife. She had power that helped her husband (name given, but forgotten). Xexals got the woman 'You'll go over there and be there for the rest of your time. If any of the coming gen. [generations] will travel over you, they are liable to lose their lives through you.' She's there now, almost middle of river."[54] Joe explained to Wells, on the other hand, "And the man's wife, this man that is supposed to come down at that time took this woman and threw her in the river. Well, this time of year you see the water boiling where this woman is supposed to be at."[55] Even though her relationship to X̱éylx̱elemòs changes from sister to wife in Joe's two versions, the teaching remains the same as in McHalsie's telling. The story provides an explanation for, and a reason to respect and be careful around the whirlpool. The personification of the whirlpool establishes a relationship to S'ch'e:il and through her, a relationship to the river itself. The story offers discursive relationality for Stó:lō people to understand their place on the land and in the world.

Each of the X̲exá:ls stories of the canyon contributes to kinship relationships to the land. Stories recognize connection to transformer rocks through shxwelí, acknowledge their role as ancestors and sí:le, and position them as symbols of history, ecological balance, community, and the dangers of power, both in people and in nature. Steven L. Point, Xwelixweltel, has referred to this symbol or mark as an inscription of X̲exá:ls teachings. The root of X̲exá:ls is 'xá:l,' meaning to write in Halkomelem; therefore, each transformation is the inscription of X̲exá:ls, describing Stó:lō people's responsibility to the land.[56] These writings do not prescribe how to take care of the environment, but define relationality to the land through story. A story and/or storyteller reads each transformer stone, interpreting X̲exá:ls teachings to Stó:lō people, and each reading holds the potential to produce a somewhat different interpretation over time. As a conduit for comprehending relationality to the natural world, stories cannot hold a static, singular meaning; they must evolve and adapt over time to new and changing contexts.

Bierwert comments on how some scholars are confused by transformer stories because they contain ancestral relations between people and land, but are historically mutable.[57] However, I argue that historical mutability is what allows these stories to actively maintain ancestral relations between people and land. For example, in an interview with Roy Point as part of the Stó:lō Heritage Project[58] in 1972, Susan Peters referred to X̲exá:ls as "Little Christ"[59]: a translation, which has an obvious Christian dimension. And Dave Johnny, in an interview with Gutierrez as part of the same project, spoke of X̲exá:ls transformations as "hypnosis,"[60] a thought-provoking translation choice that suggests a certain Western influence, but also adds a psychological aspect to transformation. As translations, these adaptations help communicate to Christian and Western sensibilities the spiritual dimension and power X̲exá:ls embodies. Such adaptation and infinite iteration allows stories to continue living and being told, leaving them open for future mobilization and use.

Viewing X̲exá:ls stories of the Fraser Canyon through a literary framework ensures that larger structures of significance and embedded sensibilities are not lost, but kept alive. A literary framework reveals the interconnected web of kinship relations between Stó:lō people and the land, ensuring that the ecology of the canyon is balanced and healthy. These stories teach how to be a good person by establishing relationships to transformation sites and strengthening Stó:lō people's responsibility to attend to those kinship bonds. This teaching cannot be prescriptive because it must be adaptive. Justice describes kinship as "what we do for family"[61]; there are no set rules or lessons for how to take care of family. Family is complicated, messy, and each one is different, but above all, we have an active, committed responsibility to family. X̱exá:ls stories of the canyon extend notions of family and kinship to include the environment and show Stó:lō people their responsibility and commitment to take care of it. Part of understanding these stories comes from attending to bonds of kinship with the land, walking the land, being on the land, and being respectful of the land. Stó:lō people also have a responsibility and a kinship connection to the stories themselves to ensure their multiplicity, complexity, and richness is not reduced or forgotten. As McHalsie put it as we ended our interview, "I have to look after [these stories] as a member of the Stó:lō people."[62]

Appendix: Sonny McHalsie's Version of the X̱éylx̱elemòs Story

So the story actually starts with X̱éylx̱elemòs and well X̱exá:ls travelling up through the, just past, well almost to Lady Franklin Rock. And the first trans-formation he does is with his cane, or his walking stick. So it's called Q'awa. And so, he got to that turn and he shoved his stick in the ground, transformed it into stone, and then he continued walking. And when he got to the river bank on the east side just opposite downriver end of Lady Franklin Rock, and he had heard about X̱éylx̱elemòs.

X̱éylx̱elemòs was a shxwlá:m or Indian doctor from X̱elhálh who used his powers the wrong way. So, what he did was he used his powers to benefit himself. Okay, because today when you ask any shxwlá:m for help or if you ask any spiritual worker like Hihiyeqwels, you're not allowed to hire them, like you can't use that word, otherwise it's insulting them. And same with you're not allowed to pay them and they're not allowed to charge you neither. So, that's why we're very careful today when we ask them for their help. We usually use that word, we ask them to help us or that we need their help. And so, we don't say, "can we hire you," you know, or anything; we don't use those words. And same with when we're thanking them. We say this is our way of thanking you. And you know, of course, in our culture when you're given something you can't turn it down, right? So that's how it's done today.

And so, this fellow then, X̱éylx̱elemòs was using his power to benefit him-self; he was getting rich off of his power. So X̱exá:ls had heard about him and he decided he wanted to set an example of him. So he went, called for X̱éylx̱elemòs and he found out that X̱éylx̱elemòs was actually up in Spuzzum visiting some of his relatives. So X̱exá:ls called for him, but X̱éylx̱elemòs wouldn't come down to do battle with him. And so that's when X̱exá:ls transformed X̱éylx̱elemòs's sister, S'ch'e:il, into stone to entice X̱éylx̱elemòs to come down. So, once S'ch'e:il was transformed into stone, and once X̱éylx̱elemòs found this out, then that's when he decided to come down and do battle.

So he's supposed to have travelled through a tunnel from Spuzzum, came out of that tunnel just upriver, right where the river turns, just on the eastern side where the river turns north—north to south, east to west—right there, that turn. And he crossed over. So he came out of that tunnel, crossed over the river to the south side or the east side, east bank. And then he crossed, walked down and he sat on a rock across from where X̱exá:ls was sitting. X̱exá:ls was sitting at a place called Th'ex̱elís. Th'ex̱elís means gritting his teeth. So right there, just opposite down the other end of Lady Franklin Rock, but on the west or north side.

So X̱éylx̱elemòs sat on the other side and X̱exá:ls was on one side and then they started doing battle with each other. And at one point X̱exá:ls cast a thunderbolt to X̱éylx̱elemòs and the thunderbolt went into the rock. And so you can still see that white vein of quartz rock. It's about two feet wide, about 80 feet long. And, but of course, he missed X̱éylx̱elemòs with that thunderbolt. That's why it went into the rock. And then eventually . . . oh, each time X̱exá:ls used his power, he put a scratch in the rock. So that's why when you go to that place there, Th'ex̱elís, you'll see where he sat. There's that little dip where he sat and then you can see where he has his legs dangling over the bank, little dip there. And then on the right side you can see scratches from his right fingernail and left side scratches from his left side. So each time he used his power against X̱éylx̱elemòs he put a scratch into the rock. So that place is called Th'ex̱elís, meaning gritting his teeth, because he was sitting there when he was using his powers, gritting his teeth at the same time, and also at the same time whistling too. So that's why you say that you can still see his whistle. When he whistles you can see the little waves in the water in the river, so they still call that X̱exá:ls and that's X̱exá:ls's breath when he's sitting there whistling, causing those little waves.

So eventually he transformed X̱éylx̱elemòs into stone and that's the big rock there that's known as Lady Franklin Rock. X̱éylx̱elemòs was also known to have a third eye, a third eye on his forehead, so when he was transformed into stone his third eye was transformed into stone as well, and it's on the south side or what you call the east bank side of the island. And we're not allowed to look at that rock otherwise we could suffer from what we call in our language xo:lí:s. Xo:lí:s is described by Rosaline and Elizabeth saying that if you're told not to do something, but you go and do it anyways, then you could suffer from that: suffer from twisting up or causing you to twist up and die from doing something you're not supposed to do. So that's what that eye is on the back of that mountain or that rock there.

So that's the story of X̱éylx̱elemòs, well a whole bunch of stories; it's Q'awa, Th'ex̱elís, X̱éylx̱elemòs, and S'ch'e:il. And I can't remember the Halkomelem word for the thunderbolt, but there's a word for that as well.

Notes

1 X̱ex̱á:ls are four sibling black bears, three brothers and one sister, who made the world right through transformations. In the distant past, the world was chaotic; people could communicate with animals, and animals could take off their coats to become human. X̱ex̱á:ls punished people by turning them to stone, rewarded people by turning them into local resources, and fixed people, animals, and land features into their permanent forms. X̱ex̱á:ls are sometimes referred to in the singular form X̱á:ls, a variation that suggests Christian influence. Stories about X̱ex̱á:ls are classified as sx̱wōx̱wiyám in Halkomelem: oral histories that describe the distant past. Keith Thor Carlson, David Schaepe, Albert "Sonny" McHalsie, et al., eds., *A Stó:lō-Coast Salish Historical Atlas* (Vancouver: Douglas and McIntyre/Chilliwack: Stó:lō Heritage Trust, 2001), 6.

2 Franz Boas, *Indian Myths and Legends from the North Pacific Coast of North America*, eds. Randy Bouchard and Dorothy Kennedy, trans. Dietrich Bertz (Vancouver: Talonbooks, 2002), 108; Johnny Bob, interviewed by Marian Smith, 16 July 1945, Transcription of Field Note Pads, 268:2 No. 20, Marian Wesley Smith Collection, MS-2794 BC Archives, Royal British Columbia Museum, 8–9; George, "Transformer II," in *Lower Fraser Indian Folktales*, collected by Norman Lerman, typescript 1950-1, 145–7; Charles Hill-Tout, *The Salish People: The Local Contribution of Charles Hill-Tout, Vol. II: The Squamish and the Lilloet*, ed. Ralph Maud (Vancouver: Talonbooks,1978), 128; Mrs. August Jim, interviewed by Oliver Wells, in *The Chilliwacks and Their Neighbours*, eds. Ralph Maud, Brent Galloway, and Marie Weeden (Vancouver: Talonbooks: 1987), 64–5; Bob Joe, interviewed by Wilson Duff, summer 1950, in Wilson Duff, Fieldnotes, Notebook No. 3, Wilson Duff Papers, BC Archives, Royal British Columbia Museum: 27–8; Dave Johnny, interviewed by Matilda Gutierrez, June 23, 1972, Stó:lō Heritage Project, transcript of tape no. 35, 3–5; Sweetie Malloway quoted in Crisca Bierwert, *Brushed by Cedar, Living by the River: Coast Salish Figures of Power* (Tucson: University of Arizona Press, 1999), 54; Susan Peters, interviewed by Roy Point, 29 February 1972, Stó:lō Heritage Project, transcript of tape no. 10, 3.

3 Albert McHalsie, interview by author, Chilliwack, BC, 28 May 2013.

4 Julie Cruikshank, "The Social Life of Texts: Editing on the Page and in Performance," *Talking on the Page: Editing Oral Texts*, ed. Laura J. Murray and Keren Rice (Toronto: University of Toronto Press), 98.

5 Clem Seymour, interview by author, Seabird Island, BC, 28 May 2013. Many Stó:lō people feel that it is taboo to talk about X̱ex̱á:ls stories. Seymour stated that these stories have been put away until people are ready to hear them and truly understand their meaning. I have tried my best here to stress the importance of learning these stories from elders and on the land in order to understand them in the fullest sense.

6   Ibid.

7   Ibid.

8   James A. Teit, "Tales from the Lower Fraser River," in *Memoirs of the American Folklore Society* XI (1917), 129.

9   "Up about 3 miles [from Yale], on this side, he came upon a young woman, about 12 or 13, swimming. She saw him, ran, and lay down on a rock, and he turned her to stone. She can still be seen at low water. 'Can see everything.' She is about 9' tall, has colored fine grass, which never dies, growing on her pubic region." Patrick Charlie, interviewed by Wilson Duff, summer 1950, in Wilson Duff's fieldnotes, Notebook No. 2, Wilson Duff Papers, BC Archives, Royal British Columbia Museum: 3.

10   Teit spoke fluent Thompson, having married a Nlaka'pamux woman and lived in Spences Bridge. Wendy Wickwire, "Teit, James Alexander," *Dictionary of Canadian Biography*, http://www.biographi.ca/en/bio/teit_james_alexander_1884_15E.html.

11   Robert Bringhurst, *A Story as Sharp as a Knife: The Classical Haida Mythtellers and Their World*, 2nd ed. (Vancouver: Douglas and McIntyre, 2013), 338.

12   Cruikshank, "Social Life of Texts," 99.

13   Ibid., 107.

14   David Schaepe, "Stó:lō Identity and the Cultural Landscape of S'ólh Téméxw," in *Be of Good Mind: Essays on the Coast Salish*, ed. Bruce G. Miller (Vancouver: University of British Columbia Press, 2007), 250.

15   Albert "Sonny" McHalsie, "We Have to Take Care of Everything that Belongs to Us," in *Be of Good Mind*, ed. Miller, 104–5.

16   Cruikshank, "Social Life of Texts," 117.

17   Ibid., 114.

18   Keith Thor Carlson, John Lutz, and David Schaepe, eds., "Turning the Page: Ethnohistory from a New Generation," *University of the Fraser Valley Research Review* 2, no. 2 (Spring 2009): 1–8, 1.

19   Clifford Geertz, "Deep Play: Notes on the Balinese Cockfight," *Daedalus* 134 (Fall 2005): 56–86, 83.

20   Clifford Geertz, "Thick Description: Toward an Interpretive Theory of Culture," in *Interpretation of Cultures, Selected Essays* (New York: Basic Books, 1973), 9.

21   Bierwert, *Brushed by Cedar*, 67.

22   Seymour, interview.

23   Lee Maracle, "Toward a National Literature: 'A Body of Writing,'" in *Across Cultures/ Across Borders: Canadian Aboriginal and Native American Literatures*, eds. Paul DePasquale, Renate Eigenbrod, and Emma LaRocque (Peterborough: Broadview, 2010), 90.

24   See Anastasia Tataryn's "Stó:lō Ancestral Names, Identity, and the Politics of History" in this collection for a detailed examination of the importance of carrying ancestral names and their role in reinforcing accountability to family and community.

25   McHalsie, interview.

26   Hill-Tout, *Salish People*, 128.

27   X̱elhálh, which means "injured person" in Halkomelem, is a settlement site adjacent to Lady Franklin Rock, just upriver from Yale. Boas, *Indian Myths and Legends*, 108n77; Carlson et al., eds., *Stó:lō-Coast Salish Historical Atlas*, 152.

28 Boas, *Indian Myths and Legends*, 108. Boas also mentions Beaver (Sk:Elá'o), the first chief of Spuzzum, digging an "underground passage" to X̱éylx̱elemòs's house. This passageway could refer to the tunnel that McHalsie discussed in his version of the story (see Appendix).

29 Galloway, quoted in Boas, *Indian Myths and Legends*, 108n78.

30 Bierwert, *Brushed by Cedar*, 64.

31 McHalsie, "We Have to Take Care of Everything," 103.

32 Ibid., 104.

33 Ibid., 105–6.

34 Schaepe, "Stó:lō Identity," 253.

35 Daniel Heath Justice, "Go Away Water!: Kinship Criticism and the Decolonization Imperative," in *Reasoning Together: The Native Critics Collective*, eds. Craig S. Womack, Daniel Heath Justice, and Christopher B. Teuton (Norman: University of Oklahoma Press, 2008), 150.

36 Ibid., 166.

37 Ibid., 150–1.

38 Bierwert, *Brushed by Cedar*, 83.

39 Teit, "Tales from the Lower Fraser River," 129.

40 Bob, interview, Smith Field Note Pads, Marian Wesley Smith Collection: 8.

41 Charlie, interview, in Duff fieldnotes, Notebook No. 1, Wilson Duff Papers: 2.

42 Seymour, interview.

43 Charlie, interview, in Duff fieldnotes, Notebook No. 2, Wilson Duff Papers: 44.

44 McHalsie, interview. McHalsie mentioned the flood of 1948, where the Harrison River ran backward because the Fraser was so high, as an example.

45 Keith Thor Carlson, *The Power of Place, The Problem of Time: Aboriginal Identity and Historical Consciousness in the Cauldron of Colonialism* (Toronto: University of Toronto Press, 2010), 53.

46 For example, in Haida culture the orca is the power of the ocean incarnate and the primary visible form of spirit-beings. Bringhurst, *A Story as Sharp as a Knife*, 122, 248.

47 McHalsie, interview. Patrick Charlie and Dave Johnny both talked about another transformation, in roughly the same area, of two women. Charlie said that you can still see their faces on the rock and Johnny told Gutierrez, "right back at the other side of the tunnel at Yale they say there's two rocks like this shaped just like two women, and this man used to hypnotise the people that were fighting and the only people we see are those two women, that were climbing the mountains there he just done this to his hand, he hypnotise them and they became rock they say it's still there, but I never see it myself." Charlie, interview, in Duff fieldnotes, Notebook No. 2, Wilson Duff Papers: 3; Johnny, interview transcript, 3–4.

48 Bierwert, *Brushed by Cedar*, 71.

49 Ibid., 54.

50 Jim, interview, in *The Chilliwacks*, 64.

51 McHalsie, interview.

52 Bierwert, *Brushed by Cedar*, 71.

53 McHalsie has heard a version of the salmon woman story where S'ch'e:il was the salmon woman and X̱exá:ls created a storm, blew her into the air, and spun her around and down into the water, where she was turned to stone. McHalsie, interview.

54   Joe, interview, in Duff fieldnotes, Notebook No. 3, Wilson Duff Papers: 28.

55   Bob Joe, interviewed by Oliver Wells, in *The Chilliwacks*, 121. Joe also mentioned that X̱éylx̱elemòs's canoe was transformed as well. To Duff he described that X̱éylx̱elemòs "had got close to his canoe, which is up on its edge against the rock. There is moss on his back and on canoe. Anytime it's hot, scrape moss off back and rain will come or clouds will come in." Joe, interview, in Duff fieldnotes, Notebook No. 3, Wilson Duff Papers: 28.

56   McHalsie, interview; Bierwert, *Brushed by Cedar*, 73; Keith Thor Carlson, "Orality about Literacy: The 'Black and White' of Salish History," in *Orality and Literacy: Reflections Across Disciplines*, eds. Keith Thor Carlson, Kristina Fagan, and Natalia Khanenko-Friesen (Toronto: University of Toronto Press, 2011), 61.

57   Bierwert, *Brushed by Cedar*, 72.

58   See Ella Bedard's "'Bringing Home All That Has Left': The Skulkayn/Stalo Heritage Project and the Stó:lō Cultural Revival" in this collection for a full description of this project.

59   Peters, interview transcript, 1.

60   Johnny, interview transcript, 3.

61   Justice, "Go Away Water!" 167.

62   McHalsie, interview.

2

Relationships: A Study of Memory, Change, and Identity at a Place Called I:yem

AMANDA FEHR

Eayem Memorial 1938 AD, Erected by the Stalo Indians.
In memory of many hundreds of our forefathers buried here,
this is one of our six ancient cemeteries within our five
mile Native fishing grounds which we inherited from our
ancestors. R.I.P.

— Text on 1938 I:yem Memorial[1]

The I:yem memorial was erected in 1938 by the Stó:lō Coast Salish to honour their ancestors and as a monument to their fishing grounds in the Fraser
Canyon, British Columbia. Located four kilometres north of Yale, British
Columbia, the I:yem memorial represents the first time that Indigenous people
of the Fraser River Valley and Canyon publicly displayed the name Stó:lō in
reference to themselves.[2] The "five mile fishing grounds" highlighted on the
memorial refers to the banks and rocks of the lower Fraser Canyon, which
are one of the most productive fishing grounds in the Pacific Northwest, as
well as the only place in all of British Columbia where salmon can be reliably
wind dried.[3]

Seventy years later, in October 2008, some members of the Yale First
Nation used a backhoe to push the I:yem memorial into the Fraser Canyon,
making their own independent claim to the territory where their ancestors also
fished and were buried. What it means to be, and who should be considered,
Stó:lō remains contested today.

With the ratification of the Yale treaty by the federal and provincial governments and the Yale First Nation, it appeared that Yale authority over I:yem

and the canyon fishery was solidified. The Yale First Nation, which shares a common language and culture with the other downriver Stó:lō communities, had long claimed exclusive rights to the canyon fisheries, in spite of a long history of joint use and despite the fact that Stó:lō leaders have continued to assert their own claims to the canyon fishery.[4] Since then, the Yale First Nation has rethought its position and has not yet implemented this aspect of its treaty, pending further discussions with its Stó:lō neighbours. The I:yem memorial was reconstructed and put back in place by the Yale First Nation, in collaboration with the Stó:lō Nation and Stó:lō Tribal Council, in April 2016.[5]

Contemporary interpretations of the memorial, its creation, destruction, and reinstallation alternately emphasize the need to re-establish and maintain personal connections to canyon places, and the memorial's relationship to the ongoing questions of identity and territory between the Stó:lō Nation/Tribal Council on the one side and the Yale First Nation on the other. I:yem is a Stó:lō place and a Yale place, but perhaps more importantly it is experienced and interpreted by particular individuals and families.

Ethnohistorian Keith Thor Carlson concludes his article "Innovation, Tradition, Colonialism and Aboriginal Fishing Conflicts in the Lower Fraser Canyon" with a brief discussion of the I:yem memorial, proposing that it was principally created to honour the memory of the ancestors "whose remains had been re-interred after developments associated with the building of Canada's two transcontinental railways"; it represented "a bold assertion of shared Stó:lō collective identity and a broad communal title to the canyon fishery"; and it "signified a recognition that the principal threat to Aboriginal fishing rights now came from non-native interest, and implicitly that internal disputes should be handled internally."[6]

Building upon Carlson's assessment of the significance of the monument in 1938, what follows is an exploration of some of the ways the Indigenous people of the Fraser Canyon and Valley have understood I:yem and its memorial more recently. While the memorial may have been built at a time when the principal threat to Indigenous fishing rights was from non-Indigenous interests, more recent events around the I:yem memorial allow us to explore the at times con-flicting Stó:lō and Yale efforts to protect and regain connections with canyon places. After a brief discussion of my approach and scholarly inspirations, my analysis begins with some individual interpretations of I:yem before turning to the collective relationships that the political entities of the Stó:lō Nation and Yale First Nation have had with each other and the canyon places they continue to view as their own.

Indigenous alter servers and Catholic clergy at the dedication of the I:yem memorial. *Vancouver Sun*, 20 August 1938.

This discussion is primarily based on oral interviews that I conducted ten years ago during the joint University of Victoria–University of Saskatchewan Ethnohistory Field School in June 2007, and incorporates earlier interviews from the Stó:lō Nation Archive's Oral History Collection, court records, political agreements, and newspaper articles. I was not able to speak with anyone from the Yale First Nation and the focus of this paper is on Stó:lō voices prior to the destruction of the memorial.[7] I am a settler woman and have spent the majority of my life in Saskatchewan. The 2007 field school was my introduction to British Columbia and Stó:lō history and culture, and it was during this time that I conducted five interviews with community members that became the basis for this paper.[8] I expanded on my original field school project for my master's thesis at the University of Saskatchewan.[9] This paper is an updated synthesis of that original work, and does not include additional interviews with Stó:lō community members.[10]

This discussion of I:yem draws upon several bodies of literature, including works specific to the Coast Salish and the Fraser Canyon, place making, memory studies, and a variety of anthropological and historical theorists. Sonny McHalsie, Bruce Miller, Keith Thor Carlson, David Schaepe, Wayne Suttles, and Crisca Bierwert have noted the importance of place to the Coast Salish people, and the role of places in validating social and political status and determining personal and collective identities.[11] Less attention has been given to considering what happens when stories of place and Indigenous identities come into conflict, or in exploring the nuances of personal experiences and identities that at times complement but at others conflict with tribal-based political affiliations. While several works acknowledge diversity within Coast Salish communities,[12] little has been done to specifically explore differences within and between Coast Salish groups. While only focusing on the fractures in and between communities is not beneficial, being aware of them and the variety of interpretations of I:yem and its memorial is still important.

In addition to scholarship relating to the Stó:lō and Coast Salish, this analysis seeks to contribute to a broader body of academic literature on place making,[13] suggesting how places themselves may be inherently powerful rather than simply social constructs, and considering what happens when places become sites of conflict between Indigenous groups. Exploring the reciprocal relationships between people and their places illustrates how individuals gain power and authority from belonging to certain places and how they in turn use that power to maintain connections within those places in the present and for the future. To this end, the relationships with the Fraser Canyon itself are what is important, and become the basis for competing claims to the canyon fishery.

"In memory of . . . "

I:yem, which means "strong" or "lucky place,"[14] changed considerably in the seventy years since the memorial was erected there. In 2007, Stó:lō elder Mabel Nichols described the "white picket fence no longer white, two small grey crosses with nothing written on them, and the larger one with the gaping spot where the plaque had been."[15] A casual visitor might have inferred that the memorial has been forgotten; indeed, some of the elders I spoke with required some prompting to understand what place I was interested in learning about. Yet, I:yem surfaces every so often in a process of reinterpretation, and most recently conflict, as understandings of the memorial have been shaped by people's visions for their future and ongoing assessments of the past.[16] Naxaxalhts'i (Sonny McHalsie),[17] who at the time of my research was the codirector of the Stó:lō Research and Resource Management Centre at Stó:lō Nation, suggested that I:yem was already being forgotten in 1938, and that the memorial, and more significantly the plaque, were created to preserve its memory and history.

The community members that I spoke with in 2007 frequently referred to the importance of the memorial's plaque. In the context of more recent intertribal political conflicts, it is this text that is of particular significance. Grand Chief, Judge (and former lieutenant governor of British Columbia) Steven Point emphasized the political and economic significance of "rediscovering" the memorial through people's "own lens," as it provided important evidence for the Stó:lō in their ongoing disputes with the Yale First Nation over territory.[18] Further highlighting the importance of the text, self-described "fisher-lady" and Stó:lō elder, Rita Pete,[19] shared how upset she was when she discovered that the plaque had been stolen. It was the plaque, she explained, that provided the memorial with significance: "whoever we bring up there, they wonder what it means. So we let them read it and then they go around reading the other ones. It [is] just important and now everybody knows that it's there and everybody wanted to know what it said. Now there's no plaque to read."[20] Mrs. Pete's comments demonstrate how, in many ways, the plaque had become the memory of I:yem. Building on Sonny McHalsie's suggestion that I:yem was already being forgotten in 1938, and that the memorial (and more significantly the plaque) were created to preserve its memory and history, these statements provide glimpses of how people have begun to reclaim the memorial and, with that, to reassert their rights and claims to territory. In this way the memorial, while providing evidence of past relationships with I:yem, served as a reminder of the need for those who identify as Stó:lō to forge their own connections with I:yem. The significance of the plaque and the power of its words are further demonstrated when one considers that the monument was destroyed at the very time that some Stó:lō people were planning a ceremony to replace it. When the ceremony continued in spite of the memorial's destruction, charges of trespassing were threatened.[21] In the fall of 2008 the plaque's text supported the claims of Stó:lō leaders, but challenged the position of the Yale First Nation.

"This is one of our six ancient cemeteries"

According to Sonny McHalsie, the memorial's creators "didn't want us to forget about the burial grounds."[22] Those who continue to fish in the canyon, and still have some connection or relationship with these places, have not forgotten about the cemeteries in the five-mile Native fishery. In fact, Rita Pete, who in 2007 had been fishing at I:yem with her family for about sixty years, also looked after the gravesite there.[23] Her family has cleaned the cemetery at I:yem every year since they began fishing there, and before that they cared for a graveyard across the river at Aseláw where they had fished.[24] Thus, Mrs. Pete and her family have continued the practice of looking after the ancestors buried in the canyon, with the significant exception that they do not know who any of the people are that are buried in the cemeteries. Mrs. Pete suggested that the ancestors were forgotten because they died so long ago and that "nobody thinks of them or anything."[25] Her connection with I:yem and the cemetery there has developed because it is next to her fishing spot rather than through connections to specific ancestors who are buried there.[26] Although those buried at I:yem (and their stories) have been forgotten as individuals, they continue to be remembered as ancestors and treated with respect.

"Many hundreds of our forefathers"

This concept of having a connection to particular places and those who used them in the past is often emphasized, as is the sense that it has been lost and needs to be regained. The need for meaningful connection between the Stó:lō and the Fraser Canyon is outlined by Sonny McHalsie: "When I talk about I:yem as a place name that's an important place, it's a fishing place, it's a fishing ground. But when I start talking about Dennis S. Peters[27] setting up the memorial I start talking about my grandfather fishing at that one place and that's my connection to the spot.... That's the really important part of it. I think that is what's missing today.... I think that the only people that have a really big connection up there is to the fishing grounds."[28] McHalsie describes the changing relationships between the Stó:lō and I:yem as it transformed from a village site, to a place where people returned to be buried, to a site where some people now fish. This suggests that, increasingly, it is only those Stó:lō people who have continued fishing in the canyon who identify with canyon places like I:yem and see them as key parts of their Stó:lō identity. He proposes that it is through stories of past connections and specific familial rights to places that regaining relationships with particular places in the present might be possible.

"Within our five mile Native fishing grounds"

I:yem was a good place to catch salmon. According to Matilda (Tillie) Gutierrez, whose grandparents fished at I:yem, "the reason why they all loved going up there is because the water is so rough and the fish is easy to catch because they used dip nets."[29] She went on to explain, "I guess that's what it really means, the memorial of that place there, I:yem, that fish was easy to get because the water is so rough."[30] To Mrs. Gutierrez the significance of I:yem and the memorial connected to it is directly linked to her own experiences there.

I:yem, and the other fishing sites above Yale, were an important component of the traditional fishing economy,[31] yet as described by Mrs. Gutierrez, the value of the fishery went beyond economics. People's memories of fishing in the canyon demonstrate personal connections with places themselves and the people with whom they share them. To Tillie Gutierrez, I:yem is linked with memories of spending time drying fish with her grandmother and pulling in a big spring salmon when she was thirteen or fourteen years old (to the delight of people fishing across the river). There is a sense of community created by the people from nearby fishing spots. I:yem was where she met her husband, Alan Gutierrez, who was also fishing there with his grandparents, and a place where they fished together when they were first married.[32] Mrs. Gutierrez explained, "I loved that area so much and today I still do—that's why these place names stick right in my mind—all the heavenly places I grew up."[33] It is through these experiences and relationships that Mrs. Gutierrez remembers and interprets I:yem. In this way, the personal aspects of understandings of I:yem often result from familial and interpersonal relationships that were maintained there. Mrs. Gutierrez's love of I:yem is partly derived from the place itself, but also from the time spent there with others.

I:yem is more than simply an "easy" place to catch fish, as fishing (and therefore I:yem) is associated with other elements of Stó:lō culture. Tillie Gutierrez explains that it was at I:yem that they[34] caught the salmon for the sacred First Salmon Ceremony by lowering themselves down through a rocky arch that used to be there.[35] Sonny McHalsie believes that this is significant as, through I:yem and learning about that place, people have been able to relearn elements of the First Salmon Ceremony that were nearly lost.[36] Aspects of Stó:lō culture and history literally exist within certain places and the memories that they evoke. Memories and experiences are connected to places, and it is through returning to those places that they can be regained.

Mrs. Gutierrez emphasized how her family's fishing area at I:yem was destroyed when the stone arch was blasted away "when they put those fish ladders in there."[37] The construction of concrete fish ladders by the International Salmon Commission in response to river blockages in the late 1950s showcases what are at times conflicting interests between band control over reserves and family connections to particular fishing places. Notably, in 1961, Yale Chief Peter Emery was advised that the International Salmon Commission wished to use a portion of Yale Indian Reserve 22 to set up an air compressor in connection with the proposed removal of twenty feet of two rocky pinnacles—the arch previously referred to by Mrs. Gutierrez. Because I:yem is on reserve land, the commission required permission from the Yale Band to access the territory. Although Chief Emery had originally "shown considerable concern over the possibility of their excellent fishing pool at this point being ruined,"[38] a band council resolution was passed giving the commission free access to do their work.[39] As Tillie Gutierrez and her family were not members of the Yale Band they were not consulted regarding this matter, and as a result their fishing spot as they knew it was forever altered. Mrs. Gutierrez explained: "Now there's nobody who can do any fishing there anymore, so actually the only thing we own is the site but no more fishing ground; it's all ruined."[40] Specifically, this statement illustrates how Tillie Gutierrez viewed I:yem. To her, I:yem was specifically her grandparents' fishing spot rather than a broader area including other fishing sites—such as where Mrs. Pete continues to fish. More generally, she highlights how people of her generation view canyon places primarily as fishing grounds. To Mrs. Gutierrez, I:yem, as she knew it, was ruined by the destruction of their fishing spot. Accordingly, testifying before a judge in a 1980s fisheries case, she said, "there *used* to be a place there they called I:yem."[41]

In stating that I:yem is no more, Mrs. Gutierrez raises questions about place and memory, and how changes to places affect people's memories of, and connections to, them. The I:yem that Tillie Gutierrez loved no longer exists. Her connections to that place are now primarily through her memories. The memorial too serves as a reminder of the way that I:yem was; however, rather than existing only in memory it exists in space and time.

Relationships between the Stó:lō and their canyon fishing places have changed even while people continue to fish in the spots of their ancestors. In the early 1950s, Wilson Duff noted that the "time tested Aboriginal technology of dip nets and drying salmon in the canyon, though still in limited use" were "rapidly giving way to gill nets and home canning."[42] No doubt such transformations in human activities were partially due to changes to the landscape itself, as well as government regulations and developments in transportation and technology. Rita Pete spoke of how she had seen the fishing fluctuate in the past sixty years and explained that "not that much of us dry fish these days."[43] She attributed this to people passing away, and although she recognized that "some of the kids go up there yet," she noted that, "some don't bother."[44] Although it might be more efficient and economical to can salmon, something is potentially lost when families do not gather together over the course of several weeks to wind dry salmon. The storytelling, the sharing of memories, and the significance of I:yem are the sorts of things that technological change can obscure.

Individual fishing spots within the five-mile fishery have been, and continue to be, contested. Even the fishing site at I:yem used by the memorial's creator, Dennis S. Peters, was disputed.[45] Today Mrs. Pete fishes at that same spot. Although she explained how Dennis S. Peters's son, Oscar Peters, gave the site to her mother Lillian (and that she had later taken it over), she admitted that others had recently tried to claim the site. It seems that when disputes arise within groups, rather than open conflicts, people question someone else's right or authority to use a particular spot to which they regard themselves as having a superior claim. For example, Sonny McHalsie has noted the controversy around his aunt Rita's[46] claims to the spot where his grandfather fished, explaining, "they [Mrs. Pete's family] actually should be fishing across the river where I fish and I should be fishing where Rita fishes because my grandfather [Robert Peters] fished there."

Even in this controversy, the way in which Mrs. Pete and her family use the spot is significant. As McHalsie has noted, the year he wanted to start fishing, "she [Mrs. Pete] was already fishing there. She already had her family there, you know the dry rack, cabin, and she was quite comfortable."[47] Seen in this light, it is most important that the fishing spot remains a Stó:lō place where someone with a claim, albeit from some people's perspectives not necessarily the best claim, continues to fish and dry in a *proper* way. It is her earlier and ongoing use of the site that gives Mrs. Pete authority to use the spot.

Belonging to I:yem

From the perspective of some of the Stó:lō people I interviewed, people are regarded as *belonging to places* as much as *places belong to people*. Mrs. Gutierrez explained that when some people[48] tried to claim the spot where her daughter continues to fish, "the spirit" protected her from being hurt because her daughter belonged to that area—the ancestors that inhabit that place recognized her daughter as also belonging to that fishing spot.[49] In this regard, by drawing attention to the ancestors buried in the Fraser Canyon, the memorial at I:yem is a reminder of this connection between the Stó:lō and the canyon as well as their corresponding rights to fish there. The idea that certain people belong to the canyon emphasizes that for the Stó:lō meaning exists within these places and is not simply ascribed to them.

While some Stó:lō people are seen as belonging to certain places and their relationships with the Fraser Canyon can be viewed as protected, the places themselves have been and continue to be threatened and changed. It is difficult for an outsider like myself to understand how Tillie Gutierrez's daughter's relationship with her canyon fishing place was preserved because she belonged to that place while I:yem itself (as Mrs. Gutierrez knew it) was destroyed by cement fish ladders in the early 1960s. Such changes are further evident in the vandalism that has occurred in the cemetery at I:yem, which included the theft of the memorial's plaque and, more recently, the destruction of the monument itself. Yet, while canyon places change, for some the meaning that is inherent in them remains, as does the need for certain people and families to continue to return to them. In attempting to reconcile ideas of belonging with obvious changes to canyon places, I suggest that it is the relationship with the canyon itself that the Stó:lō view as the most important—demonstrating continuity in the midst of change.

Statements of belonging to the Fraser Canyon go beyond articulating an emotional attachment and can be seen as providing authority to particular claims to these places. It is because individuals and their families belong to their canyon places that they argue their claims are superior to those of others. By articulating this relationship, they actively maintain connections with their canyon places. Nonetheless, competing claims over these places remain, as do competing authorities. While places may own certain people and grant authority to their claims, legally and politically these same places are under the control of groups to which these individuals may not belong. This is most evident in the Yale First Nation's role in acceding to the creation of the fish ladders that destroyed Mrs. Gutierrez's family's fishing spot. Even though Mrs. Gutierrez's family believed they belonged to I:yem, as part of a Yale Indian reserve it was under the authority of the Yale Indian Band, to which she did not belong.

Authority derived from both belonging to particular places as well as from legal and political structures continues to be invoked in negotiating Indigenous relationships with canyon places. Both the Yale and Stó:lō see themselves as belonging to the Fraser Canyon and are actively engaged in protecting their connections to certain places. These themes of belonging and authority will be further explored as the focus of this analysis turns to the collective relationships that the political entities of the Stó:lō and Yale have with I:yem and with each other, as well as some understandings of these relationships.

Rediscovering I:yem: I:yem as a Contested Place

The memorial at I:yem continues to be significant as it relates to larger disputes between the Yale First Nation on the one hand and the Stó:lō Nation and Tribal Council on the other over fishing rights in the canyon. Since 1938 the legal climate for Aboriginal rights has changed, creating opportunities for land claims and the formation of political organizations to pursue them—including the different incarnations of the Stó:lō Nation, the Stó:lō Tribal Council, the Yale Band, and the Yale First Nation.[50] As Carlson explains, "occasionally colonialism creates a context where Indigenous interests clash with one another, and within which both sides invoke history to justify innovative means to traditional ends."[51] Thus, the dispute between the Stó:lō and the Yale First Nation is intertwined with their relationships with the federal and provincial governments and the history of colonial changes to the Fraser Canyon.

It is in such a context that the memorial has been "rediscovered," taking on a new political and economic significance. According to Steven Point,

> [The I:yem memorial] became politically significant at a time [in the late 1980s and early 1990s] when the Stó:lō were being asked to get a licence to fish up there [in the Fraser Canyon] from the Yale Band.[52] And the Yale Band was trying to get control of the fishery there and our chief was going "why should we get a licence from you when this is our fishery?" There was internal conflict there, and so the memorial became important just to show that the Stó:lō have been up there fishing for a millennium, for a long, long time.[53]

The potential for the memorial to help the Stó:lō regain important fishing grounds made it potentially significant for Stó:lō fishers and leaders and potentially harmful to members of the Yale First Nation. Similarly, each group has distinct understandings of the canyon fishery.

The Stó:lō Nation/Stó:lō Tribal Council on the one side and the Yale First Nation on the other have been in court multiple times since 1992, disputing who should control access to and regulate the canyon fishery—and by implication who should be considered Stó:lō.[54] The Stó:lō groups emphasize that access to the canyon fishery was and is based upon customary familial rights to particular fishing stations and that the Yale First Nation is indeed a Stó:lō band. The Yale have argued that their chief and council has the right to control access to the canyon fishery and that members of other First Nations, including the Stó:lō, require their permission to use sites in the "Yale fishery."[55]

When the Yale First Nation Final Agreement was introduced in the House of Commons for ratification on 31 May 2013, Stó:lō leaders questioned not only the agreement but the treaty process itself, taking the matter of their overlapping claims to the five-mile canyon fishery to court.[56] Part of the final agreement outlines that the Yale First Nation would determine who has rights to harvest fish in their territory. In addition to the allocation of these resources, the Yale First Nation would become responsible for setting out methods, timing, and location of fish harvesting, with the potential for commercial opportunities, and determining access to lands for hunting and fishing.[57] Beyond rights and access to the canyon fishery, this agreement could be seen to officially solidify the position of I:yem as an area under the control of the Yale First Nation rather than the Stó:lō collectively. As Stó:lō Nation Grand Chief Joe Hall explained in response to the Yale treaty, "This is not what treaties are about. Treaties were meant to create harmony among, not just the First Nations, but also the non-aboriginal people. And what they've done, unfortunately, is forced us to go to the courts to have this resolved."[58] While court battles are ongoing, the larger significance for this discussion of I:yem is the various and continued efforts by the Yale and Stó:lō to use government treaty processes and the Canadian courts to maintain their authority over and access to the canyon fishery, and the limits of these processes for dealing with conflicting Indigenous claims. At the time of revising this paper in 2017, the final agreement has yet to be carried out. Changes in the Yale First Nation's chief and council have led to community deciding not to implement the agreement.[59] This draws further attention to the familial and individual differences within Stó:lō and Yale communities and the complexity of the current treaty process.

Court cases and treaty negotiations contribute to how people are able to relate to the Fraser Canyon and demonstrate the role of Canadian law in shaping understandings of I:yem and its memorial. These decisions and negotiations continue to define Indigenous places, and can be seen as a continuation of the mapping and remapping of Indian reservations in British Columbia that began in the mid-nineteenth century.[60] Similarly, more recent negotiations affect how people relate to places and one another—especially in their assertions over to whom the canyon belongs and what types of rights Indigenous people have to certain places. Recent court cases and land claims emphasize that the Fraser Canyon is partially a legal space that continues to be defined by processes that are never entirely within Indigenous control. In this way, the current conflict raises broader issues about the role of courts and the treaty process in determining who can form relations to particular places, and how they are able to do so.

The conflicts between the Yale First Nation and the Stó:lō Nation/Tribal Council relate not only to who should have rights to fish in the Fraser Canyon, but to who should be considered Stó:lō. As such, they are also about assertions of authority and collective identity. Individuals' understandings of places are often conceptualized in comparison with others. Carlson has noted that in contemporary Indigenous conflicts, "a group will often assert that its claim to a particular resource is superior to another's because it is more 'traditional.'"[61]

In this conflict between the Stó:lō and the Yale, in addition to invocations of tradition and history, the Indigenous peoples of the Fraser Canyon and Valley tend to undermine their opponent's claims by dichotomizing the economic motives of the two sides. Both sides speak of what the other stands to gain from controlling the canyon and what their own group stands to lose. Some members of the Stó:lō First Nation have suggested that the Yale decided "they weren't Stó:lō anymore," when it became politically and economically prudent for them to do so.[62] Yet, when referring to their own claim, these Stó:lō spokespersons typically focus on the personal aspects of their connections to canyon places.[63] Chief Robert Hope of Yale provides a counter-argument, asserting that the people at Yale were only included in the Stó:lō group by the Department of Indian Affairs and Northern Development as an "administrative convenience."[64] Ironically, Steven Point explained the government's placement of the canyon fishing reserves under the authority of the Yale Band as also a matter of "administrative convenience."[65] Statements emphasizing the need for individuals and groups to have meaningful relationships with their places while denying others that same connection reveal that both the Stó:lō and Yale draw upon their personal connections with these places to add authority to their own claims.

While both sides emphasize their personal connections to canyon places and the role of these connections in their group identities, the clear economic benefits of the canyon fishery seem (to an outsider's eyes) glaring and contradictory. As such, they raise questions about my own assumptions in interpreting information that has been shared with me. Identities and cultures are inherently political and typically promote the interests of their members. Yet, whereas my own biases accept economic self-interest as a driving motivation for people vying for control over valuable canyon resources in the past, the present claims, which stand to financially benefit one Indigenous nation over another, seem less palatable to me. Significantly, the relationships of the

Stó:lō and the Yale to their canyon places have been articulated and mobilized primarily in the more adversarial settings of the courtroom, treaty negotiating table, local media, and other political forums. This public dispute has been characterized by outsiders as Indigenous nations "vying for control of the lucrative Canyon fishery in the courts and at the treaty table,"[66] or alternatively as only a "rivalry skirmish and contest between Indian bands over where they might catch their given allocation of salmon."[67]

Such normative assessments tend to dismiss the conflict. They are also reductionist, narrowing the conflict to what people stand to gain economically.[68] It is important, however, to avoid simple answers derived from outside cultural perspectives and to take the economic aspects of these relationships with place seriously. Consequently I must reconsider the testimony of those individuals and groups whose self-interest is easiest to critique, as well as the accounts of those, such as Mrs. Gutierrez, whose claims of personal connections are easy to accept uncritically. Just as commercial fishers may have more complex personal relationships with their fishing places, those who have emphasized the inherent personal meaning of the places may also benefit economically from the fish that they and their families catch there. While acknowledging the validity of economical aspects of relationship to places, questioning how representative an individual's testimony is of the Stó:lō or the Yale, their family, and their own personal perspective is necessary. This conflict, which has at times been violent,[69] is not, however, simply about fish. It is also, and I argue more fundamentally, about maintaining important relationships to particular places, even when fishing elsewhere could be more convenient and just as profitable, given changes in technology. In this way, Indigenous relationships with the Fraser Canyon are not only about access to fish or tribal identities, but also about the continued meaning of the canyon itself, and the need of both the Yale and Stó:lō to maintain their connections with those places.

Yale Stories of I:yem

Even the broader political conflict cannot be separated from the personal aspects of place. This is especially evident in statements made by respected Yale elder Lawrence Hope regarding the canyon fishery—statements that are inherently political, yet fundamentally personal.[70] Like Tillie Gutierrez, Sonny McHalsie, and Rita Pete, Mr. Hope emphasizes his own personal connections with and experiences in the Fraser Canyon. He establishes his authority by asserting, "I think I am the only one that grew up in the canyon that is left. I am the only one that truly lived in the canyon, in the fishing ground that saw things."[71] It is these experiences that legitimize his claims and add to his own status, while denying others that same authority. Furthermore, his childhood experiences of spending time in the canyon with his family inform his current understandings of these places.

It is interesting to explore Lawrence Hope's description of the Stó:lō asking permission of the chief at Yale to fish in the canyon. As Mr. Hope explains, in the past a person would not say "I want to come here to fish."[72] Rather, he reminisces that:

> When I was a young boy, I remember that before anyone went fishing they always dropped in to say hello and pay their respects to my grandfather.[73] This was a customary way of asking permission to fish in our territory. The arrival of guests into our territory for purposes of fishing was a cause of celebration, they would stay over night with the chief before going to the river and would visit us again on their departure. This happened on a yearly basis.[74]

Lawrence Hope's understandings of the canyon are shaped by his relationships with his family, especially his grandfather, and also by his interactions with those who fished there at the time. Although this statement outlines proper protocols between insiders and outsiders (suggesting that the territory belongs to those at Yale), it is essentially about relationships between people and the places they share. Mr. Hope's sentiment that such connections have been lost is evident in the simple statement, "but those days are gone."[75] Lawrence Hope's conceptions of the Fraser Canyon, shaped by his relationships with those that he experienced it with, are similar to Mrs. Gutierrez's memories of the I:yem of her childhood that has ceased to exist in the present. Furthermore, his interpretation complements that of Sonny McHalsie, as both stress a sense of loss and change, and the need to regain connections with places and between the people who share them. While articulating seemingly different political perspectives, Lawrence Hope and Sonny McHalsie share concerns over their respective communities' lost connections to the Fraser Canyon and seek to reassert their attachments to those places.

I:yem as a Stó:lō Place and a Yale Place

Building on Lawrence Hope's personal understandings of the Fraser Canyon, I will now explore how the broader community at Yale may relate to, and interpret, this place. In attempting to look at I:yem as a Yale place in addition to a Stó:lō place, it is necessary to take seriously and historicize the Yale's claim of not being Stó:lō. This exploration of the heretofore underexamined experiences of those who stayed in the Fraser Canyon rather than migrating downriver in the late nineteenth century[76] offers some insight into how they responded to changes to their places and came to view themselves as a distinct Indigenous people of both Stó:lō and Nlaka'pamux heritage.[77] Newspaper articles, public statements, and earlier oral interviews with members of the Yale First Nation reveal that the Yale's interpretation of their history is fundamentally shaped by particular familial connections. Over time, the families at Yale have changed and by 1952, there were only three family groups that were a part of the Yale Band.[78] The majority of men who stayed in the canyon married Nlaka'pamux women from upriver and their "families negotiated membership in both 'communities.'"[79] Anthropologist Andrea Laforet has noted that in the 1970s, the Indigenous people at Yale were of both Upper Stó:lō and Nlaka'pamux descent.[80] As familial connections and rights to certain places can be seen to centre a person's own spatial orientation, changes to particular families over time would affect their members' understandings of their places.

Such an upriver focus of the leaders and major families at Yale would have differed from how those who moved downriver for agricultural opportunities related to the territory.[81] Over time identities shifted and ethnogenesis potentially occurred as the descendants of the Emerys, Charlies, and Hopes learned the Nlaka'pamux language and associated histories of their grandparents.[82] This is not to say, as has been claimed in court, that the Stó:lō do not have ancestral links to the Fraser Canyon and familial rights to its fishery. Evidence from reserve commissions, oral history, and the memorial itself notes that those who moved downriver considered themselves to have retained their canyon fishing rights. Nevertheless, it is important to consider how the disputes between the Yale and the Stó:lō might be linked to their changing relationships with particular places, and that the formation and articulation of new identities could be seen as legitimate responses to such changes.[83]

This exploration of Yale understandings of the canyon sheds light on some of their differences with the Stó:lō, especially the contested claim that the Stó:lō require the Yale chief's permission to fish in the canyon. According to tribal historian Bob Joe, who in 1962 shared his memories of the creation of the I:yem memorial with amateur ethnographer Oliver Wells, the memorial asserted the right of all of the Stó:lō people to fish in the five-mile fishery above Yale. In contrast, he noted the different relationship that the Nlaka'pamux had with the area, as they needed to get permission before fishing there.[84] This explanation offers a possible reason as to why more recent chief and councils of the Yale Band, individuals with Nlaka'pamux heritage, believed that other groups, such as the Stó:lō, required permission to fish in the canyon. This is reflective of how their ancestors and families understood outsiders to relate to the fishery.

The memorial at I:yem was seen as a threat to the Yale First Nation as it was not representative of their familial and political identities. However, for the Stó:lō this memorial, which for decades seemed to have sat forgotten, has recently become an important representation of their identity and a claim to the canyon resources. The Yale First Nation destroyed the memorial in 2008 to show their control over the territory. In response to this recent destruction, a group of Stó:lō people placed a new stone plaque (with the same inscription as the 1938 original) into the ground where the memorial once stood, demonstrating their continued claim to this place, in response to which Yale threatened to lay trespassing charges against the Stó:lō.[85] This dispute goes beyond politics, as all involved are concerned about angering their ancestors who fished and were buried in the canyon. These events emphasize the arguments I have made about the continuing need for both the Stó:lō and the Yale to maintain and protect particular relationships with I:yem and the Fraser Canyon.

I:yem Beyond the Courtroom

It is important not to overemphasize the contest over being Stó:lō. While this conflict over fishing rights is significant, it does not capture the complexity of the various relationships that the Indigenous people of the Fraser Valley and Canyon had and continue to have with the Fraser Canyon and I:yem. The perspectives of the Yale and Stó:lō are also interconnected. They draw on a common history, though they often favour different aspects. In their relationships to place, members of both groups emphasize the role of government regulations and other colonial changes and the continuing importance of kinship in regulating access to the canyon fishery. Both groups continue to creatively respond to perceived threats to their relationships with the canyon fishery. There is not a single Indigenous perspective, or Stó:lō, or Yale voice for that matter. By looking at some of the specific relationships that people of the Fraser Canyon and Valley have had with I:yem, and how these relationships have continued and changed over time, it is possible to start exploring differences within and between Indigenous communities, rather than simply colonial relationships between Indigenous peoples and the settler state. Fundamentally, it is the Indigenous people of the Fraser Canyon and Valley that have and will continue to set the parameters of what aspects of the canyon can change and what must be preserved, ultimately defining their own relationships with this place.

Although there is a difference between such a general political significance and the personal connections that Tillie Gutierrez, Rita Pete, Lawrence Hope, and Sonny McHalsie emphasized, these differing views (while not necessarily informed by one another) cannot be completely separated. Tillie Gutierrez, Rita Pete, and Archie Charles had little to say about the political conflict between the Yale First Nation and the Stó:lō, and Archie Charles, who fishes for food and not commercial sale, reported never having problems with the Yale Band.[86] Their connections to I:yem and the fishery were personal. To Tillie Gutierrez, I:yem was her grandparents' fishing spot. To Rita Pete, I:yem is where her own fishing spot and dry rack are located, as well as the graveyard that she is responsible for looking after. Then again, even those who emphasized more personal relationships with I:yem have also been involved in the more political aspects of things and vice versa. Mrs. Gutierrez testified in the Van der Peet case regarding Aboriginal rights to sell fish commercially that eventually went to the Supreme Court of Canada.[87] Archie Charles, who was the chief of Seabird Island for many years and served as one of the grand chiefs of the Stó:lō, was personally named in the court cases between the Yale and the Stó:lō over fishing in the Fraser Canyon. Even Mrs. Pete referred to some trouble with the Yale First Nation, noting that although her fishing spot at I:yem is not on reserve land, members of the Yale Band "came there measuring it."[88] In contrast, Steven Point, whose interpretation of the I:yem memorial was the most overtly political, conducted a sacred burning ceremony at I:yem for Mrs. Pete. Most notably, Lawrence Hope's testimony and affidavit, while providing the foundation for the Yale First Nation's claim, is especially personal. Finally, even though Sonny McHalsie recognizes the political significance of the memorial and its implications for Stó:lō collective identity and history, has conducted research for claims, and testified in court, I:yem is where his ancestors lived, fished, and where his great-grandfather built a memorial—by extension, this is a place where he belongs.

Conclusion

Conflicts between the Yale First Nation and the Stó:lō Nation/Tribal Council relate not only to who should have rights to fish in the Fraser Canyon, but to questions of whether, and how, Indigenous peoples can define their identity. Authority derived from personal connections to particular places as well as from legal and political structures has been (and continues to be) invoked in negotiating Indigenous relationships with these canyon places. Considering the creation, destruction, and reconstruction of the I:yem memorial enables an exploration of some of the ways that competing claims of authority over the canyon's history and resources have been mobilized and challenged by the Stó:lō and Yale, while recognizing the complexity of the various relationships that the Yale and the Stó:lō had and continue to have with these places.

I:yem is not only a place that is politically significant for the Stó:lō and the Yale First Nation, it is also personally meaningful to many of the people who were interviewed for this project. It is this need for meaningful relationships with places that seems to link the personal and the political, the tangible and the intangible, and to maintain relationships between the dead, the living, and those yet unborn—demonstrating continuity in a place that has changed and will continue to do so. I:yem is a Stó:lō place and a Yale place, but beyond that it is experienced and interpreted by particular individuals and families. The ways in which Sonny McHalsie, Tillie Gutierrez, Archie Charles, Rita Pete, Steven Point, and Lawrence Hope spoke of I:yem and the canyon demonstrate the importance of connections to places, memory, belonging, authority, ancestors, and fishing for both personal and political reasons. Meaning is never simply something that is ascribed to places—it also exists within them. This is especially true at I:yem, where people's ancestors are located and where they themselves feel like they belong. It is through the process of returning to these places that aspects of memory and identity are regained and new connections with the landscape created, and why the possibility of being denied access to these places becomes such a point of conflict.

Notes

1   In 2007, when I conducted my research for this paper, the plaque had been missing from the I:yem memorial for several years. This text was taken from an older picture of the memorial. The use of older spellings of "Eayem" and "Stalo" are as inscribed on the memorial; throughout the rest of the paper these terms appear in the form standardized in *A Stó:lō-Coast Salish Historical Atlas* unless quoting directly from an earlier source.

2   Albert "Sonny" McHalsie believes that the memorial marks the first time the term Stó:lō was publicly displayed by the people themselves, with the exception of the *Dream Book of the Stó:lō Chief*. See Albert "Sonny" McHalsie, interview by Amanda Fehr, Hope, BC, 24 June 2007. Copies at SRRMC.

3   Keith Thor Carlson, David Schaepe, Albert "Sonny McHalsie, et al., eds., *A Stó:lō–Coast Salish Historical Atlas* (Vancouver: Douglas and McIntyre/Chilliwack: Stó:lō Heritage Trust, 2001), 26.

4   Paul Henderson, "Sto:lo Lawsuit Names Feds and Province in Treaty Fight," *Chilliwack Times*, 25 June 2013, http://www.chilliwacktimes.com/news/ 245072611. html.

5   X. Y. Zeng, "Desecrated Monument Restored," *Hope Standard*, 14 April 2016, http:// www.bclocalnews.com/news/375628511.html.

6   Keith Thor Carlson, "Innovation, Tradition, Colonialism and Aboriginal Fishing Conflicts in the Lower Fraser Canyon," in *New Histories for Old: Changing Perspectives on Canada's Native Pasts*, eds. Ted Binnema and Susan Neylan (Vancouver: UBC Press, 2007), 168.

7   Despite efforts to meet with and interview members of the Yale First Nation while I was in the Fraser Valley in 2007 and again briefly in 2008, I was unable to talk with anyone who officially represented that community as their treaty negotiations were ongoing at the time I was conducting my research. Notwithstanding this, every effort has been made to include the perspectives of members of the Yale First Nation using alternative sources.

8   All but one of my interviews were conducted with other field school students, meaning that several topics were covered in a single interview. With the exception of Sonny McHalsie, I met those that I interviewed only once, often building on relationships that they had with the Stó:lō Nation, the host of our field school, or former field school students.

9   I:yem and the memorial there was the subject of my MA thesis, in which I focused on the political significance of the memorial, the associated fishing rights it called for, issues of Stó:lō collective identity, and ideas of place making. Amanda Fehr, "The Relationships of Place: A Study of Change and Continuity in Stó:lō Understandings of I:yem" (MA thesis, University of Saskatchewan, 2008).

10   A version of this paper was originally published in 2009. I have updated the paper to address more recent events related to the I:yem memorial, but have not conducted additional interviews. See Amanda Fehr, "Relationships: A Study of Memory, Change, and Identity at a Place Called I:yem," *University of the Fraser Valley Research Review* 2, no. 2 (2009): 9–35. More recently I considered the Catholic elements of the I:yem memorial in a separate article. See Amanda Fehr, "A Subversive Sincerity: Christian Gatherings and Political Opportunities in S'olh Téméxw," in *Mixed Blessings*, eds. Tolly Bradford and Chelsea Horton (Vancouver: UBC Press, 2016).

11   See David Schaepe, "Stó:lō Identity and the Cultural Landscape of S'olh Téméxw," in *Be of Good Mind: Essays on the Coast Salish*. ed. Bruce G. Miller (Vancouver: UBC Press, 2007); Carlson, "Innovation, Tradition, Colonialism and Aboriginal Fishing Conflicts in the Lower Fraser Canyon"; Keith Thor Carlson, *The Power of Place, the Problem of Time: Aboriginal Identity and Historical Consciousness in the Cauldron of Colonialism* (Toronto: University of Toronto Press, 2010); Bruce G. Miller, *The Problem of Justice: Tradition and Law in the Coast Salish World* (Lincoln, NE: University of Nebraska Press, 2002); Albert "Sonny" McHalsie, "Halq'emélem Place Names in Stó:lō Territory," in *A Stó:lō–Coast Salish Historical Atlas*, eds.Keith Thor Carlson, David Schaepe, Albert "Sonny" McHalsie, et al. (Vancouver: Douglas and McIntyre/Chilliwack: Stó:lō Heritage Trust, 2001); Wayne Suttles, "The Persistence of Intervillage Ties" in *Coast Salish Essays*, ed. Wayne Suttles (Vancouver: Talonbooks, 1987); Albert "Sonny" McHalsie, "We Have to Take Care of Everything

that Belongs to Us" in *Be of Good Mind: Essays on the Coast Salish*, ed. Bruce G. Miller (Vancouver: UBC Press, 2007); Crisca Bierwert, *Brushed by Cedar, Living by the River: Coast Salish Figures of Power* (Tucson: University of Arizona Press, 1999).

12   The roles of social networks, villages, and families has been highlighted in Suttles, "The Persistence of Intervillage Ties"; Miller emphasizes a tendency for communities themselves to perpetuate the idea of a harmonious past while deemphasizing social conflict in the present in order to manage relationships with the outside world (Miller, *The Problem of Justice*, 13); Carlson notes current tensions regarding fishing within Stó:lō communities suggesting that there are two dimensions to them: conflicts between families and those between the Yale First Nation and the Stó:lō (Carlson, "Innovation, Tradition, Colonialism and Aboriginal Fishing Conflicts in the Lower Fraser Canyon," 145). In a different context Carlson explains that there are similarities/commonalities among this group of people in addition to differences, and chooses to focus on the former while acknowledging the latter. Keith Thor Carlson, "Introduction," in *A Stó:lō-Coast Salish Historical Atlas*, eds. Keith Thor Carlson, David Schaepe, Albert "Sonny" McHalsie, et al. (Vancouver: Douglas and McIntyre/Chilliwack: Stó:lō Heritage Trust, 2001), 1–2.

13   A significant amount of scholarship has centred on the various relationships between memories and particular places. These studies demonstrate that places are important sites of memory, that memory lives as long as it serves a social role, and that it is possible for multiple and equally valid meanings to be attached to particular sites. See, for example, Keith H. Basso, *Wisdom Sits in Places: Landscape and Language among the Western Apache* (Albuquerque: University of New Mexico Press, 1996); Fernando Santos-Grenaro, "Writing History into the Landscape: Space, Myth, and Ritual in Contemporary Amazonia," *American Ethnologist* 25, no. 2 (1998): 128–48; Lesley Fordred Green and David R. Green, "From Chronological to Spatio-Temporal Histories: Mapping Heritage in Arukwa, Area Indígena Do Uaçá, Brazil," *History and Anthropology* 14, no. 3 (2003): 283–95; Julie Cruikshank, *Do Glaciers Listen? Local Knowledge, Colonial Encounters, and Social Imagination* (Vancouver: UBC Press, 2005); William Turkel, *The Archive of Place: Unearthing the Pasts of the Chilcotin Plateau* (Vancouver: UBC Press, 2007).

14   See Wilson Duff, *The Upper Stalo Indians of the Fraser Valley British Columbia*, Anthropology in British Columbia Memoir No. 1. (Victoria: British Columbia Provincial Museum, 1952), 30; McHalsie, "Halq'emélem Place Names in Stó:lō Territory," 142.

15   Mabel Nichols, personal communication, 6 October 2007.

16   This is essentially the idea of historical consciousness, by which I mean, "individual and collective understandings of the past, the cognitive and cultural factors that shape those understandings, as well as the relations of historical understandings to those of the present and future." Sharon Macdonald and Katja Fausser, "Towards European Historical Consciousness" in *Approaches to European Historical Consciousness*, ed. S. Macdonald (Hamburg: Koerber Stiftung, 2000), 10, as quoted in Peter Seixas, "Introduction," in *Theorizing Historical Consciousness*, ed. Peter Seixas (Toronto: University of Toronto Press, 2004), 10.

17   Sonny McHalsie is the great-grandson of one of the memorial's creators, Dennis S. Peters. McHalsie, interview.

18   Steven L. Point, interview by Andrée Boisselle and Amanda Fehr, Chilliwack, BC, 29 June 2007. Copies at SRRMC.

19 Mrs. Pete was born in 1935 and lived at Skam reserve when I met with her in 2007. Her fishing spot was located at I:yem. For more on the Pete family relationship to I:yem, see Whitney Bajric, "On Experiencing Place: A Biography of a Stó:lō Family's Fishing Site in the Fraser Canyon of British Columbia" (Master's major research paper, University of Victoria, 2015). On file at SRRMC.

20 Rita Pete, interview by Amanda Fehr and Katya MacDonald. Skam, BC, 29 June 2007. Copies at SRRMC.

21 "Sto:lo Ceremony Delayed After Grave-Site Pedestal Destroyed," *The Vancouver Province*, 3 November 2008, http://www.canada.com/story.html?id=5dce7690-793d-4347-a3c1-1debffc01971 (accessed September 2015).

22 McHalsie, interview.

23 In 2007 Rita Pete was still fishing at age seventy-three. It was Mrs. Pete's mother, Lillian, who had connections to I:yem. See Pete, interview.

24 Ibid.

25 Ibid.

26 However, due to the relationship between fishing spots and family connections, it is likely Mrs. Pete has some connection, albeit in a distant way, to those buried at I:yem.

27 Stó:lō political activist Dennis S. Peters was instrumental in erecting the I:yem memorial with his brother-in-law, Chief Isaac James of Ruby Creek. Dennis S. Peters was Sonny McHalsie's maternal great-grandfather. See McHalsie, interview.

28 McHalsie, "We Have to Take Care of Everything that Belongs to Us," 93.

29 Matilda "Tillie" Gutierrez, interview by Amanda Fehr and Amber Kostuchenko, Chawathil, BC, 26 June 2007. Copies at SRRMC.

30 Ibid.

31 Ibid.

32 Ibid.

33 *R. v. Van der Peet*, Proceedings at Trial, Provincial Court of British Columbia, File No. 43322T, 1989. Copies at SRRMC.

34 It is clear that here Mrs. Gutierrez is referring to her family at least.

35 Gutierrez, interview, 26 June 2007; McHalsie, interview; McHalsie, "We Have to Take Care of Everything that Belongs to Us," 90.

36 McHalsie, "We Have to Take Care of Everything that Belongs to Us," 90.

37 Matilda Gutierrez, as quoted in McHalsie, "We have to Take Care of Everything that Belongs to Us," 90.

38 J.S. Dunn, Superintendent New Westminster Indian Agency, to Mr. Lloyd A. Royal, Director International Pacific Salmon Fisheries Commission, New Westminster, BC, 26 January 1961, Department of Indian Affairs and Northern Development Fonds, RG10, vol. 13300, 153/31-5-33-22, Library and Archives Canada (LAC).

39 Band Council Resolution, Yale Indian Band, New Westminster Indian Agency, 27 March 1961, Department of Indian Affairs and Northern Development Fonds, RG10, vol. 13300, file 167/31-5-41-11, LAC.

40 *Regina v. Dorothy Van der Peet*, 17.

41 Ibid, 30. Emphasis added.

42 Duff, *The Upper Stalo Indians of Fraser Valley British Columbia*, 13. Some changes to technology have led to confusion over the ownership of fishing stations. Carlson has noted that whereas 100 years ago it was commonly understood that Stó:lō fishing

spots were their fishing rocks next to the eddies where people could dip net, today it is the eddies where people place their gill nets that are considered to belong to particular fishers and their families. See Keith Carlson, "History Wars: Considering Contemporary Fishing Site Disputes," in *A Stó:lō-Coast Salish Historical Atlas*, eds. Keith Thor Carlson, David Schaepe, Albert "Sonny" McHalsie, et al. (Vancouver: Douglas and McIntyre/Chilliwack: Stó:lō Heritage Trust, 2001), 78.

43 She explained that only fourteen families currently dry fish in the canyon. Pete, interview.

44 Ibid.

45 See Mrs. Vincent Peters, in Marian Smith Fieldnotes, MS 268: 4 (15) and 268: 4 (9), Marian Wesley Smith Collection, MS-2794, BC Archives, Royal British Columbia Museum.

46 Mrs. Pete is McHalsie's mother's second cousin. See McHalsie, "We Have to Take Care of Everything that Belongs to Us," 95.

47 Ibid.

48 Mrs. Gutierrez did not specify whom.

49 Gutierrez, interview.

50 Paul Tennant, *Aboriginal People and Politics: The Indian Land Question in British Columbia, 1849–1989* (Vancouver: UBC Press, 1990), 122. Stó:lō bands participated in the Chilliwack Area Council that began when the federal government transferred jurisdiction over their social assistance program to the council in 1974. Significantly, in 1975 the "self-proclaimed Stó:lō Tribes of the Lower Fraser Watershed drafted and adopted the Stó:lō declaration," which was essentially "a statement of Aboriginal title and rights to all land and resources within their collective tribal territory." By the early 1980s the political tribal council, the Stó:lō Nation, was formed. The Yale Band was a member of this tribal council, until it withdrew its membership by a Band Council Resolution on June 6, 1983. This was not the only conflict within the Stó:lō Nation, and in 1985 its member bands split to form two tribal councils—the Stó:lō Nation Canada and the Stó:lō Tribal Council. It is significant that following this split both political entities still considered themselves to be Stó:lō and would unite in the pursuit of common causes and goals. These organizations amalgamated in 1999 before fracturing again in 2005/2006. See Miller, *The Problem of Justice*, 125; Schaepe, "Stó:lō Identity and the Cultural Landscape of S'olh Téméxw," 235; Affidavit of Robert Hope, *Chief Robert Hope v. Lower Fraser Fishing Authority and others*, BC Supreme Court Vancouver Registry. File No. c92-4333. Signed 8 July 1992, 2; "Yale First Nation Paid Advertisement," *Chilliwack Progress*, 3 July 1999.

51 Carlson, "Innovation, Tradition, Colonialism and Aboriginal Fishing Conflicts in the Lower Fraser Canyon," 145.

52 The people from Yale refer to themselves as the Yale First Nation because they view themselves as separate from the Stó:lō. The use of the term Yale Band here promotes the view that they remain a Stó:lō community.

53 Point, interview.

54 This public conflict was sparked by the efforts of the downriver Stó:lō communities to negotiate an Aboriginal Fishing Strategy (AFS) and pilot sales agreements with the Department of Oceans and Fisheries. See *Chief Robert Hope v. Lower Fraser Fishing Authority and others*, Reasons for Judgment of Mr. Justice K.C. MacKenzie, BC Supreme Court Vancouver Registry, 17 July 1992; *Yale First Nation v. Her Majesty the Queen In Right of Canada et al.*, Reasons for Judgment of the Honourable Madam

Justice Dorgan, BC Supreme Court Victoria Registry, 22 May 2001, Reasons for Judgments Database, http://www.courts.gov.bc.ca/jdb -txt/sc/01/07/2001bcsc0746. htm (accessed 2009).

55   See *Chief Robert Hope v. Lower Fraser Fishing Authority and others,* Reasons for Judgment of Mr. Justice K.C. MacKenzie, 2; See also *Yale Indian Band v. Aitchelitz Indian Band et al.,* Reasons for Order of Prothonotary John A. Hargrave, Federal Court Vancouver BC, 24 June 1998, File T-776-98, Federal Court Decisions, http:// decisions.fct-cf.gc.ca/en/1998/t-776-98_4083/t-776-98.html.

56   Jennifer Feinberg, " Sto:lo head to BC Supreme Court Over Yale Treaty," *Chilliwack Progress,* 20 June 2013, http://www.theprogress.com/news/212403421.html.

57   "Yale First Nation Treaty Negotiations Agreement in Principle," 47, 50. Yale First Nation Final Agreement, https://www.aadnc-aandc.gc.ca/eng/1336659639099/ 1336660353801#chap7.6.

58   Henderson, "Sto:lo Lawsuit Names Feds and Province in Treaty Fight."

59   Peter O'Neil and Rob Shaw, "Yale First Nation Puts Hold on Treaty Implementation," *Vancouver Sun,* 2 November 2016.

60   Cole Harris has noted the legal realities of the "arbitrary boundaries identified on the reserve maps." Cole Harris, *Making Native Space: Colonialism, Resistance and Reserves in British Columbia* (Vancouver: UBC Press, 2002), 271.

61   Keith Thor Carlson, "Toward an Indigenous Historiography: Events, Migrations, and the Formation of 'Post-Contact' Coast Salish Collective Identities," in *Be of Good Mind: Essays on the Coast Salish,* ed. Bruce G. Miller (Vancouver: UBC Press, 2007), 139.

62   According to Steven Point, the fight between the Stó:lō and the people at Yale began when selling fish became legal. The Yale did not want the Stó:lō Nation to be controlling what they viewed as their industry, "that's why they aren't Stó:lō." Point, interview.

63   For example, Ken Malloway, a Stó:lō commercial fisherman, emphasized that the "dispute is not just about 'property,' in the European sense. It is about family, and personal identity; about the need for cultural survival. We are borrowing the land and the resources from the children who are yet unborn." See Ken Malloway, as quoted in Mark Falkenberg, "Family Feud: Stó:lō Say Fight Over Fishing Rights with Yale Band Comes Down to Respect for Traditional Fishing Patterns," *Chilliwack Progress,* 17 April 1998, 9.

64   *Chilliwack Progress,* 17 March 2006, as quoted in *Fraser Valley Treaty Advisory Committee Local Media Excerpts to March 31st, 2006,* online, http://www.fvrd. bc.ca/NR/rdonlyres/37719ADD-6E99-4634-BD00-B53E396C7D86/928/ LocalMediaReporttoMarch3106.pdf.

65   Point, interview. Issues of government mistakes in naming reserves are not new, as they were raised in the 1950s by Mr. and Mrs. Lorenzetto from Hope, who explained to Wilson Duff that X̱elhálh was put under the Yale band by mistake. The Lorenzettos explained that the "Commissioner going by didn't land there, and Liyik travelling with him, said he'd take care of their other places out of his kindness. Commissioner said he'd come back, but didn't so X̱elhálh stayed with Yale band, not foreseeing trouble at present." See Mr. and Mrs. Lorenzetto, 1950, Wilson Duff, Fieldnotes, Notebook No. 7, Wilson Duff Papers, BC Archives, Royal British Columbia Museum. Copies at SRRMC.

66   Robert Freeman, "Bands Feud Over Canyon Cleaning," *Chilliwack Progress,* May 18, 1999.

67 *Yale Indian Band v. Aitchelitz Indian Band et al.*, Reasons for Order of Prothonotary John A. Hargrave, 1998, p. 7.

68 There is also a tendency for some scholars to be critical of Indigenous groups that seem to prioritize more local band-based identities in the pursuit of economic advantages. For example, lawyer and historian Alexandra Harmon has explained, "people of Native ancestry have related their histories in order to show that they meet government definitions of Indian, tribe or band and are therefore entitled to particular resources." Alexandra Harmon, "Coast Salish History," in *Be of Good Mind: Essays on the Coast Salish*, ed. Bruce G. Miller (Vancouver: UBC Press, 2007), 46–48. See also Miller, *The Problem of Justice;* Tennant, *Aboriginal People and Politics*; and Harris, *Making Native Space.*

69 For example, Ken Malloway has referred to violent confrontations between the Yale and Stó:lō over the fishery. He has also emphasized that, "our people [the Stó:lō] would die for those fishing spots, literally, our people would die for those fishing spots." Ken Malloway, interview by Katya MacDonald and Sarah Nickel, Sardis, BC, 22 June 2007, transcript, 10. Copies at SRRMC.

70 Lawrence Hope was born in the 1920s at Seabird Island. Although his grandfather, George Hope, had moved the family to Seabird from Yale to farm, the family seasonally returned to the Canyon to fish. Lawrence Hope's mother, Lena (née Charlie), later took over the farm. Mr. Hope explained that the farm "wasn't much of a success, so we more or less moved to Yale all the summer months." Lawrence Hope is the father of Chief Robert Hope. Lawrence Hope, interview by Sonny McHalsie, Randel Paul, and Richard Daly, Albert Flat's Reserve, 25 November 1988, SRRMC Oral History Collection, 88SR46-49, 4.

71 Ibid, 13.

72 Affidavit of Lawrence Hope, *Yale Indian Band v. Aitchelitz Indian Band et al.*, section [30].

73 Mr. Hope is referring to his mother's stepfather, who was Chief Jimmie Charlie. Jimmie Charlie was a brother-in-law to Dennis S. Peters and Isaac James.

74 Affidavit of Lawrence Hope, *Chief Robert Hope v. The Lower Fraser Fishing Authority and others*, BC Supreme Court Vancouver Registry, File No. c92-4333, July 1992: 5. For similar statements see also "New Head of Fisheries Meets Canyon Band," *The Hope Standard*, 13 July 2000; Affidavit of Lawrence Hope, *Yale Indian Band v. Aitchelitz Indian Band et al.*, section [30]; Affidavit of Lawrence Hope, *Yale Indian Band v. Aitchelitz Indian Band et al.*, section [33].

75 Ibid.

76 Carlson has extensively explored the role of large migrations from the Fraser Canyon in the formation and consolidation of a collective Stó:lō identity among those who moved to more arable lands further downriver. See Carlson, *The Power of Place ,the Problem of Time*; Carlson, "Toward an Indigenous Historiography"; Carlson, "Stó:lō Migrations and Shifting Identities."

77 See Hope, interview; Yale First Nation Treaty Negotiations Agreement in Principle.

78 J. C. Letcher, Superintendent New Westminster Agency, BC, to W.S. Arneil, Indian Commissioner for British Columbia, 28 January 1952, Department of Indian Affairs and Northern Development Fonds, RG10, Vol. 7128, File 987/3-5, Pt. 2, LAC.

79 Andrea Laforet and Annie York, *Spuzzum: Fraser Canyon Histories, 1808–1939* (Vancouver: UBC Press, 1998), 137. Notably, the families of Patrick Charlie and Maggie Emery negotiated memberships in Spuzzum and Yale. The Hope family prominent at Yale at the time of my research also has links to both communities. See

Irene Bjerky, "First Peoples of Yale and Spuzzum," *Colourful Characters in Historic Yale*, http://www.virtualmuseum.ca/ pm.php?id=story_line&fl=0&lg=English &ex =00000150 &sl =5044&pos=15.

80 Andrea Laforet, "Folk History in a Small Canadian Community" (PhD diss., University of British Columbia, 1974), 33.

81 As early as 1945, Fred Ewen explained to one of Marian Smith's students that the Talti't or Yale People were a joining of the Halq'emélem and "Thompson people in the Stalo." See Fred Ewen and Marian Smith, Fieldnotes, Summer 1945, 268:2:1 (13), Marian Wesley Smith Collection, MS-2794, BC Archives, Royal British Columbia Museum.

82 The use of language and history in families of both Nlaka'pamux and Stó:lō heritage would likely influence understandings of place. There is a link between language and the names of particular places, and the knowledge of those places that can be derived from their names. In this way the prominence of the Nlaka'pamux language in these families is directly tied to understandings of places and their history. See, for example, Elsie Charlie, interview with Sonny McHalsie, Richard Daly, Randel Paul, and Peter John, Richard Hope's Camp, Spuzzum BC, 2 August 1988, SRRMC Oral History Collection, 22; Hope, interview, 6–7.

83 This discussion fits into a body of literature that rightly describes the Coast Salish as a "fluid, supratribal society." However, some scholars seem to privilege Indigenous identities and affiliations that grow to be more expansive over those that become narrower. Arguably, current interpretations of the Yale's identity and understandings of place, while narrower than those of the Stó:lō, still fit into a context of fluidity and flux that involves both expansions and contractions. See Harmon, "Coast Salish History," 47–48; Suttles, "The Persistence of Intervillage Ties"; Miller, *The Problem of Justice*; Carlson, "Toward an Indigenous Historiography."

84 Bob Joe, "Bob Joe at Tzeachten February 8, 1962" transcript, in Oliver Wells Interview Collection (1961–1968), SRRMC, 103.

85 Robert Matas, "Taking it to their graves," *Globe and Mail*, 5 November 2008, and 13 March, 2009, http://www.theglobeandmail.com/news/national/taking-it-to-their-graves/article662715/.

86 Archie Charles, interview by Amanda Fehr, Amber Kostuchenko, and Katya MacDonald. Seabird Island, BC, 28 June 2007. Digitally Recorded. Copies at SRRMC.

87 Mrs. Gutierrez provided testimony in 1989. The Stó:lō supported Dorothy Van der Peet and brought the case all the way to the Supreme Court. Although the Supreme Court did not find in favour of Mrs. Van der Peet in 1996, the case resulted in the court providing criteria for establishing Aboriginal rights.

88 Pete, interview.

3

Crossing Paths: Knowing and Navigating Routes of Access to Stó:lō Fishing Sites[1]

KATYA C. MACDONALD

The Fraser River is a central feature in arguments about Stó:lō histories and contemporary political and daily life, and as such, it forms an important place of access. Of particular significance is the fishery with which the river is so closely associated. Euro-Canadian intervention here has added and complicated paths of access to twentieth-century Stó:lō fishing practices, meaning that fishers have found it necessary to articulate publicly why and how they access the river when they seek to fish there. Some aspects of the fishery have been maintained over time, while others have been adapted in response to changing circumstances, thereby also affecting interpersonal and intertribal relationships. I aim to expand the idea of access beyond simply physical usage of fishing sites to also encompass intellectual and social access to protocols and ideas of tradition; access to political knowledge to circumvent, discuss, or adapt to government restrictions; and, above all, access to collective and individual histories and the arguments for identities that accompany them. While each of these routes of access exists with its own history and consequences, all are interdependent as well. Stó:lō fishers have argued and established that fishing and its centrality in Stó:lō histories has had important links to a wide range of other discussions within and about their communities, and as a result, access to the fishery is, naturally, vital. Navigating the various paths that lead to the Stó:lō fishery involves negotiating with various people, groups, and situations along the way. Thus, to Stó:lō fishers, the fishery represents a particular Stó:lō history, not only because of the fishery's extended history as an activity that matches the Fisheries Act's description of food, social, and ceremonial functions of fishing, but also because it is situated at the axis of access routes formed by a history of long-standing and ongoing relationships.

These histories of interactions are complex, but they fall into a handful of broad categories or circumstances; that is, they travel certain paths of access most frequently. I explore here four interlocutors in discussions about fishing through the examination of familial, governmental, financial, and what some fishers call (somewhat as a shorthand for a multiplicity of historical understandings) cultural modes of access to fishing sites. Families have historically been, and continue to be, the most immediate mode of access to hereditary fishing sites and they also shape a fisher's understandings of fishing technologies and protocols. With the advent of governments' regulation of Indigenous fishing practices, fishers began to find that the sharing and interpretation of family histories was, at least at times, rerouted through governmental interpretations. This, in turn, required an understanding of non-Indigenous laws and political climates, and, perhaps more significantly, made it more difficult to find effective ways of evaluating the legitimacy of families' and individuals' access to sites. Canadian and provincial government intervention also created an Aboriginal fishery that separated fishing for economic reasons from fishing for sustenance, and this dichotomy has created an aspect of the fishery where financial viability and gain form a central route of access, while often referring and responding to governmental bans or regulations. Accessing fishing sites has not been restricted to any single path, and the navigation of a series of paths, both simultaneously and in sequence, can help to point out the motivations for a particular fisher to access the river. These intertwining histories of access point to a desire among fishers for a more broadly and politically Stó:lō narrative of fisheries history, and by extension to fishing practices that some Stó:lō fishers have defined as distinctly Stó:lō, such as wind drying salmon.

"The Fishery Defines Who We Are": Situating Fishing Sites in History and Historiography

During my field school experience in 2007 as a student about to enter an MA program, I interviewed several Stó:lō fishers with a range of experience in fisheries.[2] Our conversations were loosely structured around my questions regarding ownership and handing down of their families' fishing sites, interactions with other fishing families, and what they would do with the fish once they had been caught, along with other similar topics that arose. It is important to note that although the field school environment allows for significant and long-standing institutional relationships between the universities and interested members of the Stó:lō Nation political body, as an individual participant, I had the chance to meet with most of my interviewees on only one occasion, ten years ago now, prior to writing this paper. This has meant that my analysis is necessarily focused on broad, at times politically driven themes. Furthermore, especially because I am a settler scholar, my aim here is to explore the ways that some Stó:lō fishers have responded to colonial intrusion over time, rather than to provide a comprehensive overview of Stó:lō experiences or histories. The discussion that follows stems directly from the conversations and contexts of my 2007 field school work.

The fishers I met all noted the importance of fishing to themselves, their families, and their sense of history, and this conviction was often expressed during discussions of their access to the fishery. They highlighted ways of reacting to or circumventing restrictions on fishing, whether these limitations were enforced by governments, other families, physical ability, or a lack of knowledge of historical and social protocols of access. Speaking about fishing in these terms highlights the many interactions that are involved with the apparently simple act of catching fish. Recognizing that their statements represent individual understandings of their own experience rather than any generalized Stó:lō history, I include some of my interviewees' observations here in order to reinforce the strong connections between Stó:lō interactions with people and people's (or peoples') interactions with fishing sites, and to demonstrate the multifaceted nature of access even within a single Indigenous group. Their analyses have shaped my understanding of fishing as a central point of access through various conduits.

The issue of access remains salient not only because, as Stó:lō fisher, political activist, and leader Ken Malloway has noted, fishing "defines who [the Stó:lō] are,"[3] but also because of the ways in which the Aboriginal fishery has been defined, as well as challenged and changed by European intervention. In his exploration of the history of relationships between humans and nature along the Columbia River, historian Richard White comments that "claims to salmon are so passionately made and defended because they are so much more than economic."[4] Access to fishing sites involves more than physically being there and more than the implication of physical, tangible gain; it requires and engages both the natural and social aspects of the river. Furthermore, for the fishers I spoke with, access represents an important feature of what they saw as uniquely Stó:lō histories, as well as, particularly in the past, a source of livelihood. As a result, the changes brought about by European regulation served

Stó:lō family at fish camp, near Yale, BC, c. 1890. Postcard by T.N. Hibben and Co., in Keith Carlson's private collection.

to highlight fishing as a subject of particular urgency and often controversy, especially for the Indigenous people affected. A significant cause and outcome was an environment of interactions where Indigenous and non-Indigenous interests were often perceived as belonging to a dichotomy of "traditional" and "progressive" peoples. Yet beyond these nineteenth-century social Darwinist tropes, within any interest group were a multitude of interpretations of how best to access the fishery. As historian Keith Carlson has commented, sometimes "colonialism creates a context within which indigenous interests clash with one another, and within which both sides invoke history to justify innovative means to traditional ends."[5] In other words, debates over access to fishing are also debates over histories of access. These "innovative means" of maintaining access to the fishery have taken diverse forms, some of which I discuss in this paper, but they all have common catalysts.

When considering fishing, the colonial context to which Carlson refers had its beginnings in two key pieces of 1880s legislation. The 1868 Salmon Fishery Regulations were a provincial government initiative meant to foster non-Indigenous commerce in British Columbia by prohibiting the sale of salmon caught in non-tidal waters (where the Stó:lō fishery takes place), and banning certain Indigenous fishing technologies such as fish weirs and dip nets. In effect, this served to equate the Aboriginal fishery with fishing for food, social, and ceremonial—not economic—purposes, creating an artificial distinction. Secondly, a federal law passed in 1884 (often referred to in shorthand as the potlatch ban) made property-transfer gatherings illegal, which removed the forum through which the Stó:lō had previously claimed and passed down ownership of fishing sites.[6] These circumstances were not only causes of changes in the fishery; they were also symptomatic of broader non-Indigenous views of Indigenous people's livelihoods. In both formal and informal ways, these conditions set the stage for ongoing histories of accessing the fishery, with all of the complexities involved with and implied by them.

A fishing site, then, is both a site of and a metaphor for historical interactions that occur at and in reference to it. Anthropologist Crisca Bierwert has noted that when she writes about places, she also necessarily describes interwoven layers of relationships in the landscape. This includes interactions with physical surroundings, but also social practices, histories, and conflicts that inhabit those spaces.[7] The particular significance of a site was and is determined by the reasons that historical actors past and present have considered it important; changes to a place often result in changes in the ways people relate to that place, as well as to each other, and in turn how they use the site. Exploring fishing histories can help to trace the significance of these changes over time. As anthropologists Akhil Gupta and James Ferguson have argued, aspects of a culture are changed and reworked in response to political and historical processes, and as a result, culture itself, "a space of order and agreed-on meanings," also changes. This is a singular definition of culture that does not wholly encompass the dialogic and at times contested nature of communities and their activities, but Gupta and Ferguson's idea nevertheless provides a useful lens through which to view the negotiation of Stó:lō fishing sites over time: the fishery exists as more than common features, it also encompasses—and at times creates—differences among people.[8] Examining these differences, and often conflicts, over space and time can offer social depth to what may appear to be largely political issues, and can highlight the political discussion that has taken place domestically or locally, beyond the public eye. These are histories that include discrepancies among individuals, families, communities, and governments, and while these various perspectives sometimes give voice to tension, they can also serve to highlight the many ways of accessing the fishery, thereby speaking to the complexity of Stó:lō fishing.

In its most basic form, Stó:lō fisheries are individual or familial affairs, but ones that necessarily refer and respond to outside influences, making fishing an area of broader, collective concern among the Stó:lō and other Indigenous groups. Indeed, access to fishing sites often manifests itself in the various ways that people have responded to these external influences, which have most often taken the form of law or government policy. Legal historian Douglas C. Harris has suggested that law has been an ongoing structure in British Columbia fisheries; regulations have always been in place, but colonialism has changed who they affect and how.[9] The potlatch, in particular, was an Indigenous legal space that enabled people to govern their resources.[10] British colonial law transformed these spaces, acting as an instrument of control and a way of defining the colonies as "a source of raw materials and labour."[11] Whether Indigenous or colonial or some combination of the two, the law has always acted as a collective voice and structure to which individuals relate. Accessing fishing sites, then, engages legal spaces, as well as their consequences for smaller-scale interactions. The routes that access takes can be a means of evaluating the effects of colonialism by serving as a constant reference point to which fishers can relate their experiences.

Many of these experiences have been common to Indigenous fishers in British Columbia, who have all been subject to the same histories of regulation. Historian Dianne Newell has traced Indigenous fishers' encounters with government intervention from British Columbia's early political history through to the 1990s, discussing how the Aboriginal fishery as a political entity was "invented" through the separation of subsistence fishing from managing fishing activity or fishing for purposes other than purely for food.[12] This policy, she suggests, created for policy makers an image of Indians as "simple subsistence people who were quite unlike the commerce-minded Euro-Canadians."[13] Histories of regulations and their consequences were ways of defining and attempting to control how access to fishing sites occurred, and so Indigenous responses to government management reflected which forms of access were important, and to whom. The broader history of regulation and responses that shaped historical events and processes have, in turn, helped to define fishing and fishers' desire for it. Their experiences ultimately involve fishing at a particular site, but those sites imply an extensive network of historical interactions that have brought and anchored fishers and their activities there.

"He's Got a Family Now, So He'd Probably Try and Get Out Fishing": Inheriting Histories of Access

Contemporary and historical Stó:lō fishers alike have cited family histories as a key link in the chain between individuals and fishing spots on the Fraser River. Similarly, anthropologist Wilson Duff argued in 1950 that the Fraser Canyon and its great potential for fishing formed the basis of Stó:lō society both historically and in the period in which he was undertaking fieldwork. He commented, "offering, as [the canyon] did unparalleled conditions for the catching and drying of salmon, its importance in Stalo economy and prehistory would be difficult to overemphasize."[14] Duff's statement speaks to the deep roots that these activities have in Stó:lō territory, an immense backdrop to the non-Stó:lō intervention in fishing that would take place in the late nineteenth and twentieth centuries and beyond. This economic aspect of fishing history is not only significant because of its depth, but also because of its direct role in providing access to the fishery. Economic and family access have become closely intertwined. Anthropologist Wayne Suttles has noted that, historically, the lower class of Stó:lō society lived physically separated from the upper class, and were regarded as "people who had lost their history"; that is, they had no ancestral claim to resource areas, no inherited privileges, and "no private knowledge [or] moral training."[15] These history-less, or s'téxem, people historically had their own leaders, family names, and healers, yet although s'téxem individuals existed since the dawn of time, their collective social class was a result of specific, relatively recent (following the smallpox epidemics that began in 1782) group migrations. Thus, while s'téxem individuals may not have histories that are deemed legitimate by others, collective s'téxem communities can.[16] In practical terms, then, access to fishing spots was and remains dependent, at least in part, on having and claiming worthy families.

It is important to note here that, given the compressed time frame of the field school environment in which the research for this paper took place, I spoke mainly with Stó:lō people who either fished themselves, or who had family members who did. By definition, then, the perspectives presented here are the historical interpretations of people with "good" histories according to Stó:lō metrics, and successful access to fishing as a result. Furthermore, several of the people I interviewed have held political positions as well. Even though, as I note later in the paper, these histories have at times been limited and contested by people from within and outside of Stó:lō communities, they are nevertheless histories of people whose access to fishing has been deemed largely legitimate by others. There remains a need and an opportunity for considering histories of the Stó:lō fishery from the perspectives of those who consider themselves Stó:lō, but who have held more marginal positions in their communities.

To be able to trace a clear historical link to a desirable fishing site was to have a legitimate path of access to that place, which in turn would provide one with property, fish, and a physical symbol of status. Indeed, the same remains true today. Even when one person's access to fishing is interrupted, family connections continue to link relatives to that site. Tony Malloway (brother to Ken Malloway, mentioned above) is part of a family with a strong fishing presence in the Fraser Canyon, and he has become involved with monitoring the fisheries. Because to fish himself while carrying out this work would be a conflict of interest, at the time of our interview in 2007, he had not been fishing since he was hired as a monitor. Nevertheless, because of the prominence of his family's historical claim to fishing, his family's access route remains relatively open, despite these gaps in his individual access. Discussing the transfer of fishing sites from one generation to the next, he commented: "I was planning to pass [the site] on to my son, Ivan, but he's kind of in the same boat as me right now—he's into [fisheries management], he's having a hard time getting up there to fish, because he's working. But he's got a family now, so he'd probably try and get out there too."[17] Families, then, are an important reason to maintain a connection to fishing sites, particularly because they are a conduit through which one can access these spots, and because having access to this place acts as a record of the particular history that links people to each other and to their fishing activities. To be separated from this history would mean physical separation from access to the fishery as well.

One specific way of recording and passing on rights is through hereditary names. Historically, the more genealogical details that accompany the explanation of a name during a public naming ceremony, the greater the legitimacy of the rights associated with that name.[18] The name, then, refers not only to a person, but also to historical precedents that delineate rights and territory.[19] Because naming ceremonies were prohibited by the 1884 potlatch ban, the ownership of these rights sometimes became more nebulous, but Stó:lō people today continue to recognize the salience of names and their functions in families and communities. Ken Malloway is one of the hereditary chiefs of the Chilliwack tribe, and he discussed the significance of his inherited name not only for himself but for his people:

> One of the things that I was told when I got my name [Wileleq] was, they told me I was one of a long line of hereditary chiefs, so

I took that quite seriously, and they said if you don't do it [live up to the obligations of the name], we'll give that name to somebody who's more worthy, we'll take it from you. You don't own a name outright—if they think that you're not living up to your obligations, we'll take that name and give it to someone more worthy to carry that name. . . . That's one of the things we're told when we get our Indian name, especially a hereditary chief's name, if you don't look after the name properly and you don't carry it properly, and you don't look after your people and your territory, we'll take that name from you. . . . They always tell us you're not allowed to drag your name in the mud.[20]

Names thus act as public, ongoing reminders that access is not only physical; it must also be accepted by a community and supported by a family in order for the benefits of that access, such as the status afforded by the knowledge of history, to emerge. While names are unique to a particular family, they also involve other fishers implicitly, who may acknowledge others' rights to fishing spots or present a threat to access to a site.

Relationships among histories and modes of access can be informal, negotiated among people who encounter each other in the various environments where discussion of fishing occurs, or they can be "institutionalized" in families and marriages. Given that fishing access results from various sources involved simultaneously, it follows that interactions among people, not solely the assertions of individuals themselves, help to describe how that access came to be granted. Suttles has explained that in Coast Salish societies, weddings have been an event at which wealth, in the form of physical objects as well as access to inherited privileges, is exchanged between the two newly united families.[21] However, particularly in a more recent historical period, what is not necessarily shared is an "agreed-on meaning" of ownership. Each family has come to this point of access through a separate set of circumstances that inevitably inform their respective understandings of how that site will be passed along and used in the future. Chief Sid Douglas of Cheam recounted the movement of a fishing site from his family into the Malloway family:

One of the fishing grounds that belongs to our family came to my father when he got married. His grandfather, whose name was Louis Squawtits, handed it down to him when he got married. So after that, my oldest brother [Sam] used to fish there . . . before he got into the commercial fishery, he got Ed Victor up with him. . . . But when they [Sam and his father] got into that, Sam also became a commercial fisherman, so when we left the grounds there, Ed Victor continued fishing; his family continued . . . and our uncle Felix got with Sweetie Malloway. That's when the Malloway family started to fish those fishing grounds. They still fish them to this day.[22]

He went on to note, however, that the Malloway family understands the site differently: "we haven't really sat down to talk to them [the Malloway family], but they know [it belongs to the Douglas family]."[23] Ken Malloway described a nearby family fishing spot in these terms: "There's a place in the Fraser Canyon that's near Steamboat Island, the area is called I:yem, it means 'strong wind,' but some of the elders call that place Yakweakwioose—Frank Malloway lives on Yakweakwioose, that's just up by Chilliwack . . . but his family has been there so long that they call the [fishing site] Yakweakwioose. So my great-grandmother and her husband fished there, and their grandparents before them fished there."[24] When the paths of the Douglas and Malloway families crossed, so too did their means of access to a specific fishing site. Both recognized the potential economic and social value of these spots, but through their understandings of the families' histories required to legitimate access, they trace different paths to people who can and should use these sites today. What is at stake is not only the ability or inability to acquire fish, but also whose family history is more accurate or influential.

"I Guess If I Was On Welfare I'd Do That": Navigating Through, Around, and Alongside Government Restrictions

Certainly, knowledge of family and broader cultural history is important in acquiring the right to access a fishing spot, but intervening circumstances may impede that knowledge or change how fishers interpreted it. In the Stó:lō fishery, such rerouting of knowledge occurred frequently in the twentieth century, and has often been a result of government regulation of Indigenous people and fishing practices. Because physical access to fishing sites has always been dependent on the transfer of rights across generations, it follows that if physical access is limited in some way, then those interpersonal and interfamilial interactions will also change.

The creation and subsequent reduction of reserves along the Fraser River was an early instigator of such changes. As private, non-Indigenous property ownership increased along the river, access to resources decreased,[25] so that, as historical geographer Cole Harris notes, for the Indigenous population, "life became a matter of working out spatial strategies that would allow them to survive in such circumstances."[26] As Ken Malloway has explained, changes in physical space had long-lasting consequences to the way people conceptualized their place within the Stó:lō and within the broader society:

> I use the term "bands" kind of loosely, because I'm just used to calling them bands. Some of them call themselves First Nations, and some of them call themselves villages, but I don't really believe that they're First Nations. Stó:lō Nation is the nation, and Indian bands are just Indian bands that were created in my area—that's Skowkale and Yakweakwioose and Tzeachten. It used to be one village, just one community at the time. We were part of the Chilliwack tribe, but Indian Affairs came in and drew circles around our villages .... There's seven villages that are part of the Chilliwack tribe, but we ended up being separated into different bands. A lot of people get offended if you say Indian bands, but it doesn't bother me, it's just a creation of the Indian Act. And some of them want to be called First Nations, but they're not actually a nation unto themselves, just part of the Stó:lō Nation.[27]

Ken Malloway's argument about the political makeup of Stó:lō identities suggests that the political reaches of the fishery extend beyond fishing itself, to address the changing ways that governments and Stó:lō people themselves have defined themselves collectively. These redefinitions of people's sense of belonging and place that Malloway describes have had a direct impact on ideas of access to fishing.

In 1972, Marilyn Bennett conducted a survey of Indigenous fishers on the Fraser River, in which 89 percent of respondents said that the band of which they were members had fishing places that had been used for many years.[28] The study included Indigenous groups besides the Stó:lō, some of whom may have a history of managing fishing sites communally rather than within a family, meaning that the statistics are not necessarily accurate when considering only Stó:lō practices. Regardless, the statements hint at a disconnect between family-based access to fishing sites and access that may be politically or governmentally legitimate but, as Ken Malloway argues, socially artificial. In such an environment, it may be difficult to determine which methods of securing access, and the specific aspects of knowledge required to do so, are most legitimate.

Throughout the history of government interventions in the fishery, the desire to fish has remained strong. What has resulted is a merging of "outside" and "intra-Stó:lō" knowledge and practices, sometimes done intentionally by fishers and sometimes resulting from circumstances beyond their control. One such incidence of the latter was the closure of the Fraser River to Indian fishing between 1919 and 1921 in order to protect commercial fishing interests. Indigenous communities were promised compensation for this loss of livelihood, but were not permitted to harvest any fish from the river.[29] While this proviso took into account the importance of fish as sustenance, fishing was, and is, the foundation of many social interactions as well; eliminating the need to fish for food did not eliminate the need to fish to maintain the relationships, knowledge, and sharing of history that allowed fishers access to catch food. Both the government and Stó:lō responses to the effects of the ban reflected an understanding that the fishery's significance reached beyond salmon. Government officials did not enforce the ban uniformly, as they had realized that it was nearly impossible to prevent resistance, such as dip-netting at night to avoid detection, that was widespread on the river.[30] However, while it remained possible for the Stó:lō to access the fishery, the form this access took referred at least as much to government parameters as it did to Stó:lō ways of monitoring and managing access.

Indeed, having to respond to government intervention meant that these outside structures sometimes inserted themselves into already-existing means of regulation, usually within families and communities. Ernie Crey, a Stó:lō activist who has been heavily involved in recent fishing-related and other sociopolitical discussions and agreements with governments, has suggested that ongoing intervention in the fishery has changed conceptions of who can legitimately offer access. He has noted that, increasingly, Siya:m (respected family leaders) no longer decided fishing times, sites, and techniques. Instead, this role fell to fisheries officers, making them, in a sense, Siya:m themselves—at least in terms of the power they held, though likely not in terms of the respect that Siya:m would typically garner.[31] Reorganizing familial and community interactions in this way could create a vacuum among families where custodial confusion and, potentially, conflict fill the void. A 1988 proposal for fishery co-management between the Stó:lō and governments noted the importance of having a process in place to resolve internal disputes. The proposal identified differences in harvesting patterns among bands, family or individual rights to sites, and fish populations as potential areas of conflict.[32] These represent various levels or forms of access to the fishery. By noting possible discord within families and their historical rights of access as well as in areas with broader significance, the proposal sought to inscribe fishers' understandings of Stó:lō histories and customs in the wider fishery. It merged rules governing physical access with access to the knowledge of the past that governs how fishers interpret their access rights. Government regulation of the fishery did not create a parallel form of access to fishing sites; instead, it complicated and rerouted existing means of access.

Government involvement in Stó:lō fisheries has sparked changes in the ways fishers have considered their access to their sites, and the goal and meaning of access has, at times, also changed in response. Marilyn Bennett's study of Fraser River fishing found that 86 per cent of those surveyed believed that more people fished when their grandparents were young, around 1900. The most common reasons given for greater fishing involvement in the past were: lack of employment or social services, a greater abundance of fish, and a lack of regulations or restrictions.[33] These results point to a focus on fishing for economic support, though it is perhaps not entirely clear whether respondents' assessments of their grandparents' values reflect their understanding of history, a projection of their own concerns onto the past, or some combination of the two. However, it is clear that fishing provided access to economic benefits, and for some, perhaps even financial sustenance. In discussing the banning of the potlatch, historian Tina Loo has stated that even when the law appears to work to a group's disadvantage, it is nevertheless "a space for argument that, when creatively employed . . . gives them a means to transform their own relationships," and individuals may also be able to use the law for material gain and its associated status.[34] Ray Silver, a Stó:lō elder from the Sumas First Nation, recalls acquaintances who have done just this, even while it remained illegal for fish to be bought from or sold by Indigenous people: "There's lots of Native fishermen that caught lots—they had other people working for them ... it was big business, running fish into Vancouver or wherever—I heard they were even taking them down south to the States. I never did that because I was always working here. I guess if I was on welfare I'd do that, I would have did that."[35] Unlike some of his contemporaries, Ray Silver's employment at the brick plant meant that he did not need to fish to supplement his livelihood, and that position highlights his focus on fishing as a primarily economic pursuit. Fishing with the intention to sell the catch provided a way for fishers to achieve independent financial support for themselves, but it also reinforced connections among Stó:lō people. Though catching fish remained restricted to food purposes, by circumventing this law, sellers of fish were able to emphasize the importance of fishing to their families and communities. Just as fishing sites were places to access food, the illegal sale of fish was a conceptual place where food provided access to the broader economy while continuing to acknowledge fishing's less tangible importance as well.

Ray Silver's equation of welfare with the need to sell fish mirrors a statement by Kimberly Linkous Brown, who has written of Stó:lō fishing histories that "the business of fishing need not be separated from the Stó:lō tradition of fishing, whether conducted illegally in the shadows of night or legally in the light of day."[36] No matter what route was required to access the fishery, the activity remained a link to the history that shaped the multifaceted significance of fishing. Indeed, the law that created the Aboriginal food fishery also defined a "traditional" economy, but it was "a traditional fishery that had no precedent in Native society"; it had never been categorized or limited in that way.[37] As Bierwert notes, "the presence of outlaw fishing expresses the market power of a knowledge that law did not completely curtail."[38] Fishing remained central to Stó:lō life because the connection to it was based on family histories as well as on physical access to sites; the law could regulate the latter but not the former.

Responses to fishing or sales bans tended to employ multiple routes of access concurrently. Sometimes the physical, family-governed, and economic aspects of the illegal fish market intersected at the very spot where the fish were caught. Tony Malloway remembered: "When we first started fishing in Yale we used to take the train from Chilliwack to Yale, and once we got into Yale we had to catch one of them little speeders to our fishing camp, and the speeders are them little things that work on the railroad tracks. Then it was against the law to sell fish, so we'd have some trains even stop there buying fish, and speeders would be buying fish. Sometimes by the time you got home you wouldn't have much fish left, because you'd sell them all."[39] Such instances serve as very tangible illustrations of the various forms of access that fishing both requires and offers. Because physical, economic, and assorted other benefits of the fishery are so closely intertwined, they may be accessed in several ways from a single space.

Often, occupying the same region meant that sales of fish were conducted between people who already knew each other, or who had come to know each other through previous transactions.[40] This would reinforce the ties among these people, thereby strengthening a social fabric that was created, surrounded, and supported by the fishery. Ray Silver sold fish on a small scale, and he describes this involvement with an evident sense of connection to his customers: "Mostly what I used to do, with people like myself, ordinary guys, they're working hard, and they bought fish off of me. . . . When I first started selling them, I think I got about ten cents each for a sockeye, ten or fifteen cents, and then it went to two bits, twenty-five cents, fifty cents, a dollar. It was a dollar for many, many years, a dollar a fish, and that was a lot of money to me, and a lot of food for my friends."[41] In the midst of illegal fish sales, the fishing site remained the point from which all related activity stemmed. While names and family connections allowed access to that site, the fish procured at that spot acted as a means of access to reinforce social and historical relationships and narratives. These relationships sometimes doubled as a market for the fish, providing fishers with some financial benefit and once again drawing them back to the fishing site.

"They Didn't Understand the Concept of Family Grounds and Protocols": Intersections of Money and Histories

During the years when selling fish was illegal, fishers retained a widespread desire for the legal right to do so, pointing to another path of access to the fishery: financial access. This desire was, at least partially, realized in 1992 with a Pilot Sales Agreement that granted permission to certain British Columbia Indigenous groups, including the Stó:lō Tribal Council and Stó:lō Nation, to sell fish, subject to allocations and management agreements, in order to test such a program and identify potential problems.[42] With this sanctioning of catching fish for sale came an increased interest in fishing. For those who had fished the river even without the option of making a legal profit, the influx brought with it a certain degree of tension. As well as stolen gear and overcrowding, there were concerns over the potential loss of fish for those who intended to fish largely for personal consumption.[43] Sid Douglas, a member of a particularly politically active family from Cheam, described the drastic change on the river: "Before the pilot sales came in, there was only between 200 and 300 registered fishermen from Langley to Yale, and then when the pilot sales came in, and that meant there was money involved, there was a lot of other people that wanted to cash in on the money. Our fisherman list went up to about 1,500, and we weren't prepared for that. A lot of the new fishermen, they didn't understand the concept of family grounds and protocols."[44] For fishers like Douglas with experiences of powerful histories and relatively uncontested access, the pilot sales arrangement became the site of arguments over the nature of tradition. While the pilot sales were an acknowledgement of an activity that many argue has always been an Indigenous right and practice, they also illustrated ways in which different ideas of access can cause conflicts around fishing sites. For the new fishers on the river, access to the sites was, in effect, granted by the government; without that impetus, it is possible that some would not have investigated their families' hereditary rights to fishing spots. Further, established fishers such as Sid Douglas interpreted the newcomers' motives as being largely monetary. Even so, accessing the sites involved many of the same social structures and connections that it always had. Once the fish had been caught, however, the aspects of society to which they connected was often quite different between those who fished for profit and those whose priorities for fishing lay in a desire for access to traditions, family, or subsistence.

This is not to say, however, that "traditional" and other, perhaps more recent reasons for access are mutually exclusive categories. Carlson has argued that tradition is not a static concept; invoking it does not preclude the use of innovative fishing methods, nor does innovation automatically imply assimilation.[45] Indeed, with the fishing site as the place to which all fishing activity refers, fishing for economic reasons and fishing to maintain certain cultural values are, in many ways, inseparable. Whether legal or not, the sale of fish has provided economic benefits for both sellers and buyers, thereby providing an incentive to continue the inherently Stó:lō activity of fishing. Yet the location of some fishing sites necessitates that the owners have the economic means required to transport themselves to these spots. Previously, the Canadian National Railway (CNR) and Canadian Pacific Railway (CPR) had each run their trains on separate sides of the river, but in the 1970s, the weight freight ceased on the CNR side.[46] Many Stó:lō fishers had used these trains as inexpensive transportation to fishing sites in the canyon that had no road access, sometimes paying six sockeye as their fare.[47] Without this means of access, fishers usually needed to acquire a powerful motorboat,[48] an investment that in 2007 Ken Malloway estimated could cost a fisher as much as $20,000.[49] Interestingly, between 1930 and 1932, when salmon canneries, and thus also the demand for fish, were in the depths of the Depression, fishing boat licences increased, with the number of gasoline-powered boats growing the most.[50] It is unclear how many of these boats belonged to Indigenous fishers, but the trend suggests reasons for fishing that went beyond the purely monetary. Despite its potentially high start-up costs, fishing was clearly an activity to be maintained even during times of economic hardship. Thus, fishing for profit and fishing for cultural reasons were, in many ways, inseparable; financial gain from fish enabled transportation to the fishing site, which in turn allowed for further gain.

Economic gain can be achieved through access to fishing, but affluence can also reinforce Stó:lō social organization and interactions. Ken Malloway points out that "everyone has equal opportunity, but some fish harder than others and some have better fishing spots."[51] The "equal opportunity" described here refers to the fact that every Stó:lō person has the Aboriginal right to fish, but each fisher has a unique path of access through family, political, or financial conduits, some of which result in more satisfactory fishing results than others. Similarly, Suttles has argued that the effectiveness with which individuals subsisted in their environment affected their ability to distribute wealth at a potlatch, and thus to achieve or maintain a degree of prestige in society.[52] Sharing food was and remains, to an extent, a direct means of access to high status,[53] and so those who are financially and physically able to use their fishing sites are also more likely to be granted esteem by other fishers and community members. The connection between food, status, and wealth became true in a more formal sense with the introduction of the Pilot Sales Agreement. Those who fished on behalf of others often turned the highest profit, as experienced fishers would set nets for their younger relatives in exchange for a percentage of the proceeds.[54] Within this monetary structure, however, fishing and sharing continued to promote family ties and maintain historical connections to fishing, including the granting of status to those who had access to enough food to share.

"I'll Have to Write a Letter for My Kids to Keep that Place": Crossing Cultural Paths

Those who provided food also provided access for others to their communities and culture; this, certainly, would be a reason for the esteem in which providers were, and are, held. Rita Pete, a self-described "fisher-lady" and Stó:lō elder, noted that "there's some on the reserve who can't go fishing, so we give some [fish] to them ... the old people that can't go out."[55] Testifying in the landmark court case *R. v. Van der Peet*, in which the Stó:lō defendant was charged with selling fish illegally, the late elder Tillie Gutierrez recalled from her youth that this practice is not new: "[Fish] was never hoarded, this is mine, I'm not sharing any of it. No, this would never happen. It was always given."[56] It is unsurprising, then, that she would continue to find the practice of sharing so valuable: "The elders' camp dried fish and they gave it to us so we appreciate that very much and we have a few friends that give us salmon."[57] The fish themselves are a way of accessing and maintaining one's place in a group. For those who are unable to access fishing spots, sharing the produce of others' sites connects them to the history that first established them as legitimate fishers and respected members of a fishing community.

It follows, then, that a desire to stake out a place in a community would be linked to claims to fishing sites, particularly given the problems, both potential and real, that have arisen when fishers and regulations interact. Families' differences in interpretation of rights, economic or governmental restrictions, and one's own physical or financial limitations all require a fisher to find ways beyond physically harvesting salmon from the river to eke out a place along the canyon, and thus also a place within a particular fishing-based culture. Prior to the 1992 pilot sales, one way of marking a spot was simply to leave one's fishing equipment at the site. This would ensure that other fishers realized the place had a definite owner, but with the influx of fishers, crime increased as well, perhaps proportionally. As Ray Silver observed, "it's getting hard for us now to launch our boats. See, you can't leave anything in the river anymore. In the old days we used to leave our canoes there, our nets, everything, right there in the river, and nobody would touch them. You could go back there the next week and they're still there."[58] Today, other ways of noting ownership carry more weight. Although, as Tony Malloway noted, "there's sort of a thing on the river that's unwritten ... it's just like everybody knows whose spot is whose,"[59] some fishers regard written confirmation of ownership as being more secure. Rita Pete plans to keep her site in her family by ensconcing it in print: "I'll have to write a letter. I'll have to write a tape and a letter for my kids to keep that place—years from now." She has also considered "homesteading" her fishing grounds.[60]

This is not entirely a new strategy; in 1903, a Stó:lō fisher named Billy Swallsea sought to purchase fee simple title to an acre of land along the river, which included a disputed fishing spot that Swallsea was claiming as his own. This act was met with support from the Department of Indian Affairs, who eventually decided to grant Swallsea the title, but with considerable resistance from some other Stó:lō fishers, led by Paul Skitt, who also claimed hereditary rights to that site.[61] Carlson notes that the dispute illustrated "innovative means to traditional ends," but that outside agencies' mediation was not necessarily deemed legitimate by Stó:lō people involved in the conflict.[62] Today, however, while rights to a fishing site are not frequently maintained through written means involving non-Indigenous granters of access, the influx of new fishers and, perhaps, the presence of government in other issues involving Indigenous land, such as treaty negotiations, have led some fishers to seek out ways of securing their access to sites in an environment where Canadian laws and governments can provide "back-up" proof of ownership if a family's history is called into question by other fishers. Physical access to a fishing site remains central to all other relationships and activities that surround the fishery. It follows, then, that marking the site physically and tangibly as one's own would be seen as central to providing access to the history and links to a specific definition of "cultural identity" implied by the users of fishing grounds.

Dry racks, situated at fishing spots for wind drying salmon, represent the intersection of historical and physical claims to a site. They provide evidence that the owners of the spot are using and maintaining it; not to do so could be interpreted as a forfeiture of ownership.[63] Perhaps because the dry racks act as physical reminders of more intangible concepts of history and culture, "the wind-dry fishery has come to be considered a hallmark of traditional Stó:lō life and the dry-rack families the keepers of that tradition."[64] This is, of course, only one possible interpretation of ideas that, like that of tradition, are mediated situationally, but for Rita Pete it was the practice of wind drying that provided her direct access to her current fishing site: "It was my dad there; he said, 'Well,' he said, 'You'd better take over that spot,' he says, 'You're drying salmon all the time,' and I says, 'Yeah, okay.' So I just went up there and started drying salmon."[65] Her practical knowledge of fishing and drying warranted ownership of her own place, where, through her family's historical ties to the spot, her knowledge would be imbued with the cultural significance attached to wind drying. The dry racks indicated to others that, as the site owner, Rita Pete took seriously the responsibilities of her role, and because wind drying is the product of shared historical knowledge of techniques, practising those techniques was a way for her to access the specific cultural and personal histories that connect fishers to particular sites.

Conclusion

Fishing sites are not only places where fish are caught. Spheres of individuals, families, governments, cultures, histories, and, of course, salmon orbit around these rocks and eddies, so that in order for Stó:lō fishers to access any one of these agents, one must refer to the fishing grounds. Thus when conflicts and changes regarding fishing sites emerge, they necessarily involve all of the parties and factors associated with these places. Access to sites is sometimes a complex path, requiring one to navigate through histories of rights, protocols, and regulations, as well as through various interpretations of such knowledge. Over the course of these histories, fishers have sought to assert their place along the river, and, by extension, in Stó:lō society and interactions. In so doing, they have drawn connections to their collective and individual histories in numerous ways: by interacting with other fishing families, by circumventing or adapting to government restrictions, or by carrying out activities that reinforce links to a site. All of these aspects of history carry with them various voices of interpretation and changes that create dialogue around central sites of Stó:lō activity and identity. Access, then, is not a single path, or even a series of parallel paths. Like fishing itself, it is both a process and an ability that develops out of a history of shared interactions.

Notes

1   An earlier version of this paper was originally published as "Crossing Paths: Knowing and Navigating Paths of Access to Stó:lō Fishing Sites," *University of the Fraser Valley Research Review* 2, no. 2 (2009): 36–53.

2   In addition to those fishers I cite here specifically, I would also like to acknowledge the other Stó:lō people I interviewed during the course of my research for this paper (Archie Charles, Jack Lawrence, Ivan McIntyre, and Mabel Nichols) for their valuable contributions to my understandings of Stó:lō fishing, histories, and communities during my field school work in 2007.

3   Ken Malloway, interview by Katya MacDonald and Sarah Nickel, Chilliwack, BC, 22 June 2007. Recording available at Stó:lō Archives, Stó:lō Research and Resource Management Centre, Chilliwack, BC.

4   Richard White, *The Organic Machine* (New York: Hill and Wang, 1995), 91.

5   Keith Thor Carlson, "Innovation, Tradition, Colonialism, and Aboriginal Fishing Conflicts in the Lower Fraser Canyon," in *New Histories for Old: Changing Perspectives on Canada's Native Pasts*, eds. Ted Binnema and Susan Neylan (Vancouver: UBC Press, 2007), 145.

6   Ibid., 150.

7   Crisca Bierwert, *Brushed by Cedar, Living by the River: Coast Salish Figures of Power* (Tucson: University of Arizona Press, 1999), 59.

8   Akhil Gupta and James Ferguson, "Culture, Power, Place: Ethnography at the End of an Era," in *Culture, Power, Place: Explorations in Critical Anthropology*, eds. Akhil Gupta and James Ferguson (Durham, NC: Duke University Press, 1997), 5.

9   Douglas C. Harris, *Fish, Law, and Colonialism: The Legal Capture of Salmon in British Columbia* (Toronto: University of Toronto Press, 2001), 3.

10 Ibid., 6.

11 Ibid., 188.

12 Dianne Newell, *Tangled Webs of History: Indians and the Law in Canada's Pacific Coast Fisheries* (Toronto: University of Toronto Press, 1993), 62.

13 Ibid., 62.

14 Cited in Keith Thor Carlson and Sarah Eustace, "Fraser Canyon Fishing Rights: Canadian Law and the Origin and Evolution of an Intertribal Dispute," draft paper prepared for Stó:lō Nation, Chilliwack, BC, (1999), 4.

15 Wayne Suttles, "Affinal Ties, Subsistence, and Prestige among the Coast Salish," in *Coast Salish Essays* (Seattle: University of Washington Press, 1987), 17.

16 Keith Thor Carlson, *The Power of Place, the Problem of Time: Aboriginal Identity and Historical Consciousness in the Cauldron of Colonialism* (Toronto: University of Toronto Press, 2010), 49.

17 Tony Malloway, interview by Katya MacDonald, Chilliwack, BC, 28 June 2007. Recording available at Stó:lō Archives, Stó:lō Research and Resource Management Centre, Chilliwack, BC.

18 Carlson and Eustace, "Fraser Canyon Fishing Rights," 9.

19 Suttles, "Affinal Ties," 21.

20 Ken Malloway, interview.

21 Suttles, "Affinal Ties," 17.

22 Sid Douglas, interview with Keith Carlson, Katya MacDonald, and Sarah Nickel, Chilliwack, BC, June 22 2007. Recording available at Stó:lō Archives, Stó:lō Research and Resource Management Centre, Chilliwack, BC.

23 Ibid.

24 Ken Malloway, interview.

25 Cole Harris, *Making Native Space: Colonialism, Resistance, and Reserves in British Columbia* (Vancouver: UBC Press, 2002), 288.

26 Ibid., 274.

27 Ken Malloway, interview.

28 Cited in Kimberly Linkous Brown, "To Fish for Themselves: A Study of Accommodation and Resistance in the Stó:lō Fishery" (PhD diss., University of British Columbia, 2005), 89.

29 Reuben M. Ware, *Five Issues, Five Battlegrounds: An Introduction to the History of Indian Fishing in British Columbia, 1850–1930* (Sardis, BC: Coqualeetza Education Training Centre, for the Stó:lō Nation, 1983), 32.

30 Ibid., 33.

31 Cited in Linkous Brown, "To Fish for Themselves," 85.

32 Stó:lō Tribal Council, "Fisheries Co-Management Proposal for the Lower Fraser River Watershed," 1988, 48.

33 Marilyn G. Bennett, "Indian Fishing and its Cultural Importance in the Fraser River System," Fisheries Service, Pacific Region, Department of the Environment and Union of British Columbia Indian Chiefs (1973), 14.

34 Cited in D. Harris, *Fish, Law, and Colonialism*, 198.

35 Ray Silver Sr., interview with Emmy Campbell, Katya MacDonald, and Lesley Wiebe, Sumas, BC, 27 June 2007. Recording available at Stó:lō Archives, Stó:lō Research and Resource Management Centre, Chilliwack, BC. See Bierwert, *Brushed by Cedar*, 240, for a discussion of the banning of Indigenous fishing.

36 Linkous Brown, "To Fish for Themselves," 187.

37 D. Harris, *Fish, Law, and Colonialism*, 203.

38 Bierwert, in D. Harris, *Fish, Law, and Colonialism*, 248.

39 Tony Malloway, interview.

40 Bierwert, in D. Harris, *Fish, Law, and Colonialism*, 245.

41 Silver, interview.

42 Linkous Brown, "To Fish for Themselves," 102.

43 Ibid., 108.

44 Sid Douglas, interview.

45 Carlson, "Innovation," 147.

46 Caroline F. Butler, "Historicizing Indigenous Knowledge: Practical and Political Issues," in *Traditional Ecological Knowledge and Natural Resource Management*, ed. Charles R. Menzies (Lincoln, NE: University of Nebraska Press, 2006), 113.

47 Linkous Brown, "To Fish for Themselves," 185.

48 Tony Malloway, interview.

49 Linkous Brown, "To Fish for Themselves," 186.

50 Newell, *Tangled Webs of History*, 103.

51 Quoted in Linkous Brown, "To Fish for Themselves," 196.

52 Suttles, "Affinal Ties," 16.

53 Ibid., 20.

54 Bierwert, in D. Harris, *Fish, Law, and Colonialism*, 252.

55 Rita Pete, interview by Amanda Fehr and Katya MacDonald, Skam, BC, 29 June 29, 2007. Recording available at Stó:lō Archives, Stó:lō Research and Resource Management Centre, Chilliwack, BC.

56 Tillie Gutierrez, witness for the defence, *R. v. Van der Peet*, Proceedings at Trial, Provincial Court of British Columbia, 31 May 1989, 14.

57 Ibid., 27. The late Grand Chief Archie Charles of Seabird Island donated his fishing site in the Fraser Canyon for the common use of Stó:lō elders in an effort to facilitate their access to all of the aspects of the fishery discussed in this paper.

58 Silver, interview.

59 Tony Malloway, interview.

60 Pete, interview.

61 This was a dispute that involved considerable correspondence among Swallsea, a series of Indian agents, the Dominion Land office, Skitt, and several notable Stó:lō leaders over the course of two years. See Carlson, "Innovation."

62 Carlson, "Innovation," 167.

63 Carlson and Eustace, "Fraser Canyon Fishing Rights," 10.

64 Linkous Brown, "To Fish for Themselves," 155.

65 Pete, interview.

4

Stó:lō Ancestral Names, Identity, and the Politics of History

ANASTASIA TATARYN

Preface[1]

In the conclusion of his 2010 book, *The Power of Place, the Problem of Time*, Keith Carlson emphasizes the importance of an (ethno)historical research methodology that challenges the metanarrative that is common in historical writing, where the impact of colonialism on Indigenous people is interpreted from within the colonial framework.[2] In spite of the positive efforts to include Native history, this historical inquiry is quickly appropriated by the dominant culture. In such a framework, research on Stó:lō ancestral names is analyzed for what it offers to Canada, in other words non-Native Canadians learning about the history and diversity of Canada. Yet non-Natives do not *need* to learn about Stó:lō ancestral names in order to *help* Canadian history, which is invariably history written from a newcomer perspective. Instead, researching and writing about Stó:lō ancestral names is important in order to offer a deeper understanding of Stó:lō teachings. These teachings have not been protected from the impact of colonialism. Nevertheless, exploring current efforts to revive naming practices demonstrates how carrying ancestral names reinforces a tangible link to a different worldview. For non-Native researchers, a study of Stó:lō ancestral names offers an example of what Argentinian philosopher Walter Mignolo refers to as *pluriversality*, providing clear evidence that there is not one single universal claim or truth that has either been assimilated or rejected in relation to the colonial project. The Western modern/colonial framework that claims to be "universal" shatters in the face of current practices that incorporate and value the role of ancestral names in Stó:lō identity. Instead of *universal* truth,

Mignolo suggests thinking of a plurality of cosmologies that are experienced and continue in contemporary local practices around the world.[3]

The current significance of Stó:lō ancestral names to Stó:lō identity is an example of local politics with global significance; global because local experiences and actions that are happening within the regular lives of Stó:lō people cause politics, law, and culture to be rethought "from the perspective of difference."[4] Moreover, the ethnohistorical methodology itself is an attempt to disrupt colonial discourses[5] that are easily perpetuated by historical studies that, notwithstanding their importance and contribution, nevertheless distil complex lived experiences into simplified non-Native chronologies of colonialism and postcolonialism. Because, as will be elaborated below, names must be honoured and kept clean for future generations, the names and their holders participate in the reproduction of living history. Names connected to places, and genealogy, provide currency and connection.[6] This is a currency and connection within existing systems of power and order, not external to them. For instance, the naming ceremonies of the twenty-first century are massive events that take months of planning, fundraising, and organization. These ceremonies, similar perhaps to the events of the Winter Dances, may not outwardly change the quotidian pattern of a person's life, but naming and naming ceremonies reflect a plural world experience, the *pluriversality* mentioned above.

While listening to the details of a recent naming ceremony, held in early 2015, I was struck by how much I could identify with and relate to the family conflicts, importance of minute organizational details, efforts of planning, and need for community involvement. Current naming ceremonies are not insular experiences detached from other expressions of community identity, and neither are they attempting to simulate a past distinct from the lived experiences of Stó:lō today. For instance, in his role as researcher at the Stó:lō Nation, Sonny McHalsie often helps families to trace their genealogies and facilitates knowledge of which ancestral names elders can give in a naming ceremony.[7] In the past, the elders held this role; however, while elders may know the names, they do not have McHalsie's expertise with the genealogy. Furthermore, many elders do not know the Hal'qemeylem language. Thus the revival of ancestral names and naming ceremonies resonates with both the traditional teachings and with present-day realities of many Stó:lō. Ancestral names can be seen as tools that help Stó:lō to cope with, or succeed in, the dominant non-Native political-legal-cultural-economic system.

Therefore, what this study of Stó:lō ancestral names offers is not necessarily a radical new way to understand Canadian history and identity. Rather, this chapter seeks to contribute to emerging methodologies that bring attention to the subtle, ongoing practices whereby Stó:lō are rekindling teachings and traditions in order to make sense of the world, here and now. Ancestral names reinforce a link between past, present, and future that circumvents non-Native linear associations between family and individuals. The connections to ancestors that are established through naming ceremonies make explicit responsibilities and obligations between individuals, their families, and their community that are different from the discourses of citizenship, state, and civic community that have dominated Western modern colonial histories and shaped twenty-first-century identities. Undeniably, the resurgence of naming ceremonies and genealogical mapping holds political and strategic importance. However, whatever their "use," the importance of these ceremonies and of carrying ancestral names is now perhaps more fundamentally what these ceremonies and traditions repeat, recite, and speak out loud: the teachings passed down through the elders, the gathering of the family and community, the honour bestowed upon individuals receiving names who have to *earn* the names and remain accountable to the family and community. Knowledge of this version of what it means to be Stó:lō shapes identities, interpretations, and experiences as a *pluri-history*, not simply an "other" experience.

Introduction

The systems of remembering and demonstrating genealogical lines of descent in Stó:lō pre-colonial history and tradition, and in the Hal'qemeylem language, are complex and often confusing to non-Stó:lō researchers. Xwelitem (non-Native newcomers of European descent) researchers and scholars, often unconsciously, seek to place Stó:lō pre-colonial history, post-"contact" narratives, and individuals' personal histories into the type of historical package that "white" academic, and popular, culture is accustomed to.[8] As researchers from outside the Stó:lō /Coast Salish community, Xwelitem scholars instinctively look for linear, clear-cut chronological histories that are familiar to our own worldview. Often this Xwelitem paradigm fails to incorporate the gravity of personal relationships to ancestors or the urgency of demonstrating hereditary lineage to a certain deceased chief. By exploring the fundamental ways in which Stó:lō people identify themselves and carry their history, one can begin to address the stalemate of understanding which can result from contradictory worldviews and confusing cross-cultural exchanges.

Trying to make sense of some Stó:lō "family trees," with the multiple layers of relations, brings to mind Geertz's statement that "coherence cannot be the major test of validity for a cultural description."[9] Geertz argues that scholars need to see not just the broad but also the deep layers of cultural meaning and must avoid judging the validity of cultural and historical understanding based on preconceived definitions. Stó:lō family histories and the role of ancestral names in Stó:lō society reveal a deep, multilayered, interwoven history—a history that is not necessarily coherent and comprehensible from an "outsider" perspective.[10] Ancestral names, and their importance in Stó:lō and Coast Salish identity, provide an intersection of past, present, and future wherein an exploration of identity, meaning, and history can be pursued.

Currently, Stó:lō are reviving traditions of naming ceremonies and carrying ancestral names following a period, beginning in the early to mid-twentieth century, where Stó:lō were in many cases disconnected from their families and history.[11] Ancestral names are elemental to the construction and preservation of Stó:lō social organization, social hierarchies, and history as they give form and meaning to Stó:lō identity. In other words, ancestral names are critical to the existence and organization of Stó:lō culture and are the tangible mani-festation of a Stó:lō person's history and connection to ancestors, past and future. The event of a naming ceremony is an opportunity to affirm and repeat Stó:lō teachings. Great care is required to select names from the names that are "owned" by the family. Individuals are then given a name by their elders, who remain the "owners" of the name: the name belongs to the family, not the individual bearing it.[12] According to Sonny McHalsie, during the naming ceremony it must be carefully explained to the people gathered—there can be up to 300 people in attendance—who the name came from and how the person receiving the name is in direct lineage to this ancestry. When the names are announced, the names must be pronounced correctly, especially if someone else in the family already holds this name. If someone already has this name, they are called forward to be present when the name is given to the new receiver. Moreover, the person receiving the ancestral name does not know the name in advance of the announcement. The explanations and genealogical tracing would traditionally be done by the elders, and supported by the witnesses called upon by the speaker; as above, it is the role of the elders to pass on the names within the family. However, currently tracing the genealogy of ancestral names requires more work and expertise, thus Sonny McHalsie himself is often asked to facilitate the gathering of information on the names and lineage, particularly where elders do not read or speak the Hal'qemeylem language.[13]

Methodology

Contemporary ethnohistorical research requires an awareness of the researcher's ideological context, which can be achieved by shifting the lens of analysis away from a primary focus on the Other towards the researcher. Scholars must acknowledge the relevance of multiple historical frameworks and ensure that their ethnohistorical analysis does not favour one framework over another, for example a Stó:lō framework or Western perspective. Not only are these frameworks false absolutes, they stifle the potential for creative ideas and understanding to emerge in the research process. As Stó:lō oral histories indicate, history is a dialogic process, serving multiple needs, audiences, and purposes. All stories and histories are constructed by social interactions, and demonstrate layers of experience, diverse worldviews, and various ideological/ spiritual contexts. Only by recognizing the intertextuality of historical experience and historical expression can one begin to engage with other cultures and make meaningful "contact."[14]

The use of ancestral names in Stó:lō culture and the role they play in political, social, and economic interactions is indicative of a cultural paradigm different from a Western ontology. Working from a framework that recognizes and seeks to understand these differences is essential. This research brings to light an aspect of Stó:lō conceptualizations of history that needs to be acknowledged in order to facilitate multi-levelled and cross-cultural understanding.

Ancestral names in Stó:lō tradition and their importance are explored in this paper through interviews, transcripts of earlier interviews conducted with Stó:lō elders held in the Stó:lō Nation archives, and the ethnography of the Stó:lō and other Northwest Coast peoples, such as the work of Franz Boas, Charles Hill-Tout, Wayne Suttles, and more recently scholarly work by Jay Miller, Christopher Roth, Crisca Bierwert, Keith Carlson, and John Lutz. Offering historical background, these sources situate the tradition of carrying and giving ancestral names, as well as the origins of current "name disputes."[15] Interviews and conversations with members of the Stó:lō Nation, from elders to young adults, conducted in the spring of 2005, demonstrated the persistent importance of ancestral names. Further, the individuals interviewed reflected on the pivotal role ancestral names played in past generations, and how these names form a critical aspect of Stó:lō identity by linking present, past, and future.

This research is, however, limited by the small number of interviews conducted in 2005 and the ever-present fact that interview-based research uses certain individuals' beliefs and experiences used to represent a whole. The people interviewed, although intimately connected with the Stó:lō Nation, are not all Stó:lō themselves, but represent other Coast Salish groups such as Thompson and Ts'ymsen as well. In subsequent studies, a wider range and greater number of interviews would provide a more comprehensive illustration of the role and importance of ancestral names in Stó:lō culture and history. Also, the conspicuous role of an ethnographer, or "outsider" interviewer questioning Stó:lō or other Northwest Coast peoples about their intimate understanding of self and history may inevitably result in some answers that are tempered and/or framed to satisfy the listener. Real communication and trust between an interviewer and interviewee in most cases requires substantial time to be established.[16] The time limitations of this initial fieldwork meant that these relationships had only begun to develop when the interviews took place.

Family Histories and Ancestral Names

Generally speaking, Stó:lō and other Coast Salish groups have historically, both pre-contact and continuing into the twentieth century, identified themselves by "Indian" ancestral names.[17] Ancestral names were pivotal in identifying individuals as Stó:lō and were used to define individuals according to their family lineage. Through carrying an ancestral name, individuals gained a place in their family histories. These histories were often linked to epic stories where great individuals and their great actions formed a larger supratribal history. If an individual's name connected them to the supratribal history, then their social status was augmented and, further, their historical knowledge and/or their interpretations of history gained greater legitimacy within the community. According to Wayne Suttles, amateur ethnographers' initial recorded observations at the time of Europeans' contact with Coast Salish and Stó:lō peoples, and later observations by professional ethnographers all noted that Coast Salish societies were organized and socially stratified.[18] Ancestral names were key to this social organization as names demonstrated status, ensured resource allocation according to family connections, and regulated personal behaviour. Knowledge of one's history, which was gained through ancestral names, was pivotal to establishing social status in Stó:lō society. This is reflected in the terms for the upper class, the "worthy" people who were referred to as smela:lh, "those who know their history," and s'texem, meaning the lower-class, "worthless" people.[19]

Name Disputes

Many of the individuals who were interviewed note that caution is paramount when giving ancestral names, because by carrying an ancestral name, one carries the family's history. There is a fear that if given to the "wrong" person, history may be told (and ultimately unfold) badly, not only jeopardizing the people exposed to this "bad history" but also dishonouring the ancestral name and all implicated ancestors. Stripping an individual of their name was, and remains, a serious disgrace; therefore great care continues to be dedicated to choosing and giving names.[20] Naming necessitates discernment in order to prevent the granting of a name to someone who might potentially pollute that name. Harley Chappell, a Stó:lō man and father, maintained that the name must be "kept clean for future generations."[21]

In his article "Reflections on Indigenous History and Memory: Reconstructing and Reconsidering Contact," Keith Carlson discusses in greater detail the convergence of truth, fiction, reality, and embellishment in Stó:lō criteria for legitimate histories. He provides an example where history was manipulated in an individual's narrative in order for him to claim genealogical connections and therefore rights to history and resources. At the time of carrying out the interviews in 2005, controversies abound when individuals claim certain family names. For example, a priority for Stó:lō elder Joe Aleck and his family was to document genealogical links to a prominent historical figure, Chief Alexis, as they feared other families were attempting to illegitimately claim the ancestral name and its inherent rights. This case, and presumably others like it, involve a multitude of factors that cannot be understood without first examining the fundamental role of ancestral names in Stó:lō tradition.

Stó:lō Worldview—Language and Spiritual Forces

Stó:lō/Coast Salish concepts of time—past, present, and future—do not follow a Western or European linear chronology. Many authors, notably Bierwert, Miller, and Carlson, have explored how in Stó:lō and other Coast Salish belief systems, human beings are sites of "multiple spiritual forces."[22] Affected by the metaphysical spirit world, humans are understood as fluidly linked in various ways to their ancestors, as well as to future generations. Vocabulary in the Halq'émeylem language demonstrates this belief. In the *Stó:lō-Coast Salish Historical Atlas*, Carlson uses interviews with Stó:lō elders and documentation of Halq'émeylem words to describe and illustrate how there is one and the same word for great-grandparents (great-aunt/uncle) and great-grandchild (great-niece/nephew): sts'o:mqw. The use of a common word for both ancestor and future relative continues on until great-great-great-great-grandparents and great-great-great-great-grandchildren, who are referred to as tomiyeqw.[23]

This terminology illustrates the belief among the Stó:lō that "people from a parallel past and future generations, up to seven times removed from current living relatives, are considered to hold the same relationship with the current living generation."[24] Many of the people interviewed for this paper, particularly Harley Chappell, discussed how the individual living in the present with an ancestral name plays a central role in linking an entire tradition, both past and future. The power of these metaphysical connections is remarkable compared to an Xwelitem (non-Indigenous person) worldview that is rooted in linear beliefs and generally sees little intrinsic connection between generations.

The Naming Process: Ceremony, Status, and Gender

Charles Hill-Tout, in 1902, noted that ancestral names were given through a naming ceremony when a youth passed into adulthood.[25] Hill-Tout's observations were confirmed by current oral histories, which explained how in "the past" naming ceremonies, like potlatches, represented a family's wealth and status; by hosting a big ceremony a family indicated their wealth and subsequent worthiness to carry a particular name. Isadore Charters and Irene Aleck both confirmed, in separate interviews, that in the past naming ceremonies included up to two or three days of feasting, speeches, and giveaways, and people gathered from faraway villages to act as witnesses and to carry the news of the naming to their homes.[26] In the most recent example of a naming ceremony in 2015, the naming ceremony was held on one day, but the time of year purposely coincided with the time of the Winter Dances. During this ceremony, over 300 people were present, and witnesses, dancers, and singers were invited from other families.[27] In the past, the naming depended on receiving the consent of the gathered community, and if consent was not given, the name would either be given up or the family would be expected to hand out more gifts in order to convince the community of their worth and the worthiness of giving that name.[28] This is interesting as it demonstrates that wealth could potentially "buy" a name, regardless of historical entitlement. Ancestral names conceivably organized Stó:lō society by fixing class divisions, as lower-class Stó:lō were prohibited from accessing high-class names due to their lack of status and wealth.

According to Bob Joe in an interview with Oliver Wells in 1962, a father's name was always given to his oldest son.[29] Wayne Suttles, in his discussion of the Katzie, describes the sons as being the ones to succeed their fathers' "inherited names." However, names were also given to daughters as "part of their dowries to be used by their sons to show their mother's origin."[30] In the Thompson tradition it was the duty of the matriarch, the grandmother, to name the children born into the family. According to Isadore Charters (who is Thompson), naming young children was based on the child's physical or personality resemblance to a deceased ancestor, regardless of gender.[31] Among various Coast Salish groups women carried multiple names that would then be distributed to their sons to represent matrilineal lineage.

Through the multiple layers of families, marriages, and intermixing, individuals could, and currently continue to, trace their lineage to several groups and ancestors. For example, Wayne Suttles worked with Simon Pierre, who traced his lineage to "Saanich communities at Patricia Bay and Brentwood Bay and with people at Tsawwassen." He was also connected through uncles and aunts to Scowlitz at Harrison River, Lillooet, and with "descendants of white settlers."[32] In 1894 Boas similarly observed that among the Stó:lō "names [were] given by both paternal and maternal relatives" and an individual could carry more than one name.[33] The interwoven webs of ancestry are therefore complicated by the various naming practices and identities acquired through receiving ancestral names. Further, an individual became connected through each name to a specific place.

Name and Place

Names were and are integrally linked to their place of origin. Franz Boas's work, as well as current oral histories, affirms that names could be associated with a certain location or village.[34] Some Stó:lō and Coast Salish people have discussed how an ancestral name could belong to the village and the tribe, as the ancestor was part of that particular tribe, rather than to the individual. Thus, when in a particular village an individual personified a certain ancestor to those people in that place, she or he was given that name regardless of other names the individual might carry. The name and place stayed together, while the person embodying that name in that place changed with the generations.[35]

Association with ancestral names was key to establishing communities within villages and identifying the members of a tribal group.[36] Isadore Charters maintained that, "Without a[n ancestral] name it's almost like going without an ID."[37] Names served, and serve, to identify individuals and their role or position in the community. In the past, the purpose was primarily to define communities within villages. Currently persons are still recognized for their ancestral links and given status based on their role within a community and family. A twenty-first-century example of this is given by Tíxwelátsa (or Herb Joe). He explained the reasons he received his name, Tíxwelátsa, a name that "goes back to the beginning of the Ts'elxwéyeqw people":

> I was given the name by an Elder in our family who decided that because of my position in the community—I was a newly elected, very young, chief, I was working for the federal penitentiary service, with supposedly a totally First Nations case load—so he said that it was important that I carry a traditional name, a family name, so that when I was at big chief's meetings, he said that the other families from the other tribes would recognize who I am and recognize me. The only way that they would recognize me is through the names. Because what he asked was, "Who knows Herb Joe? We know Herb Joe because you're our family but who else would know you? No one! So we put a name on you then everybody will know you.[38]

Similarly, the late Amelia Douglas stated that she was "accepted by Abel Joe" because of her name, Siya:mia. Abel Joe told Amelia that they must be related because "they have a *Siya:mia* in their family."[39] Thus, even now, Stó:lō connect, reconnect, and fall into prescribed relationships, according to the ancestral names they carry.

Ancestral Names and the Web of Reciprocal Relationships

Harley Chappell believes that the basic premise of holding an ancestral name is the relationship that forms between the people who carry and have carried that name. He explains, "the person whose name you receive is the closest to you in the family," even if they may be separated by up to seven generations; they are your mentor, your role model, and your guide through life.[40] This was evident in conversations with several individuals. Isadore Charters (Yen MoCeetza), when speaking of the man he was named after, provided intimate details about his ancestor's personality and characteristics: "Yen MoCeetza was old, was a traveller, a sort of shaman . . . he was an awesome storyteller and a fiddler. He knew lots of legends and stories about the Creator, and he believed in the higher power, and so every time he went into different homes, he would be like, he would be helping, he would help chop wood, gather wood, do a lot of different things that needed to be done and people liked him so they let him stay. So he travelled, he was from the States, Coleville area. . . ."[41] Generations removed, Isadore nevertheless spoke of Yen MoCeetza with personal fondness and profound respect.

Naming, the giving and receiving of ancestral names among the Stó:lō, forms a web of reciprocal relationships and responsibilities that bind communities and families together, transcending physical time and space. Similarly, Jay Miller observed that for the Ts'mysen ancestral names provide the "mortal-immortal connection."[42] Among the Ts'mysen, sharing names is believed to "sustain and enhance the status" of both the contemporary individual and the ancestor. Carrying a name obligates one to act honourably and respectfully towards that ancestor. However, in return one can also depend on having guidance not only from that ancestor but also from the elder who gave the name and, essentially, the entire community that was present when that name was given.[43] For Chappell, ancestral names mark the cycle of history; they represent "how we [Stó:lō] keep our history going."[44] Names not only show an individual to whom she or he belongs, affirming identity and membership in a collective community, names also ensure that family roots remain and will not be lost. Ancestral names keep history alive.

"Names Feed People"

Among the Stó:lō there is a parallel to Miller's observation that "names feed people."[45] This is because names connected individuals to their rights to land and resources. Miller furthers this, saying, "in this manner, the immortal sustains the mortal,"[46] demonstrating the living relationship between the ancestor and the person carrying their name. Miller offers insight into naming ceremonies and the importance of ancestral names for individuals and their families/tribes. He explains that in the Ts'mysen tradition, each house (the family/genealogical lineage) owned "a corpus of immortal names"[47] that were passed down through the matrilineal line. The chief of the house held a leading name, which carried with it the responsibility of reciting the adawx, or the epic: the history and events that came with that name, the history of the descendants of that name—similar to the "genealogy founders" in the Stó:lō tradition.

The smela:lh, those high status Stó:lō who knew their ancestors and where they came from, also enjoyed social, economic, and political advantages.[48] An ancestral name gave individuals rights to inheritance, resource locations, fishing sites, songs, and dances that had been part of that line of descent for centuries. Also, people who carried different names from the different villages where they had relatives had access to even greater wealth and resources as each of the names provided for them.[49]

Ancestral names in Stó:lō living tradition may play different roles. However, whether they serve to connect family, mark genealogies, or give rights to ancestral places and resource sites, names remain central to Stó:lō identity. Ancestral names indicate family and thus connect individuals to people they have never encountered.[50] Ancestral names can bridge gaps within and between families, creating vast, complicated webs of relations.

Halq'émeylem and the Organization of Relations

Halq'émeylem has extensive vocabulary to explain relatives and different familial connections. The language distinguishes between matrilineal and patrilineal relatives and has, as well, words for half-siblings, relatives of separated spouses, illegitimate children, adopted children, orphans, widowed individuals, and so on.[51] In an interview he conducted with the late Amelia Douglas, Sonny McHalsie mentioned how in English the words cousin, aunt, uncle, and grandparent do not indicate which side of the family they are from, whereas in Halq'émeylem these relationships are made clear. Amelia Douglas responded to McHalsie's statement saying that without knowing the Halq'émeylem words, the only way she came to understand how she had so many relatives was when her mother "got some matches, she set out matches and there was two up on top, from the two they branched out, spread out so that's the only time I know of that I realized that Bob, Alex and Oscar were my third cousins."[52] When Amelia was little, her parents "couldn't seem to explain who their relatives were," so everyone was referred to as siyo:ye, which she later learnt meant your relative or your relation. Through this, Amelia discovered that she has family all over Fraser Valley and that "most of the Fraser Valley is related somehow." This is interesting not only in terms of examining a particular Stó:lō understanding of history and family, but is also noteworthy in that Amelia Douglas came to understand her family lineage in "European" terms rather than Stó:lō, perhaps a result of growing up in the period where there was a profound intrusion of Xwelitem (non-Stó:lō) ideas and education into Stó:lō life.

To further illustrate these complex familial linkages through ancestral names one can look at Amelia Douglas's explanation of her grandmother's name, Siya:mia, which is the ancestral name Amelia inherited and carried. Amelia Douglas's grandmother, whose English name was Lucy, was married three times. Amelia's mother was Josephine. Josephine's father's name was Siyemtel and Amelia's first cousin inherited that name. Lucy's other two husbands were William and Waleseluq from Iwowes—Waleseluq "maybe" is Alan Gutierrez's great-grandfather. Lucy's name began as Siya:mia, from her first husband, and then with her second husband (who she noted was also respected and wealthy) her name changed to Luxsiya:mia once "the sxwyo:yxwoy mask was in the family." In the case of Agnes Kelly, she had three husbands and with each of these marriages came rights to pass on ancestral names to children, as well as rights to berry-picking sites, fishing sites, and so on.[53]

Names and Land Rights

Perhaps most important politically is how ancestral names connect individuals to rights to land. According to Roth, names link Ts'msyen members to their past as well as to "the land upon which that past unfolded."[54] Connection to land, made through names, is particularly important for the Ts'msyen in their treaty negotiations and land claims. Roth explains, "hereditary names connect individuals to corporate descent groups."[55] He uses the example of the court case *Delgamuukw v. British Columbia* to show how the entire house of Delgamuukw was called on for the case—generations and generations of people that call on the rights inherent in that hereditary name.[56] Earlier, Boas noted that each of the Stó:lō ancestors remembered through names is connected to a village, a certain place. The connection to a particular location is further accentuated in cases where the ancestors were turned into a physical element such as a rock (a transformer site), often found close to the village.[57] Of vital importance to the Stó:lō is that ancestral names remain in the place of their origin. Contemporarily, in *You are Asked to Witness*, Frank Malloway discusses the names of four original chiefs of the Ts'elxeyeqw people. One of the names, Wili:leq, problematically, according to Malloway, "went to [a person in] Victoria"; it was given to an aunt's grandson. According to Malloway, this is regrettable because a Chilliwack name that is part of the history of the people in Chilliwack should never leave that territory.[58]

Claiming Descent

Claiming descent from ancestors is a complex process. European genealogical mapping systems, which assert legitimacy and connection to an ancestor on a purely linear, chronological level do not work. Instead, among the Stó:lō family lineage is remembered through the oral telling and retelling of stories. In his work on the origins of the Katzie people, Suttles provides an example of how difficult it would be to find the "authentic" original groups of the Katzie. According to Suttles, the Katzie came from three original groups: Pitt Lake, Sturgeon Slough, and Port Hammond people. However, Suttles's respondent, Simon Pierre, named ten "tribes" or "families" settled at Katzie.[59] Potentially, one could claim descent from any of these Katzie settlements, thus connecting oneself with the original ten tribes, and thereby claiming rights to the land in that area. Similarly, Boas's recorded seven generations of the original Stó:lō tribes. However, these tribes no longer exist and various Stó:lō now claim to be "returning" to their homeland.

On the one hand, some Stó:lō are claiming names and rights they believe are inherently theirs, while on the other hand, other Stó:lō see them as illegitimate invaders of their own rightful land. Fishing disputes also are connected to ancestral names as conflicts arise between people who believe that their claims to fishing locations are "more traditional, and therefore more legitimate, than someone else's."[60] Proof of legitimacy and authenticity are difficult to determine within the web of oral history, interwoven family genealogies, and changing, inconsistently documented names.

The Aleck Family

The case of Joe Aleck and his family's desire to document their hereditary links to Chief Alexis (chief of Cheam 1867–88) accentuates the precariousness of attempting to justify one's claim to history. Their claim to ancestral rights to Chief Alexis's name is arguably similar to what Carlson refers to in his article as history disputes—where one group challenges another's assertion of hereditary rights and prerogatives, calling into question fact, fiction, truth, and reality.[61] Elder Joe Aleck (Siyamalalexw) and his family claim to be descendants of Chief Alexis, who was the first listed chief of Cheam in Department of Indian Affairs records and who played a vital role in early Stó:lō interactions with the Canadian/British government and missionaries, and in early Stó:lō land claims petitions.[62] The Alecks' link to Alexis is made through Joe's great-grandmother, Lucy Olale, who is believed to be a descendant of Alexis. However, to date genealogical links have not been firmly established by Stó:lō Nation genealogists and researchers.

The inability to consolidate this family's genealogy results primarily from inconsistencies of surnames and dates in marriage, birth, death, baptismal, and census records, as well as the aforementioned layers of relations in Stó:lō families. For example, as listed in the Stó:lō Nation genealogical files, Chief Alexis Srouchelaleou (b. 1843) and his wife Pauline Marie Steyroula (b. 1843) had nine children—four of whom were listed carrying the surname Alexis, while four others are listed with the surname Sruetslanough, and the seventh child is listed with the surname Edwards.[63] Also, while some records claim that Chief Alexis's father was Louie Skw:etes, the Stó:lō Nation's genealogical

Joe and Irene Aleck. Photo courtesy of Keith Carlson.

database shows Alexis's father to be Mathieu Hielamacha. There is no mention or record of Skw:etes—who apparently is the ancestor linking "many of the people of the Stó:lō Nation." The book *In the Shadow of Mount Cheam* asserts the families of Cheam—Alex, Casimer, Douglas, Edwards, Harris, Louie, Murphy, Shaw, Thomas, and Victor—are all connected through Louie Skw:etes, Chief Alexis's father; however, genealogical data compiled by the Stó:lō Nation fails to reflect this.

While this topic requires more detailed research and analysis, it is important to note the urgency with which Joe Aleck and his family wish to consolidate their link to the Alexis name. This is presumably due to tension with another family on the Cheam reserve, who some Stó:lō believe have been given the name Alexis illegitimately. Relatives of Joe Aleck have even recently changed the spelling of their surname from "Aleck" to "Alexis" to assert their hereditary right to the name. In the limited information gained for this paper, the reasons why the Alexis name was so desired were not made clear exactly. Yet, one can imagine that due to his vital political role, Chief Alexis is among the great "genealogical founders" of the Stó:lō nation, and thus holds a highly respected and honourable name.[64]

Reflecting the Ancestors

In addition to their role in sustaining familial heritage and family linkages, many believe ancestral names are given according to personality traits and/or to a person's (usually a young child's) resemblance to an ancestor. In this case, the elders' responsibility is to remember the ancestors and their personalities, and to match young individuals with appropriate names. Isadore Charters notes how, in his Thompson tradition, grandmothers always name the young children. They will look at the young baby, reflect on the past, and choose a name according to the child's visible personality. These names go on to influence the individual's own life. For example, the name, Yen MoCeetza, guides Isadore to follow the path set by his ancestor who was the original owner of the name. Similarly, in an interview in 1988, Matilda "Tillie" Gutierrez discussed how grandparents can give Stó:lō names at birth because of the baby's resemblance to a deceased relative or because the name is not occupied: there is "nobody standing for that name."[65]

Some Stó:lō believe, however, that giving names to babies is unwise, as the full knowledge of the responsibilities inherent in carrying a name are not known to that baby. To assign ancestral names to babies before seeing what kind of people they will become is believed to be too great of a risk. Thus, some contend names should only be given once individuals have demonstrated they are responsible enough or have accomplished something special—ancestral names must be earned.[66] Others, however, believe names and carrying an ancestral name is a "matter of fate." With the proper guidance and support, children will grow into the name and its requisite responsibilities and obligations.[67] In 2015, naming ceremonies are generally held for persons who have moved through puberty and into adulthood and have demonstrated that they have "earned" the name, that they lead a "good life" and will not act in a way that drags that name through the mud. This is not to say, however, that some families do not seek ancestral names for younger family members, perhaps in an attempt to use up the ancestral names with their corresponding territorial or hierarchical claims before other family members claim the names.[68]

Names to Non-Stó:lō

Ancestral names are sometimes given to non-Stó:lō people. Richard Wilson's name was given to him by a Stó:lō elder, although he himself is Ts'msyen, married to a Stó:lō woman. The name was given not to connect Richard with his direct ancestors, but to reflect his special abilities and his role in the Stó:lō community. Richard's name, Si:yo Laylex, means Spirit Singer and is integral to Richard's identity and daily life. As a drummer and singer, Richard, through his name, carries a responsibility to his community to drum and sing whenever and wherever he is needed. He admits that, "Sometimes I think my name is a jinx, but I'm really honoured and I'm really happy to be able to carry the name that I do, because I love to drum and sing. Like I said, I originally come from Kitimat and up there we rarely do cultural stuff, like we do down here. And down here it's every day for me."[69]

In this way, Richard's name vitally connects him to a community not of his ancestry. For Richard and others, carrying an ancestral name involves enormous responsibility. A recurrent theme when discussing ancestral names is the challenge, and the responsibility, an ancestral name entails to "not drag it [the name] through the mud."[70] This theme demonstrates the continuous commitment among Stó:lō to honour and respect the responsibilities that come with accepting an ancestral name. Although ancestral names are negotiated in different ways to give meaning to Stó:lō identity, the recognition of the power inherent in ancestral names is constant.[71] This responsibility is arguably the primary motive to receive or not receive ancestral names, as one must live carefully to do the name justice and dishonour neither the elders who gave the name nor the ancestors implicated and reflected in that name. Many Stó:lō youth and adults refuse or decide not to carry a name, often because they feel they are not living in the way they would like to as carriers of an ancestral name.[72] Moreover, even in the planning for the naming ceremony itself families will take into account who they invite as witnesses, masked dancers, singers, and receivers so as not to discredit the naming ceremony itself by inviting people who are not leading a good life but have chosen a reckless path.[73] Thus great care and attention is given to every aspect of granting names and receiving them, including the honour of all those present at the naming ceremony, who in turn share responsibility for those individuals and their ancestors.

Interestingly, at the time of the interview with Richard Wilson, his mother in Kitmat was preparing to pass on to Richard, her eldest son, a hereditary chief's name. Among the Ts'msyen, with a chiefly name comes a "mandate to authority and a deed of sovereign land title."[74] Richard discussed the honour, but also the immense pressure that comes with holding a chief's name. According to Roth, the successors to a name are accountable for their predecessors' actions: "the agency and accountability associated with an action transcended the lifetime of a mortal individual and pertained not to a biological self, but, rather, to an onomastic one."[75] That name must not only be carried with honour, but also must be carefully passed down to someone who will equally respect and honour the name. It is similar among the Stó:lō. The ancestral name Harley Chappell carries is from an ancestor who was a leader and a guide. With this name, Harley feels he must "live up to my name,"[76] and therefore strives to be a guide and leader in his community and family.

Belonging to a Name

An ancestral name does not belong to the person; rather the person belongs to the name. Roth quotes a Ts'msyen elder who stated, "People are nothing ... it's the names that are really real."[77] He goes on to explain that names are "social actors who constitute a social order that transcends their holders."[78] According to McHalsie, the names are owned by the family and given by the elders.[79] Similarly, Chappell asserts that ancestral names are precisely "how we carry our history. That's how we carry our culture."[80] It is interesting to witness how naming ceremonies, and carrying ancestral names, are gaining prominence in contemporary Stó:lō society after a period where ancestral names were generally not used and were forgotten. Interviews from the late 1980s, with elders Elsie Charlie, Matilda (Tillie) Gutierrez, Agnes Kelly, and Amelia Douglas, indicate that although "Indian" names were a topic of discussion, many elders were unsure as to the specific meaning of their names and often only close family members referred to them by their ancestral name. For example, when asked what her "Indian name," Themset, meant, Elsie Charlie replied, "something about the little pools in the river something like that [Sonny McHalsie: How long have you had the Indian name?] I guess since I was a little girl ... nobody seemed to call me by that name ... just my sister."[81]

Generations of Stó:lō

The generational difference that Elsie Charlie reflects above is noteworthy. A young Stó:lō woman expressed that carrying an ancestral name means carrying an understanding of history—"so that when an elder or someone asks what your name means, or where it comes from, you should be able to give an informed answer."[82] When I was gathering information for this paper, the "younger" generation of Stó:lō were quick to explain exactly where and from whom their names came, while the older generation did not all know such specifics.

In elder Irene Aleck's case, only as an adult has she reclaimed her name, Tiaktenaw Slaholt. She points to her experience at boarding school as being the reason why people's "Indian" names were forgotten and taken away.[83] In an informal conversation with a Stó:lō elder from a reserve near present-day

Chilliwack, the elder mentioned how she sees the value placed in names and family ties in Stó:lō culture clash with Western ideas of the individual. She contended that the experience of residential schools has had such a lasting imprint on Stó:lō people, teaching people to forget who they are, forget their identity as Stó:lō, and forget their ancestors and history: all aspects contained within an "Indian" name.[84] Similarly, Irene Aleck stated, "We didn't know who we were, just little brown white people."[85]

Significant disagreements amongst family members have also contributed to ancestral names not being given and naming ceremonies not being organized until more recent years (2000s). These disagreements can involve elders not knowing what the traditional teachings are; for instance, assuming that names can be given to whomever they choose, notwithstanding whether that individual has earned the name or not.[86] Furthermore, the lasting impact of a generation who did not learn to speak or read the Halq'émeylem language makes it difficult for elders to be able to trace and research their genealogies.

Current Reclamation of Ancestral Naming

Many Stó:lō are now reclaiming their language, history, and roles in Stó:lō society by reclaiming their ancestral names. However, even while living in a contemporary and predominantly "Western" culture, Stó:lō are "immersed in subjectivities imponderably alien to non–First Nations understandings."[87] Contemporary Stó:lō identity needs to be negotiated to bridge traditional and contemporary realities. Irene Aleck stated that names are vitally important as they show people who they are and they allow "Salish" people to be who they are. She explained:

> I think that [now] more of the younger generations know of who they are and what they are, what we believe in, what our traditions are. That gives them the strength; it gives them strength to be a better person. Give them an Indian name and say that's an old, old name and there's about twenty people lined up behind you that had that name, and they're going to guide you and help you, so you don't rub that name in the mud. You carry it with pride. Be proud of who you are, that name is strong and you have to behave in a way that all these ancestors will expect you to behave.[88]

Harley Chappell maintains that Stó:lō youth need to acknowledge their identity; they need role models as they struggle to transcend their present circumstances to "start to live instead of just surviving." He believes that carrying ancestral names and nurturing cross-generational connections provides what is necessary: identity, role models, and cultural grounding. Through ancestral names, Stó:lō youth "learn to be better people than their parents."[89] And the nation, through remembering its history, is kept alive.

In current Stó:lō tradition, naming ceremonies continue to be significant events for families. Reflecting the enduring importance of community gatherings and cultural celebrations, Richard Wilson explained his experience at his naming ceremony:

> That's where you find out where your family is, or who your family is. People that you helped before will come back and they'll thank you and then they'll help you during that time, during a naming ceremony. We were told [for his naming ceremony], that we gotta call witnesses and people who help us, we gotta pay them. So we had to save a lot of money and we thought we were going to be short. Because I had a hundred and fifty dollars in quarters and that wasn't enough and then and then there was, like I said there was people that come up and say you're part of their family, they claim you, or they want to repay you for what you did for them. They'll come up and they'll help you out with money or blankets, so by the end of the night, by the end of the naming, and after we paid everybody off, I still had a hundred and fifty dollars in quarters [laughs] …'cause so many people came up to help. And that's, that's the way it is around here.[90]

Naming ceremonies and the enduring tradition of giving and receiving ancestral names offers a sense of belonging, security, and affirmation, as well as responsibility and obligation to a family, genealogy, and community beyond the individual. Although not ubiquitously, ancestral names can generate dignity and empower Stó:lō people and others in the Stó:lō community to serve and nurture their community and family in a way that is honourable and consistent with Stó:lō traditions and history.

Conclusion

For many Stó:lō, there is a sense of obligation "to past and future generations to ensure that our identity and our connection to the land lives on."[91] Ultimately, from the limited interviews that I conducted, it is evident that it is through the conscious reclamation of ancestral names and the continuous ritual cycles of naming that Stó:lō are remembering who they are and where they come from. This process is nurturing a revivification of meaning in Stó:lō culture.

It is vital that studies of Stó:lō ethnohistory include a recognition, and seek to understand the power of, ancestral names in Stó:lō identity. Although not universally used and by no means uniformly interpreted, Stó:lō ancestral names and the relationships between past, present, and future exemplified in the Halq'émeylem language embody a worldview, a narrative, and a relationship with history that differs significantly from the one guiding the "Xwelitem" (mainstream popular cultural) paradigm. By recognizing and seeking to understand these multilayered differences, mutually positive and mutually beneficial contact can and does occur.

Notes

1   I conducted the interviews referred to in this chapter in 2005, and wrote the original article in 2008. The main claims of the article have not significantly changed over the past nine years. Consequently, except for minimal additions, the text remains the same. However, a recent conversation with Sonny McHalsie about a naming ceremony held by the McHalsie family prompted this preface as a reflection on the ongoing significance of the study of Stó:lō ancestral names.

2   Keith Thor Carlson, *The Power of Place, the Problem of Time: Aboriginal Identity and Historical Consciousness in the Cauldron of Colonialism* (Toronto: University of Toronto Press, 2010), 274.

3   Walter Mignolo, "Delinking," *Cultural Studies* 21, no. 2 (2007): 500. See also Arturo Escobar, "Worlds and Knowledges Otherwise," in *Globalization and the Decolonial Option,* eds. Walter Mignolo and Arturo Escobar (Abingdon: Routledge, 2010), 37. According to Arturo Escobar, Western (Eurocentric) modernity, "as a particular local history," has produced specific global designs that have "'subalternized' other local histories and their corresponding designs."

4   Escobar, "Worlds and Knowledges," 54.

5   Discourse is defined by Ernesto Laclau and Chantal Mouffe as "an attempt to dominate the field of discursivity, to arrest the flow of differences, to construct a centre." Ernesto Laclau and Chantal Mouffe, *Hegemony and Socialist Strategy: Towards a Radical Democratic Politics* (London: Verso, 2001), 112.

6   See Wayne Suttles, "Affinal Ties, Subsistence and Prestige among the Coast Salish" in *Coast Salish Essays* (Seattle: University of Washington Press, 1987); and John Sutton Lutz, *Makúk: A New History of Aboriginal-White Relations* (Vancouver: University of British Columbia Press, 2008).

7   Sonny McHalsie, personal communication, telephone conversation, 28 July 2015.

8   See Christopher Miller and George Hammell, "A New Perspective on Indian-White Contact: Cultural Symbols and Colonial Trade," *Journal of American History* 73, no. 2 (1986): 311–328.

9   Clifford Geertz, "Thick Description: Toward an Interpretive Theory of Culture," in *Interpretation of Cultures, Selected Essays* (New York: Basic Books, 1973), 17.

10   Further discussion of insider/outsider researchers can be found in Kirin Narayan, "How Native Is a 'Native' Anthropologist?" *American Anthropologist* 95, no. 3 (1993): 671–86.

11   I would argue that factors involved in contact with Europeans such as migration, disease, residential schools, and the concentration of Indigenous populations into urban centres all contributed to a tendency away from carrying ancestral names and following Stó:lō tradition. See Keith Thor Carlson, "Reflections on Indigenous History and Memory: Reconstructing and Reconsidering Contact," in *Myth and Memory: Stories of Indigenous-European Contact*, ed. John Sutton Lutz (Vancouver: University of British Columbia Press, 2007); and Keith Thor Carlson, David Schaepe, Albert "Sonny" McHalsie, et al., eds., *A Stó:lō-Coast Salish Historical Atlas* (Vancouver: Douglas and McIntyre/Chilliwack: Stó:lō Heritage Trust, 2001).

12   Lutz, *Makúk*, 56; Suttles, "Affinal Ties"; Albert "Sonny" McHalsie, "We Have to Take Care of Everything that Belongs to Us," in *Be of Good Mind: Essays on the Coast Salish*, ed. Bruce G. Miller (Vancouver: University of British Columbia Press, 2007), 97.

13   McHalsie, personal communication, 2015.

14   By "contact" I refer to John Lutz's discussion of contact as a series of "encounter moments," or the site, the zone at which the "stories begin." See John Sutton Lutz, ed., *Myth and Memory: Stories of Indigenous-European Contact* (Vancouver: University of British Columbia Press, 2007), 13–14.

15   Carlson, "Reflections," 49. Carlson notes that claiming descent and showing genealogical ties to "genealogy founders"—often heroes, protectors, or transmitters of epic stories—is important to Stó:lō today.

16   The brief time I spent as a field school student researching in British Columbia did not allow for these relationships to be fully established. However inadequate, this introductory paper is intended to provide background for further research on Stó:lō family histories and a context for current attempts made by Stó:lō individuals to document their genealogy. In contrast, the phone conversation with Sonny McHalsie in July 2015 was an exception to the previous interviews from 2005. I have not maintained contact with Sonny or this research throughout the years; however, despite the years that have passed, the trust and ease with which I felt we were able to speak meant that our conversation did not follow the format of an interview, but rather Sonny generously explained and shared with me details of his family's recent naming ceremony. Thinking back to 2005, it is worth noting that the conversations I had that were included as interviews in this research project were all experiences of listening and learning as individuals generously recounted their stories, teachings, experiences, and opinions, for which I am ever grateful.

17   See Franz Boas, "The Indian Tribes of the Lower Fraser River: On the North-Western Tribes of Canada." *American Anthropologist*. Report – 1894; Charles Hill-Tout, "Ethnographical Studies of the Mainland Halkömë'lem, a division of the Salish of British Columbia," in "Report on the Ethnological Survey of Canada," British Association for the Advancement of Science (1902), Early Canadiana Online, http://eco.canadiana.ca/view/oocihm.14331.

18   Suttles was part of the dialogue as to whether social stratification and a significant "lower class" existed in what was referred to as Coast Salish society at "contact." He concludes that this "Coast Salish" society was stratified. See Wayne Suttles, "Private Knowledge, Morality, and Social Classes among the Coast Salish," in *Coast Salish Essays* (1972, repr. Vancouver: Talonbooks, 1987).

19   Ethnographers and anthropologists who observed Stó:lō and Coast Salish groups in the late nineteenth and early twentieth centuries and noted social organization are discussed by Wayne Suttles in *Coast Salish Essays*. Carlson also discusses the use of the term *smela:lh* to delineate high- and low-class status Stó:lō in Carlson, et al., eds., *A Stó:lō-Coast Salish Historical Atlas*, 27 and "Reflections," 49. See also Suttles, "Private Knowledge," 6–9; diagram of social stratification, 12.

20   According to Sonny McHalsie (personal communication, telephone conversation, 28 July 2015), taking away someone's name is not as common now as it seems to have been in the past (100 years ago or so). Having said that, Sonny remembers a recent situation where a person was stripped of their ancestral name not, as traditionally was the case, because of being unworthy or disgracing the name, but because of inter-familial disputes and political agendas and strategies to claim a particular ancestral lineage and to prevent another family member from establishing that desirable connection.

21   Harley Chappell, personal communication, e-mail, 30 June 2005. A name carried with it the actions and behaviours of all those who have held it previously. With a name one also inherits the actions of its predecessors.

22   See Crisca Bierwert, *Brushed by Cedar, Living by the River: Coast Salish Figures of Power* (Tucson: University of Arizona Press, 1999); Jay Miller, *Lushootseed Culture and the Shamanic Odyssey: An Anchored Radiance* (Lincoln, NE: University of Nebraska Press, 1999); and Keith Thor Carlson, "Expressions of Collective Identity," in *A Stó:lō-Coast Salish Historical Atlas*, eds. Keith Thor Carlson, David Schaepe, Albert "Sonny" McHalsie, et al. (Vancouver: Douglas and McIntyre/Chilliwack: Stó:lō Heritage Trust, 2001), 28.

23   Carlson, "Expressions of Collective Identity," 29; and Brent Galloway, *Dictionary of Upriver Halkomelem* (Berkley: University of California Press, 2009). Available online at http://escholarship.org/uc/item/65r158r4).

24   Carlson, "Expressions of Collective Identity," 27–8, plate 8c.

25   Hill-Tout, "Ethnographical Studies of the Mainland Halkömë'lem," 63; Keith Thor Carlson. ed., *You Are Asked to Witness: The Stó:lō in Canada's Pacific Coast History* (Chilliwack, BC: Stó:lō Heritage Trust, 1997), 167.

26   Isadore Charters, interview by Anastasia Tataryn, Chilliwack, BC, 19 May 2005; and Irene Aleck, interview by Anastasia Tataryn, Cheam Reserve, BC, 26 May 2005.

27   McHalsie, personal communication, telephone conversation, 28 July 2015.

28   Briam Thom, *Stó:lō Traditional Culture: A Short Ethnography of the Stó:lō People* (Chilliwack, BC: Stó:lō Curriculum Consortium, 1996), 35.

29   Bob Joe, interview by Oliver Wells, in *The Chilliwacks and Their Neighbours*, eds. Ralph Maud, Brent Galloway, and Marie Weeden (Vancouver: Talonbooks, 1987), 113–23.

30   Wayne Suttles, "Katzie Ethnographic Notes" in Anthropology in British Columbia, Memoir No. 2, ed., W. Duff (Victoria: British Columbia Provincial Museum, 1955), 28.

31   Charters, interview.

32   Suttles, "Katzie Ethnographic Notes," 28.

33   Boas, "The Indian Tribes of the Lower Fraser River," 5.

34   Richard Wilson, interview by Anastasia Tataryn, Chilliwack, BC, 19 May 2005; Charters, interview; also Frank Malloway, interview by Heather Myles, in *You Are*

Asked to Witness: The Stó:lō in Canada's Pacific Coast History, ed. Keith Thor Carlson (Chilliwack, BC: Stó:lō Heritage Trust, 1997), 3–26.

35 Interviews with Charters and Wilson, and the author's interview with Harley Chappell: Harley Chappell, interview by Anastasia Tataryn, Chilliwack, BC, 25 May 2005. See also Suttles, "Affinal Ties"; and Lutz, *Makúk*.

36 Boas, "The Indian Tribes of the Lower Fraser River."

37 Charters, interview.

38 Herb Joe, interview by Liam Haggerty, Heather Watson, and MacKinley Darlington. Chilliwack, BC, 20 May 2005.

39 Amelia Douglas, interview by Sonny McHalsie, Randel Paul, Richard Daly, and Peter John, 16 August 1988, Stó:lō Archives, Stó:lō Research and Resource Management Centre, Chilliwack, BC.

40 Chappell, interview.

41 Charters, interview.

42 Jay Miller, "Tsimshian Ethno-Ethnohistory: A 'Real' Indigenous Chronology," *Ethnohistory* 45, no. 4 (1998): 671.

43 This point came up in a few interviews, specifically Wilson and Chappell, and an informal conversation with a Stó:lō elder from a reserve near Chilliwack, B.C., 24 May 2005. It was also reaffirmed in conversation with Sonny McHalsie, personal communication, telephone conversation, 28 July 2015.

44 Chappell, interview.

45 Miller, "Tsimshian Ethno-Ethnohistory," 671.

46 Ibid.

47 Ibid., 662.

48 Carlson, "Reflections," 49.

49 Thom, *Stó:lō Traditional Culture,* 35; Boas, "The Indian Tribes of the Lower Fraser River," 3.

50 Chappell, interview. He also added that this makes dating so much harder, because you never know who you are actually related to—another impetus to research family genealogies.

51 Carlson, "Expressions of Collective Identity," 27–8; Galloway, *Dictionary of Upriver Halkomelem*; Suttles, "Affinal Ties," 18–19.

52 Douglas, interview.

53 Agnes Kelly, interview by Sonny McHalsie, Randel Paul, Leona Kelly, and Peter John, 10 June 1988, Stó:lō Archives, Stó:lō Research and Resource Management Centre, Chilliwack, BC.

54 Christopher Roth, "'The Names Spread in All Directions': Hereditary Titles in Tsimshian Social and Political Life," *BC Studies* 130 (2001): 69.

55 Ibid., 70.

56 *Delgamuukw v. British Columbia*, [1997] 3 SCR 1010.

57 Boas, "The Indian Tribes of the Lower Fraser River," 1.

58 Frank Malloway, interview.

59 Suttles, "Katzie Ethnographic Notes," 10.

60 Carlson, et al., eds., *A Stó:lō-Coast Salish Historical Atlas*, 58.

61 Carlson, "Reflections," 68.

62 See "Appendix 2: Stó:lō Petitions and Letters," in Carlson, et al., eds., *A Stó:lō-Coast Salish Historical Atlas*. Letters signed by Chief Alexis include: 1870 petition to governor, 1874 petition to superintendent, 1875 letter to Mr. Lenihan, Indian Commissioner in Victoria, (May and September), 172–4.

63 Spouses are only listed for the first child, but Pauline (Chief Alexis's wife) is not listed as carrying her husband's surname, leading me to believe that the difference in surnames is not reflective of the children's spouses.

64 I hesitate to touch on this topic as briefly as I am doing; however, I was not able to conduct the interviews with Joe Aleck and his family members as I had anticipated. I do not want to present the case falsely, but only wish to demonstrate the current desire among Stó:lō individuals to have their genealogies documented, as well as the difficulties encountered when conducting genealogical research.

65 "And I feel the power of my name. And I got it right when I was born. My grandfather and grandmother named me Qw'olamot right away. . . . You see they gave it [the name, Qw'olamot] to me as soon as I was born because my grandfather's mother was dead long time ago. . . ." Matilda Gutierrez, interview by Sonny McHalsie, Randel Paul, and Richard Daly, 20 September 1988, Stó:lō Archives, Stó:lō Research and Resource Management Centre, Chilliwack, BC.

66 Informal conversation with a Stó:lō woman living in Chilliwack, BC, 29 June 2005.

67 Chappell, personal correspondence, e-mail, 30 June 2005.

68 McHalsie, personal communication, telephone conversation, 28 July 2015.

69 Wilson, interview.

70 Ibid.

71 I had originally hoped to interview a wider variety of people. However, due to time constraints, this was not possible. In further studies it would be valuable to explore alternative perspectives on Stó:lō identity and ancestral names among Stó:lō youth, adults, and elders.

72 Wilson, interview. This also came up in the interview with Harley Chappell and other informal conversations with young Stó:lō people.

73 McHalsie, personal communication, telephone conversation, 28 July 2015.

74 Roth, "'The Names Spread in All Directions,'" 70.

75 Ibid., 78.

76 Ibid.

77 Ibid., 69.

78 Ibid., 75.

79 McHalsie, personal communication, telephone conversation, 28 July 2015.

80 Chappell, interview.

81 Elsie Charlie, interview with Sonny McHalsie, Richard Daly, Randel Paul, and Peter John, Richard Hope's Camp Spuzzum, BC, 2 August 1988, Stó:lō Archives, Stó:lō Research and Resource Management Centre, Chilliwack, BC.

82 Informal conversation with young Stó:lō woman in Chilliwack, BC, 29 June 2005.

83 Aleck, interview.

84 Informal discussion with Stó:lō elder, 24 May 2005.

85 Aleck, interview.

86 McHalsie, personal communication, telephone conversation, 28 July 2015.

87 Roth, "'The Names Spread in All Directions,'" 71. While Roth was referring to the Ts'msyen, I feel this statement fits a Stó:lō context as well.

88 Aleck, interview.

89 Chappell, interview.

90 Wilson, interview.

91 Albert "Sonny" McHalsie, "Halq'emélem Place Names in Stó:lō Territory," in *A Stó:lō-Coast Salish Historical Atlas*, eds. Keith Thor Carlson, David Schaepe, Albert "Sonny" McHalsie, et al. (Vancouver: Douglas and McIntyre/Chilliwack: Stó:lō Heritage Trust, 2001), 134.

5

Caring for the Dead:
Diversity and Commonality Among the Stó:lō

KATHRYN MCKAY

The events that precipitated my participation in the Stó:lō Ethnohistory Field School began one year prior to my actual attendance. In 1999 the RCMP collected a solitary human cranium found by a clean-up crew in an old shed at an abandoned gravel quarry in the central Fraser Valley. The first sojourn of these remains was the laboratories of the provincial coroner's office, where they were ascertained to be of some antiquity, as belonging to a person of First Nations ancestry, and not of interest to the RCMP as either a possible contemporary homicide or missing persons case. Consequently, the remains were turned over to Stó:lō Nation Archaeologist Dave Schaepe, with whom the RCMP has worked on other archaeological issues. The remains were accepted as those of an ancestral community member by the Stó:lō Nation, in whose collective territory they were found. In accepting the remains, the nation took responsibility for their caretaking. This return to the Stó:lō, however, was not the conclusion of the journey.

In the fifteen years since I attended the Stó:lō field school, there has been a significant shift in both the academic and the public perception and treatment of First Nations burials. Universities incorporate Indigenous world views into their curriculum and frequently partner with First Nations peoples on research initiatives.[1] After years of public dispute, the province of British Columbia transferred title of Grace Islet, a known Penelekut burial site, from private hands to the Nature Conservancy as a means to preserve the sacred site from development.[2] As well, the Musqueam First Nation, in conjunction with the University of British Columbia's Museum of Anthropology and the Museum of Vancouver, produced the exhibition *c̓əsnaʔəm, the city before the city* to explore what is commonly known as the "Marpole Midden."[3] Rather than focus on the display of artifacts, the thrust of the entire exhibition at all three sites was devoted to illustrating the connection between the living and the dead through the oral narratives of the Coast Salish peoples. While none of these developments are without some controversy, they do signal a significant change in thought regarding the rights of First Nations peoples in Canada.

The study of death and its rituals reveals more than just how a people die, it also reveals how they live. Social, religious, and cultural ideas that motivate the living are reflected in the manner in which a people perceive death. Changes in these practices do not necessarily represent the evolution or progress of a culture, nor do they signal a loss of traditional values. Rather, they depict the ability of a culture to live and adapt in a changing world. Rituals and ideas that remain stable over time establish continuity and are not necessarily restraints; rather, they illustrate integral parts of a lasting cultural identity. A discussion of the perceptions and practices of a number of modern Stó:lō with a comparison to ethnographic and archaeological studies confirms that many of the practices of the past have continued into the twenty-first century.

The purpose of this article is to discuss the manner in which the Coast Salish attitude towards death and burial has been reflected in their cultural practices and oral traditions over time. The main objective is to incorporate archaeological and ethnographic information with interviews to produce a description of these attitudes through an examination of the practices that changed before the arrival of Europeans, some that changed as a result of "contact," as well as others that remained constant for thousands of years. My argument focuses on the idea that Coast Salish culture has, for centuries, recognized the existence of a community between the living and the dead and has emphasized this connection through both continuity and change in burial rituals. Continuity is represented in the wrapping of bodies and the feeding of the dead. Transformation is evident in the shifts in outward burial customs.

This article is organized into three interlocking discussions of community and identity as outwardly manifested in burial traditions. The first section, "Investigating the Past," reviews information on burial practices as they were described by the early ethnographic and archaeological studies undertaken during the late nineteenth and early twentieth centuries. It also addresses more recent archaeological studies and examines the conclusions published concerning burial practices during the late twentieth and early twenty-first centuries.

The second section, "Let Me Give You a Story," offers the words of the modern Stó:lō regarding the respectful treatment of the ancestors. The third section, "Diversity and Commonality," concentrates on the recent past and investigates the controversies that arise in relation to the treatment of human remains.

Investigating the Past

Archaeological evidence indicates that the Coast Salish peoples have followed a number of different types of inhumation in the past. The earliest method documented in the archaeological record was midden burials, followed by mounds and cairns. At the time of extended contact during the later portion of the eighteenth century, the Coast Salish practice was to place the dead on a raised platform or tree to hasten decomposition. During the past 250 years a number of explorers, missionaries, ethnographers, and archaeologists have collected evidence concerning Coast Salish and Stó:lō burial practices. However, information from the earliest times has the disadvantage of being rather speculative and often contains the strong prejudices of the writers. Mindful of these limitations, an amount of useful information can be teased out of these works.

The earliest European explorers to the Northwest Coast observed that the Coast Salish put their dead on a raised platform or in a canoe that was then placed in a tree. Once the body had decomposed, the bones were generally wrapped in blankets and buried in the ground. One of the earliest records of this type of inhumation comes from the journal of Manuel Quimper, who explored the coast for Spain in 1790. While anchored off what is now Sooke Harbour on southern Vancouver Island, Quimper's pilot went ashore to explore. Quimper reported that: "At the mouth of the river he saw three canoes with a dead Indian in each one. This is the mode of burial these natives practice."[4] Over 100 years later, in 1899, the practice had changed very little. A Kwantlen woman reported a similar type of ritual:

> It was the custom of our villagers to bury their dead within an hour of death. They were in most cases placed in a tiny house raised on posts; but, if there was no house ready, or if they were a distance from the "dead houses" they were wrapped in skins and blankets and placed in pole platforms high above the reach of animals, or in trees. With the dead were placed pipes, bowls, hammers or such things as he made or might require to start life in the next world. Before the burial-house was placed a stone or wooden figure to guard the dead from evil spirits.[5]

Grave markers in the Shxw'ōwhámél Cemetery. Photo courtesy of Keith Carlson.

Myron Eells, a missionary writing in the 1880s and 1890s, described scaffold burials. He considered that this was a variation of canoe burial and was a response to the actions of unprincipled white gold seekers who stole both canoes and grave goods from burials that they encountered along rivers in the Pacific Northwest. According to Eells these thefts "incensed the Indians and caused a change in their mode of burial. They collected their dead in cemeteries and because enough trees could not be obtained . . . they built scaffolds . . . instead of using canoes, they made boxes and elevated them on a frame."[6] He reports that when canoes were used, they were rendered useless by punching many holes through them. Eells's report of these modifications did not signify a break with past tradition, but rather suggested that the Coast Salish were adapting the outward appearance of their customs in the face of cultural insensitivity.

The texts of some of the early twentieth-century authors, such as Harlan Smith and Charles Hill-Tout, offer some interesting insights into the mortuary rituals of the more distant past. Unlike recent studies that focus on scientific data, these early works describe the human ingenuity needed to construct these mortuary edifices. Both of these men wrote a great deal about the burial mounds and cairns, most probably because of their prominence in the landscape.

Smith, working with Gerald Fowke, published "Cairns of British Columbia and Washington" in 1901. This short article described the excavation of a number of burial cairns in coastal areas. Smith concluded that: "data tends to show that at one time the cairns were the burial places of the makers of the shell heaps nearby, but on other occasions and in the same region people who used the shell heaps did not bury in cairns." He also mentions that the great deal of effort needed for and care evident in the construction of cairns contrasted with the traditions that he saw practised by the Coast Salish of his time. Smith's conclusion that the Coast Salish of the early twentieth century were less concerned about the dead most probably stemmed from his own lack of knowledge concerning the ability of the Coast Salish to practise their customs unmolested, rather than indifference on their part.

Charles Hill-Tout discussed the mounds of the Marpole culture. Unlike his colleagues, Hill-Tout noted that the absence of grave goods was "remarkable in the face of the fact that in all disposals of the dead among modern indians ... stone, bone and other objects were commonly buried ... with the corpse."[7] He also reported the changes that he saw in the construction of the mounds and stated that some "were undoubtedly formed when a mode of burial prevailed very different from that practiced by the natives of this region ... it is well known that established customs rarely change radically among primitive people."[8] Although Hill-Tout believed there was some connection between the early inhabitants and the Coast Salish, he considered that the Coast Salish knew little or nothing of the early inhabitants. Further, he believed that the Salish of his time were "quite unconcerned at their (burial mounds of the earlier inhabitants) being opened or disturbed. This indifference in the face of the zealous vigilance they exercise over their own old burial grounds ... becomes the more striking."[9] However, what Hill-Tout considered as indifference could have been reticence on the part of his informants to approach the site because of concerns about their ability to do so safely.

Hill-Tout described a number of mounds and noted that certain mounds often had a layer of charcoal between the layer of stones and that of the soil and clay and speculated that these were the remains of some sort of ritual fire.[10] What is significant is that he noted the presence of charcoal and evidence of ritual burnings that corroborates the idea that the current practice of burning provisions for the dead has been an important practice for generations. Importantly, even at this relatively early date of archaeological exploration in the area, the evidence of the longevity of these mortuary practices was evident.

One aspect that was briefly mentioned in both of these papers was the association of burial mounds and cairns with the remains of long-dead cedar trees. Both authors commented on the cedar's longevity and used this quality to place the construction of the burial structures in the distant past.[11] Hill-Tout wondered if the tree, in some way, shielded the human remains from the elements. It is interesting that neither author suggested that these trees could have been deliberately planted for both the physical protection of the burial and as a symbol of the afterlife. As well as providing many of the necessities of life for the coastal peoples, the ability of the cedar to seemingly re-sprout from dead remains could possibly have expressed the idea of the afterlife and the connection between the living and the dead. Further, if these trees were used in early burials, it is possible that the tree burials of the contact period were a modification of this practice.

More recent archaeological studies have the benefit of both advanced technologies, such as means to accurately date materials, as well as a more culturally sensitive outlook. Archaeological evidence demonstrates that significant changes in the manner of burial have occurred from 2,500 BC until the present. During this time, the Coast Salish buried their dead in middens, mounds, and cairns, and in above-ground interments. As well, this archaeological evidence demonstrates that many of the religious or spiritual ideas of the Coast Salish have their roots in earlier eras and that these concepts have persisted in the ethnographic record.

The Arcas study of Marpole phase midden burials in Tsawwassen reports that bodies were wrapped in a cedar mat or blanket and often placed in a cedar box.[12] Once the body was dressed and wrapped, it was buried in an unused area in the midden. In some cases, there is evidence that food and other goods were burned at the gravesite. The authors speculate that this practice is related to the feeding of the dead.[13]

Information from the site at Scowlitz on the Harrison River, the location of a large settlement approximately 2,000 years ago, also suggests the continuity of some burial traditions. Despite the age of this settlement, the Stó:lō connection to these ancestors is supported by Nicole Oakes, who states that "by 2000 years ago, if not earlier, the cultural ancestors of the Stó:lō were practicing life ways which closely resembled those observed by early European visitors to the area."[14]

This short summary of a few of the important archaeological studies indicates that there were changes in the mortuary rituals of the Coast Salish in the pre-contact era, and also that many of the rituals which are still central to Coast Salish people have their roots in the distant past.

Let Me Give You a Story

Death and burial are personal and religious subjects and many people do not feel comfortable discussing this topic with outsiders. This section will not examine directly the intricacies of modern practices; rather, it will address the evidence that the age-old practices of wrapping the body and feeding and burning goods for the dead are still important to the Stó:lō. In order to distance the discussion from the mention of the recently deceased, these topics will be examined in the context of the reburial issue.

In a larger sense, the issues that concern reburial also relate to a definition of the community that encompasses both the living and the dead. This conceptual framework maintains that a certain amount and type of interaction between these two states of being is necessary in order to keep the world right. In essence, this section will examine current practices that concern reburial and the treatment of human remains by looking into the past for guidance into the future.

While attending the field school during the summer of 2000, I interviewed five Stó:lō people for my project concerning the development of the Stó:lō Heritage Policy Manual. Two elders, Rosaleen George and Elizabeth Herrling, were frequently interviewed and respected as sources of the Halq'eméylem language, customs, place names, and other aspects of traditional Stó:lō knowledge. Jeff Point worked as a cultural interpreter in the Longhouse Extension Programme run by the Stó:lō Nation at Coqualeetza. Betty Charlie and Helen Joe worked directly with academics involved in scientific excavations. All were involved in the preservation of Stó:lō rituals such as the proper means for burial and reburial and the tradition of the longhouse. The questions I asked of this group included the propriety of testing remains, the spiritual power of remains, the length of time for genetic studies, the protocol around such studies, and the respectful treatment of remains.

In an informal conversation, Stó:lō cultural advisor Sonny McHalsie also related the experiences of another Stó:lō man, now deceased.[15] As well, the attitudes of many of the Stó:lō elders were evident in a discussion of the treatment of human remains that took place on 25 May 2000 at the meeting of the Stó:lō Elders Council or "Lys" at the chambers on the Coqualeetza grounds. These interviews provide a variety of opinions on treatment of human remains.

This discussion should in no way be considered a presentation of a monolithic set of Stó:lō beliefs. Like most groups, the Stó:lō are a diverse people with a variety of attitudes and beliefs, unified by a sense of community.

In order to understand the Stó:lō attitude towards human remains, the Stó:lō perspective on the dead needs some discussion. The Stó:lō view life and death as cyclical, which is made evident in their language. For example, in Halq'emeylem the word for "great-grandfather" is the same as for "great-grandson."[16] Thus the underlying sense is one of connection between ancestors and descendants. This cyclical relationship imbues the Stó:lō perspective with respect and responsibility for the dead as well as the living. Ancestors, no matter how long they have been dead, must be treated with respect.

This connection between the living and the dead is illustrated in a story recounted by elder Rosaleen George. She tells of a group of men who were instructed by an owl to find the remains of a long-dead Stó:lō:

> They were all sitting around the campfire and it was hunting season. They were hunting for deer. There was an owl and it was making noise. These men were kind of annoyed with that owl and one of them says [about another member of the party] well he's a Doctor.[17] He should be able to understand what the owl is saying. So they told him why don't you do something and find out what he wants. So he left the group and went further back, and it was dark by this time and the owl said I've been here a long, long time and I am tired. I am tired and I want to rest. So they didn't hunt, they went around looking for this thing, this dead body where the owl said it was. And when they found it . . . there was nothing but bones left. . . . I don't know if they found out who he was.[18]

This story emphasizes the idea that it was more important for these men to find the remains than it was for them to hunt for food for the living.

Many modern-day Stó:lō have continued to practise their rituals despite the adoption of Western practices. Unless there are extenuating circumstances, the dead are buried four days after death has occurred.[19] The body is usually washed, dressed, and wrapped in a blanket. Following the ceremony, a feast is held. At this feast many of the goods of the deceased are distributed to friends and family. As well, a "burning," an important aspect of the feast, is performed. Food and goods, such as clothes, are burned in order to feed and clothe the deceased. The Stó:lō maintain that the act of burning allows the essence of the goods to move from the worldly, physical plane to the spiritual plane. Helen Joe, who often conducts these burnings, explains:

> A burning itself is a way of providing for our people who have passed on. It is a belief . . . [that] we take care of one another. It is kind of understood that once the people get to the spirit world there are different things they do—but they don't have means to feed and clothe themselves. They don't have the material means, but because they are used to these things, they still need them. So, it is our job here on the earth to set the table and call them. So we have the food that is there, the water, the tea, the juice that they used to drink. . . . We prepare it, we cook it, we cut up the fruit . . . take the candies out of the wrappers. When everything is ready we have the fire. Once it goes into the fire and you see the smoke going up from the fire, that means that a part of that food and anything else that goes into the fire, once you see the smoke going up that means the spiritual part goes to the spirit world so the spirits there can partake in the meal. . . . It is like any other meal with your family.[20]

She further explains that if the deceased is not hungry, the spiritual food is shared with others in the spirit world who do not have anyone to take care of them, or who have been forgotten by their descendants. The dead, then, just as the living, share goods among the members of their community.

The ritual of the burning is not limited to the post-burial feast, but is considered the main method for the living to continue to take care of the dead. The Stó:lō feel that the deceased are able to communicate directly with the living and request additional goods and food to be burned. Betty Charlie related the story of an ancestor who was cold and requested another blanket be burned for her use in the spirit world.[21] Betty also considers that burnings should be done as a means of showing respect for the dead in places that are being studied, such as at Scowlitz: "Burnings should be done, mostly for the people at the site, because we are invading their territory. It is out of respect."[22] Burnings, then, provide spiritual sustenance for the dead and are seen as acts of common courtesy acknowledging the responsibility that the living have towards those in the spiritual realm.

Respect for the dead, both for their physical remains and spiritual essence, is of prime importance. Jeff Point maintains that: "If human remains are mis-treated, respect is lost for both parties [the dead and the living]. If they are treated with respect [then] generations down the line, our children, will see that, then they will have respect. All remains should be treated with respect. We should respect our past [ancestors], no matter how long ago they passed on."[23]

Most importantly, if respect for human remains is not maintained the interaction between the dead and the living can become dangerous for the living, especially for children. Elder Rosaleen George tells a story concerning the mistreatment of a skeleton. In this situation, the spirits of the people came back and interacted with children, attempting to coax the children to follow them to the spirit world:

> There was a skeleton rolling around. They don't know that it would affect lots of people. These little people, they lived on the earth. [My niece] was playing with this little spirit, it was one of the little skeletons that have been rolling around. The little ones can be coaxed away. I phoned around and no one had heard anything [about the bones]. Finally Frank Malloway said that he heard that I was concerned. And I said, "I am, they are our little people." So he went and asked the chief if we could bury them in the cemetery, so that's where they are now. And those little people didn't come around anymore. Ever since they put them in the ground, they have been at peace.[24]

This preoccupation with the safety of children also suggests the connection that the Stó:lō feel exists between the generations. Children, as more recently reborn spirits, may have a greater affinity with the spirit world than adults who are more accustomed to the physical world.[25]

Betty Charlie addressed another aspect of danger in her first-person experience concerning a white academic who did not believe that any danger was involved at the Scowlitz site. The man was sent to cut weeds with a weed-eater near an open excavation. Despite warnings, he did not apply temelth, the red ochre paint that is considered by some to have protective qualities, nor did he behave in a respectful manner. According to Betty:

> Andrew was a student and he was over there and he kept asking questions about spirit and stuff. And he told us that he didn't believe in stuff like that—that he was cool and didn't have to wear the temelth. And they were clearing one day and he went out to an area, like a wall of rocks—a platform. And his job was to clear out the nettles and he was over there by himself. And that should never have happened. Students shouldn't be over there by themselves.

And he had the weed-eater, he was over there cutting nettles and we were in area A and the next thing I saw was Andrew coming out of the stinging nettles without his weed-eater and he was screaming that there was a man standing there on the platform. And I said that that was okay, it was probably just the man from mound one. He asked if it is okay to go back to work and I said yes. So he did. So the next thing, he was coming out of the nettles and he was white and pouring sweat. He got over to area A and he dropped on the ground and he stayed there. And they took him over to the hospital by boat and the doctors couldn't find anything wrong with him. His body temperature was below normal and his blood pressure was high and they couldn't explain it. He was okay, but the elders came and they talked to him. They explained that he had to go back to the job because he started it. It was hard, but he did it. But he wasn't allowed to use the weed-eater, he had to use a machete because the elder told him that the people there didn't like the sound of the weed-eater. He got sick because he didn't believe. He didn't believe that there was anything over there. He was just over there for school, and then he got hit with whatever was over there and now he believes. When we are working over there in those mounds, we hope that they don't find anything. As soon as somebody said there was a skull, we were out of there. It was really hard.[26]

One of the most eloquent points that Helen Joe makes is that spirit power is much stronger than physical power. It is for this reason that dealing with the dead can be dangerous. She offers:

I'll give you a story. There was an incident from my mother's people down in the States. They had some remains that were returned back to the community and I'm not sure where they came from but they had evidence that one person that was there was a woman because they found this comb and it was carved and when they saw the comb I guess there were ones who were working there who wanted to duplicate it. So they asked a group, it was a group of elders, I guess they had an advisory group, if they could duplicate it. And they had the go ahead to duplicate it but they had to make sure that the comb, the original comb was put back with the remains before they were buried. But from what I have heard they put the duplicate in with the remains and there was a group that was involved with that. And one lady that was involved with it ended up having a stroke and she's not healthy, she lost the use of one side. Another man has had numerous surgeries and his health is just not right. The man, who was supposed to have duplicated the comb, actually carved the comb and then put it back and apparently it was not the original that went back, he has died. There was another spiritual person who was in the community who wasn't really involved but he was kind of on his last stages of leukemia and they always say that the spiritual part of your being sometimes gets much greater at that period of your life because you are getting ready to go to the spiritual part of the spiritual world. So they say that the spirits sometimes get extra strong or have that extra energy to take your spirit to the other side. This man, while he was laying in his bed in his home he said this old lady came and she said "I didn't mean to hurt anybody, I just wanted my comb." And this was the day that they had the young man's funeral who died . . . the comb needs to be returned, if the process isn't taken care of properly then people could get hurt. There have been no problems at the Scowlitz site because they have been taking care of those people by doing a burning [when necessary]. I have been involved in some of the burnings over there.[27]

Helen continues this discussion with a reference to burnings and an admonition that even a hug given in love by a deceased person can be dangerous to the living recipient:

I guess to go on, the spiritual part of our lives is much stronger than our own human one, much greater. Not just stronger but greater. . . . When we used to have our burnings we would fix the plates cause we prepare the plates for our people and we would have them just heaping, and we would have all kinds of stuff and we would have just everything on them. And he [an elder] told us, he said, you know you don't need to have that much food. We're putting a normal portion of fish and a normal portion of smoked fish and maybe a normal-sized, one medium potato, and a vegetable and cake and fruit and everything else, and we had it all on the plate and he said, that's too much for them; he said if you can look at a piece of fish that is maybe a half an inch that's like giving the spirits a whole fish. That's how great their size and strength, whatever it is that they have, that's how great it is compared to us. So he said you only need to give them a little bit of each. One little inch-square piece each of fried bread is like giving them a whole piece. So those kind of things, like portions, we had to learn how to fix. And then when you go up to a child or you go up to someone in your family and you give them a hug and you give them a good hug, a hug that feels good, we all enjoy being hugged, you like hugging your family. But if you were to experience that from a spiritual being, that hug would almost squeeze you to death, because that energy is so strong. You know so he said we have to understand that the spiritual strength and the spiritual part of our people is so much greater than the human being and we have to be careful.[28]

This remark makes the point that the dead are not evil or malicious but are simply more powerful than the living.[29] Further, it explains some of the wariness with which the Stó:lō approach their dead. Rosaleen George explains: "It all depends on how these people were when they were on earth. If they were very possessive, it's pretty hard to take something away from them. . . . Our grandparents never let us take anything away from the cemetery. Sometimes they hung things on the cross and my grandmother always said 'don't you fancy anything in the graveyard. Don't think of anything—just be happy that it's there.' That's one thing my sister and I were told by my grandmother."[30] The respect shown to the dead, then, is both an aspect of concern for the ancestors as well as an acknowledgment of their enhanced spirit power.

Diversity and Commonality

None of those I interviewed agree with the excavation of human remains simply for study; however, they generally concur that graves could be moved for a proper reason, and if the movement was done with respect. Sonny McHalsie relates a story from the late 1930s that was included in an interview he conducted with Henry Murphy. As a youth of approximately twelve years, Henry was playing on a hillside and found what he knew to be human remains. Realizing the significance of his find, Henry promptly told his father and uncle. Rather than rebury the remains in the same place, they moved the bones to a place where they would be more secure. Sonny notes that the important issue was the respectful reburial of the remains in a place where they would not be disturbed rather than interment in the same spot. According to Sonny, this was done without the intervention of any state authorities.[31] This story suggests that work done at sites, such as at Scowlitz, is acceptable to those Stó:lō who define it as a rescue operation rather than solely a scientific expedition.

The ability to move graves was reiterated by three of the participants. Betty Charlie stated that if the dead are apprised of the reason that they are to be disturbed, they have the same capacity for reason as do the living. The elders also compared the dead to those who are sleeping. Betty Charlie felt that if the dead are gently made aware of the situation, rather than yanked out of their beds, they will respond in a positive manner. Rosaleen George states that: "The spirits are bothered when they are moved around. What if you were sleeping and someone just came along and bothered you. They just wake them up, that's what they do to those skeletons."[32] Jeff Point mentions practices from the past:

> My grandfather told me there was a great big box of them [bones] and our people used to move them if they were moving, migrating from one place to another, they would drag this big box with them. And on my grandmother's side—they had a house similar to this one and there were shelves and they stayed in there. Now to get to that point of view, you see our people didn't bury people, it wasn't until the Europeans came here. So they buried them all. So now I always tell them, to me if we wanted to keep these remains in a little box to me it's okay. But it's not up to me. There are people older than me and if they say it is wrong, we have to abide by it. This is all I can say about it.[33]

Elder Vince Stogan comments on the role of the government in the movement of graves: "We had huts, fence around it, they just put people in those huts, pile them up, one family in each hut. We have to destroy all those, bury the bones in the modern cemetery. Government said it should not be done like that. The huts were made of cedar. The spirits live on, they are always around."[34]

While graves should not be moved for capricious reasons, influences such as environmental degradation validate their movement. Again, colonial practices have often caused quite a disturbance among the dead.

The subject of incidental discoveries, as opposed to archaeological investigation, elicited an interesting historical point. The Stó:lō maintain that there are a variety of explanations for the discovery of remains outside the bounds of established cemeteries. While some were simply buried before the establishment of cemeteries in the modern sense, many of the cemeteries are associated with Christian denominations. The Catholics, for example, would not bury those who were not baptized or who were considered to have clung to their heathen practices. This restriction did not allow those Stó:lō who followed the traditional religion, whether wholly or in part, to be interred in what was considered to be holy ground. Betty Charlie relates: "The elders will tell you that a long time ago they put up fences around the cemetery. The priests used to come along and baptize people. The priests would change their names. That is how some people lost their Indian names. And some of the elders wouldn't ... [so] they [the priests] would bury them outside the cemetery gates. So that's why they find so many outside the cemetery."[35]

For reasons of doctrine, Catholics did not allow the bodies of those who had committed suicide to be buried in church grounds. This prohibition pertained to all Catholics and was not meant to discriminate against First Nations peoples; however, recent revelations of the treatment of children and youths in the church-run residential schools, which have often resulted in suicide, make this discrimination doubly ironic.

The excavation of burials and the related topic of testing human remains reveal important differences of opinion. Not surprisingly, those who were involved with the Scowlitz site considered the study to be a valid one. Betty Charlie explains the situation:

> I got involved in the Scowlitz site because of [various academics] and Sonny McHalsie when they "discovered" those mounds. A lot of the elders knew about it, but when they don't want anybody coming in and vandalizing the site, they don't tell anyone about it. They had to pick two people to work with the university, and Cliff and I were those. Cliff's dad wouldn't speak to us. He was in anger. "What's the use in keeping quiet," he said "we'd have every grave digger in the Fraser Valley over there." It was mostly anger that we were going to be part of it.[36]

Those who feel that studies, such as Scowlitz, should be allowed do maintain that certain precautions must be taken. These precautions ensure that both the respect for the dead as well as the safety of those who are working at the sites are maintained. Betty Charlie suggests that a kit composed of a blanket and cedar box should be required equipment. The blanket would be available to cover any remains while the cedar box would alleviate situations, such as happened in the past, in which remains were placed in a plastic bucket. However, despite her work with the archaeologists, she admits: "We tell them that we don't really like it when they are getting close to the centre of a mound. We'll watch and tell them stories, but we don't really like it ... it does give you a funny feeling. Especially when they are getting near the centre, and you hope that there is nothing there."[37]

In contrast, Jeff Point and the elders Rosaleen George and Elizabeth Herrling feel that there are no good reasons to excavate the dead. Jeff wonders: "I mean it is kind of odd. I wonder if I went to England and started digging up the coffins. It would upset a lot of people. If it washed out . . . by all means pay respect, but there are ways of finding out [facts about Stó:lō history without excavations]. I wonder what the English would think if my people wanted to do a scientific study on them. If the tables were turned, what kind of excuse would they find? I feel that scientific excavation is wrong."[38]

Another debate focuses on testing of human remains. Jeff Point feels that testing, while wrong, could be done to determine identity or familial ties: "I actually say . . . it should be done. Basically because of what has happened to our people . . . it would be good to know whereabouts these people came from. A lot of our people went missing. So actually it is wrong to do things like that. But today for today's interest it should be done. To let the family know."[39]

In contrast, the two elders maintain that any testing is inappropriate and disrespectful. All participants feel that reburial should occur as soon as possible, hopefully within the prescribed four days, as in the burial of the recently deceased. Betty Charlie and Helen Joe maintain that any material that has been removed for testing could be reburied at a later date. Betty Charlie states: "There should be a proper ritual, but no boxes and no washing. They should be put back exactly the way they are found, except for a new blanket. If there are bones they should be numbered and graphed and put back exactly the way they are found. They should be able to take a piece of bone, like a baby finger. Once it has been dated it should be put back by someone who knows what to do."[40]

All participants believe that some sort of ritual should accompany the reburial of the human remains. Further, there is agreement that the remains should be handled as little as possible, with the exception that they should be rewrapped in a blanket. Jeff Point states: "I feel that it should be left the way it was found. Leave in that state and rewrap it, because our people wrap loved ones in blankets."[41] In general the use of a cedar box was not considered essential. Jeff Point comments that the use of the box or coffin is of recent origin and is not a traditional practice.

Although the sample group is small, clearly a number of customs that date from the earliest known times are still important. Burnings are still being practised and are considered to be one of the main ways to interact with the dead. They are a means to both care and show respect for the deceased. Feeding the dead is one of most central practices that maintain the continuity of community between the living and the dead. Wrapping of bodies, while not discussed as a separate topic, has been mentioned numerous times during the interviews.

Conclusion

The concept of transformation is central to this discussion. As mentioned, the Halq'emeylem word for great-grandparent is the same as great-grandchild. This suggests that both change and continuity are apt linguistic metaphors for the combination of tradition and variation evident in Stó:lō burial customs. Despite the notion that contact with Western culture caused the greatest amount of change, it can be seen that change is a constant, but also that the central concept, the community between the living and the dead, has not altered.

Finally, let us return to the ancestral remains being temporarily housed in the Stó:lō Nation Material Culture Repository. In May of 2000, I attended a meeting of the Elders Council at which Schaepe and McHalsie were discussing details for the reburial ceremony. One of the questions that concerned the elders was that the gender of the person was unknown. As discussed, an important component of the reburial would be the burning. Since this skeleton had not been found in an undisturbed grave and had been removed from the burial site, it was essentially naked and in need of clothing. It was a general feeling that further testing, which could ascertain the gender of the person, was not acceptable as most of the elders felt that the remains had "been through enough."

Finally, one elder remarked that this type of testing was unimportant. She suggested that any person today would be happy to wear jeans and a T-shirt. In a very modern response to a traditional question, it was decided that these modern clothes would be burned at the reburial ceremony.[42] Seated amongst the others, wearing cedar clothes or Hudson's Bay blankets, is another Stó:lō person dressed in jeans, a T-shirt, and a baseball cap, enjoying the salmon feast, reunited with the rest of the family and community.

Notes

1   See, for example, George Nicholas's "Decolonizing the Archaeological Landscape: The practice and politics of archaeology in British Columbia," *The American Indian Quarterly* 30, no. 3/4 (2006), and the PhD dissertations of Michael Klassen, "Indigenous Heritage Stewardship and Transformation of Archaeological Practice: Two Case Studies from the Mid-Fraser Region of British Columbia" (PhD diss., Simon Fraser University, 2013) and Darcy Mathews, "Funerary Ritual,

Ancestral Presence, and the Rocky Point Ways of Death" (PhD diss., University of Washington, 2014); David M. Schaepe, Susan Rowley, Stó:lō House of Respect Committee Members, Darlene Weston, Mike Richards, "The Journey Home— Guiding Intangible Knowledge Production in the Analysis of Ancestral Remains," Unpublished report, Stó:lō Archives, Stó:lō Research and Resource Management Centre, Chilliwack, BC (available at www.sfu.ca/ipinch/sites/default/files/ resources/reports/the_journey_home_ver2_may2016.pdf); David M. Schaepe, Natasha Lyons, Kate Hennessy, Kyle McIntosh, Michael Blake, Colin Pennier, Clarence Pennier, Andy Phillips and Project Members, *Sq'éwlets: A Stó:lō–Coast Salish Community in the Fraser Valley*, Virtual Museum of Canada, 2016, www. digitalsqewlets.ca.

2   "Luxury home on B.C. burial ground to be torn down," CTV News, 11 August 2015, http://bc.ctvnews.ca/luxury-home-on-b-c-burial-ground-to-be-torn-down-1.2511948; "Grace Islet home on sacred aboriginal cemetery to be demolished," CBC News, 10 August 2015, http://www.cbc.ca/news/canada/british-columbia/ grace-islet-home-on-sacred-aboriginal-cemetery-to-be-demolished-1.3186534; Lindsay Kines, "Province buys disputed Grace Islet for $5.45 million," *Times Colonist*, 16 February 2016, http://www.timescolonist.com/news/local/province-buys-disputed-grace-islet-for-5-45-million-1.1764939; Judith Sayers, Maureen Grant, Dave Schaepe, Robert Phillips, and Murray Brown, "When First Nations Burial Sites and Development Collide," *The Tyee*, 18 August 2014, https://thetyee. ca/Opinion/2014/08/18/First-Nations-Burial-Developments/; "Declaration on the Safeguarding of Indigenous Ancestral Burial Grounds as Sacred Sites and Cultural Landscapes" (2014) https://www.sfu.ca/ipinch/resources/declarations/ancestral-burial-grounds/.

3   *c̓əsnaʔəm, the city before the city*, University of British Columbia Museum of Anthropology, Vancouver, 25 January 2015–24 January 2016, http://www. thecitybeforethecity.com, http://moa.ubc.ca/portfolio_page/citybeforecity/.

4   Henry R. Wagner, *Spanish Explorations in the Strait of Juan de Fuca* (New York: AMS Press, 1971), 101.

5   Ellen Webber, "An Old Kwanthum Village—Its People and Its Fall," *American Antiquarian and Oriental Journal* 21 (1999): 313.

6   Myron Eells, *The Indians of Puget Sound, The Notebooks of Myron Eells*, ed. George Castille (Seattle: University of Washington Press, 1985): 334.

7   Charles Hill-Tout, "Prehistoric Burial Mounds of British Columbia," *Museum and Art Notes* 4 (December 1930): 120. "indians" is not capitalized in the original.

8   Ibid., 121.

9   Ibid., 120.

10   Ibid., 124.

11   Ibid., 122.

12   Arcas Consulting, *Archaeological Investigations at Tsawwassen, BC. Volume 4*, Prepared for Construction Branch, South Coast Region, Ministry of Transportation and Highways, Burnaby, BC, and the BC Archaeology Branch, Permits 1984–41, 1990–2 (Coquitlam, BC, 1991), 46.

13   Ibid., 58.

14   Nicole Oakes, "Preliminary Report on the 1997 Archaeological Reconnaissance near Harrison Mills, Southwestern British Columbia," May 1998, Stó:lō Archives, Stó:lō Research and Resource Management Centre, Chilliwack, BC, 5.

15   At the time of writing my initial paper, Sonny's transcripts of his interview with Henry Murray had been misplaced.

16   Keith Thor Carlson, *The Power of Place, the Problem of Time: Aboriginal Identity and Historical Consciousness in the Cauldron of Colonialism* (Toronto: University of Toronto Press, 2010), 44.

17   In this context, a doctor means an Indian doctor who has knowledge of spiritual matters.

18   Rosaleen George and Elizabeth Herrling, interview by Kathryn McKay, Chilliwack, 30 May 2000, tape and transcript, Stó:lō Archives, Stó:lō Research and Resource Management Centre, Chilliwack, BC.

19   Helen Joe, interview by Liam Haggerty, Heather Watson, and MacKinley Darlington, Chilliwack, BC, 20 May 2005.

20   Ibid.

21   Betty Charlie, interview by Kathryn McKay, Chilliwack BC, 29 May 2000, tape and transcript, Stó:lō Archives, Stó:lō Research and Resource Management Centre, Chilliwack, BC.

22   Ibid.

23   Jeff Point, interview by Kathryn McKay, Chilliwack, BC, 31 May 2000, tape and transcript, Stó:lō Archives, Stó:lō Research and Resource Management Centre, Chilliwack, BC.

24   George and Herrling, interview.

25   Madeline Rose Knickerbocker, "'What We've Said Can Be Proven in the Ground': Stó:lō Sovereignty and Historical Narratives at XA:YTEM, 1990–2006," *Journal of the Canadian Historical Association* 24, no. 1 (2013): 317.

26   Charlie, interview.

27   Joe, interview.

28   Ibid.

29   Ibid.

30   George and Herrling, interview.

31   McHalsie, informal discussion, Chilliwack, May 2000.

32   George and Herrling, interview.

33   The interview was conducted in a room off the kitchen used for the Longhouse. It was approximately twelve feet wide by twenty feet long. Point, interview.

34   Vince Stogan, "When I came home my Elders taught us that all our people who have passed on are still around us," in *In the Words of Elders: Aboriginal Cultures in Transition*, eds. Peter Kulchyski, Don McCaskill, and David Newhouse (Toronto: University of Toronto Press, 1999), 452.

35   Charlie, interview.

36   Ibid.

37   Charlie, interview.

38   Point, interview.

39   Ibid.

40   Charlie, interview.

41   Point, interview.

42   LYSS meeting, 25 May 2000. Notes in possession of the author. LYSS (Lalems Ye Stó:lō Si:ya:m) is also known as the House of Chiefs.

6

Food as a Window into Stó:lō Tradition and Stó:lō-Newcomer Relations

LESLEY WIEBE

> *Stan Green told me once [that] one of his elders had told him that despite the fact that, you know, the different government policies that were trying to take away our culture—and the missionaries and the diseases—despite that that elder told him that our culture is still out there. It's all around us. And . . . if we try to take it all back all at once we won't be able to handle it, 'cause we're just—we're weak, we're not strong enough because we've lost a lot of it. And so he said we have to take a little bit at a time. So each time we take a little bit of our culture back it makes us stronger so that we can take other parts, and I think that's what our people are going through right now.*[1]

Thus far, academics have explored two possible means of assessing twentieth-century changes in Stó:lō dietary practice. First, when articulating her larger thesis that British Columbian Natives' bodies were sites of struggle in Canadian colonial praxis, historian Mary-Ellen Kelm described a time (based on Stó:lō elder Nancy Phillip's recollection) early in the century when Stó:lō fished and hunted for sustenance as they adopted various non-Native foods and methods of food production.[2] She later contextualized this by referencing M.M. Lee, R. Reyburn, and A. Carrow's finding that by 1969 refined and processed foods, including bread, cereals, and soft drinks, accounted for 48 percent of Anaham adults' caloric intake—a transition newly detrimental to their health as nutritional analyses indicated Indigenous foods had formerly provided the bulk of their required protein, calcium, and vitamins. Her conclusion, given these two pieces of information, was that "Euro-Canadian culinary imperialism" symbolically and physically weakened the Stó:lō and other Indigenous targets.[3]

Second (and alternatively), anthropologist Kevin Washbrook appraised the metaphorical means by which Stó:lō people talked about plants as medicine.[4] Employed at the Stó:lō office as anthropologist, his initial research plan had been to evaluate Stó:lō discourse surrounding the roles of plants as food and technology; instead, people responded to his request, "Tell me what is important about plants," with lists of plant uses to solve health issues. This invariable response led him to believe that when informants related cure stories they were in actuality affirming the power of their traditional knowledge over the inefficacy and ignorance of "White" medical practice, emphasizing the continuity between their culture's self-sufficient past and powerful present as embodied in their elders' wisdom. So whereas Kelm described a process of historical decline via dietary change, Washbrook conversely highlighted the enduring utility of Indigenous (Stó:lō) plant customs.

My more recent discussions with Stó:lō informants, however, indicate that the discourse surrounding both "traditional" and "Western" foods does not neatly conform to one or the other line of reasoning. Rather, Stó:lō perceptions about food can be understood, as Kirin Narayan stated in a methodological piece, "in terms of shifting identifications amid a field of interpenetrating communities and power relations."[5] Specifically, Stó:lō collective consciousness relative to dietary change from the mid to late twentieth century involves spiritual and economic considerations that jointly reflect the community's current understanding of cross-cultural relations and the colonial dynamic. This mindset is best illustrated through an analysis of the foods Stó:lō identify as "traditional."

This paper (along with earlier iterations) is the result of research begun in June 2007 for the Stó:lō Ethnohistory Field School. At the time, I was invited to examine the history of changing Stó:lō dietary practices—in particular, the early twentieth-century move away from, and later-century return to, "traditional" food use. Specific points of inquiry were to include diabetes, social and cultural economies, as well as community discussion surrounding feeding ancestors at burnings. My study was to link to a previous traditional-use survey and become part of a growing body of research the Stó:lō Research and Resource Management Centre (SRRMC) has at its disposal for use in treaty negotiations.

With this purview, I completed seven ethnographic interviews over the course of the month, in addition to accessing unpublished articles and earlier interviews held at SRRMC. Stó:lō staff provided a list of possible participants based on people's perceived knowledge of the issue, and I set interview appointments with those whom I was able to contact. The majority of interviews lasted for approximately one hour and each was conducted in the presence of one to two other students. Questions were asked in an open-ended fashion as part of semi-structured interviews to give elders latitude and avoid prescriptive responses.

Following my return to Saskatoon, I researched further secondary material at the University of Saskatchewan's library and via online databases. A draft of the paper was marked prior to its submission to Stó:lō Nation archives along with interview recordings and transcripts. Variations on the paper were subsequently presented at several conferences, including the Stó:lō's People of the River Conference held in Chilliwack, British Columbia, April–May 2011. An earlier revised version of the paper appeared in the Spring 2009 issue of the *University of the Fraser Valley Research Review.*[6]

In this manner, the paper was intended to fill a research gap identified by the Stó:lō Resource Management Centre staff. Similarly, in *Edible Histories, Cultural Politics: Towards a Canadian Food History,* Franca Iacovetta and her fellow editors note that while food history is a budding field, American food historiography is prolific when compared with its Canadian counterpart. They suggest the works of staples historians (e.g., Harold Innis's work on the cod-fishery) as the upper limit of Canadian canon, though they are not food history per se.[7] Several articles within their work attempt bridgework in the realm of Indigenous food history. For example, Alison Norman explored food, recipe, and culinary information exchanges between British settler and Indigenous women between 1791 and 1867 in her article, "Culinary Colonialism in the Upper Canadian Contact Zone." She argued that British immigrants' diets changed with the increased use of "Native" ingredients like corn, wild rice, venison, etc.; conversely, First Nations adoption of settler culinary culture is framed as a "dilution" of "'traditional' culture, heritage, and identity."[8] Kristina Walters's "'A National Priority': Nutrition Canada's *Survey*" chronicles a decade-long (1964–75) national nutrition project undertaken by the Department of National Health and Welfare. Focusing on the *Survey's* design and its published results, Walters suggests it pathologized non-Western foodways when characterizing nutritional profiles of Indigenous mothers.[9]

The contributors to *Edible Histories, Cultural Politics* also briefly mention multidisciplinary scholarship on Indigenous peoples, which I will detail, given its relevance in a British Columbian context. Robert Daly's blended legal and anthropological study *Our Box Was Full* examined potlatching and the seasonal round among the Gitksan and Witsutwit'en peoples as a part of a larger analysis of historical and present-day Indigenous land management practices and stewardship. His research, of course, was conducted in connection with the well-known Aboriginal rights case *Delgamuukw v. British Columbia.*[10] Leslie Main Johnson's "Aboriginal Burning for Vegetation Management in Northwest British Columbia" (also focused on the Gitksan and Witsutwit'en peoples) investigated the role of fire in traditional land management to procure plants foods, particularly berries.[11] Within the same edited collection, Nancy J. Turner's "'Time to Burn': Traditional Use of Fire to Enhance Resource Production by Aboriginal Peoples in British Columbia" described controlled burning by Indigenous groups to enhance not only the growth of plant species but also game.[12] Both pieces are ethnographic, leaning towards ethnobotany. Douglas C. Harris's *Landing Native Fisheries: Indian Reserves and Fishing Rights in British Columbia, 1849–1925* critiques the legal construction of an "Indian food fishery" amid the quagmire of colonial dispossession in British Columbian history.[13] All of the above sources are either expressly general in focus, i.e., are province-wide studies, or centred on a particular Indigenous group (not the Stó:lō). They are also not strictly food history, but rather studies where food is discussed as an adjunct to various topics.

While each of the above has merit, the scholarship does, as SRRMC staff pointed out in their conversations with me, leave one wanting—though the ways in which it does this (which I detail below) are not necessarily what was conveyed to me. In this regard, I draw inspiration from Keith Carlson's book, *The Power of Place, The Problem of Time*, where he acknowledges the challenges researchers face when presenting a critical yet internally meaningful piece to an Indigenous readership.[14] Both Norman's and Walters's pieces draw exclusively on primary material of non-Indigenous origin; in theoretical terms, they are written productions of the colonizers. Their works make no reference to what both the past and present Indigenous peoples each scholar writes about thought of these liminal food/diet exchanges. Norman, in particular, frames the culinary exchanges between two peoples as benign to one party (British settler women) but detrimental to another (Indigenous women). Consultation with Stó:lō participants, however, reveal their perspectives on this issue are not cut and dried, and it is my hope that having a history where the Stó:lō themselves are the primary source will make it more (internally) meaningful. Likewise, the ethnographic pieces cited above tend to stray into either lists of plant foods and their harvesting locations, or are expressly legal, emphasizing jurisdictional issues and/or title to fishing spots. The intrinsic cultural and spiritual importance—beyond litigation (though this consideration, of course, backlit my research)—of "traditional" food was foremost in my work. Again, it is my hope that this emphasis will allow my paper to resonate with Stó:lō readership.

Salmon hanging on the Pettis family's dry rack in the Fraser Canyon. Photo Courtesy of Keith Carlson.

As Iacovetta and her collaborators acknowledge, foodways and memories are central to group identity formation—food is fundamental and personal to all of us because we *must* eat.[15]

When asked to comment on dietary changes he had seen over his lifetime, Stó:lō cultural leader Steven Point answered, "[W]hen we were growing up ... we ate fish all the time, eh. We just ate fish."[16] Leona Kelly of the Stó:lō community of Shxw'ōwhámél similarly answered immediately when questioned about traditional foods she ate as a child, "Well, I remember as a young girl ... supper, it would be taters [potatoes] and rice, and fish, a lot of salt fish," and later recounted that canned fish, dried fish, and deer meat were consumed in her household either more or less frequently.[17] Spiritual healer Gwen Point listed baked, dried, and smoked salmon as staples, and related that in childhood she also regularly ate "wild" meats like deer, duck, grouse, and eulachon.[18] Although also briefly mentioning deer and eulachon, Albert "Sonny" McHalsie (the SRRMC's cultural advisor) expanded on salmon's importance as a dietary mainstay:

> We try to eat as much traditional food now then we did before [sic]. Actually, we eat a lot of fish, for sure. ... Um, my mom used to can. The most jars I've seen of canned fish was like three hundred and sixty quarts ... in our pantry. The most I do nowadays is, um, about

a hundred and, um, oh it'd be about a hundred and eighty, so not even half of it. But yeah, she did, like, over three hundred quarts. And so we were eating a lot of canned fish, and then she would have, uh, you know like those freezers like from the file cabinet to here [SM gestures], about here, a big long freezer like that, half of it was frozen, and she would, um, dry, I don't know—gee, about two hundred dried fish. And she would trade her dried—some of her dried fish for smoked fish. So there's a lot of fish, uh, we ate a heck of a lot of fish when we were growing up. And I still like it. [laughter][19]

Stó:lō community members' invariable mention of either salmon or fish recapitulates what archaeologists, anthropologists, and other scholars understand concerning the historical use of resources by Coast Salish peoples. Karen Fediuk and Brian Thom,[20] for instance, citing Deur, suggested that salmon had been Coast Salish groups' primary food resource possibly for as far back as 6,000 years; they moreover reference Suttles's estimate that no more than 10 percent of the Central Coast Salish diet had been obtained through gathering (i.e., fruits and vegetables) in pre-contact times. Furthermore, after reviewing Marilyn Bennett's 1971 estimates of the pounds of salmon consumed per capita/per year in Stó:lō territory, and relevant Department of Fisheries and Oceans data on Stó:lō catches from 1956 to 1999, Fediuk and Thom concluded that during the latter half of the twentieth century Stó:lō annually took fifty-five salmon per capita with an edible weight of 253 pounds (it should be noted that their approximation deviates significantly from Bennett's original calculations).

Plant foods, although consumed in small quantities by pre-contact Coast Salish peoples, were nonetheless mentioned by current Stó:lō elders and community members when discussing "country" or traditional fare.[21] Cultural leader and spiritual healer Helen Joe noted that her grandmother had instructed her and her husband carefully about incorporating vegetables into their children's diets, and conjectured that her two eldest daughters' memories of visiting their great-grandmother would include "spaghetti, green salad, and green beans."[22] Elder Ray Silver recollected that he and his wife used to avoid purchasing tea and coffee as, in his words, "we got wild stuff here"; his grandfather would collect "swamp" tea[23] in sacks he then hung to dry, and Silver himself gathered rose hips in his youth for his mother to subsequently brew. He further recalled that at one time "tons and tons of fruit" grew on uncultivated plots locally, and listed sugar plums, blue dempseys, prunes, and egg plums to emphasize the variety formerly available.[24] Kelly likewise described picking stinging nettles as a child, along with crab apples and wild berries (she specifically mentioned blackberries), which were later made into jams.[25] And Steven Point referred to his mother's backyard garden that contained strawberries, beans, corn, cucumbers, carrots, cherries, crab apples, and egg plums, which would be harvested for canning or use in homemade preserves.[26]

Both Joe's and Point's comments about cultivated gardens with Western vegetables, within the context of a discussion of "traditional" plant foods, deviate from what might be expected. For example, foods that Kelm labelled "new-comer,"[27] and that are commonly known to have Indigenous origins elsewhere, are discussed fluidly and in tandem with other "safely" designated traditional dietary staples by both Joe and Point. And, in Kelly's case, taters and rice are listed alongside fish to comprise a typical traditional meal, despite the fact that potatoes were brought to Stó:lō territory by Hudson's Bay Company forts in the nineteenth century,[28] and Asian rice was introduced to the Northwest Coast during the 1858 gold rush. Methods of processing both gathered and grown plant foods that may also be identified as foreign similarly crop up in conversations about professed country fare. So while Steven Point discussed canned goods in a "traditional" context, Theodoratus suggested that canning, though quickly picked up by Northwest Coast Indigenous groups, was introduced by homesteaders in the late 1890s.[29]

However, for the purposes of this study, what is important is that the *ways* these plant foods were accessed and processed is consistent with longstanding Stó:lō subsistence practices; these foods are suitably "traditional" insofar as they were *gathered*, as opposed to being native to the area. Theodoratus, referencing Turner's work, observed that Salishan peoples partly cleared plots of weeds, stones, and brush by controlled burning, and that sod was lifted with digging sticks to harvest larger bulbs—neither of which is a stretch from gardening.[30] Similarly, whereas berries had been preserved in the past by sun drying, or a sped-up process whereby fruit was covered with leaves and then hot ashes,[31] canning simply comprised a new means by which to achieve the same end, i.e., retard spoiling. The importance Stó:lō people attribute to either harvesting or gathering foods in culturally appropriate manners, however, is perhaps best revealed in discussions surrounding the spiritual aspects of meat eating.[32]

When asked about traditional hunting and gathering practices, Gwen Point responded: "I don't know what it is, I just cannot eat store-bought meat. I can eat meat that comes from a man that has our teaching, that knowledge, cause it's not just going out and shooting a deer. There's a teaching that goes with it. That man has to be right in his heart, and his mind, and how he takes care of the deer, right to when the meat is brought to the people. I don't know what stores put into their meats. That's why I'm quasi-vegetarian."[33] Several noteworthy ideas spring from this passage. First, in this case—and as opposed to the above scenarios with plant foods—an obvious discursive dichotomy is established between a type of "Western" versus "traditional" food; Point is explicitly averse to store-bought meats, but she will eat game in certain circumstances. Second, the "right" contexts allowing her to eat meats involve culturally defined hunting practices, as her description is somewhat suggestive of a Stó:lō worldview that casts humans and non-humans in "reciprocal social relationships based on mutual respect and autonomy."[34] Third, and importantly, her distaste for store-bought meat is conversely the result of the suspect nature of its origins.

Paul Rozin has suggested that, on some level, the majority of people believe the adage, "you are what you eat," in the sense that individuals subconsciously judge cultures who eat boar as boar-like, turtles as turtle-like, and so on.[35] Coast Salish worldviews somewhat reflect this precept, as humans and animals are considered extended family[36]—which explains Gwen Point's declaration that "Salmon is our brother, family, was a person."[37] According to Old Pierre, as beings with vitality or thought (or in salmon's case, a soul), animals are at once both conscious and watchful of humans' actions, as well as ready to aid them in times of need; as a result, hunters must to be careful to avoid "improper treatment of game, such as the rude hurling of a hide to the ground."[38]

This two-pronged deference to animals was ritualized in certain circumstances, as exemplified in the First Salmon ceremonies historically prevalent among Coast Salish communities. In the first instance, by re-enacting those oral narratives surrounding how people acquired the knowledge to catch and process salmon, Indigenous participants reinforced what they believed was an age-old relationship between kin.[39] Alternatively, as McHalsie suggests, the ritual was undertaken so that attendants could "thank the salmon for returning every year" and respectfully petition "*him* to return again the next year [emphasis added]."[40]

These culturally prescribed codes of conduct further reveal individual and community desires to avoid spiritual contamination. Rozin also argued that the "you are what you eat" maxim heavily informs both individual and cultural perceptions of what is disgusting; as he explains it, not many people drank (during his own experimental inquiries into the matter) from a glass containing a dead, sterilized fly, as "flyness" had somehow entered its contents. "Flyness," for all intents and purposes, refers to the energy or properties passed from one to another object through touch—in anthropological jargon that concept is dubbed the law of contagion, and is integral to sympathetic magic.[41]

For Stó:lō people, object-to-object or person-to-object energy transfers occur in a variety of situations, and not just instances of physical contact. As a consequence, staring longingly at a cookie on a neighbour's plate, according to Steven Point, is enough to drain it of its spiritual value.[42] Or, as Gwen Point maintained, harbouring a negative attitude while preparing or cooking a meal can effectively contaminate the food.[43] The idea then, which she acknowledged in the above passage about hunting, is that a person should "be right in [their] heart, and [their] mind" while dealing with foods.[44] When this sort of food handling is achieved, as Joe suggests, the resultant meal provides "not only nutritional food for your body, but . . . also food for the spirit."[45]

The protocols associated with ritual burnings[46] exemplify just how much this rationale configures day-to-day Stó:lō activities. Pregnant and menstruating women, given their ritually susceptible state, are barred from preparing and cooking meals lest they inadvertently alter the spiritual nature of the food. Moreover, that prohibition applies not only to the meal preparation done immediately prior to the ceremony, but also when foods are preserved throughout the year, as canned, dried, and smoked goods may eventually serve ceremonial purposes.[47] Kelly noted that this proscription permeated her traditional education in childhood (her exact words were, "[i]t's always on our mind"), as her mother had forbade her from picking stinging nettles, drying fish, and even climbing fruit-bearing trees during menstruation.[48] Those involved in food preparation are warned to tie back their hair, as there is a sense that if a strand is burnt along with the food it will carry part of that person's spirit across to the ancestor realm.[49] More importantly, cooks must "be of good mind"—manifesting what Kelly called poise—as they complete their work because negative thoughts jeopardize both the meal and ritual overall.[50]

In light of such cultural taboos, Gwen Point's switch to partial vegetarianism seems perfectly understandable; as she states, she does not "know what stores put into their meats,"[51] meaning she is unsure about not only their physical, but also their spiritual integrity. Likewise, Steven Point's brother's advisory against eating too much hamburger seems reasonable, as any energy possibly obtained from beef is suspect.[52] To clarify, these meats are questionable from a Stó:lō perspective because they are almost certainly metaphysically contaminated in one or each of two ways: either they were inappropriately harvested, or handled, or both. Assembly line–style butchery essentially constitutes the antithesis of proper Stó:lō hunting technique, and buying meat at a grocery store disingenuously distances the meat-eater from that animal's death. For Steven Point, the problem with store-bought meat can be summed up as follows: "These kids don't know where chicken comes from. We used to see them walking around and then one day they'd be on the table. . . . We used to have to kill them all, cut the heads off, bleed them, boil them, pluck them, clean them, stuff them in bags. Then they're chicken stew the next day. You know, we *knew* where chicken came from. . . . That's one thing about the kids . . . they have this idea that there's an endless supply somewhere, that we just need to stop off and buy it from somewhere . . . you know, which is a mistake . . . they don't have an appreciation, right?"[53]

There is also a material aspect to this aversion to store-bought foods; Stó:lō people readily associate the above-mentioned historical shift from a traditional to a Western diet with a drastic reduction in their physical health. McHalsie, for example, blamed store-bought foods for his and his sister's medical conditions, saying: "I think that's why I have diabetes . . . because of those other foods that I used to eat. And my sister Chevy, she has some kind of a thing, she's not—she has to watch her diet too. I don't know what she has, I think she has high blood pressure, or something. . . . That's why I straightened out last, yeah, over a year now I quit—I quit all those fatty foods. I quit fast foods. Like I quit . . . sausages, quit pepperoni, quit french fries . . . ."[54] His comments are echoed by Joe's opinions concerning her husband's diagnosed diabetes and high cholesterol, as she attributed his ill health to fast foods and eating out at restaurants.[55] Steven Point, in a similar way, pointed to a community-wide concern about "store-bought" high-starch, high-sugar diets—he noted that at a particular gathering an announcement was made to henceforth ban soft drinks from ceremonies in favour of water and fruit juice.[56] Gwen Point also faulted sugar, specifically, for rotting Stó:lō people's teeth and, like McHalsie, linked her gallbladder problems to historical changes in Stó:lō dietary practices.[57]

According to scholars like Borré and Thom and Fediuk (and obviously Kelm, as cited above), their suspicions are not entirely unfounded. Borré argues that a traditional Inuit diet was healthier than its store-bought equivalent, as it was high in quality protein, polyunsaturated fats, iron, and vitamins, and constituted a healthier source of all nutrients except calcium, vitamin C, and carbohydrates. To bolster her argument she cites Schaefer and Steckle's 1980 report, which correlated an increased reliance on store-bought foods with high rates of dental caries, acne, obesity, and iron-deficiency anemia on reserves.[58] Fediuk and Thom reported that as only 57 percent of British Columbian Natives consumed meat daily in 1991, there had been drastic reduction in Indigenous *food security* following the change to a store-bought diet.[59] They suggested that statistics indicating that Hul'qumi'num infants experienced high rates of anemia due to inadequate iron intake simply reaffirmed this conclusion—as they stated, "the situation of infants reflects the poor diet of their parents."[60]

Each of these authors framed their contentions from an accessibility standpoint: Borré outlined the potentially harmful effects of recent sealskin embargos on Inuit subsistence hunting, as pelt sales previously afforded hunters with necessary cash to buy hunting supplies;[61] and Fediuk and Thom discussed Coast Salish people's shift towards "market" as opposed to traditional foods in light of government-imposed restrictions on harvesting and post-contact-era poverty.[62] Their perspectives reflect Drèze and Sen's theory of entitlement connecting social determinants and hunger (a type of prolonged food insecurity), although neither party referenced this concept directly. Drèze and Sen had determined that access to food, or *entitlement*, was based on individual command over alternative commodity bundles given prevailing legal, economic, and political arrangements. Or, put another way, they had suggested personal food security depended on both intrinsic ownership of a means to produce or gain food (*endowment*) and/ or what can be acquired through (market) exchange.[63]

Shifting food entitlements during the nineteenth and twentieth centuries had a significant impact on Stó:lō foodways. According to King, Stó:lō faced increasing restrictions on fishing at the turn of the century, whether for commercial or subsistence purposes. While the development of the canning industry in the Fraser Valley was originally a temporary boon to Native peoples (as they were able to work in the canneries due to British Columbia's small population), it later inspired limiting legislation such as A.C. Anderson's 1882 prohibition on Indian commercial fishing.[64] Furthermore, canneries' overfishing, resulting from rapid rises in production, led to observations by non-Native parties that *Indigenous* fishers took too many fish, and that Native subsistence fishing "should be dispensed with in the way of other foods, such as canned pilchards or other food products rich in iodine and oil."[65] Ensuing bans on reef nets, fish weirs, and other Native fishing technologies, along with prohibitions on Indigenous people either selling or obtaining too much deer meat,[66] severely decreased Stó:lō people's initial *endowments* as well as market opportunities to procure food by other means. Stó:lō people's use of welfare, or government food vouchers, and wage labour—or their development of "moditional" economies, to quote John Lutz[67]—in addition to subsistence activities temporarily provided for their dietary needs. So, for example, although the Department of Indian Affairs (DIA) issued relief rations in 1928 to First Nations limited to twenty-four pounds of flour, two pounds of sugar, and whatever beef, pork, fish, bacon, or beans $2.00 could buy, a standard Seabird Island menu even decades later incorporated country salmon along with lettuce and potatoes to comprise a healthy meal overall.[68]

After the Second World War, however, Stó:lō people lost opportunities to successfully navigate between various economic ventures. Lutz reported that British Columbian Natives' involvement in wage labour increased by 400 percent from 1940 to 1942, and that by 1945 Indigenous dependence on welfare in British Columbia had dropped to 2 from 9 percent as recorded ten years previously. During this period, when Stó:lō and other Indigenous people spent less time pursuing subsistence activities, the provincial Game Department and the federal Department of Fisheries implemented new restrictions on food licences issued to subsistence harvesters. Indigenous labourers, later ousted from their jobs when veterans returned, soon discovered that hunting and fishing were largely no longer viable.[69] Annie Alex said that whereas her family had spent a significant amount of time engaged in subsistence activities prior to the war, afterwards "they got convicted for hunting."[70] Similarly, Gwen Point suggested that the switch to a store-bought diet was precipitated by restrictions on hunting and fishing, stating: "To get store-bought bread—our families didn't get it because they wanted it, [but] because they restricted hunting, restricted our fishing more and more, restricted our areas more and more . . . our families had to rely on the local grocery guy's just small selection. And [he] charged high prices sometimes."[71]

The DIA's 1946 decision to newly emphasize protein-rich foods in their monthly relief schedule (including tinned vegetables, fresh meat, beans, and peanut butter) effectively signalled the change in the times: "never in the seventy-year history of Aboriginal welfare in British Columbia had Aboriginal people not been able to obtain sufficient protein from their traditional subsistence activities."[72] The fast-paced nature of modern living further confounded efforts to eat traditionally: Joe recalled a time when she would pick up fast food over cooking a meal, as it was easier in light of her family's busy schedule;[73] and Washbrook recounted that many informants' sole remarks about plants as food were that people were too "rushed" or "live too fast now" to bother with their collection.[74]

Conclusion

Neither Kelm's historical account nor Washbrook's symbolic assessment of Stó:lō "talk" about (plant) food entirely encapsulates Stó:lō perceptions regarding traditional dietary practices. In discussing the historic shift from a country to a store-bought diet, Stó:lō community members both highlighted the spiritual

superiority of their traditional foods—or more accurately, methods of food production—and their people's ill health in the later twentieth century. Day-to-day
rhetoric among Stó:lō conversationalists holds up healthier and metaphysically
pure traditional foods over physically and spiritually contaminated store-bought
foods. Certain plant foods tentatively bridge an interesting theoretical middle
ground in the sense that newcomer fruits and vegetables can fit a traditional
mould provided they are still harvested and/or processed in accordance with
Stó:lō custom.

With this plurality of meaning and context borne in mind, it becomes apparent that the entire debate between traditional vs. store-bought foods forms
a part of a larger Stó:lō discussion about the effects of contact—if "contact"
is defined as "a series of moments that occurs repeatedly, and yet somewhat
distinctively each time people speak across cultures."[75]

When Stó:lō people talk about the power of traditional foods they are
articulating instances of beneficial liminal exchange between their and new-
comer cultures. For example, when Gwen Point described her white classmates'
enthusiasm over her salmon and bannock lunches,[76] she was also relating a case
of cultural indemnification and affirmation. Conversely, when Stó:lō people
thrash out the negative consequences of the move away from traditional food
use, they are in actuality discussing contact gone badly, or the adverseness of the
colonial encounter. This dynamic plays out in both concrete and, alternatively
(and perhaps simultaneous), metaphysical senses: when Gwen Point states, "I
don't know what stores put into their meats," she could at once be discussing
the health implications of injected water, fillers, and dye to make the meat more
appealing for sale, as well as the culturally inappropriate treatment of the animal; and when Steven Point says, "these kids don't know where chicken comes
from," he is both identifying their lack of practical knowledge of butchery as
well as an overarching sense of cultural loss.

Part of a conversation with Helen Joe about traditional food use provides
an exemplary case in point of these shifts of signification. The Stó:lō label
for Europeans, xwelitem (which loosely translates to "the hungry ones"), was
brought up, but with only a passing reference to the meaning inherent in its
original usage.[77] Instead the term was contextualized to (playfully) tease my
fellow researcher and me about our seemingly insatiable desire for knowledge:
for the moment, food "talk" was used to jokingly characterize a particular and
recurring aspect of Native-newcomer cases of contact—white people are incor-
rigibly curious and constantly questioning. When asked about a possible third,
implied meaning of the word involving European "hunger" for and exploitation

of resources, Joe reflected that "that [attitude]'s taken over some of our culture as well. Overfishing and logging by some people—it's how they learned to survive. Traditionally, people only took what they needed. They would only smoke so much salmon because they would only eat so much."[78]

She then added disapprovingly that she had partly adopted consumerist mannerisms towards food use, as she occasionally purchases more groceries than needed and currently had year-old, unused fish in her freezer (a practical issue).[79] A discussion that originally concerned traditional dietary practices, therefore, quickly and fluidly turned within the course of several minutes to broader dialogue on cross-cultural relations in which the power dynamic flip-flopped between Indigenous peoples on top (in the joke) to unfavourably affected (following the acquisition of negative cultural traits), with quotidian details in the mix.

Significantly, this contact scenario comprises just one among many contacts between Stó:lō and newcomers where food is of central importance; the true ramifications of this fluctuating and heterogeneous discourse on diet are apparent only when one considers that Albert "Sonny" McHalsie makes *daily*, historically informed decisions to eat healthier or that Gwen Point swore off store-bought meats *altogether* to gain a spiritual nutrition. The mixed sense of regret and cultural assurance discussed above regarding traditional dietary practices therefore takes on more import in light of that opening quote by Stan Green about the process of "taking back culture."

Notes

1   Albert "Sonny" McHalsie, interview by Lesley Wiebe, Chilliwack, BC, 25 June 2007, digital recording, Stó:lō Archives, Stó:lō Research and Resource Management Centre, Chilliwack, BC.

2   Phillip had briefly described her father's dairy farm. See Mary-Ellen Kelm, *Colonizing Bodies: Aboriginal Health and Healing in British Columbia, 1900–1950* (Vancouver: UBC Press, 1998), 35.

3   Ibid., 34–6.

4   Kevin Washbrook, "Plants and Medicine: Talking about Power in Stó:lō Society," 10 June 1994, Document 000390, Stó:lō Archives, Stó:lō Research and Resource Management Centre, Chilliwack, BC.

5   Kirin Narayan, "How Native Is a 'Native' Anthropologist?" *American Anthropologist* 95, no. 3 (1993): 671.

6   Lesley Wiebe, "Stó:lō Traditional Food 'Talk' as Metaphor for Cross-cultural Relations," *University of the Fraser Valley Research Review* 2, no. 2 (Spring 2009): 137–51.

7　Franca Iacovetta, Valerie J. Korinek, and Marlene Epp, eds., *Edible Histories, Cultural Politics: Towards a Canadian Food History* (Toronto: University of Toronto Press, 2012), 7–8.

8　Alison Norman, "'Fit for the Table of the Most Fastidious Epicure': Culinary Colonialism in the Upper Canadian Contact Zone," in Iacovetta et al., eds., *Edible Histories, Cultural Politics*, 32.

9　Kristina Walters, "'A National Priority': Nutrition Canada's *Survey* and the Disciplining of Aboriginal Bodies, 1964–1975," in Iacovetta et al., eds., *Edible Histories, Cultural Politics*, 433–51.

10　*Delgamuukw v. British Columbia*, [1997] 3 SCR 1010. Richard Daly, *Our Box Was Full: An Ethnography for the Delgamuukw Plaintiffs* (Vancouver: UBC Press, 2005).

11　Leslie Main Johnson, "Aboriginal Burning for Vegetation Management in Northwest British Columbia," in Robert Boyd, ed., *Indians, Fire, and the Land in the Pacific Northwest* (Corvallis: Oregon State University Press, 1999), 238–54.

12　Nancy J. Turner, "'Time to Burn': Traditional Use of Fire to Enhance Resource Production by Aboriginal Peoples in British Columbia," in *Indians, Fire, and the Land in the Pacific Northwest*, ed. Robert Boyd (Corvallis: Oregon State University Press, 1999), 185–218.

13　Douglas C. Harris, *Landing Native Fisheries: Indian Reserves and Fishing Rights in British Columbia, 1849–1925* (Vancouver: UBC Press, 2008).

14　Keith Thor Carlson, *The Power of Place, the Problem of Time: Aboriginal Identity and Historical Consciousness in the Cauldron of Colonialism* (Toronto: University of Toronto Press, 2010), 10.

15　Iacovetta et al., *Edible Histories*, 4, 14.

16　Steven Point, interview by Lesley Wiebe, Chilliwack, BC, 22 June 2007, digital recording, Stó:lō Archives, Stó:lō Research and Resource Management Centre, Chilliwack, BC.

17　Leona Kelly, interview by Lesley Wiebe, Shxw'ōwhámél, BC, 26 June 2007, digital recording, Stó:lō Archives, Stó:lō Research and Resource Management Centre, Chilliwack, BC.

18　Gwen Point, interview by Lesley Wiebe, Chilliwack, BC, 20 June 2007, digital recording, Stó:lō Archives, Stó:lō Research and Resource Management Centre, Chilliwack, BC.

19　McHalsie, interview.

20　Karen Fediuk and Brian Thom, "Contemporary and Desired Use of Traditional Resources in a Coast Salish Community: Implications for Food Security and Aboriginal Rights in British Columbia," Paper presented at the 26th Annual Meeting for the Society of Ethnobotany, Seattle, WA, 27 March 2003, 2–3, 5.

21　For a detailed list of Stó:lō plant foods, see Kevin Washbrook, "An Introduction to the Ethnobotany of the Stó:lō People in the Area Between New Westminster and Chilliwack on the Fraser River," November, 1995, Document 000625, Stó:lō Archives, Stó:lō Research and Resource Management Centre, Chilliwack, BC.

22　Helen Joe, interview by Lesley Wiebe, Chilliwack, BC, 27 June 2007, digital recording, Stó:lō Archives, Stó:lō Research and Resource Management Centre, Chilliwack, BC.

23　The plant referred to here is also known as Hudson's Bay or Labrador tea.

24　Ray Silver, interview by Lesley Wiebe, 27 June 2007, digital recording, Stó:lō Archives, Stó:lō Research and Resource Management Centre, Chilliwack, BC. It is worth noting that Stó:lō territory has elsewhere been described as a "berry-picker's Eden":

Robert J. Theodoratus, "Loss, Transfer, and Reintroduction in the Use of Wild Plant Foods in the Upper Skagit Valley," *Northwest Anthropological Research Notes* 23, no. 1 (1988): 37. For a complete list of fruits available to and used by the Stó:lō, see Washbrook, "An Introduction," 15–24.

25 Kelly, interview.

26 Steven Point, interview.

27 See Kelm, *Colonizing Bodies*, 35.

28 Wayne Suttles, "The Early Diffusion of the Potato among the Coast Salish," *Southwestern Journal of Anthropology*, 7, no. 3. (Autumn 1951): 272–88; Theodoratus, "Loss, Transfer, and Reintroduction," 35–52. It is worth noting that prior to contact many First Nations harvested the 'Indian' potato, *Claytonia lanceolata*, which is a tuber, like store-bought potatoes.

29 Theodoratus, "Loss, Transfer, and Reintroduction," 44–5.

30 Ibid., 39.

31 Washbrook, "An Introduction," 9.

32 Paul Rozin has argued, in part based on Andras Angyal's views on the matter, that culturally variable objects of disgust are almost always animal products due to both moral and health reservations. See Paul Rozin, "Why We Eat What We Eat, and Why We Worry About It," *Bulletin of the American Academy of Arts and Sciences* 50, no. 5 (1997): 38–9.

33 Gwen Point, interview by Patricia Kelly, 2004, audiotape, Stó:lō Archives, Stó:lō Research and Resource Management Centre, Chilliwack, BC.

34 Washbrook, "An Introduction," 6–7.

35 Rozin, "Why We Eat," 39.

36 Franz Boas, "Indian Tribes of the Lower Fraser River," in *The 64th Report of the British Association for the Advancement of Science for 1890* (London: British Association for the Advancement of Science, 1894), 7.

37 Gwen Point, interview by Lesley Wiebe.

38 Cited in Washbrook, "An Introduction," 6.

39 Pamela T. Amoss, "The Fish God Gave Us: The First Salmon Ceremony Revived," *Arctic Anthropology* 24, no. 1 (1987): 58.

40 Albert "Sonny" McHalsie, "Are the Spirits Addicted?" *Sqwelqwel: Stó:lō Tribal Council Newsletter* (May/June 1993): Section T.

41 See Rozin, "Why We Eat," 39–41 for a full explanation.

42 Steven Point, interview.

43 Gwen Point, interview by Lesley Wiebe.

44 Ibid., and Kelly, interview.

45 Joe, interview.

46 "Burnings" involve transferring food, clothing, and blankets to deceased Stó:lō ancestors by placing items in a ceremonial fire. They are usually conducted in the spring and fall of each year, and are considered among "the most important Sto:lo rituals": Bruce King, "White Conceptualization and Industrial Canning: The Disruption of Sto:lo Culture," 8 May 1991, Document 000503, Stó:lō Archives, Stó:lō Research and Resource Management Centre, Chilliwack, BC, 6; Albert "Sonny" McHalsie, "Stó:lō Deceased: Cemeteries, Funerals and Burnings," paper presentation, LYS Meeting, Chilliwack, BC, April 2002, 4–5.

47 McHalsie, "Stó:lō Deceased," 6.

48   Kelly, interview.

49   McHalsie, interview.

50   McHalsie, "Stó:lō Deceased," 6; Kelly, interview.

51   Gwen Point, interview by Patricia Kelly.

52   Steven Point, interview. Point's brother had implied, via gesture, that eating hamburger caused dull, witless, "cow-like" behaviour.

53   Steven Point, interview.

54   McHalsie, interview.

55   Joe, interview.

56   Steven Point, interview.

57   Gwen Point, interview by Patricia Kelly.

58   Kristen Borré, "Seal Blood, Inuit Blood, and Diet: A Biocultural Model of Physiology and Cultural Identity," *Medical Anthropology Quarterly* 5, no. 1 (1991): 57.

59   For their purposes, food security was defined as "adequate access [to] affordable, high quality foods that are culturally acceptable." Fediuk and Thom, "Contemporary and Desired Use," 6.

60   Ibid.

61   Borré, "Seal Blood," 57.

62   Fediuk and Thom, "Contemporary and Desired Use," 4–5, 10–14.

63   Jean Drèze and Amartya Sen, *Hunger and Public Action* (New York: Oxford University Press, 1989), 10.

64   King, "White Conceptualization," 15–16.

65   Ibid., 17–18.

66   Following the First World War, Indigenous hunters were restricted to harvesting three deer per annum during a four-month open season; Liam Haggarty, "A Cultural History of Social Welfare Among the Stó:lō" (MA thesis, University of Saskatchewan, 2007), 25.

67   Lutz coined the term to describe economic systems combining modern and traditional pursuits to maximize adaptability and reduce dependence on a single economic pursuit; cited in Haggarty, "A Cultural History," 19.

68   Kelm, *Colonizing Bodies*, 34–5.

69   Haggarty, "A Cultural History," 27.

70   Ibid., 28.

71   Gwen Point, interview by Lesley Wiebe.

72   Haggarty, "A Cultural History," 28.

73   Joe, interview.

74   Washbrook, "Plants and Medicine," 3.

75   Keith Thor Carlson, "Reflections on Indigenous History and Memory: Reconstructing and Reconsidering Contact," in *Myth and Memory: Stories of Indigenous European Contact*, ed. John Sutton Lutz (Vancouver: UBC Press, 2007), 54.

76   Gwen Point, interview by Lesley Wiebe.

77   Joe, interview. Joe recounted that when Indians on the Fraser first encountered Europeans they were famished and required charity in the form of food; hence, they were *literally* hungry.

78   Ibid.

79   Ibid.

7

"Bringing Home All That Has Left": The Skulkayn/Stalo Heritage Project and the Stó:lō Cultural Revival

ELLA BEDARD

As a participant in the Stó:lō Ethnohistory Field School, I spent May 2013 learning about the life of the late Stó:lō elder Xwiyàlemot, Matilda "Tillie" Gutierrez. When I asked about Xwiyàlemot, her friends and family would often recount her favourite story to me, the story of Skunk and Crane. Skunk loses to Crane in a duel and as a result loses a defining part of himself: his precious weapon, the stink sack. After much searching, Skunk is able to retrieve it with the help of some friends. I came to think of this story as an analogy for the process that Xwiyàlemot herself went through. As one of the last fluent Halq'eméylem speakers, Xwiyàlemot and other elders like her participated in a process of cultural and linguistic revival that brought the Halq'eméylem language back from the brink of extinction. In this paper, I explore Skunk-like moments of learning and re-learning that were facilitated by the Skulkayn/ Stalo Heritage Project.

Initiated in 1971 under the auspices of Skowkale Band in Sardis, British Columbia, the Skulkayn/Stalo Heritage Project was the first program of its kind in Stó:lō territory.[1] Run by Indigenous people on Indigenous land, Skulkayn employed both traditional Coast Salish and Western academic methodologies to preserve and revive the Halq'eméylem language and worldview.[2] In addition to leaving volumes of transcripts and recorded oral interviews that represent a major library of history and traditional stories, Skulkayn began a process of language revival that has produced a practical orthography for writing Halq'eméylem, a number of curriculum resources for teaching the

Tillie Gutierrez. Photo
courtesy of Keith Carlson.

language, and a dictionary that has become so popular it is now available as a smart phone app.

When looking at the period from 1969 to 1976—the immediate post–White Paper era of Indigenous activism in British Columbia—the story of the Skulkayn Heritage Project is easy to miss, wedged as it is between the rise of the Red Power movement, the formation of the Union of British Columbia Indian Chiefs (UBCIC), and the occupation of the Coqualeetza residential school site.[3] In writing this micro-history, I have tried to achieve a high level of detail without drifting into antiquarianism. To this end, I frame my study as a work of local ethnohistory. Following Keith Carlson, I seek to identify historically induced change over time within structural continuities while remaining alert to the ways structures can subsume events and make them "non-events." It is precisely this dialectical process of change and continuity that I examine here, as presented primarily through the cultural renewal of the Skulkayn Heritage Project.

As many scholars have argued, the work of cultural production—like the writing of history—is inherently political. Gloria Jean Frank, Wendy Wickwire, and several other scholars have argued that First Nations displays in traditional museums have historically legitimized the colonialist project by rendering Indigenous people in static and uncontextualized scenes of so-called "primitivism."[4] Michael Ames and Jon Clapperton have also shown how museums and cultural spaces have been redeployed by First Nations and their allies as part of a larger political project of decolonization. In fact, Ames argues that we cannot help but see First Nations efforts to take control of their own cultural resources and representation as part of a larger claim for self-determination.[5]

Although Indigenous cultural interpretive centres and education programs employ similar methods to conventional museums, they differ in significant ways. As opposed to conventional museums, which present the dominant culture's view of an "other" (the supposed "ethno"), the Indigenous-run cultural programs are self-representative. In the case of the Skulkayn Heritage Project, the aim was to present Stó:lō culture and history for a predominantly Stó:lō audience. In doing so, the project affirmed the Stó:lō way of life as a *living culture*.[6] That is, Stó:lō culture and Stó:lō identities were treated as evolving and dynamic entities; informed by their interactions with historical forces and outsider influences, but ultimately made manifest through the daily lives of Stó:lō people. In this context, "culture" refers to a system of values and meanings. More than a type of cuisine or a style or art, it is a worldview. This idea of culture is integral to the educational philosophy that became an integral part of Indigenous social development strategies during the post–White Paper era. Working within this framework, programs like the Skulkayn Heritage Project were built on the idea that the health of a community could be measured by the strength of its cultural identity and in turn, Indigenous-run cultural education programs could be used to stimulate collective healing.[7]

Thomas McIlwraith has noted that the pan-Indian "rhetoric of cultural healing" developed in the 1970s continues to be used today to build solidarity among Stó:lō people in opposition to colonialism and racism. The discourse he refers to includes the concepts of pride, survival, healing, and struggle, all of which appear frequently in the grant proposals and mid-term reports for the Skulkayn Heritage Project—my main sources for this paper. As McIlwraith acknowledges, this rhetoric would have been both familiar and acceptable to the Canadian government and funding institutions to which such proposals appealed.[8] But whereas McIlwraith argues that the pan-Indian discourse opened a door for the "intrusion" of pan-Indian cultural tropes at the expense of local traditions, I hope to show how pan-Indian notions of cultural rejuvenation, as well as the political and fiscal support of pan-Indian organizations, actually galvanized Stó:lō people to rediscover what was distinct about their culture and language. From the Skulkayn Heritage Project (SHP) interviews and my own interviews with the project's former coordinators, it is clear that for SHP participants, cultural healing was mutually supportive of both regionally based Stó:lō activism and the pan-Indigenous movements of the 1970s.

As the first Stó:lō-run cultural program in the Fraser Valley, the SHP was the foundation on which the ethos of decolonization that Clapperton and others have identified in contemporary Stó:lō cultural programs was built.[9] Cultural revival and educational initiatives like the Skulkayn Heritage Project should be seen as part of the larger social-political movement for Indigenous rights that emerged in the post–White Paper era. By laying claim to their past, the Skulkayn Heritage Project participants were also asserting their claim to a brighter future for the Stó:lō people of the lower Fraser Valley watershed.

"Indian Control of Indian Education"

Since the early twentieth century there have been several permutations of pan-Indian political organizing in British Columbia. According to Paul Tennant, such attempts at cross-tribal organizing have always been rooted in pre-existing Indigenous political structures and identities and were often inflected by more locally rooted tribal and clan affiliations.[10] Though this often made it difficult to organize province-wide political movements, the result, Tennant argues, was that British Columbia's Indigenous political movements were primarily concerned with cultural preservation, land claims, and self-governance: "Theirs was the politics of survival."[11]

When, in 1969, Indigenous people mobilized across the country in unprecedented numbers to protest the White Paper, groups in British Columbia and elsewhere made it clear that they would not merely survive—they planned to thrive. The idea, first proposed by Hawthorne's report, that Indigenous people were "citizens plus," though they were being treated like "citizens minus," became a rallying cry for Indigenous groups.[12] As Paul Tennant has shown, the outrage caused by the White Paper led to the consolidation of several pan-Indian organizations across Canada including the National Indian Brotherhood (NIB) and the North American Indian Brotherhood (NAIB), and in British Columbia, the UBCIC.[13] Bryan Palmer, on the other hand, focuses more on the anti-capitalist and far-left organizing that took place mostly among Indigenous youth. Whereas Tennant emphasizes continuity with past movements, Palmer emphasizes the influence of U.S.-based Red Power activism and contemporaneous political movements, such as Black Power and the New Left. However, neither author looks at the ways in which these forces interacted with one another and with more localized movements. In the case of the Stó:lō, we can see both the dialectics of particularity and pan-Indianism, as well as the interplay between tradition and the zeitgeist-inspired break from it.

Critical to the Indigenous critique of this era was an emphasis on education reform and the reclamation and revitalization of traditional knowledge systems. Though much of the post–White Paper activism was directed at the systemic racism and assimilative policies of the Canadian government, Indigenous people in the Fraser Valley and across Canada were also starting to turn inward, asking questions about what their communities would need to heal from the traumas of colonialism. In stark contrast to the policy proposed by the White Paper, many Indigenous people felt that community health was inextricably linked to cultural and spiritual well-being. Looking to save face after the White Paper debacle, the federal government was actually willing to listen to these ideas. A leader in British Columbia's Indigenous political and cultural rejuvenation, the Stó:lō's cultural renewal initiatives set important precedents that helped to establish a new direction for federal policy on Indigenous education in the 1970s.

In several influential policy documents put forward by Indigenous organizations, the idea of cultural renewal and (re)education was articulated as a critical unit of a larger community development strategy. In 1972, the NIB published a report, "Indian Control of Indian Education," which articulated a national strategy for Indigenous education.[14] In it, the NIB identifies the importance of local control over educational programming and the paramount importance of Indigenous cultural knowledge to community health and self-determination: "Unless a child learns about the forces which shaped him: the history of his people, their values and customs, their language, he will never really know himself or his potential as a human being. Indian culture and values have a unique place in the history of mankind. The Indian child who learns about his heritage will be proud of it. The lessons he learns in school, his whole school experience, should reinforce and contribute to the image he has of himself as an Indian."[15] From this perspective, the goal of Indigenous education reform was to teach Indigenous students "the fundamental values and attitudes which have an honoured place in Indian tradition and culture." In stark contrast to the residential school philosophy, the NIB proposal asserted that the rejuvenation of Indigenous lifeways would actually help Indigenous children survive in the colonial world. Far from being a complete condemnation of the Canadian school system, the NIB proposed to harness the "best from both cultures" in order to build confidence and pride in Indigenous individuals for the benefit of Indigenous communities.[16]

The NIB also called on the federal government to support the growing number of Indigenous cultural education programs that were emerging across the country.[17] The basic purpose of these projects was to help re-establish Indigenous systems of knowledge transfer. In addition to being a repository for specialized cultural knowledge, the Indigenous cultural education centre was proposed as a "unique organizational device" that would help facilitate intergenerational communication as a means of bolstering specific community claims to Indigenous rights and title while ensuring the continuation of Indigenous lifeways.[18] In *Citizens Plus,* a 1970 policy proposal also known as the Red Paper, the Alberta Association of Indian Chiefs (AAIC) outlined their vision for the Alberta Indian Cultural Centre, which would serve as a resource centre where all Albertan Indigenous peoples could learn about their language, history, and cultural practices.[19] Indigenous organizations in other provinces quickly followed suit, and similar proposals were submitted for cultural education centres in Saskatchewan, New Brunswick, and in British Columbia by the Stó:lō of the Fraser Valley.[20]

Since the late 1960s, cultural revival initiatives in the Fraser Valley have been highly politicized, tied up as they are with the reclamation of the Coqualeetza site in Sardis, British Columbia. As a former residential school and TB hospital, Coqualeetza had been a site of resistance, healing, and assimilation for Indigenous people from across the province. Several Indigenous leaders, including George Manuel, had attended school or been treated for illness at Coqualeetza.[21] Coqualeetza also figures prominently in Halq'eméylem sxwōxwiyám (oral history) as a site where, during a famine, selfish men were punished by their wives for withholding salmon from their suffering families.[22] At the same time, members of the Skulkayn (also known as the Skowkale) band, located in Sardis, also claimed that Coqualeetza had originally been part of their village site and should rightfully be designated as part of their reserve land.[23]

The Skulkayn band first lobbied for a cultural centre at Coqualeetza in 1968, when it was discovered that the hospital operating there was going to be closed. As an urban community situated along the Chilliwack River with plenty of desirable land for lease, Skulkayn was a relatively wealthy and socially stable band, producing several prominent Stó:lō leaders of the time. Then Skulkayn chief Gordon Hall was one of the founding member of the UBCIC,[24] while his son Bob was a Red Power activist involved in some of the more militant actions at Coqualeetza.[25] Roy Point and his sons Mark and Steven were also prominent in the Skulkayn band and deeply involved in the Indian education movement. In fact, Mark Point had joined the NIB committee on Indian education and helped write "Indian Control of Indian Education" while trying to gain more support for the Coqualeetza Education Program.[26]

Along with nine other Stó:lō bands, Skulkayn formed the Coqualeetza Education Committee in 1969.[27] However, as Mark Point explains, the group quickly realized that they would not be able to establish a claim to Coqualeetza without a broader base of support: "we did not have the strength and the numbers to convince Ottawa and the Chilliwack community and other native communities that we could occupy and use the property ourselves so we began sitting with other people."[28]

The NAIB of British Columbia was the first pan-Indian organization to support the idea of a cultural education centre at Coqualeetza in January 1968.

The following year, Skulkayn Chief Gordon Hall brought the issue before the newly formed UBCIC and 65 communities across British Columbia passed band council motions in favour of a cultural centre at Coqualeetza.[29] By 1970, six major British Columbia Indigenous organizations had joined together to appoint a three-person committee to pursue establishing First Nations control of the site.[30]

Eager to change his image and distance the Department of Indian Affairs and Northern Development (DIAND) from the assimilative policies of the White Paper, then minister of Indian Affairs Jean Chrétien showed early support for the Coqualeetza proposal. Health Minister John Munro, whose department held jurisdiction over the Coqualeetza grounds, also met the proposal with cautious enthusiasm.[31] Yet, while both the DIAND and the Health and Welfare Canada gave funding to the Coqualeetza committee to conduct a feasibility study for the site,[32] they evaded the issue for several years afterward, passing the file from one department to another.[33]

While the coalition backing Coqualeetza continued to press the federal government for a decision, local people employed a variety of tactics. At an open meeting in Chilliwack with Health Minister Munro, Henry Jack (a young Stó:lō activist) proposed that the Stó:lō occupy the site immediately, citing rising suicide rates among young Indians as a cause for urgency. In reply Munro said, "this is not about righting historical wrongs, but finding the best possible use for the building in the future."[34] Despite the Indigenous unrest caused after the White Paper debacle, the federal government was not yet willing to cede Coqualeetza as a token of redress.[35]

There were efforts at negotiation between Stó:lō leaders and the DIAND, but tension arose over who would pay the equivalent of taxes to the municipal government, which would have amounted to approximately $30,000 for the Coqualeetza property. The Stó:lō wanted the DIAND to pay the sum on their behalf and to transfer the lands over to them as a reserve. Negotiations were permanently sidetracked by the conflicting interests of the various government agencies involved (the Treasury Board, the departments of National Defence, DIAND, and National Health and Welfare, and municipal government), the Stó:lō chiefs, and the numerous parties backing the Coqualeetza committee.

Matters were further complicated by tensions within the province-wide coalition backing the Coqualeetza proposal. While some members of the coalition imagined that the centre would be able to represent all British Columbia Indigenous cultures, Skulkayn and other Fraser Valley bands were pushing for a Halq'eméylem-centred Stó:lō cultural program.[36] When, in April 1971, the

DIAND finally rejected the Education Committee's proposal as unviable, the Skulkayn band decided to initiate their own education and research program to begin the cultural revival work they had hoped to accomplish at Coqualeetza on a larger scale.

The Skulkayn/Stalo Heritage Project

Conceived in 1971, the Skulkayn/Stalo Heritage Project (SHP) was one of the first Indigenous-run cultural education projects to receive funding from the British Columbia government.[37] Given the involvement of Skulkayn band members in other aspects of Indigenous activism at the provincial and national levels, the SHP mandate was very much informed by the education philosophy articulated in "Indian Control of Indian Education" and the Red Paper. But whereas the AAIC had imagined that it would be possible to represent all of Alberta's Indigenous heritage under one roof at the Alberta Indian Cultural Centre, Skulkayn's coordinators limited their program to Stó:lō history and the cultural worldview of the Halq'eméylem-speaking peoples of the lower Fraser Valley watershed.

During its short tenure, the SHP had two roughly defined phases of operation. In phase 1, which lasted from about February to July of 1972, the SHP initiated its history and language program. In phase 2, the coordinators built on those programs and organized support for the implementation of this expanded cultural program at Coqualeetza. In the early month of the project, the SHP's most explicit objective was to preserve the Halq'eméylem language and worldview. As a draft of the project proposal asserts: "This project began with the realization that our native culture was slowly dying. A need exists for Indian people of this area to try to get up and salvage whatever remains of our people's folklore. . . . Today very few still speak the true Halkomelem language. Who is to blame, is not important anymore; what is important is that something be done now, to save what can be saved."[38] In this and other SHP documents, there is a palpable anxiety that the project may have come too late. The stories and traditions that the SHP coordinators recognized as being so integral to community wellness were fading from living memory with the last generation of fluent Halq'eméylem speakers. If the Halq'eméylem culture was going to be revived, that knowledge needed to be recorded before it was too late.[39]

Though in some respects the goals of the SHP seem to mirror the conservationist goals of salvage anthropology, the two had very different motivations and produced very different results. According to historian Paige Raibmon, the basic premise of salvage anthropology was that "Indian" culture would die

as Indigenous populations were assimilated or destroyed.[40] With some excep-
tions, anthropologists in the mid-twentieth century remained preoccupied
with the preservation of Indigenous culture and language in the abstract. In
contrast, the SHP coordinators were almost wholly concerned with the future
of their people.

The SHP end goal was to make learning more accessible and interesting
for Stó:lō students by alleviating the sense of alienation that many Indigenous
people felt toward education. They hoped to create curriculum and educational
programs that would be relevant and engaging to people of all ages. As the
program proposal asserts: "The returns of such a program may not be felt for
another generation but the initial step will have been [taken sooner]. . . . The
94% drop out rate for native students in ten years may have dropped because
our children felt more proud of their past. The penitentiaries may, in ten years,
not be overflowing with our people because by then they will have realized
their potential as people through projects such as ours. Only the Indian people
can solve their internal difficulties."[41] Through education, the "Native Identity"
would be used to build strong communities, while also giving Indigenous
people the tools and skills necessary to cope in the colonizer's world. In this
regard, the SHP's aims were very much tied up with the social justice politics
of the Red Power movement, making an explicit connection between the loss
of Stó:lō culture and political dispossession. As the preamble to the project's
proposal explains:

> For many years our people have been a sleeping people. While
> we sleep in ignorance, our land is taken away, our language and
> culture squashed in this area and our way of life altered. . . . These
> children today will be the adults of tomorrow; can we afford to
> pass on our problems to them? No! . . . First we must know and
> understand these problems. It is the feeling of our project that
> "Native Identity" is the greatest dilemma that our people of all ages
> confront each day. What is "Native Identity"? "Native Identity" is
> a feeling of pride, a knowledge of your language; and a knowledge
> of your cultural heritage. All difficulties faced by the Indians are
> some way related to the "Native Identity." . . . [H]ow can we bring
> back our culture to the foreground of our way of life for the gen-
> erations to come?[42]

In this call to action, the term "native identity" is used to refer both to "Indians"
in general, but also to Fraser Valley Halq'eméylem-speakers in particular. It

also identifies assimilation and colonialism as the main causes of Indigenous poverty and dispossession. If cultural imperialism and colonization brought Indigenous people into this mess, then the solution was to retrieve a culture- and language-based identity that could instil a sense of pride and agency in young Indigenous people *as* Indigenous people.

With his father's direction, the younger Hall applied for funding from the provincial-run First Citizens Fund in February 1972.[43] The proposal was for $67,000, which included approximately $40,000 in salaries for a nine-person staff, $12,000 for office supplies and recording equipment, $5,000 for office space, and $9,000 to purchase two vehicles and cover transportation costs. According to the proposal, the project coordinator was responsible to the band administration, chief, and council, which would also be responsible for the project's accounting and administration.[44] After the funding was approved, the Skulkayn band quickly constructed a log cabin to function as project head- quarters and hired Steven Point to manage the language and history program.

As language coordinator, Steven Point's goal was to interview and record as many elders as possible from across the Fraser Valley. However, there was a language barrier to contend with between the young project coordinator and the knowledgeable elders. The "old, old" elders, as Point calls them, still spoke Halq'eméylem as their first language, while the young project coordinators spoke only English. To facilitate interviews and group discussions, Point hired Amelia Douglas and Tillie Gutierrez as Halq'eméylem interpreters, while Steven's father, Roy Point, and Wilfred Charlie acted as "field work- ers." Having spent time in residential school, these "middle elders," as Point calls them, could read and write in English and so were able to work with the academic materials and transcribe interview recordings. They could also speak Halq'eméylem and were familiar with the cultural and social protocols that the elders were accustomed to. According to Point, this was crucial to the project's success. Having the middle elders provided the cultural link that both improved the accuracy and nuance of the interviews while also putting elders at ease, making them more willing to share their knowledge.[45]

With the help of the middle elders, Point conducted a survey of the Halq'eméylem-speaking elders to assess their varying degrees of fluency. After identifying a group of about thirteen fluent speakers, the SHP started holding weekly meetings in February 1972. The "Wednesday Meeting," as it came to be called, was held at a different elder's house each week in different parts of the territory. The SHP paid for lunch supplies and provided transportation, while the hosting elder prepared the meal. Using Charles Hill-Tout's 1902 *Report on*

Salish Languages: Fraser River Dialect, the elders developed a Halq'eméylem word list, while Point or Hall recorded the meeting. As Point explains in his interim report, they rarely got through more than two pages of Hill-Tout's dictionary because the word lists usually doubled as the inaccuracies of the written sources were refined and corrected by the elders.[46]

The goal of the language program was not just to preserve the Halq'eméylem language but to revive it as a spoken language. This necessitated the study of a Halq'eméylem grammar to make it possible to translate from English to Halq'eméylem. Furthermore, the SHP historical studies were not limited to the distant past but also included interviews about recent Stó:lō histories, such as the experience of Indigenous people working at the hop yards in Sardis. Although the SHP drew heavily on anthropological and linguistic material about the Fraser Valley, their efforts yielded very different results, due largely to the difference in emphasis and perspective that SHP participants brought to their work. According to Stephen Point, research undertaken by Stó:lō people for the benefit of Stó:lō communities were often more nuanced and complex:

> The beauty of that was that up until then the elders had been interviewed by trained anthropologists or historians, people like Oliver Wells who were just interested in history but they would always ask just sort of random questions like what colour is the sky? What is this bird called? Do the Indians eat meat? So the answer would be really brief and to the point. And sometimes the answer wasn't accurate because they wouldn't understand the question because you've got a whole different culture asking this culture, there's just a lot of cultural gap. . . . So the continuity you get is aboriginal people asking in their own language and getting answers in the context of the dialogue that was grammatically correct, linguistically correct. . . . So they were being interviewed for the very first time in their own language.[47]

The SHP interviews provided an opportunity for elders to speak to subjects which they deemed important. Interviewees were not only asked about their culture and language, but about how they lost their connection to these things and their Native spirituality; not only did this research foster a sense of community and pride among Stó:lō people, it provided the forum in which people could heal and talk about their experiences of colonization and what tradition meant to them.

From the SHP proposals and Point's mid-term report, we gain an under-standing of the project's ideals and long-term goals. By looking at interviews and field notes, however, we get a better sense of the immediate effect the SHP had on its participants.

Clearly a connection to the language was not the only thing that the project managed to build. For the "middle elder" field interpreters, cultural preservation work also helped strengthen their bond to the wider community. In a letter signed by Wilfred Tommy, Tim Point, Amelia Douglas, and Tillie Gutierrez, they explain: "the four of us, . . . we feel that the Skulkayn Project made us feel responsible towards our older members of our Indian people and also our younger generation."[48] Through the suppression of Indigenous social institu-tions and systems of governance, colonialism had weakened the wide-reaching social nets that connected disparate Stó:lō communities with each other and with other Coast Salish peoples. Retrieving and recording traditional knowl-edge required the SHP to connect Halq'eméylem-speaking elders from across the territory, many of whom lived in isolation and poverty. Through extended family networks, residential school, seasons spent hop picking, canning, or fishing in the Fraser Canyon, the middle elders had far-reaching social ties and were able to identify and make connections with elders from all across the Valley. As Bob Hall recalls of interpreter Tillie Gutierrez, "she knew everybody. You know literally, I think she knew everybody in the Valley."[49]

One of the most positive outcomes of the project was the effect it had on the elders who participated in the Wednesday meetings.[50] As the middle elders explain in their letter: "Many of those old people had never seen each other for a few years and are very happy to get out. We know one in particular, Mrs. Margaret Emery, who has never been out of her house for three months. We brought her to Agassiz dinner and she had a great time, she also seen her sister Mary Peters, who she had never seen for some time."[51]

For both the older and middle elders, the meetings provided an opportunity to reconnect with old friends and out-of-touch relatives. In addition to the Wednesday meetings, the SHP staff also conducted small-group and indi-vidual interviews with elders, especially those who had expertise in particular subject areas, such as medicines and healing. The SHP also hosted a potlatch and slahal tournament, "to bring elders together as was so often done long ago by their parents."[52]

The fieldworkers would spend at least one day a week in the office, sum-marizing the week's findings and writing reports. In her notes, field interpreter Tillie Gutierrez expresses the joys and difficulties of her work. She expresses her frustrations with the challenges of translating Halq'eméylem. It had been decades since Tillie was immersed in a community of fluent Halq'eméylem speakers, and the language no longer always came easily to her.[53] There was also the added challenge of having to negotiate multiple dialects from all parts of the Valley. This could be frustrating and Tillie often comments on the difficulties of this work in her field notes. On April 10, 1972 she writes, "Now Amelia and I have a new experience where we have to respect other people in our language. We still understand each other," and on April 11: "Again Amelia and I had the experience of different pronunciation."[54] On top of that, Tillie and the other elders employed by Skulkayn were figuring out how to write what had until then been an orally transmitted language; they were not only refamiliarizing themselves with the language, they were learning it anew.

Deciding on a system for writing Halq'eméylem was a difficult task, and one of the most symbolically important for the program. "We have decided to devise our own writing symbols," writes Point. "If it is done accurately, others (linguists and anthropologists) will have to adapt to our method instead of the other way around."[55] By founding their own writing system, the Stó:lō would be setting a precedent for future research and making a significant insertion into the academic tradition of which they had for so long been the subjects as opposed to the producers.

There were several phonetic systems available for writing Indigenous languages, but many, such as the International Phonetic System, were too complex to be used in school curricula and did not lend themselves to people using standard typewriters.[56] In an interesting reversal of the conventional scholar-subject relationship, one of the first interviews conducted by the SHP was with local historian Casey Wells, who, along with his brother Oliver Wells, had been interviewing and recording Halq'eméylem speakers since 1961.[57] Interviewing Wells was the SHP's first attempt to find a suitable orthographic system to record the Halq'eméylem language. The Wells brothers had developed a simple writing scheme called the Practical Phonetic System (PPS), which was designed for expediency, not subtle accuracy. Using the PPS, a Halq'eméylem speaker could recognize a written word and a non–Halq'eméylem speaker could roughly sound it out, but there was a large margin for error.[58] Though the SHP staff used a rough version of the PPS for transcribing Halq'eméylem interviews and writing folklore, they ultimately found it to be inadequate and continued to search for a more precise writing system.

During a trip to Victoria, the SHP team met with linguist Randy Bouchard at the provincial museum in Victoria. Bouchard and his wife, Dorothy

Kennedy, had formed an organization called the British Columbia Indian Language Project and together were visiting communities throughout the province to document Indigenous languages. In the process they had developed an orthography, the winning feature of which was that it required no phonetic symbols and thus could be easily learned and written with a standard typewriter while maintaining a high degree of accuracy.[59] By 1973, the SHP had decided to adopt a modified version of Bouchard's orthography, which had been adapted for Halq'eméylem, and Bouchard came to the Fraser Valley to train some of the elders in this new writing system.[60]

Point and the fieldworkers also went on several other field trips to visit universities in search of resources and academic allies. During trips to Vancouver, Victoria, Portland, and Seattle, the SHP team spoke with anthropologists and linguists, such as Wayne Suttles, and visited university libraries to collect resources. Of this experience Point writes: "We find pieces of our cultural heritage scattered all over the continent and even the world. As it is today our culture is deducted by the teachings of the white society. We want to strengthen it therefore by bringing home all that has left."[61]

The Stó:lō language and culture had long been studied by anthropologists and linguists, and with the SHP those findings were finally making a homecoming. Though the SHP coordinators were keen on using Western anthropological sources, such as Franz Boas and Charles Hill-Tout, they also aimed at reorienting that academic tradition. "For many years anthropologists, archeologists, and linguists have studied our language and culture and life style," writes Point in his proposal. "Though many of these reports are a credit to the Indian people, never has there been a study made from the Native standpoint."[62] As the first cultural and linguistic study run by Stó:lō people, the SHP began a tradition of Stó:lō-led inquiry; not only were they doing their own research, they had begun to set the terms and conditions for all future research done about them.

"This is Stalo Indian land"

Phase 1 of Skulkayn's language and history program began in January 1972 and carried through the fall of that year. In early 1973, the project was renamed the Stalo Heritage Project—an indication that the coordinators saw their work as part of a larger identity-building project.[63] That same year, the SHP coordinators returned their attention to the matter of Coqualeetza, looking to fulfill the SHP's mandate to "study and implement the construction of a Multi-Cultural Centre."[64] It is unclear from SHP archives and interviews if the SHP coordinators had always intended their program to be a feeder for the more ambitious plan of the Coqualeetza cultural centre. But in their last months of operation, the SHP started to again direct energy toward the development of a cultural program at Coqualeetza, which would be the inheritor of all the SHP programs and research.[65]

Back in 1971, the federal government had denied the UBCIC's bid for control of Coqualeetza because the Education Committee's implementation plan was deemed insufficient. To ensure that the same grounds could not be used again to dismiss the project, the SHP coordinators helped devise a more comprehensive strategy to implement a Stó:lō cultural education centre at Coqualeetza.

By the spring of 1973, the SHP coordinators had established an interim committee consisting of elders and community members from several bands to oversee the development of Coqualeetza. The committee planned to replace itself by establishing a Valley-wide tribal council and management board that would pursue Indigenous ownership of Coqualeetza while overseeing the expansion of the SHP, soon to be housed at Coqualeetza.

The SHP coordinators had ambitious plans for the future Coqualeetza Centre. Building on the research developed during the first phase of Skulkayn's history and language program, they hoped to produce three publications in the coming years: "a dictionary for the Stalo dialect; a cultural analysis covering lifestyle; and an anthology of legends, songs, poems and historical accounts."[66] In addition to these books, the SHP proposed to build a model Stó:lō village at Coqualeetza to animate the project's historical and archaeological findings, as well as initiate a photography program and a Halq'eméylem language school.[67] Though the SHP coordinators were responsible for outlining these ambitious projects, they did not see them through to completion. When the SHP funding ran dry in January 1974, the SHP operations were rolled over to a new "Stalo Center" at Coqualeetza. With financial support from the federal government's new Cultural/Education Program, the Coqualeetza Training and Education Centre (CETC) was established in the summer of 1974, receiving all the SHP archives as well as its project ideas and mandates.[68] Under the banner of the CETC, nearly all of the SHP's initial goals were achieved.

Now operating out of the former nurses' residence at Coqualeetza, the weekly elders meetings continued as the "Coqualeetza elders group."[69] In 1975, Coqualeetza hired linguist Brent Galloway to work with the elders group on a Halq'eméylem dictionary. Galloway had been invited to some of the SHP elders meetings and was familiar with their methodology. Building on Galloway's dissertation on Halq'eméylem grammar and the word lists developed by the elders group, the first version of the dictionary was completed using an adapted version of the Bouchard orthography in 1980.[70] Galloway and the elders group also helped to develop several Halq'eméylem teaching initiatives, including adult night classes on several reserves, and how-to audio and videotapes. In 1976, the CETC initiated a twelve-week Halq'eméylem Teacher Training Program at the Fraser Valley College, which graduated ten elders, including all four SHP field workers.[71] Several of the graduates had previously completed up to grade five or six in residential school; now they had college accreditation. Many of the graduates went on to teach on reserves and in public schools.[72]

In addition to this expanded language program, Coqualeetza also hosted and initiated a diversity of other programs, including elders' gatherings, a traditional summer Fish Camp, an ethnobotany program, and a weaving collective. One of the most significant programs was the place names survey, undertaken by the CETC Language and History Department in 1976. Of this program Galloway writes, "This study gave the best sense of Stó:lō ownership and love of the land that one could imagine."[73] In 1975, the "Stó:lō Sitel" department began to develop multimedia teaching materials and grade school curriculum that met British Columbia Education Department guidelines and were eventually used in public schools. The CETC also expanded operations to include a lending library and archive, a media centre, and later, a land claims department.[74]

While the CETC continued to flourish and expand, the Stó:lō leadership continued to push for control of Coqualeetza. The most dramatic event of this struggle, and the one that stands out most prominently in the Stó:lō collective memory, is the 1976 occupation of the nurses' residence, known as the "elders' occupation."[75] Vying for more space to expand their project and tired of the bureaucratic runaround, the CETC teamed up with the East Fraser District Council of Chiefs (EFDC), now headed by Steven Point, to resume pressure on the federal government. Organized primarily through word of mouth, the occupation began at 10:00 a.m. on 3 May, with about forty people from across the Valley, including a couple dozen members of the Coqualeetza elders group. By 5:00 p.m. the Royal Canadian Mounted Police (RCMP) were threatening to raid the building. Galloway remembers communicating by radio with the elders inside, using Halq'eméylem as a code language. At 6:30 p.m., the RCMP entered the building, shattering two glass doors. Twenty-six people were taken into custody and seventeen were charged with trespassing under the Department of National Defence Act.[76]

Whereas early on in the struggle for Coqualeetza there had been some ambiguity over who Coqualeetza belonged to and what Indigenous groups the cultural centre should serve, by the time of the 1976 occupation, there was near total consensus about who had Aboriginal title to Coqualeetza. "This is Stalo Indian land," read the protest signs mounted in the windows of the occupied nurses' residence. Five years prior, the majority of Stó:lō people may not have identified themselves as such because the "Stalo" identity, insofar as it existed, had lost its collective meaning. Bob Hall explains:

> Like we have 85 villages right here in the Valley between Langley and Hope. We didn't know that we were Stó:lō people. We always called ourselves Fraser East District, that was the name Indian Affairs gave us. Or we would just say Skowkale. We didn't know that we were part of a greater tribal entity. But that was when we all started to learn about our extended family, with the help of people like Tillie.... That was when they said that, the interpretation of the word that came out was people of the river, and that's where the name Stó:lō evolved from, the name Stó:lō came through. And that's what we started telling people, we are Stó:lō. We're not Coast Salish we are Stó:lō, people of the river.[77]

By 1976, not only were the Stó:lō referring to themselves in these terms again, they were also being named as such by the Chilliwack and Vancouver newspapers.[78] Even if the "Stalo" identity was still somewhat ambiguous—its inner dynamics and territorial boundaries more flexible than most outside observers are able to comprehend—it was also sturdy enough to mobilize support from bands throughout the Fraser Valley, as well as working as a legitimate political collective that could be recognized by the Canadian state. It was the Stó:lō, as a supratribal identity, who claimed ownership to Coqualeetza, and who continue to do so to this day.

Though the Skulkayn Heritage Project's primary and most explicit objective was to revive and preserve the Halq'eméylem language and culture, ultimately this engaged the program coordinators in several related goals, including the revival of traditional social institutions and support networks (especially for seniors); re-establishing a tradition of knowledge exchange between elders and young people; reclaiming anthropological and linguistic knowledge (and methodologies) from settler academic institutions; and developing methodological standards that would set the bar for future scholarship about the Stó:lō. Moreover, the SHP was able to build on the momentum of post–White Paper activism to help Stó:lō people rediscover the particularities of their cultural identity. Drawing on the modern democratic sensibilities and rights-based language of the growing Indigenous movements, Stó:lō people of the Fraser Valley framed their identity in terms of a language- and land-based form of local nationalism. By highlighting linguistic and territorial continuity and writing a collective history for the Halq'eméylem-speaking people of the Fraser Valley watershed, the SHP and its successor, the CETC, were laying new ground for political unity, legitimacy, and collective action. As the inheritors of the SHP vision, contemporary Stó:lō cultural institutions retain this ethos and continue to fulfill the pedagogical project of decolonization and celebration that began under the Skulkayn Heritage Project.

Notes

1   Brent Galloway, "The Upriver Language Program at Coqualeetza," *Human Organization* 47, no. 4 (Winter 1988): 292.

2   "Halkomelem" refers to the Salishan language family spoken by the Coast Salish people of British Columbia and Washington. At first contact there were as many as 12 known dialects of the language. These fall into three rough groupings: the Vancouver Island dialect (Hu'l'qumin'um), the downriver dialect (He'n'qemi'ne'm) and the upriver dialect (Halq'eméylem), spoken in the Fraser Valley watershed. The Halq'eméylem word "Stó:lō" means "people of the river," acknowledging the absolute centrality of the Fraser River to Stó:lō lifeways.

3   A note on terminology: It is difficult to determine what terminology to use when talking about this period of Stó:lō history, since it is during the 1960s and '70s that contemporary words in "practical orthography" like "Stó:lō " and "Halq'eméylem" came into common usage. Before the 1970s, the Stó:lō are referred to as Stalo, or Stahlo, or more generally as part of the Coast or Interior Salish, the Fraser Valley Indians, and later the East Fraser District. I prefer to use "Stó:lō" because that is what this group of people have chosen as their name. For the sake of clarity when talking about an earlier period when the term "Stó:lō " was not in use, I will sometimes use "Fraser Valley Aboriginal communities" or some variation on that. Or, if using a historical term, such as "Stalo" or "Indian," I will put it in quotation marks. Similarly, I use the Stó:lō 's chosen orthography when writing Halq'eméylem words, though the same words may appear differently in quotes from primary sources.

4   For an interesting review of this debate, see the exchange between Alan Hoover, Gloria Jean Frank, and Wendy Wickwire in *BC Studies*: Gloria Jean Frank, "'That's My Dinner On Display': A First Nations Reflection on Museum Culture," *BC Studies* 125/126 (Spring/Summer 2000); Alan Hoover, "A Response to Gloria Jean Frank," *BC Studies BC Studies* 128 (Winter 2000/2001); Wendy Wickwire, "A Response to Alan Hoover," *BC Studies* 128 (Winter 2000/2001).

5   Michael Ames, "Cultural Empowerment and Museums: Opening up Anthropology through Collaboration," in *Objects of Knowledge*, ed. S. Pearce (London: Athlone Press, 1990), 158.

6   Jonathan Clapperton, "Presenting and Representing Culture: A History of Stó:lō Interpretive Centres, Museums and Cross-Cultural Relationships 1949–2006" (MA thesis, University of Victoria, 2006), 79.

7   Claudia Haagen, "Strategies for Cultural Maintenance: Aboriginal Cultural Education Programs and Centres in Canada" (MA thesis, University of British Columbia, 1990), 9.

8   Thomas McIlwraith, "The Problem of Imported Culture: The Construction of Contemporary Stó:lō Identity," *American Indian Culture and Research Journal* 20, no.4 (1996): 44–5.

9   See Clapperton, "Presenting and Representing Culture"; Haagen, "Strategies"; Lisa Hiwasaki, "Presenting Unity, Performing Diversity: Stó:lō Identity Negotiations in Venues of Cultural Representation" (MA thesis, University of British Columbia, 1998).

10   There are also several examples within the history of Indigenous-settler relations in BC when Department of Indian Affairs policies unwittingly facilitated Indigenous political organizing. In residential schools, young Indigenous people from disparate communities shared common experiences and made long-lasting connections. Residential schools also had the unintended effect of producing political leaders who possessed the English literacy and skills necessary to confront the colonial state on its own terms. See Paul Tennant, *Aboriginal People and Politics: The Indian Land Question in British Columbia, 1849–1989* (Vancouver: UBC Press, 1990), 25.

11   "Pan-Indianism," as Tennant broadly defines it, occurs when Indigenous peoples from different tribal and cultural backgrounds "come to have a common awareness and to seek to act in concert," acknowledging a "broader Indian identity." In the discourse of pan-Indianism, the racialized term "Indian" is turned on its head, transformed from being a homogenizing slur into a unifying identity, and a basis for pride and political action for disparate groups of colonized peoples. As Tennant also notes, pan-Indian identities and organizations have historically been multiple. Tennant, *Aboriginal People and Politics*, 69.

12   In 1963, the federal government commissioned BC anthropologist Harry B. Hawthorn to investigate the state of Indigenous social conditions in Canada. Hawthorn's 1966 report suggested that Aboriginal title and treaty rights did in fact entitle Canada's Indigenous people to special rights that included but also went beyond citizen rights. Tennant, *Aboriginal People and Politics*, 328.

13   Ibid., 214.

14   "Indian Control of Indian Education," quoted in Harold Cardinal, *The Rebirth of Canada's Indians* (Edmonton: Hurtig Press, 1979), 57.

15   Ibid., 66.

16   Ibid.

17   Ibid.

18   Haagen, "Strategies," 31.

19   Ibid., 32.

20   Eager to gain face after the White Paper debacle, Trudeau's Cabinet formed an interdepartmental sub-committee on Indian Education in 1970 to evaluate the cultural centre proposals of the Stó:lō and other Indigenous groups. The result was the formation of the Cultural/Education (C/E) Program, which was initially approved at the Cabinet level in 1971, and later implemented in more detail by the Department of Indian Affairs and Northern Development (DIAND). The

Coqualeetza Education and Training Centre (CETC) was one of the first programs to receive funding from the C/E Program in 1974. Haagen, "Strategies," 33, 174.

21   Tennant, *Aboriginal People and Politics*, 126.

22   The name "Coqualeetza" means "cleansing place" and has special significance in the story of the sxwó:yxwey mask. Jody Wood, "Coqualeetza Legacy of Land Use," in *A Stó:lō-Coast Salish Historical Atlas*, ed. Keith Thor Carlson, David Schaepe, Albert "Sonny" McHalsie, et al. (Vancouver: Douglas and McIntyre/Chilliwack: Stó:lō Heritage Trust, 2001), 74–5.

23   Mark Point, interview by Melissa McDowell, Skowkale Reserve, BC, 30 May 2002, transcript, Stó:lō Archives, Stó:lō Research and Resource Management Centre, Chilliwack, BC .

24   "Hospital to be Indian Centre?" *Vancouver Province*, 22 December 1969, 36.

25   On one very memorable occasion, Bob Hall and Ken Malloway took a sledgehammer to the cornerstone of one of Coqualeetza's buildings. Legend had it that the cornerstone contained documents which would prove that the site had originally belonged to the Stó:lō. Indeed, Malloway and Hall did find a box containing documents from the residential school. Hall maintains that one of the papers he saw was a "signed treaty with one of the chiefs" stating that when "they no longer needed the TB hospital or industrial school they would give it back" (Bob Hall, interview by Ella Bedard, Sardis, BC, 31 May 2013). The papers were confiscated by the police, and Hall and Malloway were taken to the police station to face charges. Through a freedom of information request Keith Carlson has subsequently tracked down the police records, which include a list of the box's contents. There is no document pertaining to land rights or transfers included in the list. Additional investigation of historical newspaper records reveals that on 2 February 1949, "Wreckers Find Buried Documents: Coqualeetza Records Uncovered." The article relates how a tin box and a bottle were recovered from the concrete under the cornerstone of the burnt hospital. "They are known to contain documents and papers concerning the original building of Coqualeetza Industrial School and the rebuilding of the hospital." The box was to be officially opened the following week upon the return of the superintendent of the hospital, however no follow-up account appears in the paper. "Wreckers Find Buried Documents," *The Chilliwack Progress*, 2 February 1949, 1.

26   Mark Point, interview.

27   Haagen, "Strategies," 176.

28   Mark Point, interview.

29   Melissa McDowell, "'This is Stó:lō Indian Land': The Struggle for Control of Coqualeetza, 1968–1976," Stó:lō Archives, 2002, 10.

30   Those organizations were the National Indian Brotherhood, the North American Brotherhood of BC, the BC Indian Homemakers, the South Vancouver Island Tribal Federation, the Union of BC Indian Chiefs, and the BC Association of Non-status Indians. As the cooperation of these major organizations makes clear, the Coqualeetza reclamation was a pan-Indigenous endeavour. The Education Committee included only one Stó:lō person, Chief Gordon Hall, though the other two members were also Coast Salish.

31   "Hospital to be Indian Centre?", 36.

32   Contracted to the Western Consultants of West Vancouver, the study concluded that by providing traditional cultural knowledge as well as economic opportunities, the centre would be able to accomplish what the Department of Indian Affairs could not

by providing the impetus for social, economic, and cultural "innovation" to BC's First Nations. Ibid.

33 Pamphlet excerpt, *Vancouver Province*, 14 October 1971, 12.

34 "Before Talk of Alcatraz Type Takeover Decide Hospital Use, Indians Told," *Vancouver Sun*, 13 February 1970, 36.

35 Keith Thor Carlson, personal correspondence, 22 November 2013.

36 This debate highlighted existing divisions between the tenuous pan-Indian coalition backing the Coqualeetza Education Committee. While the UBCIC was willing to respect Skulkayn's claim to the site, the Homemakers and the North American Indian Brotherhood were not. "Skulkayn Hold the Fort: Indians call Mounties," *Vancouver Sun*, 29 April 1971, 2.

37 Galloway, "The Upriver Language Program at Coqualeetza," 292.

38 Ibid.

39 "Introduction to the Skulkayn Heritage Project," 1972, Coqualeetza Training and Education Centre Archives, Skulkayn Heritage Project (CTECA, SHP), Box 2, Skulkayn Heritage Project Administrative File.

40 Paige Raibmon, *Authentic Indians* (Durham, NC: Duke University Press, 2005), 5.

41 "Proposal: Coqualeetza Indian Centre of BC, 'Stalo Center,'" 1973, CTECA, SHP, Box 3.

42 "Introduction to the Skulkayn Heritage Project," 1972, CTECA, SHP, Box 2, Skulkayn Heritage Project Administrative File.

43 In BC, Premier W.A.C. Bennett announced that $130 million would be taken out of the 1970 budget surplus to establish permanent funds, one of which was the First Citizens Fund, allotted $25 million for "the cultural, education, and economic advancement of British Columbia's native Indians." See John Saywell, *Canadian Annual Review of Politics and Public Affairs 1969* (Toronto: University of Toronto Press, 1970), 141; Steven Point, interview by Ella Bedard, Sardis, BC, 31 May 2013.

44 "Skulkayn Stalo Heritage Project," 22 February 1972 CTECA, SHP, Box 2, Skulkayn Heritage Project Administrative File.

45 Steven Point, interview.

46 "The Skulkayn Indian Heritage Project: Progress Report," 2 May 1972, CTECA, SHP, Box 2, Skulkayn Heritage Project Administrative File.

47 Steven Point, interview.

48 Wilfred Tommy, et al., "Skulkayn Heritage Project," 9 May 1972. CTECA, SHP, Box 2, Tillie Gutierrez File.

49 Bob Hall, interview.

50 Ibid.

51 Wilfred Tommy, et al., "Skulkayn Heritage Project," 9 May 1972. CTECA, SHP, Box 2, Tillie Gutierrez File.

52 Steven Point, interview.

53 It is also interesting to note that Tillie and several of the elders involved in the Wednesday meetings were "non-status" people. This shows that part of the SHP's community building project included going beyond the Indian Act's prescriptions about legitimacy and authenticity.

54 "Tillie Gutierrez's Work Schedule," 7–19 April 1972, CTECA, SHP, Box 2, Tillie Gutierrez file.

55 "Introduction to the Skulkayn Heritage Project," 1972, CTECA, SHP, Box 2, Skulkayn Heritage Project Administrative File.

56 "The Skulkayn Indian Heritage Project: Progress Report," 2 May 1972, CTECA, SHP, Box 2, Skulkayn Heritage Project Administrative File.

57 Galloway, "The Upriver Language Program," 292.

58 In the 1960s, middle elders Richard Malloway and Alec James initiated a program to teach PPS to Stó:lō elders. Though the project floundered due to inadequate funding, it was likely that at least some of the SHP staff were already familiar with the PPS. Ibid., 292.

59 "The Skulkayn Indian Heritage Project: Progress Report," 2 May 1972, CTECA, SHP, Box 2, Skulkayn Heritage Project Administrative File.

60 This orthography has since been maintained as the standard written form for Halq'eméylem. Galloway, "The Upriver Language Program," 292.

61 "The Skulkayn Indian Heritage Project: Progress Report," 2 May 1972, CTECA, SHP, Box 2, Skulkayn Heritage Project Administrative File.

62 "Proposal: Coqualeetza Indian Centre of BC, 'Stalo Center,'" 1973, CTECA, SHP, Box 3.

63 Ibid.

64 "Project Submission: Skulkayn Stalo Heritage Project," 12 May 1972, CTECA, SHP, Box 2, Skulkayn Heritage Project Administrative File,

65 Unlike the SHP, the CETC had an explicit economic development mandate. In addition to providing jobs, the CETC hoped to train Indigenous people in marketable skills and trades. "Proposed Coqualeetza Multi-Centre Waiting for 'go' Signals," *Nesika: The Voice of B.C. Indians* 2, no. 5 (1973): 1.

66 "Proposal: Coqualeetza Indian Centre of BC, 'Stalo Center,'" 1973, CTECA, SHP, Box 3.

67 Ibid.

68 Steven Point, interview.

69 The Coqualeetza elders group continues to run to this day.

70 Galloway, "The Upriver Language Program," 295.

71 *Elder's Gathering Memory Book* (Coqualeetza Training and Education Centre, 1978).

72 Galloway and the elders also formed a "Halkomelem Teachers' Association," which pressed for Halq'eméylem curriculum in public school as well as equal pay for Halq'eméylem teachers. Galloway, "The Upriver Language Program," 295.

73 Ibid.

74 Ibid.

75 During the CETC's early years of operation, the Stó:lō continued to push for full control of the Coqualeetza site. By 1976, ownership of the site had been transferred from the Department of Health to the Department of Public Works, while the main building and former nurses' residence were rented to the Department of National Defence as soldier barracks. McDowell, "This is Stó:lō Land," 21.

76 "Coqualeetza Land Claims: Army Drops Charges, Still No Answer From Ottawa on the Return of Coqualeetza," *Stalo Nation News*, no. 10 (May 1976), Stó:lō Archives, Stó:lō Research and Resource Management Centre, Chilliwack, BC.

77 Bob Hall, interview.

78 Barb Stanbrook and Mike Doyle, "17 Natives Charged in Coqualeetza Clash: Stalo Band Lays Claim to Former Hospital," *Chilliwack Progress*, 5 May 1976.

8

Totem Tigers and Salish Sluggers: A History of Boxing in Stó:lō Territory, 1912–1985

CHRISTOPHER MARSH

Lakota scholar Philip Deloria suggested in his 2004 historical monograph that Euro-North Americans are often astounded when they encounter "Indians" in places where they do not expect to find them.[1] In early 2015, I personally experienced such a feeling of astonishment when in April, as a member of the student cohort enrolled in the Stó:lō Ethnohistory Field School, we were asked to select the research project that we wanted to pursue from a list of community-generated requests. The list included topics related to hunting and fishing, as well as old village sites, which have obvious value in land claims disputes and the treaty-making process that is ongoing in British Columbia.[2] Other topics sought to preserve knowledge of "old" Stó:lō culture—canoe racing, birthing practices, and Salish weaving—while still others considered the impact of colonialism on the health of Indigenous people and past economies. As a PhD student who had recently completed a comprehensive examination in comparative Indigenous history, I was not surprised to find topics like hunting, fishing, logging, canoe racing, crafts, and tuberculosis hospitals listed. What I was not prepared for was "The History of Boxing in Stó:lō Territory." Never had I considered that the Stó:lō might have been remotely interested in "the manly art of self-defence." I should have known better. One of my favourite books had been Deloria's *Indians in Unexpected Places*. In it, he unearthed "hidden histories" of early twentieth century Native Americans as they engaged modern American culture and technology.

To an outsider such as myself, the history of Stó:lō boxing was indeed a hidden history. However, for the Stó:lō and other Fraser Valley Indigenous peoples, boxing lives on brightly in the collective memory. On the occasions that I spoke to individuals and explained my research topic I would invariably be told that they knew many boxers. They would then commence listing off people with whom they thought I should speak with. In 2013, Darwin Douglas—Stó:lō community leader, mixed martial arts (MMA) fighter, and proprietor of the Four Directions Martial Arts Academy in Chilliwack, British Columbia—enquired of the Ethnohistory Field School leadership as to why none of the students had ever looked into the history of Stó:lō boxing. Deeply concerned with the problems facing Stó:lō youth (including alcohol and drug abuse, school drop-out rates, violence among young people, delinquency, elevated suicide rates, and a perceived lack of motivation to achieve), at our first meeting Darwin expressed hope that a book would eventually be the end result of such research, something that could be used to inspire pride in the Stó:lō past among young people. To provide a foundation for this broader project, Darwin expressed a desire to identify as many Stó:lō boxers as possible and to establish a set of standard questions for subsequent interviews. Having heard stories about boxing in the 1920–40s hop yards and at residential schools, Darwin wanted to learn about the various contexts where it had historically occurred, as well as how it had been organized and practised. Other pertinent questions were how individuals had gotten into the sport to begin with, and why they had continued to participate. Seeing the value of sport in developing healthy bodies, fostering self-confidence, and instilling the values of discipline and sacrifice, Darwin wanted to explore the physical, mental, and emotional benefits of participation in the sport. He also expressed an interest in exploring the relationship between it and Stó:lō warrior culture. However, the conception and image of the "warrior" is in itself a very complex topic and I was unable to address it in the Ethnohistory Field School report I was preparing for my class assignment, mostly because of the constraints of time.[3] It is an aspect of Darwin's question that will have to be taken up by a future student of the field school.

The study of Stó:lō boxing—and sport generally—has the potential to illuminate broad historical questions, including aspects of the strategy and execution of Canada's past colonial assimilation policy. Beginning in the mid-nineteenth century, Canada took a greater interest in remaking First Nations peoples in the image of the European as a means of gaining control of North American land and resources, as well as to facilitate the formation of a homogenous citizenry based on an individualist, capitalist, and liberal ethos.[4] More bluntly, the recent executive summary published by the Truth and Reconciliation Commission (TRC) asserts that the Canadian state embarked on a program of cultural genocide designed to completely eradicate First Nations societies, economies, and cultures. Researching and disseminating information to the Canadian public on these historical colonial relationships is of vital importance to the TRC. They believe that a lack of understanding on matters of the past maintains negative stereotypes of First Nations peoples and communities (such as the "Lazy Indian" who refuses to work) and creates an atmosphere of distrust between them and Euro-Canadians.[5] Elaborating on the history of sport, in this case boxing, contributes to the broader project of generating new knowledge about these historical relationships.

Colonialism can be interpreted as a means of governance, defined by philosopher Michel Foucault as "a form of activity aiming to shape, guide, or affect the conduct of some person or persons."[6] In the context of Canada, colonialism involved the government and society striving to change the conduct of First Nations peoples by pressuring them to emulate Euro-Canadian culture. Historians have often focused on Canada's prohibitory efforts in advancing this project, the funnelling of state power to forbid First Nations' practices: traditional economic models and strategies, political organization, religious expression, marriage and divorce customs, prestige generation (such as horse raiding on the western Canadian prairies and the potlatch on the Pacific Coast), and even traditional medicine. Such studies predominantly focus on the repression of these practices through the punitive power of the law, Indian agents, and the Department of Indian Affairs.[7] However, Foucault argued the prohibitory application of power is insufficient in keeping citizens—or would-be citizens—invested in the state and the society that it attempts to propagate. To accomplish this goal, there has to be an element of pleasure, an incentive to obey, which cannot be provided by prohibition alone.[8] Anthropologist Paul Nadasdy has illustrated the importance of the state in offering incentives to First Nations peoples in order to advance assimilation agendas. Nadasdy argues that, in the Yukon today, the Canadian government offers the Kluane an opportunity to participate in formulating conservation policy. However, if they refuse to provide traditional ecological knowledge or Indigenous cultural perspectives, government bureaucracies will draft these policies regardless, which will likely damage Kluane interests. However, participation in such processes demands that the Kluane adopt the language of science, law, and bureaucracy, as well as build organizational infrastructure that mirrors government agencies, a process that he defines as "bureaucratization." Nadasdy concludes that doing so actually undermines what he perceives to be "traditional" Kluane culture by changing language and thought. Additionally, it prevents members of the community from actually performing activities vital to their way of life, which has its basis in hunting and trapping.[9] Thus, it implicitly encourages assimilation by facilitating widespread and close interaction with Euro-Canadian government and society.

Sport has the potential to do the same by offering pleasure through the joy of physical movement, exuberant competition, and social bonding. The allure of amusement through games and the thrill of competition offered by sport are often inviting and difficult for individuals to resist. It certainly would not be viewed through the lens of suspicion that the more abrasive agents of prohibition would provoke. In the recent TRC executive summary, former residential school students expressed that physical activity and sport were bright spots in a world that was otherwise dull, depressing, and sometimes abusive. Some of the strongest—and most positive—memories of survivors are connected to sports, which they assert made their lives bearable.[10] It would not be a stretch to suggest that students remained engaged while in residential schools or later sought out interaction with Euro-Canadian communities solely due to the pleasure offered by athletics, which government officials and missionaries openly declared had a role to play in the process of assimilation. Given that repressive mechanisms often elicited widespread resistance in First Nation communities, sport likely had a significant and until recently an unacknowledged impact in this process.

Indigenous involvement in sport and its connection to the colonial enterprise is an emerging topic of interest among North American scholars. In the United States, Lakota scholar Philip Deloria has recognized the importance of athletics and athletic competition as a potential vehicle for encouraging American Indian assimilation and integration. European missionaries of the late nineteenth century believed in the "civilizing possibilities of structured games" based on a belief in "Muscular Christianity," which linked piety with physical health.[11] Americans believed that Indigenous men were naturally untrustworthy, irresponsible, lazy, and sexually promiscuous, which made them "unmanly" by Euro-American middle-class standards. Sports encouraged assimilation under the guidance of white, middle-class men, who inculcated proper expressions of masculinity, thus transforming them into individuals who valued good manners, sportsmanship, honour, grace, and "confident humility." Sports were the means to turn boys into men, transform "Indianness" into whiteness, and develop bourgeois character from "depravity."[12]

Until recently, Canadian scholarship that considered the involvement of First Nations peoples in sport has been sparse. Janice Forsythe and Audrey

Giles have recently edited a collection of essays that explores the relationship between First Nations peoples and sport in Canada.[13] The authors argue
that although the subject is understudied it is emerging as "an important
lens through which to examine issues of individual and community health,
gender and race relations, culture and colonialism, and self-determination
and agency."[14] In her contribution to the collection, Forsyth argues that in
residential schools, physical training, physical education, and sport encouraged the integration of First Nations individuals to "civil" European society by
instructing them on the values of good citizenship, patriotism, respect for discipline, deference to official authority, and appropriate masculine and feminine
behaviours.[15] Colonial officials hoped that athletics would instil a competitive
spirit among students that would work its way into everyday life. Further, by
fostering a desire for individual achievement among these children, it was
hoped that the young would disparage traditional values of their home communities, thereby ultimately undermining the very foundation of Indigenous
societies.[16] Finally, Forsyth argues that sports and games were encouraged as
a means of bringing Native and non-Native populations into contact, further
fostering assimilation into mainstream Euro-Canadian society.[17] Canadian
historians Allan Downey and Susan Neylan have also recently explored the
impact of sport as an assimilatory tool among select coastal First Nations
communities in British Columbia, where they argue it acted as "a powerful
agent of change used by representatives of settler society, whether from the
Department of Indian Affairs, church denominations, or the dominant society
more generally, in their attempts to assimilate Indigenous peoples."[18]

Although historians have done little work on Indigenous boxing outside
of the TRC's investigation,[19] the examination of other colonized peoples in
the twentieth century can shed light as to why young Stó:lō men boxed and
the impact it had on their lives and communities. Studying the experiences
of Filipino and Filipino-American men in boxing reveals the intersection of
sport, race, masculinity, class, nation, and colonialism. At the turn of the twentieth century, the United States imposed itself on the former Spanish colony
through war and intimidation, which it then went on to politically dominate
and economically exploit for more than forty years. For the Filipino people,
part of the colonial experience meant exposure to Western forms of athletics,
as Americans believed that participation in such activities would elevate the
disparagingly labelled "little brown men" through the inculcation of Western,
middle-class values. Americans favoured the sport of baseball as the vehicle
to this end but Filipinos quickly became enamoured with boxing. Australian

scholar Anne F. Tapp argues that the sport took off rapidly between 1902 and 1922 because it provided an outlet for racial tensions and became associated with ethnic nationalism as Filipinos demanded complete independence from the United States.[20] Discussing the Filipino-Australian boxing circuit just after the First World War, Rebecca Sheehan asserts that Filipinos took to boxing as a means to challenge racial and gender stereotypes held by Americans and Australians, who maintained that Filipinos were too small and "pretty" to be considered "real" men. However, a series of highly publicized bouts in the Philippines and Australia featuring Filipino fighters proved this assumption wrong. High-profile Filipino boxers, seen as national heroes by the masses, often pummelled their opponents in packed stadiums, cheered on by throngs of vociferous fans. Their victories over white men symbolized a redemption of race and nation, one that was ready for self-government.[21]

Continuing in this vein, historian Linda España-Maram argues that Filipino-American men in Los Angeles's Little Manila used boxing to assert masculinity and build cohesion within a highly mobile migrant community. Since Filipinos were often trapped in domestic and service jobs that were seen as feminine, and similarly because they were disempowered due to low wages, racial discrimination, and American political dominance of the Philippines, it was a realm where they could actually feel good about being Filipino men. Thousands of them followed the careers of Filipino-born boxing champions in English- and Filipino-language newspapers, travelled miles to see them perform, bet on the fights, and reminisced with their friends about past matches. To them, these heroes were sterling examples of Filipino strength, bravery, showmanship, and heterosexuality, as they often had beautiful Euro-American girlfriends and lovers.[22] However, some of Tapp's scholarship unintentionally reveals that not all boxers fought for Filipino masculine, racial, or national pride. In an essay detailing the life of the Philippines' first national boxing hero, Gaudencio Cabanela, Tapp demonstrates that men often took up the sport because of a lack of employment and the promise of easy money where there were few opportunities for poor, uneducated men. In Cabanela's case, he was also obsessed with the status and attention it brought him. The oft-described "arrogant" boxer loved the spotlight and revelled in his role as a national hero.[23]

Scholarship on Filipino participation in boxing reinforces what is increasingly understood to be an undeniable truth: that the introduction of foreign elements into another society and culture often has unintended effects, ones that are difficult to rein in once set in motion. Paternalistic Americans hoped that Western sport would transform the values and mores held by Filipino society so that they might be refashioned into something more resembling Euro-American ones, which Americans considered to be the pinnacle of "civilization." However, Filipinos quickly transformed boxing into a vehicle that questioned the fundamental assertions of American cultural and political hegemony itself. It was also deployed to resist an assault on the masculinity of Filipino and Filipino-American men. Ultimately, the sport was reshaped from a colonial tool into a subaltern shield, one used to withstand the blows of American imperialism and colonial ideology.

These are valuable insights that can be taken into the realm of Stó:lō history in order to answer questions as to why boxers boxed, and the impact of sport on these communities. However, there are limits to the broader applicability of these studies. Much of the scholarship on Filipino boxing concentrates on a limited number of star professionals and their community of spectators. Aside from the brief glimmers offered by Tapp, there is little effort to examine the historical experiences of everyday Filipino men and boys who actually partici- pated in the sport. That this mass participation existed can be clearly illustrated by the fact that the Philippines had become the largest foreign purchaser of American boxing equipment by 1919.[24] My study, by way of contrast, is focused on the mass participation of Stó:lō men and boys participating at the local and regional level throughout the twentieth century. Thus I offer more insight into the quotidian impact of boxing on these communities. It is evident that boxing ended up having a paradoxical effect once introduced into the Fraser Valley. Although assumed by settler society to be an assimilatory tool, in the hands of the Stó:lō it was mobilized to resist the impact of an assimilationist colonial state and an array of negative stereotypes regarding Indigenous peoples that were broadly held by Canadian society.[25] Throughout the twentieth century, boxing was used to reinforce Indigenous identity and community, to buttress the self-esteem of young men who grew up enveloped by a dominant society that disparaged Indigeneity and to withstand the temptation to seek refuge in drugs and alcohol.

Since the history of boxing in Stó:lō territory is a topic that no historian has tackled in detail, this project is heavily reliant on original primary research. My major archival source has been the *Chilliwack Progress*, which has been digitized and uploaded to the World Wide Web. The *Progress* has allowed me to find many Stó:lō and other Coast Salish boxers, information about when they participated, and the details of their achievements. It has also allowed me to identify when interest and support for boxing has ebbed and flowed, helping to identify broad eras. The newspaper has been instrumental in addressing the

Stó:lō community's first and second questions. However, it has often not been helpful in offering explanations as to why people participated or whether it had a positive impact on their lives.

To answer these questions, I turned to oral histories gathered in the Stó:lō community during May 2015. In this time I interviewed five individuals who either boxed themselves or knew boxers and heard stories from them. My first three informants represent the former: the recently passed Albert "Chester" Douglas, Alan Campbell (Tsulsimat), and Ray Silver Sr. (Xéytéleq). Chester Douglas, perhaps Chilliwack's most prolific Indigenous boxer, fought out of several boxing clubs in the 1960s and early 1970s and regularly participated in Golden Gloves tournaments throughout British Columbia, Washington, and Oregon. In 1970, he secured a spot at the Commonwealth Games as an alternate and later coached youth amateur boxing in Chilliwack. Alan Campbell began his involvement with the sport at North Vancouver's St. Paul's Residential School and boxed with the powerhouse athletic club, Totem AC, in the 1950s and early 1960s. While Ray Silver Sr.'s involvement in boxing was primarily as a coach and organizer for the Matsqui-Sumas-Abbotsford (MSA) Boxing Club and Fraser Valley Boxing Club in the late 1970s and early 1980s, as a young man in the 1940s and 1950s he boxed in hop yards and logging camps.

My other two interviewees were Stan McKay and Louis Julian of Matsqui. I had travelled there in mid-May to interview Brian Tommy, brother of Kenny Tommy, a 1966 Golden Gloves champion who, sadly, has passed on. Unfortunately, due to unforeseen circumstances, Brian was unable to meet that evening. Being new to conducting interviews, I was anxious to practise and decided to speak with Stan and Louis, despite them believing that they had little to say about boxing. They need not have worried, as both offered a community perspective outside of direct participation in the sport itself. While health issues prevented Stan from formally participating, he was friends with many boxers who resided in Cultus, Sumas, and Matsqui. He often took in amateur boxing tournaments and house shows as a spectator. Sometimes he did a little informal training in backyard rings and at boxing clubs where his friends hung out. Being born in 1977, Louis represents a generation of Stó:lō men not familiar with amateur boxing. However, he had grown up hearing stories about how popular it had been and had sometimes casually chatted with John Silver—Ray's son, a decorated Golden Gloves and Buckskin Gloves fighter in the late 1970s and early 1980s—on the subject.

It is important to note here that I do not intend this essay to be *the* history of boxing in Stó:lō territory but merely *a* history of it. Since I have used the *Chilliwack Progress* as the cornerstone of my primary research, my report is seen through its lens. Examining boxing from this perspective offers only one piece of the puzzle, as sports journalists often reported on events that transpired locally. I encountered several instances over the course of my research where *Progress* writers reported on a local event, made mention of an upcoming boxing competition in another municipality, and then never followed up on it. That is, it was not necessarily concerned with what happened in other municipalities and as such, there are evident gaps in the archival record. Making Vancouver, Langley, Abbotsford, or Hope the centre of research or merely adding these voices would likely change the narrative profoundly. Exploring the records of several residential schools—at the very least those with prolific boxing programs, such as St. Paul's in the Greater Vancouver area or St. Mary's at Mission—would also help overcome the partiality of this current history.

Still another factor is that there are many boxers who have not yet been interviewed, including members of prolific boxing families such as the Commodores and the Tommys. The nature of doing oral histories also contributes to its partiality. Incorporating community perspectives requires much effort in building interpersonal relationships between interviewer and interviewee so that there is a requisite level of trust and comfort. Interviewees have to feel safe and respected in order to be fully relaxed communicating what are sometimes deeply personal stories.[26] Collecting stories within First Nations communities often necessitates repeated visits to build these relationships, ideally beginning with meetings where interviewer and interviewee can get to know each other before delving into the former's research interests proper. However, because of the time constraints of the field school, these preliminary meetings were not always possible as I met with many interviewees only once. Many people in the Stó:lō community know about the biannual field school and community leaders vouch for it. Since it has been carried out since the late 1990s, the sudden convergence of outsider students is not as disruptive or intimidating as it would be in other communities where such pre-existing relationships do not exist. Ray Silver Sr., for example, has been interviewed many times by past participants on a variety of topics and is used to such meetings. However, not every elder has this experience and it can be disconcerting to discuss a topic of community interest with an outsider. In my case, Alan was enthusiastic to talk about boxing and was very open about his experiences.

On the other hand, it was evident to me in my interview with Chester that there were some topics that he was uncomfortable delving into with a mere acquaintance. Had I seen him on more than one occasion, Chester may have elaborated on his previous answers and revealed more about his experiences. There is much archival research to do and more discussion with community elders to be had before a history of boxing in Stó:lō territory can be considered definitive.

From Hop Yards to the Buckskin Gloves

Between 1912 and 1987, the *Chilliwack Progress* published 225 articles that mentioned Indigenous people's participation in boxing or provided background information on boxing clubs and their founders. Of these, 212 are the former, either being an article, photograph, or advertisement about a boxing event. From 1882—when the *Progress* began publishing—until 1911, there is no definitive evidence of Indigenous participation in boxing at all. Until 1944, there are a mere eleven mentions, with evidence suggesting that Fraser Valley First Nations were definitively exposed to boxing by at least September 1912, when the *Progress* reported on the annual fair. A large crowd of Euro-Canadians and Indigenous people came together to take in the weekend event, which included a boxing tournament, though there is no word as to the ethnicity of the boxers.[27] The very first confirmation that Indigenous peoples were actually participating was in October 1923, when the paper reported that "the local Indians and the other Indians here for the hop picking held their annual sports day on Sunday," indicating that this was not the first time such a sports day had been organized. It was a full sports program that included "some very good boxing matches."[28]

Recognition of the annual sports day in the hop fields was sporadic until 1929, the festivities being described that year as a multi-ethnic event at Sumas Prairies. "Canadians and Mennonites, Japanese, Chinese, and Indians" took in an afternoon of "Indian war dances, dances of the medicine men, wrestling and boxing, characteristic Indian songs, and the playing of the Indian game, lahal," which attracted several thousand spectators.[29] Articles covering the sports day, meant to celebrate the end of the hops-picking season, continued to be sporadic, receiving only slight mentions in 1937 and 1938. Using this archival record, it is clear that Fraser Valley First Nations first participated in boxing at the time of the hops harvest. In interviews, four of my informants offered support for this interpretation based on their own experience or stories heard from friends and relatives. Annual fairs such as the Chilliwack Cherry Carnival or the Hope Founding Day fair were also venues in which Indigenous boxers showcased their pugilistic skills. Downey and Neylan have recently revealed that Prince Rupert's annual Agricultural and Industrial Exhibition, held on Labour Day from 1912 until the 1940s, also included boxing at some of the "Indian Sports Days" the organizers promoted.[30]

In my first interview with Darwin, I learned that residential schools had often been an entry point into the world of boxing for Stó:lō young people. While true for some, it is not universally so. Not all residential schools had boxing programs. At Coqualeetza, Principal J.H. Ralry believed in the value of competition that athletics purportedly nurtured. To him, it was essential for moral development, fostered friendly relationships, helped students achieve maximal physical health, and generally made students more successful at life.[31] However, this was advanced by a program of track and field, soccer, badminton, softball, baseball, and shooting in 1931, not boxing.[32] In 1939, Ray Silver Sr. attended the school for a brief period and, although he was involved in fisticuffs with many of the other boys, there was no formal program of boxing administered at the school.[33] At St. George's Residential School at Lytton, the boys' supervisor, Ron Purvis, noted that none of his students were formally trained in boxing. This was demonstrated when he was able to eradicate an informal hierarchy among the boys based on fist-fighting by marshalling his own boxing training to defeat the number one "tough boy" during a match in the school gym. Purvis then banned the sport at the school altogether from 1945 until at least 1959, when his tenure ended.[34] The schools with the most prolific boxing programs were St. Paul's in North Vancouver and St. Mary's at Mission, whose students' achievements were conspicuously visible in the *Progress* during the 1950s and 1960s. St. Paul's program got its start in 1947 after naval veteran Alex Strain volunteered to take charge of the school's athletic program. Putting in four days a week on a volunteer basis, Strain established a tumbling team, then a boxing team.[35] The origins of the St. Mary's boxing program are more ephemeral. Recalling her time at the school from 1940 until 1943, Sister Mary Lucille declared that the successes of the boys in Golden Gloves boxing tournaments contributed to the school's burgeoning trophy cabinets.[36]

From 1946 until approximately 1966 is what I define as the "golden age" of Stó:lō boxing. The period saw the rise of boxing clubs in Vancouver and many Fraser Valley municipalities, widespread youth participation in amateur boxing under the auspices of British Columbia regulatory bodies, a high level of achievement, and the rise of the institution dubbed by its founders as the Buckskin Gloves. Altogether, this period is responsible for 142 mentions regarding boxing in terms of First Nations participation out of a total 212. The period 1950 to 1959 holds sixty-one mentions alone, making it the most active decade in the *Progress*. Amateur or Olympic-style boxing was the variation most prevalent among Stó:lō and other Salish peoples. It was regulated by rules affecting match protocol, equipment, and the conduct of the fighters. Additionally, it was highly organized, with specific tournaments being held annually to crown a champion. These tournaments were tiered by region, age, and proficiency. All tournaments crowned a champion and runner-up by weight class, awarded a grand title for the best boxer in show (the Bronze, Silver, or Golden Boy), and handed out a variety of special awards such as "Most Scientific" or "Best Left Hand." A tournament's "Boy," according to Alan Campbell, was a matter of some subjectivity among the judges. They were always the champions of their respective divisions, but also taken into consideration was how many matches they had fought and the calibre of their opponents. Some champions had an easier road to divisional dominance than others and this was taken into account when designating the best boxer in show.[37]

Tournaments were also tiered regionally, with associations at the sub-provincial level holding tournaments of their own, where winners and particular runners-up would go on to compete at the provincial level, then wider regional and national levels. For example, in September 1921 representatives from Chilliwack, Hope, Mission, Haney, Hammond, Cloverdale, and Kennedy petitioned the British Columbia Amateur Boxing Association, requesting permission to form the Fraser Valley Boxing Association. This would have allowed them to hold boxing tournaments to declare their own champions, as well as sanction their own shows in the Fraser Valley, making it unnecessary to seek permission from governing bodies on the coast.[38]

Thus, a hallmark of amateur boxing is hierarchy, where lower-level bodies defer to the authority of those above them. When Ray Silver Sr. coached the Fraser Valley Boxing Club in the late 1970s, he considered the bureaucratization of the sport one of the most infuriating aspects of the sport to deal with as a coach. He felt he had to constantly grovel to higher-level bodies in order to offer his developing boxers high-level training and other enriching experiences necessary to nurture champion-level calibre. For example, in September 1978, Ray took his club to Sacramento, California, for a tournament where they won the grand trophy for best team in show. Upon his return, instead of celebrating the team's outstanding achievement, he was berated by British Columbia boxing officials for not having sought permission to go in the first

Stó:lō boxing show in Chilliwack, BC, 1978.
Chilliwack Progress, 1 February 1978, 17.

place. This incident, as well as several others, influenced Ray's decision to get out of the amateur boxing game altogether, despite the good work he knew he was performing within the community.[39] The presence of the amateur boxing bureaucracy illustrates how sport can be a vehicle of assimilation, as it attempts to normalize the values of the dominant culture. In this case, Western culture often advances the idea that tiered hierarchy—in which some groups are superior to others—is natural, even inevitable, and unthinking deference to authority is desirable. These messages are disseminated to participants through mere involvement alone.

A prominent feature of Stó:lō golden-age boxing was the Buckskin Gloves tournament. Although house shows often exhibited the talents of Indigenous fighters—and it is clear from the archival record that they did fight in many Bronze, Silver, and Golden Gloves tournaments—in our interview, Alan characterized them as "white" spaces where Indigenous contenders were vastly outnumbered.[40] The Buckskin tournament exclusively showcased Native boxing talent, getting its start at St. Paul's school under the leadership of Alex Strain in 1949. The first tournament, held at the St. Paul's gymnasium, was so successful that Strain decided to make it an annual event. Squamish chief and activist Andy Paull—who Strain appeared to have a working relationship with throughout the 1950s—suggested the name of the tournament be the "Buckskin Gloves."[41] It was not simply a boxing show, but a spectacle to celebrate Indigenous achievements, culture, and other types of athletic accomplishment. Strain preferred to refer to it as a variety show that was meant to draw an audience as to raise money (likely for club expenses, as Ray Silver Sr. stated in our interview that it was a constant challenge to secure funds).[42] For example, the 1952 cavalcade featured gymnastics and tumbling by the St. Paul's school team, performances by orchestras from the Mission and Burrand Reserve, a beauty pageant, singing by "Indian Princess" Ina Joseph, exhibitions of Indigenous dancing, an autograph session with the greats of the 1936 North Shore Braves lacrosse team, and appearances by American Indian Olympic great Jim Thorpe.[43] To highlight the pageantry of the event, Thorpe's ferry was escorted to North Vancouver by a war canoe manned by eleven Squamish paddlers in colourful regalia.[44] Of course, boxing was still a significant part of the show that began on Friday evening and went all day Saturday. This included special exhibition bouts such as the "Dos-And-Don'ts" match, where two boxers would demonstrate ideal technique and honourable conduct. One fighter would exhibit dazzling footwork, agility, and precision punching while the other would attempt to fight dirty with kicks, head-butts, and low blows. In our interview, Alan was proud of the fact that he was often called upon to demonstrate to the crowd how to box the "right way."[45] The Buckskins, in content, seem analogous to what anthropologist John Dewhirst has generically described as "Salish Summer Festivals," which he argues were meant to showcase Indigenous elevation through identification with Euro-Canadian values and activities, even as they showcased "Indianness" and brought Indigenous communities together socially.[46] Recent research by Downey and Neylan suggests that these types of festivals had far earlier origins in the early twentieth century.[47]

The Buckskins drew crowds and major newspaper coverage in Vancouver and other Fraser Valley municipalities. By 1957 the Buckskin Gloves finals attracted a near-capacity crowd of 2,700 at a Vancouver venue.[48] From 1949 until the late 1960s, they were held every year in much the same format as other annual amateur boxing tournaments were. Fighters would compete to top their weight class, a Buckskin Boy would be crowned, and a host of special awards were handed out. For unknown reasons, the tournament went defunct for a few years until 1973, when it experienced a resurgence, but without Euro-Canadian organizers or patronage.[49] In 1977, the MSA Boxing Club, with Ray Silver Sr. at the helm and Chester Douglas as coach, brought the Buckskin Gloves back to Chilliwack. Although the MSA-operated show featured Indigenous dancers in full regalia at intermission, gone were the tumblers, gymnasts, bands, and singers.[50] It is unclear when the Buckskin Gloves faded away completely, but the *Progress* stopped reporting on them in 1981. Their departure robbed Fraser Valley Indigenous youth of a venue that previous generations had used as a means to generate pride and self-confidence through exclusive Indigenous athletic competition.

The Stó:lō and other First Nations communities also lost a means to come together as a broader community, one used to socialize and renew relationships, as the tournament had attracted participants from all over British Columbia, Washington, Idaho, Alberta, and sometimes even Ontario or Alaska. From the *Vancouver Sun*'s coverage of the 1952 tournament, there was much disappointment that the white community had failed to show up in a significant way, indicating that the majority of the crowd were likely First Nations peoples themselves. During our interview Alan remarked that boxing brought him and his father closer together, as the sport provided a venue for his father to visit and see him perform.[51] A common experience shared by many residential school survivors—of whom Alan is one—is the intense loneliness many of them felt being isolated from family and other relatives as the schools discouraged visitation by family members.[52] Boxing shows like the Buckskin Gloves gave parents and other relatives a reason to visit their children—who participated as gymnasts, boxers, and musicians—in a manner that school officials had little control over or was seen as a more tolerable reason for doing so by administration. Alan definitely sees the Buckskin Gloves as something that was good for Indigenous communities, stating in our interview, "It was fun. The Buckskin Gloves was really a lot of fun because you could meet Natives from all over the Fraser Valley and everything, I mean, they were from all over. . . . The Buckskin Gloves was good. It brought our people together, I mean, from all over even though we didn't like each other. I mean, because we are against you and you're in a boxing club and my boxing club [are going to have to meet in competition]. . . . We had good times."[53]

What Alan was likely getting at was the both unifying and fracturing power that boxing as a sport had on First Nations communities. The Buckskin Gloves brought communities together and encouraged them to identify more broadly as Indigenous people, united by competition because they were only open to Indigenous athletes. There would also be displays of culture such as singing, dancing, and drumming—activities that suggested a cultural identity distinct from Euro-Canadian communities.[54] Conversely, the desire to win and garner accolades individually and for their boxing clubs encouraged identification with the local community. Historian Keith Carlson has argued that, in the early colonial period in British Columbia, the Canadian government attempted to fracture a greater Coast Salish group identity by imposing the reserve system so as to isolate groups from each other and keep them politically weak. However, changes wrought by other colonial forces, such as the imposition of Christianity and the rise of new economies, inadvertently offered opportunities for community gatherings (such as annual hops harvests and Christian Passion Plays), that nurtured a supratribal identity.[55] The Buckskin Gloves operated in a similar fashion in the second half of the twentieth century, when residential schools were still being used to assault First Nations' society and culture.

Why Boxers Boxed

Judging by the animated way in which he tells his stories, it is easy to discern that boxing is something in which Alan Campbell takes immense pride. In 1957 he was runner-up at a Golden Gloves tournament in Nanaimo and received the All-Around Best Boxer award at the Canadian Championships in Camrose, Alberta, shortly after.[56] He deeply regrets that his coach, Alex Strain, would not let him represent British Columbia at a 1962 Canadian Championship in Toronto—a decision that spurred his decision to retire at twenty. He proudly declares that, had he found another boxing club where he could continue his training, there was likely no other featherweight in Canada that could have beat him.

Alan enjoys talking about boxing, so it was a bit shocking when he told me towards the end of our interview that had he actually been given a choice in the matter, he would have not chosen to box. By age ten he had already once resisted the efforts of his father to get him into the sport; however, when he attended residential school at St. Paul's, he did not believe that he had a choice in the matter. He explained that while at the school he felt that he had to obey and boxing was just another compulsory activity. At the same time, he is grateful for the training that he received, believing that without it, he would have been picked on his whole life. Alan was born with three disadvantages that would have made him a tempting target for bullies: he was small, Indigenous, and had a hearing impairment. Alan maintains that although this latter disability likely shielded him from having to hear the slurs tossed at him from racist white society, he was aware of racial tensions in North Vancouver, which he described as a "rough place." He remembers an incident in which "white boys" pointed a sawed-off .22-calibre rifle at his brother and foster brother, as well as the presence of large Native gangs who banded together for protection. Boxing granted Alan an enormous confidence in himself and the means to stand up to those who picked on him. Although he feels boxing was forced on him, he credits sports in general—including gymnastics, soccer, and softball—with giving him the strength to survive the residential school experience and to stave off a descent into drugs and alcohol, which was the fate of some of his childhood friends. In our interview he declared, "It's sports, sports, sports that lengthened my life."[57] Alan took the mental and physical toughness bestowed on him by boxing to mitigate the negative impacts of colonial impositions, notably the residential school system and the sometime despair that drove others to turn to drugs and alcohol.

In contrast to Alan, Chester sought out and enthusiastically participated in boxing out of his own volition. Although Chester attended St. Mary's residential school—which he says did have a boxing program—he never did any boxing there. He was a member of the Vedder Boxing Club in Chilliwack when he was eleven, but the club shut its doors in 1962. During his four-year hiatus from the sport, Chester was, in his own words a "delinquent" who was drinking a lot, getting into trouble, and sometimes ending up in jail on the weekend. At around fifteen or sixteen, he moved from Chilliwack to Langley to live with his sisters because of some troubles he was having at school. It was at about this time Chester decided to get back into boxing. After watching a Golden Gloves tournament, he said to himself, "I could beat all those guys," and resolved to do so. He joined the Langley Boxing Club and began training. Chester told me that he boxed for "sport, pride, and challenge," as well as for "notoriety." He wanted everybody to know and respect him. He loved the feeling of being recognized for his accomplishments, fighting in front a crowd, and being cheered on by family and friends. After he began to achieve local fame, he reported that everyone wanted to be his friend, where previously many had been antagonistic towards him simply because of his ethnicity. With a sly smile, he also told me that getting into shape—he felt that he was heavy as a youngster—and the notoriety bestowed upon him by boxing made it easier for him to meet girls. In seriousness, Chester declared that boxing had "straightened him out." The discipline required to train three to four days a week and do cardiovascular training every day could not be maintained if one was "messing around with drugs and alcohol." Overall success necessitated near or complete abstinence.[58]

Ray Silver Sr. also spoke of the racial tensions that existed between Euro-Canadians and First Nations peoples in the Fraser Valley region. Ray did all of his actual boxing outside the Stó:lō golden era: in hop yards, on communal berry-picking trips, and in logging camps in the United States during the 1940s and 1950s. Ray declares that he had always boxed "for money, never for a trophy." Ray was also forced to put his boxing skills to the test against town bullies that lurked in Abbotsford. He recalled that the town was filled with many "prejudiced guys" who "thought they were better than Native people."[59] When I asked Ray why it was important to teach kids how to box, he replied that they needed to learn how to protect themselves, that they should not have to "take shit from anyone." It is evident that Ray also wanted to alleviate some of these racial tensions. Like most town clubs, Ray's was an inter-ethnic one. He had white and Indigenous men who contributed their time and talents in instructing both Euro-Canadian and Indigenous boys and young men. However, he had no tolerance for those who were openly prejudicial and quickly got rid of those who were. During our interview, Ray recalled an incident where a concerned school principal called him up to ask "what the hell was going on" at his club. Upon investigation, it was discovered that one of the students' fathers was offering his son five dollars for "every white kid that they licked," which he seemingly responded to with gusto. In an effort to rectify the situation, Ray made it clear to his entire club that the skills they were learning were not to be used to pick on others, a mantra that he emphasized was repeated often.[60] Boxing was also important for the boys, he argued, because it built healthy bodies, instilled self-confidence, taught discipline and perseverance in the face of adversity, and steered them away from drugs and alcohol. Again, boxing was useful in alleviating the negative effects of colonialism: physical threats that stemmed from racial intolerance based on the disdain for First Nations peoples and the mental anguish that it could cause. Ray aimed to give Stó:lō youth the tools to combat both by teaching them to defend themselves and by buttressing a sense of self-worth through sport.

Conclusion

Scholars such as Philip Deloria and Janice Forsyth have illustrated that when wielded by colonial powers, sports participation and athletic competition has the potential to be a powerful tool in assimilating Indigenous peoples. They are a means to disseminate the values of Western culture in a more pleasurable context, one that is less overtly threatening and therefore less likely to provoke resistance. This incorporation of foreign values can work to undermine

Indigenous worldviews, leading to the overthrow of traditional economic models, political systems, and social customs, thereby ultimately eradicating the competing culture. At least, this is what colonizers in the late nineteenth and early twentieth centuries hoped would happen. However, it is difficult to determine why men like Alex Strain opened up boxing clubs, encouraged the participation of Indigenous youth, and organized tournaments like the Buckskin Gloves in the Fraser Valley. Perhaps, like other early industrial school educators such as Richard Pratt of Carlisle, Pennsylvania, and Fred C. Campbell of Fort Shaw, Montana, Strain believed in the assimilative power of sport and the utility of sports exhibitions to demonstrate to white audiences that Indigenous peoples could be integrated into Euro-North American societies.[61] As it stands now, there is simply no good evidence—contained in either archival records or oral histories—currently available that could help shed light on his reasons for encouraging boxing among Fraser Valley First Nations. What is clear from the testimony of members of the Stó:lō community is that, even if sports were intended to be a tool of assimilation, their effects were ultimately paradoxical, offering an example of the "trickster tale" as described by Downey and Neylan.[62] Just as new economic activities and religious impositions facilitated community gatherings and identification with a supratribal entity in the nineteenth century, so too did the Buckskin Gloves tournaments in the twentieth century. They showcased a visibly different Native culture through dancing, singing, and drumming, one that they could publicly take pride in. Because of the competition of children in sport, Indigenous people could come together to renew relationships with their children and each other. Boxing held the power to instil in these same children self-confidence and provided a means to resist the message of Canadian settler society that Indigenous peoples were inferior. It gave the youth a shield to help ward off the physical blows of the bullies that threw them, who were often motivated by racial intolerance and hatred. Finally, boxing gave communities a means to resist the scourge of alcohol and drugs, as seen in the stories of Ray Silver Sr., Chester Douglas, and Alan Campbell. Although much more investigation is required, as the balance sheet stands now, boxing was undoubtedly a positive force for the Stó:lō and other Fraser Valley First Nations communities through much of the twentieth century.

Notes

1   Philip J. Deloria, *Indians in Unexpected Places* (Lawrence, KS: University of Kansas Press, 2004), 4–10, 230–2.

2   For an illustration of the challenges of the contemporary land claims process and assertion of treaty rights, which are often adjudicated by the courts, see Arthur Ray, *Telling It to the Judge: Taking Native History to Court* (Montreal: McGill-Queen's University Press, 2012).

3   The biggest complicating factor in exploring this relationship is that Stó:lō images and impressions of the warrior have not been stable, having undergone fundamental changes since the late nineteenth century. Only in the last thirty years has the image of the warrior attained an overwhelmingly positive connotation (see Keith Thor Carlson's "Stó:lō Soldiers, Stó:lō Veterans" in *You Are Asked to Witness: The Stó:lō in Canada's Pacific Coast History* [Chilliwack, BC: Stó:lō Heritage Trust, 1996]), which may be linked to the contemporary pan-Indigenous struggle for land, resources, and cultural rights in Canada; see, for example, Taiaiake Alfred, *Wasáse: Indigenous Pathways of Action and Freedom* (Peterborough, ON: Broadview Press, 2005).

4   James C. Scott describes the process of transforming a mishmash of local, indirectly administered economies and polities—often based on communal models—into a homogenous, national system based on the individual in regards to taxation, land ownership, and labour, as imposing "legibility," a process which occurred in Europe from the seventeenth century to the mid-nineteenth century; see James C. Scott, *Seeing Like a State: How Certain Schemes to Improve the Human Condition Have Failed* (New Haven: Yale University Press, 1999). For a discussion of this colonial transformation in the context of the British Columbia interior, see Keith D. Smith, *Liberalism, Surveillance, and Resistance: Indigenous Communities in Western Canada, 1877–1927* (Edmonton: Athabasca University Press, 2009).

5   Truth and Reconciliation Commission of Canada (TRC), "Honouring the Truth, Reconciling for the Future: Summary of the Final Report of the Truth and Reconciliation Commission of Canada" (2015), 8–9 and 114–115. The report can be accessed at http://www.trc.ca/websites/trcinstitution/File/2015/Exec_Summary_2015_06_25_web_o.pdf. For an illustration of the "Lazy Indian" stereotype, see Chapter 3, "Making the Lazy Indian" in John Lutz's *Makúk: A New History of Aboriginal-White Relations* (Vancouver: University of British Columbia Press, 2009).

6   Graham Burchell, Colin Gordon, and Peter Miller, eds., *The Foucault Effect: Studies in Governmentality* (Chicago: University of Chicago Press, 1991), 2–3.

7   An example of such historical monographs are Keith D. Smith's *Liberalism, Surveillance, and Resistance* (Edmonton: University of Alberta Press, 2009) (on economic models and political organization); Katherine Pettipas's *Severing the Ties That Bind: Government Repression of Indigenous Religious Ceremonies on the Prairies* (Winnipeg: University of Manitoba Press, 1994) (on religious expression and the potlatch); Sarah Carter's *The Importance of Being Monogamous: Marriage and Nation Building in Western Canada to 1915* (Edmonton: University of Alberta Press, 2008) (on marriage and divorce customs); Shelley A. Gavigan's *Hunger, Horses, and Government Men: Criminal Law on the Aboriginal Plains, 1870–1905* (Vancouver: University of British Columbia Press, 2012) (on economic models and strategies and prestige generation via horse raiding on the plains); and Maureen Lux's *Medicine That Walks: Disease, Medicine, and Canadian Plains Native People, 1880–1940* (Toronto: University of Toronto Press, 2001) (on traditional medicine).

8   Michel Foucault, *Power/Knowledge: Selected Interviews and Other Writings, 1972–1977*, ed. Colin Gordon (New York: Pantheon Books, 1981), 119, 141. Foucault eloquently expresses this idea by writing, "Power would be a fragile thing if its only function was to repress, if it worked only through the mode of censorship, exclusion, blockage, and repression, in the manner of the great Superego, exercising itself only in a negative way. If, on the contrary, power is strong this is because, as we are beginning to realize, it produces effects at the level of desire," 59.

9   See Paul Nadasdy's *Hunters and Bureaucrats: Power, Knowledge, and Aboriginal-State Relations in the Southwest Yukon* (Vancouver: University of British Columbia Press, 2003).

10   TRC, "Honouring the Past," 112–16. American scholars have also observed this in boarding school settings; see David J. Laliberte's "Natives, Neighbors, and the National Game: Baseball at the Pipestone Indian Training School," *Minnesota History* 62, no. 2 (2010): 60–9.

11   Deloria, *Indians in Unexpected Places*, 116.

12   Ibid., 124. Other American scholars have made this connection regarding sports and the American assimilationist project. Linda Peavy and Ursula Smith do so in the context of basketball programs in "World Champions: The 1904 Girls' Basketball Team from Fort Shaw Indian Boarding School," *Montana: The Magazine of Western History* 51, no. 4 (2001): 2–25, while American football is the topic of interest in David Wallace Adams's "More Than a Game: The Carlisle Indians Take to the Gridiron, 1893–1917," *Western Historical Quarterly* 32, no. 1 (2001): 25–53. In Canada, this theme has been examined through the lens of lacrosse, which is a hot topic today in Haudenosaunee country (more colloquially known as the Iroquois Confederacy). Frank Consentio offers a brief look at the intersection of sport, race, and class, as well as First Nations participation in lacrosse, in *Afros, Aboriginals, and Amateur Sport in Pre-World War One Canada*, Canada's Ethnic Groups Series Booklet No. 26 (Toronto: Canadian Historical Association, 1998). A more recent and detailed study of lacrosse is Allan Downey, "The Creator's Game: Aboriginal Racialized Identities in Canada's Colonial Age, 1867–1990" (PhD diss., Wilfrid Laurier University, 2014).

13   Most of the literature that exists consists of special issues in academic journals, including the *Journal of Sports History* (2008), *Pimatisiwin: A Journal of Aboriginal and Indigenous Community Health* (2007), *International Journal of the History of Sport* (2006), and the *Journal of Sport and Social Issues* (2005).

14   Janice Forsyth and Audrey R. Giles, eds., *Aboriginal Peoples and Sport in Canada: Historical Foundations and Contemporary Issues* (Vancouver: University of British Columbia Press, 2013), 3–4.

15   Janice Forsyth, "Bodies of Meaning: Sports and Games at Canadian Residential Schools," in *Aboriginal Peoples and Sport in Canada: Historical Foundations and Contemporary Issues*, eds. Janice Forsyth and Audrey R. Giles (Vancouver: University of British Columbia Press, 2013), 22, 25.

16   Ibid., 31.

17   Ibid., 25.

18   Allan Downey and Susan Neylan, "Raven Plays Ball: Situating 'Indian Sports Days' within Indigenous and Colonial Spaces in Twentieth-Century Coastal British Columbia," *Canadian Journal of History* 50, no. 3 (2015): 442–3.

19   TRC, "Honouring the Past," 115.

20   Anne R. Tapp, "'Mecca of Oriental Pugdom': Philippine Boxing 1898–1921," *Pilipinas: A Journal of Philippine Studies* 27 (1996): 21, 26–7; 30.

21 Rebecca Sheehan, "'Little Giants of the Ring': Fighting Race and Making Men on the Australia-Philippines Boxing Circuit, 1919–1923," *Sport in Society* 15, no. 4 (2012): 447–8, 456–7.

22 See Chapter 3, "From the 'Living Doll' to the 'Bolo Puncher': Prizefighting, Masculinity, and the Sporting Life," in Linda España-Maram, *Creating Masculinity in Los Angeles's Little Manila: Working-Class Filipinos and Popular Culture, 1920–1950s* (New York: Columbia University Press, 2006).

23 Anne R. Tapp, "Under Flickering Shadows: The Boxing Career of Gaudencio Cabanela," *Pilipinas: A Journal of Philippine Studies* 31 (1998): 97–8, 104–8. In a more recent ethnographic study, Japanese scholar Tomonori Ishioka emphasizes the role of high unemployment, poverty, and idleness in everyday life to explain why men choose to join boxing clubs in Manila. Ishioka argues that it is not the hope for potential wealth or fame that draws men to be professional fighters but a yearning to have basic needs met (food, shelter, clothing), some kind of disposable income, and a structured daily life, which boxing clubs in Manila provide. The situation of these men today has parallels to boxers such as Cabanela, as described by Tapp. See Tomonori Ishioka, "Boxing, Poverty, Foreseeability—An Ethnographic Account of Local Boxers in Metro Manila, Philippines," *Asia Pacific Journal of Sport and Social Science* 1, no. 2 (2013): 148–152.

24 Tapp, "'Mecca of Oriental Pugdom,'" 23.

25 Generally, these stereotypes have been related to images held by Euro-North Americans regarding Indigenous peoples, including the "Drunk Indian," the "Lazy Indian," the "Primitive," and the "Savage Warrior." Spurred by social Darwinist ideals, in the past Euro-North Americans have generally considered Indigenous peoples to be inferior as they were situated on the lower rungs of the evolutionary ladder of "civilization." Brian W. Dippie's *The Vanishing American: White Attitudes and U.S. Indian Policy* (Lawrence, KS: University of Kansas Press, 1982) is a classic work on how Americans have imagined Indigenous peoples historically. Daniel Francis's *The Imaginary Indian: The Image of the Indian in Canadian Culture* (Vancouver: Arsenal Pulp Press, 1992) does the same in the Canadian context. Edward Buscombe illustrates how a variety of negative images were fostered in the twentieth century through film and other entertainment media in *"Injuns!" Native Americans in the Movies* (London: Reaktion Books, 2006). Chapter 6 of James B. Waldram's *Revenge of the Windigo: The Construction of the Mind and Mental Health of North American Aboriginal Peoples* (Toronto: University of Toronto Press, 2004) reveals how tenacious the image of the "Drunk Indian" has been not only in broad Canadian society but among researchers of the academic medical community. The aforementioned *Makúk* by Lutz explores the image of the "Lazy Indian" in the context of British Columbia.

26 For more on oral history methodology and the importance of establishing good rapport with informants, see H. Russell Bernard's *Research Methods in Anthropology: Quantitative and Qualitative Approaches*, 4th ed. (Lanham, MD: AltaMira Press, 2006), 210–50, and D. Soyini Madison's *Critical Ethnography: Method, Ethics, and Performance* (Thousand Oaks, CA: Sage, 2005), 34–43.

27 "Chilliwack's 40th Annual Fair Passed into History Last Week," *Chilliwack Progress*, 25 September 1912.

28 "Sardis," *Chilliwack Progress*, 4 October 1923.

29 "Hop Picking Season Ideal; Canadian Hop Growers Have Finished Picking," *Chilliwack Progress*, 12 September 1929. Lahal, or slahal, refers to a stick game played by many Pacific Coast peoples in Canada and the United States.

30 Downey and Neylan, "Raven Plays Ball," 458.

31 J.H. Ralry, "Foreword," *Coqualeetza Yearbook, 1931*, 2009.047.003, Chilliwack Archives.

32 George Williams, "Coqualeetza Residential School Sports," 1931, AM 456, Chilliwack Archives.

33 Ray Silver Sr., interview by Chris Marsh and Daniel Palmer, 26 May 2015, Sumas First Nation Community Hall, Abbotsford, BC.

34 Ron Purvis, *T'Shama, is an Indian Word Loosely Meaning "White Man, Staff, or Authority"* (Surrey, BC: Heritage House Publishing Company Ltd., 1994), 6–7, 44–5.

35 TRC, "Honouring the Past," 114–15.

36 Terry Glavin and the Students of St. Mary's, *Amongst God's Own: The Enduring Legacies of St. Mary's Mission* (Mission, BC: Longhouse Publishing, 2002).

37 Alan Campbell, interview by Chris Marsh, 26 May 2015, Home of Luke Pike, Skwah First Nation, Chilliwack, BC.

38 "Vote to Form FV Boxing Association," *Chilliwack Progress*, 21 September 1949.

39 "Valley Boxers Tops in USA," *Chilliwack Progress*, 13 September 1978; Interview with Ray Silver Sr.

40 Interview with Alan Campbell.

41 Emery Louis, "B.C. Indians Top Boxers," *Indian World* 3, no. 1 (1980): 46.

42 Silver, interview.

43 Dick Beddoes, "Greatest Indian since Hiawatha Coming Here," *Vancouver Sun*, 12 April 1952; "Two Mayors to Greet Thorpe; Here for Buckskin Gloves," *Vancouver Sun*, 12 April 1952.

44 "War Canoe, 8 Tugs Escort Jim Thorpe," *Vancouver Sun*, 17 April 1952.

45 Campbell, interview.

46 See John Dewhirst's "Coast Salish Summer Festivals: Rituals for Upgrading Social Identity," *Anthropologica*, New Series, 18, no. 2 (1976): 231–73.

47 See Downey and Neylan's "Raven Plays Ball," 443–4.

48 Ary Olson, "Title Belongs to Campbell," *Vancouver Sun*, 11 February 1957.

49 A trend noted by Dewhirst regarding other Salish festivals by the 1970s; see Dewhirst, "Coast Salish Summer Festivals," 261.

50 "Boxing Tourney for April 9–10," *Chilliwack Progress*, 30 March 1977; "Buckskin Tourney Hosts 60 Boxers," *Chilliwack Progress*, 13 April 1977.

51 Campbell, interview.

52 Both J.R. Miller's *Shingwauk's Vision: A History of Native Residential Schools* (Toronto: University of Toronto Press, 1996) and the TRC executive summary, "Honouring the Truth," illustrate this student experience aptly.

53 Campbell, interview.

54 An observation that John Dewhirst makes more generally in "Coast Salish Summer Festivals," 270–1.

55 See "Introduction" and "Conclusion" of Keith Thor Carlson, *The Power of Place, the Problem of Time: Aboriginal Identity and Historical Consciousness in the Cauldron of Colonialism* (Toronto: University of Toronto Press, 2010).

56 "Campbell New Golden Boy at Nanaimo," *Vancouver Sun*, 27 April 1957; Campbell, interview.

57 Campbell, interview.

58 Chester Douglas, interview by Chris Marsh and John Lutz, 20 May 2015, Home of Albert "Chester" Douglas, Cheam First Nation, near Rosedale, BC.

59 Silver, interview.

60 Ibid.

61 See Adams, "More Than a Game," and Peavy and Smith, "World Champions" respectively.

62 "Sports defy simple characterizations as either colonial intrusion, or conversely, vehicles for Indigenous cultural persistence. Throughout Canada sport has been a powerful agent of change . . . yet Indigenous peoples used these same sports events . . . to challenge, resist, and even displace colonial agendas." Downey and Neylan, "Raven Plays Ball," 443.

9

"I Was Born a Logger": Stó:lō Identities Forged in the Forest

COLIN MURRAY OSMOND

"Down here we say 'Run or bleed.'"[1] Those who did not run did not last long. That was the motto for Stó:lō loggers in the mid- to late twentieth century. Stó:lō loggers ensured their place in British Columbia's burgeoning forest industry by working hard, earning big, and staying alive. The woods were a dangerous place to work; the trees these men felled were not the skinny sticks you see on the trucks rolling down modern highways. They were big, heavy, unpredictable, and unforgiving. Trees crashing to the forest floor meant cash in the bank and food on the table, but financial gain was not the only motivator that kept these men working in the woods. Something much bigger than a paycheque was being negotiated in these stories.

Stories have power. By definition, they inform and tell. By intention, they shape and create. Some stories do so by inspiring and enlightening, others by maligning and misinforming. Many stories can, and should, exist on a single subject. In a TED Talk, Chimamanda Adichie explains that, "Stories have been used to dispossess and to malign, but stories can also be used to empower and to humanize. Stories can break the dignity of a people, but stories can also repair that broken dignity."[2] The most valuable of these stories need to be complex, inclusive, and respectful of the power and influence that they yield. As Thomas King reminds us, "stories are wondrous things. And they are dangerous. . . . So you have to be careful with the stories you tell."[3]

The popular story told of logging in British Columbia has not created room to include Indigenous people.[4] Further, the stories told by settler-descendants about Indigenous people often do not provide space to include Indigenous loggers. As such, Indigenous histories are marginalized in the stories of western

Canada. A new, inclusive logging history would not merely add Indigenous names and voices to the existing narrative, but rather provide a perspective that is sometimes oppositional, one that would enrich Indigenous history as much as it would the history of logging and wage labour. When I asked Stó:lō loggers about their stories, they often told me that nearly all of the men from their communities of their own, their father's, and grandfather's generations were loggers for at least some of their lives.[5] Many of them spent nearly all of their lives working in the woods. Some logged at home on their reserve, some plied their trade up and down the West Coast in logging camps. Some did both. The story of logging in British Columbia, however, was written to recount tales of hard work in an unforgiving and dangerous environment. When these stories were created, white academics and everyday people alike mostly accepted the myth that Indigenous people were inherently lazy and that labouring was not traditionally Indigenous: they were incapable of any kind of labour—especially wage labour. These triumphant stories of pioneer settlers conquering a wilderness helped justify, whether intentionally or not, the appropriation and colonization of Indigenous territories by white settlers.

The prominent belief of the colonial period was that Indigenous people lived within—and often as part of—an untouched, pristine wilderness awaiting the civilizing influence of settler society. Racial and ecological notions were mutually reinforcing, and Indigenous people were placed as part of these spaces—wild, savage, and in the way of progress. William Cronon argues that the marginalization of Indigenous people from both space and stories was "a necessary requirement of the narrative."[6] Recognizing that Indigenous people used, and worked in, these landscapes would have created a counternarrative that questioned the legitimacy of white privilege over Indigenous space. This meant that while Indigenous people laboured in the many wage industries in British Columbia, they were marginalized by stories that required them to be seen as lazy, unindustrious, and a part of a dying culture. Working to counter this narrative, historian John S. Lutz describes how explorers and later settlers defined "the Indian as lazy and extended [the definition] into a dominant stereotype, despite the abundant evidence of Aboriginal people being productively occupied."[7] Lutz further contends that Indigenous wage labourers were ignored in early works of British Columbian history because historians viewed "Indian" and "work" as oxymoronical terms.[8] These stories created clear boundaries of what being "traditionally" Indigenous meant: Indigenous people did not work, and they were in tune with and part of nature. This allowed them to be "othered" by white society. In these terms,

Indigenous loggers in the Fraser Valley. Courtesy of the Chilliwack Museum and Archives.

many non-Indigenous people viewed Indigenous identity as static, leaving little room for change.

The separation of work and Indigeneity, however, is a historical fallacy that obscures a much livelier narrative. Interactions between Indigenous people and newcomers throughout North American history have been shaped and informed by work. The earliest encounters witnessed explorers and merchants actively trading for the products of Indigenous labour. Once newcomers had settled in Indigenous space, work provided the grounds for cross-cultural interaction. Historian and folklorist Robert E. Walls defines early logging camps as "middle grounds," in the manner of Richard White, where Indigenous and non-Indigenous loggers exchanged ideas as they worked in the woods.[9] Walls explains that logging camps provided Indigenous men an opportunity to engage the wider cash economy. In turn, non-Indigenous loggers recognized the value of Indigenous knowledge and material goods: early logging-camp structures were often built from cedar using Indigenous architectural knowledge, and white loggers adopted elements of Indigenous clothing, such as deer-hide moccasins and snowshoes.[10] Indigenous words, place names, and knowledge about "trees, rivers and rapids, and hunting"[11] were discussed in mess halls and bunkhouses. These interactions remained central to the logging industry into the nineteenth and twentieth centuries. Indeed, once the Canadian government seg-regated Indigenous people onto reserves, workplaces like logging camps became increasingly crucial to cross-cultural engagement. Given the staggering social limitations placed on Indigenous identity, wage labour became an important avenue for Indigenous people to engage with settler society on different terms.

Many historians have studied the impacts of wage labour on Indigenous society and identity. The story of the inclusion of Indigenous loggers in the historiography of British Columbian labour history began out of a contentious publication in 1972. Rolf Knight's *Indians at Work* challenged historiographical orthodoxy by demonstrating that Indigenous labourers remained an important component of British Columbia's work force well into the twentieth century.[12] Despite Knight's findings, historians such as Robin Fisher continued to accept that Indigenous people played a "peripheral role in British Columbia's economy" after the decline of the fur trade.[13] Regardless of its discourse-shattering poten-tial, Knight's argument remained on the margins of British Columbian labour history until modern treaty negotiations revealed that Indigenous people sought much more than renegotiations of space; they sought the restoration of produc-tive economical systems that would allow them to re-engage the employment market and escape welfare dependency.

But even Knight only tangentially discussed Indigenous loggers, as have many of the historians who have discussed Indigenous labour history since then. This is not a fault—the complex field of Indigenous labour has many dif-ferent facets and occupations to discuss. Any lack of discussion of Indigenous logging is usually paralleled by equally valuable histories of Indigenous labour in other occupations. From my experience, however, many of the male members of coastal British Columbian Indigenous communities were actively involved in logging for at least some of their lives. The time has come to tell their stories.

Recent scholarship has begun to address the gaps in the historiography pertaining to Indigenous wage labour in logging. Lutz's monograph *Makúk*, for example, makes many important and original contributions. His theoreti-cal framework of "moditional economies" (*mod*ern and trad*itional*), a dynamic mixing of pre-contact economical and societal structures with the emerging capitalist economy, allows historians to consider the ways that Indigenous people controlled how they accepted or rejected certain elements of Western economics.[14] Lutz contends that since at least the 1860s "Aboriginal people made up a significant part of the logging crews,"[15] and that "the forest industry has continued to be a major employer of Aboriginal people in the province, but it is difficult to chart changing patterns after 1954."[16] The Stó:lō loggers interviewed for this study worked predominantly in the second half of the twentieth century. From their recollections, Indigenous loggers made up a significant portion of the labour force right up until the industry's decline in the late twentieth century. I intend to add their voices to the analysis, started by Lutz, that focused on an earlier era.

Anthropologists Charles R. Menzies and Caroline F. Butler, in their discussion of Tsimshian forestry and employment in commercial logging, argue for placing Indigenous people as active agents that played a significant role in the inception and development of the resource extraction industry in British Columbia.[17] Menzies and Butler highlight the Tsimshian's ability to negotiate a meaningful role in commercial logging employment from the arrival of Hudson's Bay Company traders, who sought cedar posts for fort construction, to modern heli-logging and silviculture. While their analysis focuses on the fact that Indigenous people were actively and meaningfully employed in several arenas of the logging industry (mill work, beach combing, hand logging, commercial logging), this paper aims to elucidate what working as a logger meant to individual Indigenous men. As such, Menzies and Butler's work provides the platform for this paper to discuss the intricate details of an Indigenous logger's identity, without dedicating valuable space to demonstrating the long history of Indigenous involvement in the industry.

Andrew Parnaby, in his discussion of Indigenous mill workers on the Burrard Inlet, called for historians and anthropologists to expand their focus to include wage labour as an important element in Indigenous societies. He maintains that focusing too much on traditional (or pre-contact) social and cultural elements creates a discourse that neglects the significance of wage labour to Indigenous society. Indigenous involvement in wage labour, he suggests, bolsters a "phenomenon that suggests change, not continuity; modernity, not custom," which often runs against narratives that champion self-determination and the "persistence of a customary way of life."[18]

This essay intends to build on the important contributions made by Lutz, Menzies, Butler, and Parnaby by focusing on what working as a logger meant for Indigenous men. By asking Stó:lō men about their time in the woods, I seek to complicate the ideology surrounding "traditional" Indigenous identities. Central to this paper is the questioning of what it meant for these men to identify both occupationally as a logger, and culturally as Stó:lō.

It is important to note, however, that I am not the first person to interview contemporary Stó:lō loggers about their experiences in the woods. Historical geographer Amy O'Neill spent many hours sitting and listening to Stó:lō loggers in the mid-1990s. This led to the writing of her master's thesis, "Identity, Culture, and the Forest: The Stó:lō," a discussion of Stó:lō loggers' perceptions of conflict between "traditional" Stó:lō values and forestry. For O'Neill, commercial logging was purely economical, and something that contrasted against Stó:lō spirituality and pre-contact societal customs. This precluded her from appreciating that logging was not necessarily (or even primarily) regarded by Stó:lō loggers as something that compromised their Indigeneity. In speaking to some of the same loggers O'Neill spoke with, and in reviewing the recordings she made two decades earlier, it became apparent that Stó:lō loggers had multiple motivations, and that their understanding of their identity as loggers and their participation in the logging industry did not, in their eyes, compromise their culture.[19]

Anthropologist Clifford Geertz once warned about researchers getting too caught up in their interpretation and framework to adequately assess what was actually being negotiated: "A good interpretation of anything ... takes us into the heart of that of which it is the interpretation. When it does not do that, but leads us somewhere else ... it is something else than what the task at hand ... calls for."[20] In my view, O'Neill's analysis did not fully account for the narratives that the loggers themselves were expressing. This is not to say that she did not make interesting insights and draw important conclusions. Indeed, some Stó:lō loggers clearly struggled with how their spirituality might conflict with the commercial destruction of forests, but the audio recordings reveal that some loggers became irritated with her line of questioning and her conclusions, and denied outright any connection, or disconnection, between their roles as loggers and Stó:lō spirituality. As one frustrated Stó:lō logger asserted, "Trees are alive, right ... so now I have feelings for the tree right? But the only thing that I look at while doing my work is that, number one, we need money. We need a job."[21] As ethnohistorians we need to be careful not to only seek out continuous notions of tradition after dramatic change—the pre-contact and "traditional" in the modern. The more interesting objective is to look for change in continuity, and continuity in change.[22]

Such a perspective need not lead one away from discussions about spirituality and cultural continuities in the face of colonial incursions. When I interviewed Stó:lō loggers in preparation for this chapter, for example, I thought that it might be interesting to ask these men how they felt about certain elements of Stó:lō spirituality. One oral tradition, about a generous man named Xepa:y, who in the distant past was transformed into a cedar tree upon his death so he could continue giving to Stó:lō people, sat prominently in my mind.[23] I asked Stó:lō loggers about their opinions on spirituality and forest work, and like O'Neill before me, I received little response. It soon became apparent, however, that this did not mean these men saw themselves as being out of step with tradition—or any less Stó:lō—because of it. They simply had a different discourse surrounding tradition. An analysis emphasizing the disconnect between tradition and modernity might contend that Stó:lō men were "forced" into their careers as loggers, and cut down trees in spite of Stó:lō spirituality, which in turn resulted in "an unavoidable antagonism."[24] Yet, it is clear that Stó:lō men who did not reconcile their logging work with their spiritually should not be seen as having viewed the forest solely in economic terms.

The stories Stó:lō loggers told me abounded with tradition. For these men, tradition meant working hard and taking care of your family to the best of your ability, even if it meant long stints away from home in a dangerous environment. Because these men's work meant cutting down trees with modern machinery within a capitalist economy, they did not fit into a non-Indigenous expectation and definition of mythic (and historically fictitious) Indigenous tradition. In this chapter, I argue that the stories told to me by Stó:lō loggers are truly representative of how these men saw themselves as acting within a traditional framework. For them, logging was a point of pride, and a way to honour their ancestors (their fathers, grandfathers, great-grandfathers, and uncles) by following in their footsteps and using the forest to provide for their families.

Stó:lō loggers serve as excellent examples to highlight how individuals' stories can be used to inform historical analysis; largely, it is because of the way that Stó:lō men talked about their time in the woods. All of the interviews I conducted were shaped chronologically and thematically like a story. When I sat down with Albert "Ab" Kelly, a retired Stó:lō logger, he said to me, "So you want to know about logging? I'm your man, and I've got some stories for you."[25] Kelly, and many of the other Stó:lō loggers I spoke with, described their histories as such. I have decided to embrace this structure as well. What follows is a discussion of the main elements of the stories told to me by these men.[26] This story begins at the start of their careers, as boys transitioning into the world of men, often following in their fathers' and grandfathers' footsteps. It carries along through their rise in the logging camp hierarchy and their hard work in a physically demanding environment. Through hard work and mechanical ingenuity, these men turned limited opportunities into thriving and meaningful careers in the woods. Felling massive trees gave Stó:lō loggers a way to transcend social and racial stereotypes so they could, at least some of the time, stand on equal, and sometimes even higher, footings as their white colleagues.[27] These stories describe how logging became an integral part of the formation of identity for certain Stó:lō men.

Entering the Woods

Many of the Stó:lō loggers I interviewed for this project started their careers in the woods at a young age. For some, it was an escape from residential schools and the oppressive system of cultural assimilation.[28] But this was not always the motivation. Some of the loggers I spoke with did not attend residential schools, rather they attended public schools in the Chilliwack area. And indeed, all of these loggers expressed the need to go to work to help lessen the financial burden on their families. They recognized a need to help their parents, and many of them did so by following in the footsteps of their grandfathers, fathers, brothers, and/or uncles. Each of the people I interviewed had extensive familial ties to the logging industry, reaching back several generations. For these young boys, picking up a saw (whether a crosscut saw operated by muscle, or a chainsaw driven by gasoline) was a way for them to ascend from childhood into adulthood. It was a way to provide for their families by using the forest and its resources. For some, it was a summer job that ended after graduation from high school. For others, it was the start of a long career and the formation of a distinct Stó:lō identity.

The loggers I interviewed for this chapter started work at a time when logging was largely a mechanized industry. They worked with powerful chainsaws, complex rigging equipment, and heavy machinery, but it was still tough, dangerous, and demanding hard work. Before telling the stories of these loggers, it will first be helpful to briefly summarize the logging process in which these men worked.[29] In the era under study here (roughly the 1950s–80s) the first into the woods were the fallers, the men responsible for cutting down the trees. These men often worked alone or in small teams. Buckers followed behind, limbing the trees and cutting them into uniform logs. Often, a faller would do both jobs. After the fallers and buckers finished in an area, in came the rigging crew. Either by using a sturdy "spar" tree, or a steel tower, these men rigged the equipment that would pull out the giant logs. The riggers worked as a crew: there was the rigging slinger, responsible for directing the rigging crew and maintaining safety; the high rigger, the most senior rigger, who prepared the spar tree or rigging tower; chokermen, who attached, or set, rigging cables to the logs; the chasers, those who unhooked the cables at the log dump; and the hook tender, or "hooker," the foreman of the entire crew, responsible for getting the logs from the forest to the loading area. Once the trees were off the mountain, the loaders placed the logs onto waiting trucks. Sometimes logs were dumped directly into a body of water. Here the boom men and tug boat operators would congregate logs into "log booms" and transport them to market.

Most Stó:lō loggers began their careers in the industry as chokermen. This was the entry-level position in the woods. Some stayed setting chokers for their entire career, others ascended the logging camp hierarchy into better-paying and more prestigious positions. Many did most of the jobs at different points in their career, but a strong work ethic ensured that most of these Stó:lō men came to be considered by their peers as "highballers," an industry term used for those who worked hard, fast, and therefore were the top financial earners .

Paris "Perry" Casmir Peters's logging experience started well before his first job in commercial logging in 1957.[30] Peters grew up in the bush. By age nine, he was helping his grandfather, Arthur Peters, log near their home on Seabird Island. He remembers the number of large old-growth cedars that he and his grandfather removed from the reserve. In those days, the mill at Harrison Lake ran around the clock to try to keep up with the amount of wood supplied by people like Peters and his grandfather.

When young Peters was not busy toppling giant cedars with his grand-father he worked independently, cutting cedar bolts that sawmills would purchase and then cut into shakes and shingles. After about a month of work, Peters had enough bolts cut to fill a truck, which he would then take to the local mill to sell. The proceeds from Perry's labour went to his mother. From a young age, Peters learned that everyone had a responsibility to work hard and support their family.

When Peters turned fifteen, he wanted to go work in a logging camp. In the 1960s it was not uncommon for boys as young as Peters, and often younger, to seek work in the woods. Peters, however, refused to lie about his age, and he was sent home after a few days. Undeterred, Peters dropped out of school and kept on going back, year after year, until they kept him on. He became the next in a long line of fallers; both his grandfather and his father had been fallers as well. This was the start of a long career in the woods, one that carried Perry all over the West Coast in search of adventure and bigger trees.

Albert "Ab" Kelly, an oft-described "legend in the bush," began his career in a similar way.[31] Kelly's father, Mike Kelly, was a logger who worked around the Chilliwack Lake area, and Ab realized that if he quit school and followed his father, he could help out with the household finances. Kelly was fifteen years old. He made the decision to leave school and become a logger independent of his parents. In fact, when Kelly went to find work, he went to where his father was logging. He worked for a few days before his father even realized that he was there: "He was sure surprised when he seen me!"[32] Kelly came from a logging family. His father and many of his uncles worked in the camps around Chilliwack Lake and throughout the Fraser Valley. His grandfather, Francis, never worked in the commercial logging industry, but he was a farmer who cleared his own land on the Soowahlie Reserve. Kelly told me of how his grandfather taught him the importance of hard work and avoiding laziness:

> My grandfather taught me ... "Don't be lazy, and don't dog around, because nobody likes anybody like that, you won't ever get another job ... always stay on top of everything." He was hard worker. You know, when I was growing up, I said I want to be a man just like him. Because I watched him work, man, there was no daylight under his boots, he would just give 'er ... he was a farmer ... just down here [in Soowahlie] ... Francis, my Dad's dad ... cause he had cows and horses, and he had to get the hay in. And he was right on top of everything.[33]

The Kelly family found their place in Stó:lō society through hard work and taking care of each other, and Kelly realized this at a young age—a significant portion of every cheque he earned as a young logger went straight to his mother.

Chris and Danny Francis, from Chehalis, both worked long careers as loggers.[34] Danny Francis, known widely for his mechanical prowess, began logging at fourteen in 1948. Chris Francis followed shortly after, at fifteen, in 1952. In fact, all of their brothers took up jobs in the industry. Chris and Danny Francis both spoke of their father, also named Danny, and his career as both a hand logger on the Chehalis reserve and as a commercial logger. Danny Kelly Sr. taught his children about logging at an early age, and they remember him using ancient Stó:lō methods for falling trees well into the twentieth century: "Our Dad, we had no power saw in those days, and our Dad put an undercut ... and he stuffed it with pitch and lit it ... during the day, by four o'clock in the morning ... you heard it go down and hit the ground. The next day, he was out there bucking by hand!"[35] The Francis brothers also remembered their father's success in the commercial logging industry. They remember their father, in the first year of the Great Depression, being one of few people in the Fraser Valley— Indigenous or non-Indigenous—to purchase a brand new 1929 Ford car, which is even more surprising when one considers that the only way to reach Chehalis at that time was by boat on the Harrison River.

The Francises remember their father as being an excellent provider for his family, and he did so by going off to work in the forest. When it became time for Chris and Danny Francis to work, their mother gave them some advice for surviving in the logging industry: "Just keep your hands out of your pockets and get in there and do the job and get out fast, and they'll like you.' So that's what we did."[36] When they became of age, they followed their father's and brother's footsteps.

Grand Chief Ron John of Chawathil started his logging career in 1947, at the age of twelve.[37] John was introduced to logging as a young child by working with his grandfather, using a two-man crosscut saw. He wanted to cut firewood on the reserve to make money, so he figured out an interesting way to work alone with the two-man equipment: "You usually had to have a partner at the other end of the saw, but a lot of times I didn't. But I was kind of inventive. There would be a little ... tree on the other side, I'd hook a rope on there, and I'd pull it, and the tree would come this way, and then it would pull the saw back! That's how I worked it!"[38]

John's father's generation logged locally, primarily in and around their reserve, and almost always within Stó:lō traditional territory. When John became fed up with his residential school education, because he did not like "the way they taught [and] treated First Nations people,"[39] he left to start working. After John left for a brief stint working in Washington, his father passed away, requiring him to "come home and be the man of the house."[40] He was working around his home on the reserve when a truck came by. The driver asked if he wanted to be a logger, and twelve-year-old John said yes. He knew that logging could provide the income he was now expected to provide after the loss of his father. So, like his father and his grandfather before him, John went to work in the woods.

Some Stó:lō loggers started in logging not by leaving a school, residential or otherwise, but by working during the summer months as a way to provide extra income around the house. Grand Chief Clarence "Kat" Pennier, for example, logged for a few summers before graduating from St. Mary's residential school and moving on to pursue his education in Vancouver. Kat Pennier remembers the commonality of bringing family members to work, stating that "My older brother wanted me to be a logger ... it was pretty common for them to bring their younger siblings out ... 'cause they had an in with the company, and if they needed additional workers ... they'd introduce them. Because that's the way it was, you often had different brothers or cousins all working together."[41]

Pennier stayed in school, but he remembers many of his colleagues who "got up and ran away to get to work and provide for themselves and their family."[42] Pennier left the industry shortly after graduating school, partly because his father, a well-known high rigger and faller, died in a tragic logging accident, leaving his mother to be the primary caregiver for the family.

While a tragic accident ended Kat Pennier's career, some Stó:lō loggers stayed in the woods after they finished their education. Stan McKay,[43] from Matsqui, began logging after his sister and brother-in-law insisted that he start pulling his weight by looking for a summer job: "When I was about fifteen, my brother-in-law . . . he said 'I can get you on in the logging camp, want to go logging?' [I said] Sure!"[44] After that first summer, McKay followed his family members to camps in the Fraser Valley, Washington State, and even up to Alaska.

McKay also spoke proudly of his father's work in the logging industry. He described his father's generation's work as "bull work," because of their lack of power saws and equipment. He remembers watching his father and other men from Matsqui use crosscut saws and springboards (elevated planks that allowed the logger to avoid cutting through the massive butt, or bottom of the tree) to topple cedars that were twenty feet wide.[45] He also remembers how Matsqui loggers cut the trees up into bolts, threw them into the river, and how the children then would catch them downstream and bring them to shore, readying them for shipment to the mill. As one of these children, McKay learned the value of trees and hard work at a very young age.

Chester Douglas, a Stó:lō logger from Cheam, also began his career as a fourteen-year-old boy working during his summer and holiday vacations.[46] But his experience with clearing trees began as a small child when he helped his grandfather, Charlie Douglas, clear farm land around Cheam. Douglas remembers his father, Albert Douglas, talking about his days working with steam-powered logging equipment before moving into more modern machinery. After graduating from school, Douglas went to Washington State to log with his brothers and other relatives before returning to the Chilliwack area. He remembers that logging was a mainstay for many Stó:lō men: "Oh yeah, I think that was what everybody . . . that was the main focus growing up, that you were going to go work with somebody that was already in the bush."[47]

While these men come from varied backgrounds and from different Stó:lō communities, they all expressed a certain pride that came from following in familial footsteps and working in the logging industry. For many of them, working with wood started at a very young age and carried into an early career in logging camps. Each of these men's stories reflects the complex dynamic that had developed over several generations of Stó:lō men working in the forest. And while this type of forestry work may not resonate with some notions of Stó:lō spirituality and tradition, there was something inherently traditional about the decisions these men made to work as loggers. Following in the footsteps of their fathers and grandfathers provided them with a way to work in an industry that provided for their families, and to work within a long tradition of Stó:lō men who had an association with the forest. They saw themselves as continuing a work ethic and an obligation to care for family that stretched back countless generations. Their motivation for telling these stories was how they articulated the traditionality of logging. For these men, no clear distinctions existed between Stó:lō "tradition" and working in the woods as twentieth-century loggers.

Highballers and Hard Work

Making it in the logging industry was not an easy task, regardless of any familial connections one might have had. Loggers were required to work hard, fast, and safely in an environment that often made it difficult to do so. For Stó:lō loggers, working hard and earning a reputation in the industry as a highballer provided a way for them to not only ascend the logging industry hierarchy, but also for them to stand toe-to-toe with white loggers. Stó:lō logger Henry "Hank" Pennier, Kat Pennier's uncle, noted in his 1972 memoirs that logging was "a man's work and it is risky . . . an Indian can feel as good as the next guy and from what I see in a lot of whites these days, maybe even better."[48] In a society that regarded Indigenous people as both socially and economically subpar, in need of assimilation, and as secondary citizens, logging provided an important way for Stó:lō men to transcend stereotypes and succeed, not only financially and socially, but culturally. Economic gain provides only a partial explanation for why many Stó:lō men became successful in the logging industry. Sometimes, companies would pay based on how many logs you processed, but often workers were paid a flat wage regardless of race, hard work, and number of trees cut. Stó:lō men told stories of hard work and success, but not always to highlight financial security. They often spoke of hard work and success as elements that set Stó:lō loggers apart from non-Indigenous loggers. Through hard work, Stó:lō loggers became Stó:lō men.

Many of the Stó:lō loggers I interviewed highlighted the importance of working hard to build a reputation, regardless of the job they did in the industry. Danny Francis told me that "the faster you moved, the better they liked you . . . If you didn't run, you didn't stay there."[49] Chris Francis explained that the reason

Stó:lō men were so well regarded in the industry was "because we used to run and do the job and get out of the way."[50] Ab Kelly built a reputation on hard work, and he was often called in to help companies increase their productivity. Herman Bob, a Stó:lō hook tender, was having a hard time meeting his bosses' quotas at a logging camp in the Fraser Valley. When the boss asked him why, Bob said it was because of the crew. Ab recounted the story:

> [The boss said,] "I'm not doing too good with ya Herm, I'm only getting two loads a day and I'm getting a thousand dollars a load, and that's not very good because I got to pay my crew eh." And [Herm] says, "You're not gonna get 'em [the logs] with these guys. You get my slinger from Chilliwack, Ab Kelly . . . get 'em up here, and we'll show 'em how to log." He went into the lunchroom and all his brothers were there. . . . [Herm said,] "Anyone of you know Ab Kelly?" [They said,] "Oh yeah, Chilliwack Ab? Yeah he's a logger all right." . . . So [Herm] phoned his wife, said, "Tell Ab to come up." The plane was waiting for me . . . I got up there and I started pulling rigging. We upped it from two loads to eleven and thirteen![51]

Chester Douglas remembers how important it was for a young logger to form a good reputation as a hard worker in the industry: "You would go to the marshalling area and . . . stand in what they called a bullpen. If one of the crews needed a chokerman . . . they'd go and they would size you up out there. I guess like a workhorse! Then . . . they'd send you out. And if you were any good, you stayed."[52]

For Perry Peters, being a good logger meant providing your employer with an honest day's work: "You wanted to put in a good day's work . . . you always wanted to put down enough timber to pay for your wages . . . didn't want to be known as a slacker . . . doing a good job was always a priority."[53] Peters's commitment to hard work resulted in a quick rise up the company pay grade, and in the logging camp hierarchy.[54] Similarly, Ron John explained that hard work and doing a good job allowed him to quickly move past chokerman, in only a few days on the job: "A few jobs I had . . . they always advanced me up the ladder so soon because they could see how experienced and fast I was. See, I wasn't a slow worker, I was what you call a highballer . . . a lot of people didn't even get past chokerman."[55]

Working hard and earning a reputation was an important aspect of their work experience for any logger, Stó:lō or not, but for Indigenous loggers, hard work and skill was a way to rise above stereotypes and claim an identity that was not just about being a logger, but being an Indigenous logger. Stan McKay explained that most logging camps were made up of loggers from various backgrounds and ethnicities. When asked about Indigenous people's place in the logging camp, he told me that, "Guys from all over . . . Natives, non-Natives, a mixture . . . most of the time the guys used to tell us, that they always got the First Nations because we had good balance . . . they'd rather have a First Nation guy."[56] Ab Kelly also explained that he tried to form an "all-Native" logging crew to show the bosses the differences between Indigenous and non-Indigenous loggers.[57] Both Kelly and McKay identified hard work and ability as key attributes of a Stó:lō logger's identity, and pride.

While it was important for Stó:lō loggers to forge distinct identities within the industry, this did not lead to racial divisions within the logging crews. One might expect that such competitive attitudes in a workplace would result in animosity, especially considering that these men often lived, slept, ate, and worked closely for long stretches of time in isolated logging camps. However, that is not how Stó:lō loggers remember things. When asked about camp life, these men explained that there were few problems that resulted from living in racially mixed camps. Chris and Danny Francis remember that there were "no fights" between loggers that were based on race.[58] For Ab Kelly and Kat Pennier, the dangerous nature of logging made it crucial that everyone got along because they had to be able to trust that other people would look out for them in dangerous situations:

> Kat Pennier: It was mixed . . . when I was with my brother in the gypo[59] outfit it was mostly Indians from a couple of our communities . . . Well I didn't face any discrimination myself, but I guess people had to get along because they had to look after each other up there, you know, when you were in the camps and you were doing your various jobs, you had to make sure that safety was paramount, because in those days logging was a dangerous job.[60]

> Ab Kelly: Everybody got along. They didn't tolerate it if there was anybody like that. Because we had to get along, you know. If we worked with a guy, we had to look after him . . . protect them with your life. That was my job, eh?[61]

A sense of camaraderie developed between loggers that allowed the social and racial elements of life outside of the logging camp to disappear. For Stó:lō loggers, it was an opportunity to develop unique identities within a structure that cared little if you were Indigenous or not, as long as you could do your job efficiently and safely. This facilitated the formation of identities that could be both Indigenous and occupational. Stó:lō men ascended logging company hierarchies not because they were Indigenous or in spite of their Indigenous identities, but because they valued hard work as something inherently important about being a Stó:lō logger.

Reflections on Life in the Woods

In this chapter, I have suggested that Stó:lō loggers negotiated their identities by defining logging as something that was traditional and therefore consistent with being Indigenous. I have argued that these men felt that by taking up the occupations of their ancestors, working hard, and using the forest to provide for their families, they were not necessarily working in ways that were in opposition with Stó:lō tradition and spirituality. Further, working in an industry where Indigenous men were often viewed as highly skilled allowed them to form an occupational identity that broke down social stereotypes. In making this argument, I am breaking away from earlier historical interpretations that tried to fit contemporary Stó:lō people into categories based on an assumed, and historically fictional, unified Indigenous traditional and spiritual identity. Focusing on tradition with too tight a lens potentially creates a framework that marginalizes people who do not fit into these rigid categories. To be clear, I am not arguing that clear-cut logging is a traditional Stó:lō activity. Using trees to increase societal power and provide for families, however, is very much a part of both ancient and modern Stó:lō people's identities. Moreover, within Stó:lō society people consider ancestors' decisions to have been informed and therefore worthy of contemplation and replication. The fact that the loggers I interviewed had fathers, grandfathers, and great-grandfathers who logged helped them understand logging as an acceptable traditional activity that had been endorsed by their ancestors.

One does not need to look far to discover how materially and socially important trees are to Stó:lō culture and identity. Earlier in this chapter I mentioned Xepa:y, the Stó:lō man who was turned into a cedar tree when he died so that he could continue to give to the Stó:lō people. Stó:lō people use trees for housing, transportation, clothing, baskets, ropes, tools, and weapons, and in a variety of spiritual ways.[62] Some of these uses do not require cutting down a tree. Many of them do. Turning trees into social power is something traditionally Stó:lō. Ethnographer Homer Barnett, in his efforts to document the pre-contact practices of several Coast Salish communities, noted that "Everybody knew something of woodworking ... it required considerable training and some men found it convenient and profitable to devote more than a common amount of time to it. Just as a good hunter could achieve prominence and material gain by supplying meat for feasts (either his own or those of others), so the expert woodworker could expect to reap social and material rewards from the product of his industry."[63] Barnett also pointed out that most of the goods produced and valued by Indigenous people in pre-contact periods "consisted of such directly utilizable items as boards, canoes, household utensils, weapons, [and] wearing apparel."[64] Stó:lō people have been using and profiting from trees within their own society prior to, and independently of, wage labour in commercial logging.

Obviously, the clear-cut method of modern commercial logging cannot directly be compared with the ways that Stó:lō loggers processed and consumed wood before the commercial logging industry. We also have to remember that the modern forestry crises developed out of the mechanical ability to process trees in a largely unsustainable way. For many modern Stó:lō loggers, the destruction of forests was not something that they considered during their logging careers. Chester Douglas said that taking too many trees "was never a concern. It was just a general attitude that the resource was there and it would never go away."[65] Douglas believed that it was international demand, not domestic and local consumption, that provided the market for overconsumption.[66] Chris Francis stated that he "never thought of it" and that "there is still enough timber out there . . . and they are replanting every summer."[67] For Perry Peters, it was not the act of logging, it was the modern method that was problematic: "I don't like clear cuts. It's better to take a patch and leave the rest . . . Those big trees will always come back again . . . Mother Nature, she knows what she is doing."[68] Similarly, Ron John believes that it was a lack of planning that resulted in overconsumption and advocates the tactic of cutting in logging strips rather than clear-cutting.[69]

These loggers' reflections show that during their careers it was unfathomable that the forestry industry would reach a point where it was unsustainable. We need to remember that it has not been that long since loggers used axes, saws, and muscle to extract timber from the forest. And, while it may have been obvious to some, it is not hard to imagine that a logger in the mid-twentieth century, deep in an isolated forest surrounded by trees, would have a difficult time believing the industry would become unsustainable. Much as it is important to realize that applying an assumed pre-contact Indigenous traditional identity to modern Stó:lō people is problematic, we need to imagine a mid-twentieth-century logger's perspective without our current knowledge of the degradation caused by commercial logging. If not, we risk not seeing the forest for the trees.

The stories these Stó:lō loggers told me complicate the non-Indigenous historical narratives surrounding forest use, logging, and Indigenous identity. Indeed, these stories are powerful. The narrative I have formed here is a summary and blending of these men's histories. In my research on Coast Salish loggers, governmental records and correspondence confirm the importance of logging to the Stó:lō. Yet, these men's stories add much nuance and provide so much more than proof of participation in an industry. Working as a logger served an important function for these men. To them, it is much more than a job and a paycheque. It is part of their identity.

One story, told to me by Stan McKay, has sinews that weave a common thread between what many of these Stó:lō men told me. Cutting down trees, for them, was a way of life and a way to provide their families with better lives. Rather than explain what I think Stan McKay's message was, from my perspective as an outsider, I will give him the final word:

> It is a sacred wood, cedar, to the First Nations people. They used it ...
> our ancestors used the bark, the wood, they built canoes, they made
> bows, they made bowls . . . lots of carvers made big bowls. They
> used cedars. Any of our carvings are in cedar, usually red or yellow
> ... It gave us life. And I work in cedar every day, and I think that's
> why I feel good too. At the age I am, I hear everybody complaining
> down there. They don't understand that we are all connected to the
> world. Whatever is around us, we are connected to, wherever we are.
> Whether we are breathing the same air, drinking the same water,
> or whether we are working with the same sacred wood. You know,
> I feel that the wood I work with is sacred because it has given me
> the life that I have been looking for, in order to raise my family. If it
> wasn't for the cedar, I wouldn't have a job, I wouldn't have brought
> up my children, watch my children bring up their children. Some
> of my kids worked down there, you know. Now we are into the
> great-grandchildren, and they are just little, but it's up to them to
> understand the way we talk about cedar. Understand that it was
> our lifeline at one time.[70]

Notes

1   Albert Kelly, interview by Colin Osmond, Soowahlie, BC, 2 June 2015. Running, in the logging industry, is a reference to loggers who work as hard and as fast as they can to get as many logs in as possible in a day's work.

2   Chimamanda Ngozi Adichie, "The Danger of a Single Story," filmed July 2009, *TED Global*.

3   Thomas King, *The Truth About Stories: A Native Narrative* (Toronto: House of Anansi Press, 2003), 9–10.

4   In this article, I use several terms to reference Indigenous people. Where appropriate, I use the specific name of a cultural or geographical group (for example, Stó:lō, Matsqui, Chehalis, etc.).

5   The interviews conducted for this paper were done as part of the Stó:lō Ethnohistory Field School, 2015.

6   William Cronon, "A Place for Stories: Nature, History, and Narrative," *The Journal of American History* 78, no. 4 (1992): 1365.

7   John S. Lutz, *Makúk: A New History of Aboriginal-White Relations* (Vancouver: UBC Press, 2008), 34.

8   Ibid., 31.

9   Robert E. Walls, "The Making of the American Logger: Traditional Culture and Public Imagery in the Realm of the Bunyanesque" (PhD diss., Indiana University, 1997), 130; Richard White, *The Middle Ground: Indians, Empires, and Republics in the Great Lakes Region, 1650–1815* (Cambridge: Cambridge University Press, 1991).

10   Ibid., 131.

11   Ibid.

12   Rolf Knight, *Indians at Work: An Informal History of Native Indian Labour in British Columbia, 1858–1930* (Vancouver: New Star, 1972), 11–12.

13   Robin Fisher, *Contact and Conflict: Indian-European Relations in British Columbia, 1774–1890* (Vancouver: UBC Press, 1977), 210.

14   Lutz, *Makúk*, 23.

15   Ibid., 185.

16   Ibid., 215.

17   Charles R. Menzies and Caroline F. Butler, "Working in the Woods: Tsimshian Resource Workers and the Forest Industry of British Columbia," *American Indian Quarterly* 25, no. 3 (2001): 410.

18   Andrew Parnaby, "'The best men that ever worked the lumber': Aboriginal Longshoremen on Burrard Inlet, BC, 1863–1939," *The Canadian Historical Review* 87, no. 1 (2006): 53.

19   Amy O'Neill, "Identity, Culture and the Forest: The Stó:lō" (MA thesis, University of British Columbia, 1999).

20   Clifford Geertz, "Thick Description: Toward an Interpretive Theory of Culture," in *The Interpretation of Culture: Selected Essays* (New York: Basic Books, 1973), 18.

21   Jack Mussel, interview by Amy O'Neill, qtd. in O'Neill, "Identity, Culture and the Forest," 36.

22   In his book on Stó:lō social structures and identity, *The Power of Place, The Problem of Time: Aboriginal Identity and Historical Consciousness in the Cauldron of Colonialism* (Toronto, University of Toronto Press, 2010), 27–28, Keith Carlson draws upon Marshall Sahlins's complication of historical "event" and "structure" to explain that "historical events can become ethnographically intelligible through the study of change rather than stasis. Instead of looking for continuity in change [Sahlins] challenges us to seek change in continuity."

23   Albert "Sonny" McHalsie, "We Have to Take Care of Everything that Belongs to Us," in *Be of Good Mind: Essays on the Coast Salish*, ed. Bruce Miller (Vancouver: UBC Press, 2007), 104.

24 O'Neill, "Identity, Culture and the Forest," 111.

25 Kelly, interview.

26 What is presented here is my understanding of the histories these men presented to me. As much as possible, I tried to honour the integrity of their own narrative frameworks. My role as a listener was to weave together the common threads of these stories. A chapter such as this definitely has methodological shortcomings. I rely on what these men told me to form my analysis. Therefore, any critique of what I argue can be seen as a direct critique of the men who told me these stories. Regardless, my goal in writing this essay is less about historical fact checking and rigorous archival work (although both remain important to the crafting of this chapter). I am much more interested in listening to what logging meant to these men's lives, something which would be hard (if not impossible) to derive from other sources. In this respect, these men are the experts, and it is not my place to analyze their own interpretations of their individual identities.

27 I do not mean to suggest that there were only Indigenous and white loggers in the industry. Rather, I use the term "white" to highlight the differences between Indigenous and settler societies, which were the basis of racist and assimilative policies towards Indigenous people. Interesting analysis could be done on the role of race within the logging camp in a much broader context, but for the purposes of this article I chose to simplify the racial diversity of the logging industry to highlight Indigenous loggers.

28 Several of the loggers interviewed for this chapter attended residential schools and found that working in a logging camp provided them with an alternative that allowed them to escape the oppressive nature of the schools, while also providing much-needed income for their families. I have also listened to similar narratives while conducting ethnohistorical research with Tla'amin loggers (on the Sunshine Coast of British Columbia, several miles north of Powell River), which are included in my master's thesis, "Giant Trees, Iron Men: Masculinity and Colonialism in Coast Salish Loggers' Identity" (MA thesis, University of Saskatchewan, 2016).

29 For a more detailed description of how this logging system worked, see Henry Pennier's *Call me Hank: A Stó:lō Man's Reflections on Logging, Living, and Growing Old*, eds. Keith Carlson and Kristina Fagan (Toronto: University of Toronto Press, 2006), 90–7.

30 Paris "Perry" Casmir Peters started his career in commercial logging in 1957. Amazingly, he still works falling trees at the time of the writing of this paper. Paris Peters, interview by Colin Osmond, Seabird Island, BC, 2 June 2015.

31 Albert "Ab" Kelly logged from 1956 until 1991.

32 Kelly, interview.

33 Ibid.

34 Chris Francis logged from 1952 until 2002, and Danny logged from 1948 to 1997.

35 Chris Francis and Danny Francis, interview by Colin Osmond, Chehalis, BC, 22 May 2015.

36 Ibid.

37 Ron John began his logging career in 1947 and retired in 2002.

38 Ron John and Patricia John, interview by Keith Carlson, Michelle Brandsma, and Colin Osmond, Chawathil, BC, 21 May 2015.

39 Ibid.

40 Ibid.

41 Clarence Pennier, interview by Colin Osmond, Sardis, BC, 20 May 2015.

42 Pennier, interview.

43 Stan McKay began his career while still attending high school in Chilliwack (roughly the late 1960s), and he still works in the cedar mill near Matsqui.

44 Stan McKay, interview by Noah Miller and Colin Osmond, Matsqui, BC, 19 May 2015.

45 Ibid.

46 Chester Douglas began working as a logger in 1964, and changed occupations in 1976. Although he no longer worked in the industry, Douglas still cut down trees to create agricultural space around Cheam, and he also cut cedar trees to make dugout canoes. Sadly, Chester Douglas passed away shortly after I heard his stories. I would like to acknowledge him for graciously inviting me into his home and taking valuable time to help me research this paper. He also helped several other field school students with their projects (he was especially influential in the researching of Chris Marsh's "Totem Tigers and Salish Sluggers," which also appears in this collection).

47 Chester Douglas, interview by Davis Rogers and Colin Osmond, Cheam, BC, 22 May 2015.

48 Pennier, *Call Me Hank*, 58–9.

49 Chris and Danny Francis, interview.

50 Ibid.

51 Kelly, interview.

52 Douglas, interview.

53 Peters, interview.

54 Ibid.

55 Ron and Patricia John, interview.

56 McKay, interview.

57 Kelly, interview.

58 Chris and Danny Francis, interview.

59 The term "gypo" refers to a small logging outfit, as opposed to a large corporation. Gypo outfits were usually short-term contract logging jobs.

60 Pennier, interview.

61 Kelly, interview.

62 For a detailed discussion of how Coast Salish people used cedar trees, see: Hilary Stewart, *Cedar: Tree of Life to the Northwest Coast Indians* (Vancouver: Douglas and McIntyre, 1984).

63 Homer Barnett, *The Coast Salish Indians of British Columbia* (Eugene: University of Oregon, 1955), 107.

64 Ibid.

65 Douglas, interview.

66 Ibid.

67 Chris and Danny Francis, interview.

68 Peters, interview.

69 Ron and Patricia John, interview.

70 McKay, interview.

10

"They're Always Looking for the Bad Stuff": Rediscovering the Stories of Coqualeetza Indian Hospital with Fresh Eyes and Ears

NOAH E. MILLER

Since the Truth and Reconciliation Commission characterized residential schools as a central element in the Canadian government's attempt to extinguish Indigenous peoples "as distinct legal, social, cultural, religious, and racial entities," scholars have been working with renewed purpose to locate the provision of health care in relation to this legacy of "cultural genocide."[1] Focusing on racially segregated Indian Hospitals, the most recent scholarship argues that this subject matter is often represented within "powerful fictions" about the "progressive march towards improved health care for Canadians and the seemingly intractable ill-health in Aboriginal communities."[2] Historian Maureen K. Lux further suggests that the separation of these two narratives obscures other meanings of Indian Hospitals, in particular how the "putatively colonized" may have used Western medical institutions "in ways and for reasons never intended by the colonizer."[3] Similarly, the words of Yakweawioose First Nations Chief Frank Malloway challenge the way in which historians have tended to portray these hospitals. Malloway says "people are always looking for the bad stuff" when conducting their research, and adds that many have approached him with a particular interest in "the sensational."[4] Together, the remarks of Lux and Malloway challenge scholars to create more space for nuance.[5] Indeed, an ethnohistorical examination of the hospital at Coqualeetza in Sardis, British Columbia, indicates that it was the site of a diverse range of social experiences and cultural interactions from its establishment as a "center for native hospitalization" until the time when newspapers reported "modern drug usage and detection techniques ... [had] brought [tuberculosis] under control."[6] This paper takes the above-noted concerns with prevailing narratives seriously and examines how existing scholarship can provide the basis for portraying a refined history of Canada's Indian Hospitals at a theoretical level. Furthermore, it suggests that by drawing from local discourse, contained in recently digitized newspaper archives and oral history interviews, we are able to assemble a more diverse image of the Coqualeetza hospital's past.

Frank Malloway. Photo by Sonny McHalsie.

Scholarship pertaining to health care among First Nations has generally tended to focus on the epidemiology of disease or the consequences of colonization on Indigenous well-being. Initially, the principal challenge facing historians studying this history in twentieth-century Canada was to understand the relationship between Indigenous people and colonial settler society. Corinne Hodgson's groundbreaking article, for instance, posits that the Canadian government and Indigenous people interpreted the meaning and purpose of "Indian Hospitals" in dichotomous ways. Within this framework, the government viewed the hospitals as "a humanitarian movement conducted in the manner typical of the time (i.e. long-term institutionalization)."[7] By contrast, Native Canadians are portrayed as viewing treatment as "tardy, motivated by white society's own (i.e. self-protective) interests, and carried out in a manner threatening to the continuity of native families and communities."[8] Acknowledging that "[not all] native groups would necessarily view these developments in the same way," Hodgson ultimately concludes that Canada's Indian Hospitals were an instrument of "medical paternalism."[9]

Hodgson's work, however, is based principally on a close reading of primary sources left behind by government agents and Western medical officials. In other words, it does not directly engage with Indigenous peoples' lived experiences or historical consciousness. It does, however, leave the door open to deeper examinations of Indigenous views by clarifying that "further studies are needed to probe more deeply the full range of cultural and social meanings of these different perspectives, as well as their ramifications upon subsequent behaviour."[10]

Works that emphasize cultural encounters as "dialogue" provide a model for filling this gap. Historian John S. Lutz, for example, delineates how "the interactive aspect of speech" can be applied to "exchange more generally."[11] Inspired by scholars such as Michael Harkin, Lutz demonstrates that "dialogue is a process of negotiation of meanings, presentation, and representation of self and other" and, as Harkin himself writes, its currency includes "speech acts, symbolic actions, material exchange, violence, marriage, imitation, legislation," with "each utterance transform[ing] the dialogue, and to a greater or lesser degree, the lifeworlds of the interlocutors."[12]

Despite a growing emphasis on interaction, historical scholarship has generally continued to focus on the meaning of the colonial government's actions in its accounts of Canada's Indian Hospitals. For example, an article by Maureen K. Lux places the creation of Indian Hospitals within the context of "long-standing . . . policy [that] aimed to isolate Aboriginal people on re- serves and in residential schools" and access to medical care that was "limited by government parsimony and community prejudice."[13] While Lux clearly illustrates that these people were regarded by white society as "a menace to their neighbours and a danger to the nation," Indigenous perspectives themselves are noticeably underrepresented.[14] Using the Charles Camsell Indian Hospital in Edmonton as a case study, Lux depicts a one-sided power relationship by suggesting that Indian Hospitals are best understood as "a very public dem- onstration of the state's commitment to define and promote a 'national health' by isolating and institutionalizing Aboriginal people."[15]

Elsewhere, scholarship has sought to balance the perspectives found in government-produced written records with the voices of Indigenous people themselves. Mary-Ellen Kelm's book *Colonizing Bodies*, for example, presents a refined view of power dynamics in which "Aboriginal bodies were not simply buffeted by the forces of colonization and resistance but [rather] emerged from the interstitial spaces of the body politic of twentieth century British Columbia, moulded by patterns of subsistence, education, belief, and healing that were, at once, centuries old and rapidly changing."[16]

Beyond this, Kelm's book supplements documentary evidence with oral sources and the archaeological record. Centring a macro-scale study of Indigenous bodies, Kelm argues that "Euro-Canadian medicine . . . served [the] colonial agenda."[17] However, especially within her discussion of Indian Health Services (IHS) in British Columbia, Kelm's oral sources do not always appear to contribute towards, or check, the overarching argument that IHS "supported the Indian policy of the Canadian government."[18] Testimony drawn from Frank Malloway, for example, is used in one chapter to elaborate on the characteristics of a "typical patient."[19] In a review article, Keith Carlson,

Melinda Marie Jetté, and Kenichi Matsui observe that this approach yields "a penetrating analysis," but go on to suggest that—even still—the Indigenous · perspectives Kelm presents sometimes appear "overly simplistic in light of recent anthropological literature."[20]

The ethnographic technique championed by Clifford Geertz, however, offers historians a way to build on Kelm's efforts. In his essay "Thick Description: Toward an Interpretive Theory of Culture," Geertz suggests scholars turn their attention to "the flow of behaviour," where he argues "cultural forms find articulation."[21] Within this framework he observes that one ought to approach "broader interpretations and more abstract analyses from the direction of the exceedingly extended acquaintances with extremely small matters."[22] Beyond examining the "microscopic," Geertz suggests that our aim should be to interpret behaviours within "webs of significance," located, in part, through selecting, and establishing a rapport with, informants.[23] Soucy corroborates the value of this approach by arguing that "the valuing of a particular kind of knowledge . . . ignores the social context and dynamics from which . . . explanations emerge."[24] In line with this perspective, this paper has sought to include, and balance, the voices of First Nations people against other sources.

The above-noted Geertzian methodology is particularly suited to the task given the availability of new materials. The recent digitization of the local *Chilliwack Progress* newspaper, when combined with the wealth of primary source material housed at the Stó:lō Nation archives in Chilliwack, British Columbia, sketches an intersectional image of hospital life at Coqualeetza that both extends and challenges Hodgson's, Kelm's, and Lux's generalizations about the nature of the provision of Indigenous health care.[25]

Such an approach has at least one distinct advantage. Raymond DeMallie's work on the Lak'ota, for instance, demonstrates how newspapers and promotional material can engrain any study with bias. DeMallie observes that "most of the contemporary written materials present outsiders' viewpoints" because "the authors of these documents . . . represented a cultural tradition [that was] very different" from that of the Indigenous people they describe.[26] While he argues that these observers can be "sympathetic" to Indigenous views, he also notes that "underlying the writings of Euro-Americans was the assumption that Indian culture must inevitably pass away before the march of civilization."[27] Regna Darnell points out that even the most sceptical anthropologists and historians admit that oral traditions are useful to confirm and expand on the information available in archival records.[28] Darnell, moreover, suggests that oral testimony can "transcend the absence of conventional written documents representing 'the other side of the story.'"[29] Similarly, as the research of Alice M. Hoffman and Howard S. Hoffman indicates, taken on their own, "eyewitness accounts are subject to considerable distortion by factors that occur after the events they describe."[30] However, the Hoffmans' experiment also reveals that archival documentation can be used to substantiate or "flesh out" oral testimony. The outcome of such a "hybrid" approach is described by commentator Brent Slife as having the potential to find "remarkable intersubjective agreement ... both across time (in the sense of reliability) and across sources (in the sense of validity)."[31]

However, this approach is not without its challenges. As D. Soyini Madison notes, "observations and analysis often accompany the oral history interview to signify its embedded implications as well as the complexities of its surface (or obvious) meanings."[32] This is problematic in that it can ironically silence the very voice the ethnohistorian is trying to incorporate. To expand on this Madison explains, "the authoritative voice and heavy hand of the researcher overshadows the voice and presence of the narrator; it 'upstages' the narrative thereby leaving the narrator's actual words as only whispers against the booming volume of the researcher's interpretation."[33] Despite this, Madison insists that this approach to analysis can nevertheless deepen one's engagement with narrative text as well as "unravel context and connections."[34]

Laurie Meijer Drees's recent book, *Healing Histories*, provides historians with one model of implementing this approach within the specific context of Indian Health Services. By focusing on individuals instead of systems, she "juxtaposes stories and perspectives."[35] The results are different than the image of the institutions generated by Lux's, Kelm's, and Hodgson's earlier emphases on the colonial nature of the relationship between Indigenous communities and the government. For example, tying together accounts from the Indian Hospital in Nanaimo and from the Charles Camsell Hospital in Edmonton, Drees portrays how, from the perspective of some discharged patients, "leaving ... friends behind was particularly difficult," while for others their stay in the Indian Hospital was "both physically and emotionally hurtful."[36] She outlines how engagement in occupational therapy programming could be advantageous in that it allowed patients who were otherwise secluded "to see one another on a regular basis."[37] Moreover, she provides evidence that "some patients dared to defy hospital rules and routines to sidestep visiting restrictions."[38] According to Drees, "the patient's condition and degree of separation from family and community," as well as "the location, size, structure, and staffing of the hospital," are all factors that need to be considered when making claims regarding meaning of these places.[39] Lastly, Drees draws attention to the fact that "Aboriginal peoples in western Canada participated actively in Western medicine as health care workers, caregivers, and support staff" and that their experiences could encompass everything from "racism and underappreciation" to recognition and praise for their abilities as "capable health care workers."[40] In short, Drees's work suggests to us that experiences "varied tremendously."[41]

The sheer relative size and historical significance of the Coqualeetza Indian Hospital makes it a worthy next topic of investigation within this historiographical vein. When the Indian Affairs branch of the Department of Mines and Resources converted the old Coqualeetza Institute into a sanitarium "for Indian patients all over the province" in 1941, it was "more than three times the size of the new 52-bed Chilliwack hospital."[42] As Reverend Scott wrote, "the new wing is beautifully furnished and well-equipped. It affords the advantages for all patients who come in for treatment."[43] Shortly thereafter, patients began pouring in from around the province. Dr. W.S. Barclay, medical superintendent at Coqualeetza, remembers that "many applications for treatment from Indian patients all over the province were awaiting attention and as we built up our staff, more wards were opened and more patients were brought into the hospital so that by the end of 1941 we [had] about one hundred in our care."[44] Dr. Barclay would later tell the *Chilliwack Progress* that he considered the opening of the hospital at Sardis "a definitive step" in the fight against tuberculosis.[45]

That this so-called "definitive step" receives little direct attention in existing scholarship is perplexing. Prior to becoming a nonsectarian hospital, Coqualeetza was "long noted as a center of Indian education in the province."[46] According to a speech delivered by staff member Dr. J.D. Galbraith in 1943, after it was converted the hospital constituted 170 of Canada's 800 beds dedicated to fighting tuberculosis among Natives.[47] Aside from housing a large proportion of Canada's Indigenous population who were afflicted with the disease, Coqualeetza was seen as on the cutting edge of modern medical treatment. In 1946 the *Chilliwack Progress* reported that the hospital was "the first complete tuberculosis unit of its kind ... in Canada."[48] This was largely tied to its occupational programming, which according to the *Chilliwack Progress*, did "much to improve the attitude of patients and to help their adjustment to normal living."[49]

However, it was not just that Coqualeetza innovated these new programs, but rather that it established a precedent that was then adopted by similar institutions, that makes it significant. A newspaper article written in 1948 indicates that, "Coqualeetza was the 'parent hospital' for the school system carried out in six other Indian hospitals in western Canada."[50] The idea that Coqualeetza set the bar for these other institutions of the same type is further corroborated by *Coqualeetza Story*, a historical pamphlet that acknowledges that while the hospitals later established at Miller Bay and Nanaimo operated as "distinct units ... Coqualeetza remained the headquarters for all tuberculosis records and for the general direction of the overall program for the province."[51] Moreover, *Coqualeetza Story* notes that the sanitarium was the "center of operation" for tuberculosis fieldwork within a "zone which extend[ed] from Williams Lake to the Southern Border and from the West Coast to the Eastern Border of BC."[52]

By 1957 Coqualeetza was also something of a gold standard in medical care more generally in that it was "the only fully accredited hospital in the Fraser Valley."[53] According to the *Canadian Hospital Administration Journal*, when Coqualeetza won accreditation for the sixth straight year in 1963, "less than twenty-five per cent of Canada's 1,243 hospitals enjoy[ed] full accreditation."[54] Coqualeetza was furthermore a gathering place for health workshops in the Pacific region.[55] If the provision of medical services to Native people indeed serves to "justify, legitimate, and sustain Canada's internal colonial relations with the First Nations," the nature of their experiences at this hospital are clearly relevant.[56]

While these descriptions of the hospital are useful in setting context, they fall short in addressing the significance of the hospital to the people who received treatment or worked there. In a letter to *Indian Time* in 1953, Mrs. Rose Abbot, a patient at Coqualeetza, praises the "beautiful" grounds for "bringing encouragement and hope."[57] She continues her correspondence by applauding the staff for their "help and understanding" and even goes as far as to characterize them all as "one big family."[58] Comments contained in the hospital's official newsletter suggest that this feeling was reciprocated by at least some of the staff. In the January 1959 issue of the *Coqualeetza Courier*, Dr. A.G. MacKinnon addresses the patients as "dear friends" and expresses his appreciation for having learned about their "way of looking at things."[59]

In retrospect, in his conversations with me, Frank Malloway remembered Coqualeetza as a "good place for all [his] people" in that it "cured a lot of [them]" and "kept them from dying."[60] At the same time, Malloway associates certain aspects of his memory of the hospital with mundanity. For example, he describes various aspects of his ten-year tenure as a nursing orderly: cleaning, prepping, feeding the patients, collecting bedpans and sputum boxes, and making beds.[61] In addition to the beneficial aspects of the hospital and its monotonous daily routine, Malloway further describes that the hospital could, at times, be depressing as it was the place he learned how to prepare bodies for the morgue "because there were so many deaths."[62] Others associate the hospital with even worse experiences. One Stó:lō woman, for instance, claims that she was sexually abused by one of the other female patients and further-more describes there being "not much difference" between residential schools and hospital life when she was at Coqualeetza in the late 1940s.[63] One can conclude, therefore, that even upon initial inspection, the institution occupies a wide gamut of meanings within local discourse.

As such, Coqualeetza may be regarded as a site of contested meanings. This can be more clearly illustrated in how patients understood the behaviour of medical staff. In 1985 Chief P.D. Peters, for example, described how doctors, in his experience, "didn't care" and were involved merely to "line their pockets."[64] By contrast, others, like Frank Malloway, remember a doctor who "used to feel really bad and get depressed when he lost a patient."[65] Differing interpretations can also be found in the way children were handled when a fire "gutted 60 percent of Coqualeetza hospital" in November 1948. Reporters crafted headlines like "Nurses Carry Dozen Babies to Safety in the Night."[66] However, Bev Julian remembers this event somewhat differently. She describes how those standing outside "could see—the volunteers were just tossing the babies . . . down the line and people were catching them and putting them in the vehicles to bring them to their safety."[67]

The point here is not to present a rosy revisionist interpretation of Indian Health Services and its connection to a colonial agenda. Indeed, if researchers search out sources that verify Hodgson's, Kelm's, and Lux's theses about the negative consequences upon Indigenous culture within the specific context of Coqualeetza, they will find plenty. For instance, the *Chilliwack Progress* contains numerous examples of paternalistic attitudes among the staff. One article discusses the "philosophical outlook of the Indian" and the need for them to be "educated in western medicine."[68] Outlining the work done by the hospital in 1943, W.S. Barclay characterizes the "opening of the Hospital at Sardis" as a "definite step forward" in the "breaking down of the prejudice of the Indian towards the hospitals."[69] Evidence exists that suggests these attitudes persisted well into the 1950s. For example, in the July 1953 issue of the *Coqualeetza Courier*, Barclay writes about "rights and privileges" in the rhetoric of medical paternalism identified by Hodgson. He opines that "the government did not have to provide free hospital care for people with TB, but as they are anxious to help them, good hospitals have been built and all necessary forms of treatment provided."[70]

Beyond the staff themselves, the body of evidence generated from patient testimony seems to corroborate a narrative centred upon the ill effects of a polarized hospital. Some patients recall it as being firmly divided along racial lines. Theresa Pierre, for example, says that when she was at Coqualeetza "all the nurses and doctors were white people" and "the ones that did the cleaning were the Native people."[71] In her memoir, Bev Sellars recalls being laughed at by two nurses for repeatedly picking out blue clothing. She says, "I did not want them thinking I was so dumb that I didn't know any other colours. . . . I got embarrassed and blushed with shame."[72] Sellars adds that "blushing is a curse that has plagued [her her] entire life but the first time [she] remember[s] experiencing it was at Sardis."[73] Moreover, Stan McKay remembers how the use of a newly developed drug adversely "affected [his] growth."[74]

However, even a preliminary exploration of the larger body of evidence is suggestive of a more complex power dynamic within the hospital. In 1951, Chief Paul highlighted the existence of tensions within racial groups by saying: "We who are here know that this hospital helps us very much. But there are some people who do not want to come to the hospital. They do not want to know that it can help them."[75] Beyond highlighting divisions within Indigenous communities, this also serves to support George Jasper Wherrett's idea that Natives were active participants in this discourse and that "there was tangible evidence that the Indians were adapting themselves to changed conditions and were taking an interest in medical services."[76] Indeed, in some cases, hospital staff were reliant on Indigenous translators.[77] In addition, white attitudes towards the hospital were not monolithic either. For example, the *Chilliwack Progress* chronicles a schism between the Chilliwack city council and Ottawa in terms of allocation of resources to support the hospital.[78] During 1968, the newspaper also contained a series of articles that demonstrate a division in attitudes about the use of Coqualeetza moving forward, one columnist arguing that "what must first be decided is what better use could be made of Coqualeetza in terms of overall health service to the Indian people."[79]

Individual accounts that address the effects of the hospital on the Indigenous populace seem to obscure its image further. For example, Frank Malloway remembers encountering racism at the hospital. He describes a couple of nurses who would "treat the white orderlies nice" but would pick on him by "reporting [him] to the matron for something [where] there [was] nothing to it."[80] However, in his telling of the story, Malloway does not describe himself as a passive recipient. He goes on to suggest that he insulated himself from the staff who were racist by opting to transition to a different shift.[81] In addition, Malloway concedes that at the same time he possessed a measure of respect, even appreciation, for staff who provided improved care for his ailing grandmother.[82]

Beyond demonstrating the complex nature of the positions and attitudes that can be held by individuals, Malloway illuminates how conflict could, in certain situations, transcend racial boundaries. For example, he remembers conflict between nurses and doctors coming to a head when a woman from the Chilcootin died of cancer. He describes how one time "the nurses were mad because [they felt] the doctors weren't examining often enough for other diseases. And the nurses were upset about it because that old lady was . . . just like a mother to them."[83]

A key part of Corinne Hodgson's argument is that the delivery of health care was "bought" at the price of "familial and community integrity and/or continuity."[84] According to Hodgson, this "disruption of family life" was "repeated in Native communities throughout Canada."[85] In her book, *They Called Me Number One*, Bev Sellars supports this idea by equating the Sardis hospital with loneliness. She writes that on 17 November 1960 she was sent to Coqualeezta, "more than two hundred miles south of [her] home."[86] She elaborates that she has "many memories" including "the vivid memory of standing at the window in the hospital and looking out in different directions wondering which way was home."[87] Upon returning home at the age of seven, Sellars says she "had forgotten [her] family" and that it took her a while to "put the right name to the right person."[88] By contrast, Stan McKay recalls his transfer from Vancouver General to Coqualeetza as reducing that sense of loneliness. He remembers being brought "closer to home" and can recount those he knew who would frequently come talk to him as a result.[89] "It picked my world up that I knew someone who came from my reserve," says McKay, "it started to make me feel better there because there were people there who knew me."[90] Others suggest that feelings of homesickness were often enmeshed with other perceptions. For example, an article in *Native Voice* describes one Christmas morning at the hospital, when patients' "feeling[s] of homesickness" were combined with "exclamations of delight."[91]

Frank Malloway's illustrations of how the Stó:lō could turn the relocation of people from around the province to their advantage causes one to stray even further from traditional colonial narratives. Malloway describes one "good part of his job at Coqualeetza" as "meeting people from all over BC," some of whom became close friends.[92] He recalls a former patient's grandson becoming quite attached to him years after his time at the hospital "because [Malloway] looked after his grandfather."[93] In addition to providing parking space in front of his longhouse in exchange for wind-dried salmon, Malloway recollects being asked by the grandson to open a meeting of the Union of British Columbia Indian Chiefs with a prayer. He recalls opening the meeting and then going for a smoke break. He describes how "this other guy" followed him and asked him: "are you Frank Malloway from Chilliwack?"[94] After indicating in the affirmative, Malloway narrates how this man was at one time a fellow patient from Bella Coola, who was "almost the next bed" to him and who would "wake up in the morning smiling" despite being "so far from home."[95] As Malloway sums up, "I still see patients today that spent time there."[96] He further suggests that the people at Coqualeetza forged stronger connections with communities across the province in all sorts of ways; he reflects, with a chuckle, "we've got relatives all over now because of marriages."[97] Clearly, then, Coqualeetza Indian Hospital was not something that was simply "imposed" on British Columbia's First Nations communities, but rather it was something that could be co-opted by those communities and, in some limited ways, turned to their advantage.

The bureaucratic nature of the institution also resulted in hospital policies that sometimes confounded its own aims. With specific regard to educational programming, the Department of Indian Affairs intended to have instruction of Indigenous children continued during their hospitalization. While educators at Coqualeetza were recognized for their "promotion of humane education," hospital protocols meant there were significant restraints on the ability of patients to take part.[98] Evidence drawn from local discourse suggests that this tension contained a kind of ebb and flow. The *Coqualeetza Story* claims that "in the early days" school work was "more or less haphazard," but later on young patients would be able "to return to school well fitted to compete with children of their own age."[99] However, the oral history testimony of several patients suggests a different reality. Theresa Pierre, for example, recalls the hospital having schooling up to Grade 6. "It was pretty hard," she says, "because nobody helped [students]; they were totally on their own in there. They would send in their schoolwork and nobody was there to teach them."[100] This is corroborated by Bev Julian, who claims she "didn't have teachers that much" and "maybe once a year" she would see one. As a result, Julian says, she "never learned very much."[101] Frank Malloway had a similar experience and went as far as to say that "TB interrupted [his] education."[102] He remembers going to school for "half an hour a day" and completing "one grade in three years."[103] By contrast, Stan McKay remembers a time just a few years later when he was attending school classes "for four or five hours a day."[104] As the hospital teacher, Anne

Robertson, later admitted to the *Chilliwack Progress*, "teaching in a classroom is one thing, but teaching school in a hospital ward is quite a different story. Each child is very definitely an individual and must have work given . . . as such."[105] Therefore, Coqualeetza could, in some cases, frustrate as much as aid the paternalistic and humanitarian intentions of government officials.

The hospital's occupational programming may be understood as another area where dominant narratives require revision. Bronwen Midtdal has argued that occupational therapy was primarily "a means of recovering funds for the hospital . . . disguised as diversionary work, and a method of connecting with one's culture."[106] While newspapers can corroborate that part of the profits from the sale of craft items were turned into a fund "to purchase more materials," they also indicate a portion of these funds went to the patients themselves. An article in the *Chilliwack Progress* claims female patients earned anywhere "from $0.60 to $10 a week in 'spending money' for their efforts."[107] This does not necessarily contradict Midtdal's line of argumentation, but does seem to suggest that it may be overstated.

However, there are two important underpinning issues with Midtdal's line of argumentation. First, it rests solely upon personal correspondence between prominent government officials and hospital administrators and, in doing so, excludes other voices and perspectives when there are many readily available. Some of the Indigenous voices claim to have participated in these activities simply because "it ma[de] them happy."[108] Newspapers reporting on events at the hospital further note the apparent therapeutic emphasis of occupational therapy and how it was "doing wonders in the recovery of tuberculosis patients."[109] Second, Midtdal's argument can be understood as encased in what historian John Langbein refers to as a "legitimation trick." Within a legitimation trick, explains Langbein, "evidence that cuts against the thesis is dismissed as part of a sub-plot to make the conspiracy more palatable to its victims, to legitimate it."[110] In other words, within Midtdal's historical framework, any positive Indigenous appraisals of the programming at Coqualeetza are meaningless as they stem from a kind of pernicious front emanating from an underlying cultural hegemony. Such a reconstruction privileges the voices of society's elite and precludes the possibility of a history in which voices of the Stó:lō matter and the exercise of Indigenous agency is even possible.

If scholarship pertaining to boarding school education in the United States is any indication, however, these different approaches do not necessarily need to diverge. In the introduction to *Away From Home*, Frank Goodyear Jr. laments that "it is curious and disappointing that the history of America's Native peoples is not . . . better integrated into American history."[111] He suggests to us that misguided policy "had a devastating and lasting impact on Native peoples," but at the same time "there were as many experiences as there were students."[112] Lomawaima and McCarty have elsewhere suggested that while historical analysis "reveals a patterned response to cultural and linguistic diversity" it also has "the potential to nourish 'places of difference.'"[113] Therefore, perhaps the "bad stuff" referred to by Malloway is not so much inaccurate as it is incomplete.

To scholars studying Canada's Indian Hospitals, the process of colonization has largely been regarded a force that has "played out *on* Aboriginal bodies in particular ways."[114] This paper has attempted to add a layer of complexity to this argument both by acknowledging the ways in which long-held narratives about colonization endure and, following Drees, by drawing attention to the individual experiences these narratives can be balanced against. The resulting portrait of the Indian Hospital at Coqualeetza shows that the settler society sometimes acted as an oppressive enemy towards Indigenous populations, but also that, in certain circumstances, it behaved like an ally. The *Chilliwack Progress* clearly depicts both Indigenous people and descendants of white settlers fighting for the hospital to remain in Sardis after a fire destroyed large sections of it in 1948.[115] It also chronicles non-Indigenous residents seeking consensus, arguing in the late 1960s that "if Coqualeetza is not required for Indian Health Services [the government] should have agreement from the Native people themselves on the point."[116] Examination of local discourse, therefore, reveals that life at the hospital was remarkably intersectional and could encompass a whole range of experiences. It also suggests that in practice, paternalistic and racist policies were both present and in some sense self-contradictory in that they sometimes frustrated their own explicitly stated aims.

Notes

1   Truth and Reconciliation Commission of Canada, "What We Have Learned: Principles of Truth and Reconciliation" (2015), 5. http://www.myrobust.com/websites/trcinstitution/File/Reports/Principles_English_Web.pdf.

2   Maureen K. Lux, *Separate Beds: A History of Indian Hospitals in Canada, 1920s–1980s* (Toronto: University of Toronto Press, 2016), 18.

3   Ibid., 5.

4   Frank Malloway, interview by Noah E. Miller, Matsqui, BC, 19 May 2015, Stó:lō Archives, Stó:lō Research and Resource Management Centre, Chilliwack, BC.

5   What Chief Malloway is describing might appropriately be considered early phases of the "expectancy effect," which, H. Russell Bernard explains, is "the tendency for experimenters to obtain the results they expect, not simply because they have correctly anticipated [a] response but rather because they have helped to shape that response through their expectations." Robert Rosenthal and Donald B. Rubin, "Interpersonal Expectancy Effects: The First 345 Studies," *Behavioral and Brain Sciences* 1, no. 3 (1978): 377, qtd. in H. Russell Bernard, *Research Methods in Anthropology: Qualitative and Quantitative Approaches*, 5th ed. (Lanham, MD: AltaMira Press, 2011), 233.

6   "To Change Coqualeetza into 'San,'" *Chilliwack Progress*, 28 August 1940, 1; "Coqualeetza Hospital Will be Closing September 30," *Chilliwack Progress*, 10 September 1969, 1.

7   Corinne Hodgson, "The Social and Political Implications of Tuberculosis Among Native Canadians," *Canadian Review of Sociology* 30, no. 4 (1993): 509.

8   Ibid.

9   Ibid., 507. Hodgson writes that, "although it may be well-intentioned and/or have benevolent effects, medical paternalism can be defined as 'interference with a person's liberty of action, where the alleged justification of the interference is that it is for the good of the person whose liberty of action is thus restricted' (Buchanan, 1978: 371). The medical paternalism exhibited in tuberculosis sanatoria ranged from a strictly scheduled daily regime (e.g. Whittaker, 1978) to the forcible detention of 'recalcitrant' patients (Linwell, 1956; Glass, 1959)."

10 Ibid., 509.

11 John S. Lutz, *Makúk: A New History of Aboriginal-White Relations* (Vancouver: UBC Press, 2008), 23.

12 Lutz, *Makúk*, 23; Michael Harkin, *The Heiltsuks: Dialogues of Culture and History on the Northwest Coast* (Lincoln, NE: University of Nebraska Press, 1997), viii, also qtd. in Lutz, *Makúk*, 23.

13 Maureen K. Lux, "Care for the 'Racially Careless': Indian Hospitals in the Canadian West, 1920–1950s," *Canadian Historical Review* 91, no. 3 (September 2010): 407. Lux's more recent work, *Separate Beds*, appeared after the submission of this paper and, as a result, is not dealt with at length here.

14 Ibid.

15 Ibid.

16 Mary-Ellen Kelm, *Colonizing Bodies: Aboriginal Health and Healing in British Columbia, 1900–50* (Vancouver: UBC Press, 1998), xix.

17 Ibid., xx, xix.

18 Ibid., 128.

19 Ibid., 123–5.

20 Keith Thor Carlson, Melinda Marie Jetté, and Kenichi Matsui, "An Annotated Bibliography of Major Writings in Aboriginal History, 1990–99," *Canadian Historical Review* 82, no. 1 (2001): 162.

21 Clifford Geertz, "Thick Description: Toward an Interpretive Theory of Culture," in *Interpretation of Cultures, Selected Essays* (New York: Basic Books, 1973), 17.

22 Ibid., 21.

23 Ibid., 6.

24 Alexander Soucy, "The Problem with Key Informants," *Anthropological Forum* 10, no. 2 (2000): 182.

25   See, for example, "Big Occupational Program at Coqualeetza," *Chilliwack Progress*, 6 November 1946, 11.

26   Raymond J. DeMallie, "'These Have No Ears': Narrative and the Ethnohistorical Method," *Ethnohistory* 40, no. 4 (1993): 515.

27   DeMallie, "These Have No Ears," 515.

28   Regna Darnell, "2009 Presidential Address: What is 'History'? An Anthropologist's Eye View," *Ethnohistory* 58, no. 2 (Spring 2011): 214.

29   Darnell, "2009 Presidential Address," 214.

30   Alice M. Hoffman and Howard S. Hoffman, "Reliability and Validity in Oral History: The Case for Memory," in *Memory and History: Essays on Recalling and Interpreting Experience*, ed. Jaclyn Jeffrey and Glenace Edwall (Lanham, MD: University Press of America, 1994), 127.

31   Ibid., 134.

32   D. Soyini Madison, *Critical Ethnography: Methods, Ethics, and Performance*, 2nd ed. (Thousand Oaks, CA: Sage, 2012), 35.

33   Ibid.

34   Ibid., 35–6.

35   Laurie Meijer Drees, *Healing Histories: Stories from Canada's Indian Hospitals* (Edmonton: University of Alberta Press, 2013), xvii.

36   Ibid., 81.

37   Ibid., 83.

38   Ibid., 87.

39   Ibid., 77.

40   Ibid., 161.

41   Ibid., 77.

42   "Conversion of Coqualeetza to Sanitarium Half Completed," *Chilliwack Progress*, 5 February 1941, 1.

43   Reverend Scott, *Foundations and Progress*, qtd. in Stó:lō Nation Site Tour Source Book, Stó:lō Archives, Stó:lō Research and Resource Management Centre, Chilliwack, BC.

44   W.S. Barclay, qtd. in H. Edmeston, ed., *Coqualeetza Story* (Sardis: n.p., 1956), 10, 96–122, Stó:lō Archives, Stó:lō Research and Resource Management Centre, Chilliwack, BC.

45   "Barclay Outlines Work Done By Coqualeetza," *Chilliwack Progress*, 4 August 1943, 1.

46   "Conversion of Coqualeetza to Sanitarium Half Completed," *Chilliwack Progress*, 5 February 1941, 1.

47   "Dr. J.D. Galbraith Speaks to Kin: Coqualeetza Important in Tuberculosis Fight," *Chilliwack Progress*, 17 November 1943, 8.

48   "Big Occupational Program at Coqualeetza Hospital," 11.

49   Ibid.

50   "Six Hospitals Follow Coqualeetza System," *Chilliwack Progress*, 28 January 1948, 17.

51   Ibid.

52   Edmeston, *Coqualeetza Story*, 11.

53   "Coqualeetza Hospital Accredited," *Chilliwack Progress*, 8 August 1957, 9.

54   "Coqualeetza Hospital: Win Accreditation For 6th Time," *Chilliwack Progress*, 27 November 1963, 17.

55   "Health Workshop at Coqualeetza," *Chilliwack Progress*, 18 March 1964, 24.

56   Mary-Ellen Kelm, *Colonizing Bodies: Aboriginal Health and Healing in British Columbia 1900–50* (Vancouver: University of British Columbia Press, 1998), 100.

57   "November 29 Letter from Mrs. Rose Abbot," *Indian Time*, September-December 1953, 19.

58   Ibid.

59   A.G. MacKinnon, "Hail and Farewell," *Coqualeetza Courier*, January 1959.

60   Malloway, interview, 19 May 2015.

61   Frank Malloway, interview by Noah E. Miller, Sardis, BC, 25 May 2015, Stó:lō Archives, Stó:lō Research and Resource Management Centre, Chilliwack, BC.

62   Malloway, interview, 19 May 2015.

63   Bev Julian, qtd. in "Coqualeetza Indian Hospital," Stó:lō Nation Site Tour Source Book, Stó:lō Archives, Stó:lō Research and Resource Management Centre, Chilliwack, BC.

64   Chief P.D. Peters, interview by Larry Commodore, 21 July 1985, transcript, Stó:lō Oral History Project, 20 85-SR4, 13, Stó:lō Archives, Stó:lō Research and Resource Management Centre, Chilliwack, BC.

65   Malloway, interview, 25 May 2015.

66   ". . . all that remains," *Chilliwack Progress*, 24 November 1948, 1; Stó:lō Nation Site Tour Source Book.

67   Bev Julian, qtd. in "Coqualeetza Indian Hospital," Stó:lō Nation Site Tour Source Book.

68   "Coqualeetza Important in TB Fight," *Chilliwack Progress*, 17 November 1943, 8.

69   "Barclay Outlines Work Done by Coqualeetza," 1.

70   W.S. Barclay, "Rights and Privileges," *Coqualeetza Courier*, July 1953, 2.

71   Theresa Pierre, interview transcript, Stó:lō Archives, Stó:lō Research and Resource Management Centre, Chilliwack, BC, 2.

72   Bev Sellars, *They Called Me Number One: Secrets and Survival at an Indian Residential School* (Vancouver: Talonbooks, 2013), 26.

73   Ibid. In discussing boarding schools in the United States, Frank H. Goodyear Jr. reminds us that in the context of policy that "had a devastating and lasting impact on Native peoples," Indigenous experiences are "human stories filled with tears, tragedy, and lasting pain" alongside "laughter, perseverance, and joy." Frank H. Goodyear Jr., foreword to *Away From Home: American Indian Boarding School Experiences, 1879–2000*, eds. Margaret Archuleta, Brenda J. Child, and K. Tsianina Lomawaima (Phoenix: Heard Museum, 2000), 10.

74   Stan McKay, interview by Noah E. Miller and Colin Osmond, Matsqui, BC, 19 May 2015, Stó:lō Archives, Stó:lō Research and Resource Management Centre, Chilliwack, BC.

75   "Liet.-Gov. Inspects Institution: His Honor Pays Neighborly Call to Coqualeetza Hospital," *Chilliwack Progress*, 20 June 1951, 7.

76   George Jasper Wherrett, *The Miracle of Empty Beds: A History of Tuberculosis in Canada* (Toronto: University of Toronto Press, 1977), 106.

77   Interview with Mary Uslick, interview by Nicola Campbell, 4 March 1994, transcript, Stó:lō Nation Traditional Use Study, UM-i-1, Stó:lō Archives, Stó:lō Research and Resource Management Centre, Chilliwack, BC, 11–12.

78   "Will Send Fire Trucks to Sardis," *Chilliwack Progress*, 3 June 1942, 10; "Will Not Fight Fires At Indian Hospital," *Chilliwack Progress*, 9 December 1942, 1; "Township Fire Protection," *Chilliwack Progress*, 24 November 1947, 2.

79   See "Chilliwack Progressive Conservatives: Claim Federal Bungling Concerning Coqualeetza," *Chilliwack Progress*, 18 December 1968, 1; "Fate of Coqualeetza Discussed," *Chilliwack Progress*, 22 January 1969, 1; "Coqualeetza Storm," *Chilliwack Progress*, 23 December 1968, 12.

80   Malloway, interview, 19 May 2015.

81   Ibid.

82   Ibid. Malloway describes how one nurse assigned a ward aide to work with his grandmother "all morning, all afternoon" in order to "bathe her" and "fix her up." Offering up additional context, Malloway explains how his grandmother had previously resided in a rest home and was "not taken care of" because the facilities were not intended to provide "extended care." He furthermore articulates his belief that his grandmother "received very good care on her last days" and how he was "grateful for that."

83   Ibid.

84   Hodgson, "The Social and Political Implications of Tuberculosis," 509.

85   Ibid.

86   Sellars, *They Called Me Number One*, 23.

87   Ibid.

88   Ibid., 26.

89   McKay, interview.

90   Ibid.

91   *The Native Voice* iv, no.1 (January 1950), Document 01679, Stó:lō Archives, Stó:lō Research and Resource Management Centre, Chilliwack, BC.

92   Malloway, interview, 19 May 2015.

93   Malloway, interview, 25 May 2015.

94   Ibid.

95   Ibid.

96   Malloway, interview, 19 May 2015.

97   Ibid.

98   "Six Hospitals Follow Coqualeetza System," *Chilliwack Progress*, 28 January 1948, 17; "Coqualeetza teacher wins Letham Poster Prize," *Chilliwack Progress*, 26 May 1947, 12.

99   Edmeston, ed. *The Coqualeetza Story*, 17.

100 Pierre, interview transcript, Stó:lō Archives, Stó:lō Research and Resource Management Centre, Chilliwack, BC.

101 Bev Julian, qtd. in "Coqualeetza Indian Hospital," Stó:lō Nation Site Tour Source Book.

102 Malloway, interview, 25 May 2015.

103 Ibid.

104 McKay, interview.

105 "Community Portrait: Anne Robertson . . . hospital teacher," *Chilliwack Progress,* April 23, 1952, 2.

106 Bronwen Midtdal, "Models of Health: An Examination of Aboriginal Wellness at the Coqualeetza Indian Hospital," unpublished paper, Simon Fraser University, 2002, Document 1250, Stó:lō Archives, Stó:lō Research and Resource Management Centre, Chilliwack, BC, 16.

107 "Big Occupational Program at Coqualeetza," 11.

108 Ibid.

109 Ibid.

110 John H. Langbein, "Albion's Fatal Flaws," *Past & Present* 98 (1983): 114.

111 Frank H. Goodyear Jr., foreword to *Away From Home,* 9.

112 Ibid, 10.

113 K. Tsianina Lomawaima and Teresa L. McCarty, "When Tribal Sovereignty Challenges Democracy: American Indian Education and the Democratic Ideal," *American Educational Research Journal* 39, no. 2 (2002): 279.

114 Lux, "Care for the 'Racially Careless,'" 408, emphasis added.

115 See "Battle on for Coqualeetza," *Chilliwack Progress,* 16 February 1949, 9, particularly subheading 'Everybody objects.'

116 "Coqualeetza Storm," 12.

Next Steps in Indigenous Community-Engaged Research: Supporting Research Self-Sufficiency in Indigenous Communities

ADAM GAUDRY

In *Decolonizing Methodologies* (1999), Linda Tuhiwai Smith famously remarks that "research is probably one of the dirtiest words in the Indigenous world's vocabulary.... The ways in which scientific research is implicated in the worst excesses of colonialism remains a powerful remembered history for many of the world's colonized peoples."[1] Because so many Indigenous communities have had negative experiences with academic researchers, many now dread the idea of being subjected to someone else's research project. While this observation remains true in many respects, research norms in the social sciences and humanities have also undergone significant transformation in the past two decades—owing mainly to the pressure of Indigenous communities and Indigenous scholars demanding researchers adopt collaborative approaches to produce relevant scholarship in partnership with communities. These practices, now increasingly institutionalized, have led in many cases to fundamentally different kinds of academic research projects—research that has community-defined research questions, community oversight, and community engagement and underlying values. But, as the benefits of Indigenous community–engaged research become clear, I think that researchers must also push themselves to a deeper form of engagement with community, one that further empowers Indigenous research practice and supports Indigenous peoples in creating *research self-sufficiency* in our communities.

The reluctance of communities to engage academic researchers is not, I think, an inherent issue of scholarly research, but rather *the normalization of exploitative and extractive research* as standard scholarly research practice.[2] Indeed, in research settings where Indigenous communities have substantial input and involvement in research projects, there are many examples of productive collaborations and a general willingness to engage researchers in projects that benefit the community. Notwithstanding the power disparities that continue to affect research in Indigenous contexts, an important shift towards community-engagement practice has taken hold, exemplified in the many ethically minded and community-engaged research projects presented in this volume.

Due to sustained pressure from Indigenous communities and Indigenous academics, there is greater research accountability built into research project design. Research ethics protocols are in place at every Canadian university, all of which require the explicit consent of Indigenous communities before research can begin. These institutionalized requirements have (theoretically) ensured greater Indigenous community oversight and involvement in academic research and have (ideally) led to a research culture shift in how academics approach their research projects. In addition to university research ethics reviews, many Indigenous nations also have research ethics reviews of their own, which in most cases must be completed before the university will approve the research project. As such, many research projects that involve Indigenous communities now require some form of community authorization and approval to get off the ground. This gives Indigenous communities substantially more input into the development of research partnerships as they are ultimately in a position to accept or reject projects.

While problems remain, these shifts in process have led to a shift in thinking and, as this volume shows, a shift in outcomes as well. Although the old way of doing research frustratingly persists, researchers who avoid community participation are more likely to be challenged in intellectual spaces, to face cutting criticism at conferences or public talks, and to be critiqued in hushed tones by scholars and community members for circumventing Indigenous community processes. With a growing number of Indigenous scholars and a growing recognition by our non-Indigenous colleagues of the ethical necessity of Indigenous community–engaged research, the likelihood of researchers working collaboratively in community spaces is growing each and every year.

Collaborative research partnerships have transformed the research landscape in important ways as well. Growing out of major research undertakings such as the Royal Commission on Aboriginal Peoples and numerous court cases (particularly in British Columbia), collaborating with community research partners to advance community interests has largely been effective in connecting outside researchers with Indigenous communities. In the best cases, communities determine research questions, researchers draw extensively on community intellectual sources—oral histories, elders, worldviews, and local archives—in order to ensure that these knowledges are treated with the respect that is due. In engaging with elders, archives, and community members, researchers can also generate new knowledge, develop research capacity, and protect this information for future generations.

The work in this volume represents the field-leading community-engaged research projects of the Stó:lō Ethnohistory Field School. The work of these researchers has contributed to fundamental shifts in conceptualizing academic research as something that occurs *in* Indigenous communities to discussions around conducting academic research *with* Indigenous communities. The success of the field school's collaborative research approach is in blurring the lines between research conducted for academic projects and research for community knowledge production. Sharing research through potlatches, observing protocol with Stó:lō elders, working on community-defined projects on community-defined time frames has a transformative impact on how research is done and how researchers conceptualize the boundaries of scholarly research. Gone, thankfully, are the days when objectivity was the goal of most social science and humanities scholarship, and it is this type of interpersonal investment that links research activities with older forms of relationality. The best research projects put into practice treaty- and kinship-like relations when working collaboratively with Indigenous communities, defying over 150 years of doing otherwise. By acting as good relatives, the best practices in research are intrinsically connected to struggle, working to undercut colonialism and return power and respect to Indigenous philosophies and ways of being. It supports a resurgence of Indigenous knowledge, predicated on a cultural resistance and an intellectual insurgency defying a system that has long dismissed these knowledges.

Collaborative research therefore serves vitally important community needs, but it can also support research capacity building in Indigenous communities to ensure that community members are fully engaged in conducting research *of their own*. Researchers practising community-engaged scholarship utilize a partnership approach, usually pairing skilled outsiders with community knowledge-holders to accomplish community-set goals and meet community ends. While this is impactful and important, I would argue that outsider researchers must also go further by working to empower Indigenous researchers, support the development of community skill sets, increase local community research capacity, and ensure that the community need not always rely on skilled outsiders to conduct research. And perhaps that is the next stage of community-engaged research: supporting research self-sufficiency in Indigenous communities.

Practically speaking, research is not a new phenomenon for Indigenous peoples, rather research practices are integral to Indigenous knowledge systems, all of which have longstanding research protocols put in place that determine who can access particular knowledges, what is required to learn from knowledge holders, what information can be shared, who is able to speak with authority on a given topic, and how knowledge is best shared among a community of learners. Most Indigenous communities, for example, still regularly observe the health of their ecosystem, they have processes in place for keeping track of markers of salmon run health or caribou herd size, and through regular dialogue of multiple observers have ways of systematizing these observations. This knowledge is disseminated throughout the community through accepted processes of discussion and dialogue, usually resulting in a consensus on the status of keystone animal species, which can affect community hunting or fishing practices, and families can adjust their behaviour accordingly. Some communities work collaboratively with scientists on these projects, others choose not to. Either way, there is still longstanding Indigenous research practice working to produce knowledge, disseminate it, and govern behaviour based on research-informed knowledge. However, these processes are not always respected as research, given the ongoing presumption that Indigenous knowledge is less sophisticated than European-derived knowledges universalized as "science" and "knowledge." Yet as many of the projects in this volume demonstrate, these approaches are not only valid, but also produce information that other ways of doing research cannot.

In reviving Indigenous research self-sufficiency, Indigenous communities face a two-fold challenge. Over centuries, Indigenous peoples have faced a concerted attempt by Canadian and British authorities to undercut our ability to transmit knowledge across generations. Despite the best efforts of imperial agents, bureaucrats, and Canadian officials, they have largely failed to eliminate intergenerational knowledge transmission—although it has been weakened substantially. Even with a massive power imbalance and invasive cultural narratives about Indigenous inferiority, knowledge transmission persists, and with the proper supports can, over time, once again transmit knowledge throughout whole communities. Therefore, the long-term survival of Indigenous knowledge ultimately rests in the hands of Indigenous people. For our intellectual traditions to be fully solidified, we need to ensure our own people are the ones guiding the process, and there is no time like the present to begin work shoring up the capacities of our peoples to protect, transmit, and generate knowledge.

Academic researchers have a responsibility to support Indigenous communities in achieving research self-sufficiency. Some cutting-edge research projects have begun by hiring Indigenous community researchers to work alongside academic researchers—particularly community youth—who are empowered with the skills, support, and confidence to take the reins on future research projects. Community-engaged research must ensure that the capacities of partner communities are strengthened through collaborative research development, leaving the community stronger at the end of the project than at the beginning. Researchers can hire local youth to conduct fieldwork and work with university-based researchers to share archival research skills. Research projects can provide scholarships for community members to attend university programs and build them in as part of research grants. Collaborative research projects can think long term to ensure that when a research project ends the community can continue on with it in ways determined by the community. Developing Indigenous community research self-sufficiency is the next stage of community-engaged research, one that calls upon researchers from universities and Indigenous communities to work towards a deeper and more transformative level of community empowerment.

Notes

1   Linda Tuhiwai Smith, *Decolonizing Methodologies: Research and Indigenous Peoples* (London: Zed Books/Dunedin: University of Otago Press, 1999), 1.

2   I have written about this more extensively in Adam Gaudry, "Insurgent Research," *Wicazo Sa Review* 26 (2011) and in Adam Gaudry, "Researching the Resurgence: Insurgent Research and Community-engaged Methodologies in Twenty-First Century Academic Inquiry," in *Research as Resistance: Critical, Indigenous, and Anti-Oppressive Approaches*, 2nd ed., ed. Leslie Brown and Susan Strega (Toronto: Canadian Scholars Press, 2015).

ACKNOWLEDGEMENTS

We are indebted to all those who supported the field school over the years. In particular, our hands go up to the Elders and Knowledge Keepers who trusted us and who shared their cultural traditions and oral histories; to the Chiefs and leaders who invited us into their communities and who suggested research topics; to the families who hosted students in their homes and welcomed them into their hearts; to the staff and management at the Stó:lō Research and Resource Management Centre who made the local accommodation and facilitated the research; and to the administration at the University of Saskatchewan and the University of Victoria who consistently supported the field school.

For helping make this collection possible, we are indebted to the Provost's Office at the University of Saskatchewan for providing funding for the symposium where the authors workshopped their chapters; to the staff at the University of Manitoba Press for all their work shepherding this book to publication; to the anonymous reviewers whose thoughtful suggestions meaningfully contributed to improving the collection; and to the University of the Fraser Valley's *Research Review* journal for permitting four of the contributing authors to this collection to revise and expand their journal articles for inclusion here.

Each one of the authors and editors deeply appreciates the support, encouragement, and patience shown by their families throughout the research and writing process.

BIBLIOGRAPHY

Oral Histories and Unpublished Sources

Aleck, Irene. Interviewed by Anastasia Tataryn. Cheam Reserve, BC. 26 May 2005. Tape.

Bajric, Whitney. "On Experiencing Place: A Biography of a Stó:lō Family's Fishing Site in the Fraser Canyon of British Columbia." Master's major research paper, University of Victoria, 2015. On file at the Stó:lō Resource and Research Management Centre, Chilliwack, BC.

Bennett, Marilyn G. "Indian Fishing and its Cultural Importance in the Fraser River System." Prepared for Fisheries Service, Pacific Region, Department of the Environment and Union of British Columbia Indian Chiefs, 1973.

Bob, Johnny. Interviewed by Marian Smith. 16 July 1941. Transcription of Field Note Pads. MS 268:2 No. 20, Marian Wesley Smith Collection. Royal Anthropological Institute Library. [microfilm copy in BC Archives, Victoria]

Campbell, Alan. Interviewed by Chris Marsh. Chilliwack, BC, 26 May 2015.

Carlson, Keith Thor, and Sarah Eustace. "Fraser Canyon Fishing Rights: Canadian Law and the Origin and Evolution of an Intertribal Dispute." Draft paper prepared for Stó:lō Nation, Chilliwack, BC, 1999.

Chappell, Harley. Interviewed by Anastasia Tataryn. Chilliwack, BC. 25 May 2005.

Charles, Archie. Interviewed by Amanda Fehr, Amber Kostuchenko, and Katya MacDonald. Seabird Island, BC. 28 June 2007. Digitally Recorded. Copies available at Stó:lō Archives, Stó:lō Research and Resource Management Centre, Chilliwack, BC.

Charlie, Betty. Interviewed by Kathy McKay. Chilliwack, BC. 29 May 2000. Tape and Transcript. Stó:lō Archives, Stó:lō Research and Resource Management Centre, Chilliwack, BC.

Charlie, Elsie. Interviewed by Sonny McHalsie, Richard Daly, Randel Paul, and Peter John. Richard Hope's Camp, Spuzzum, BC. 2 August 1988. Tape, Oral History Collection, Stó:lō Archives, Stó:lō Research and Resource Management Centre, Chilliwack, BC.

Charlie, Patrick. Interviewed by Wilson Duff. Summer 1950. Wilson Duff, fieldnotes. Notebooks Nos. 1 and 2. Wilson Duff Papers, BC Archives, Royal British Columbia Museum, Victoria, BC. Copies at Stó:lō Archives, Stó:lō Research and Resource Management Centre, Chilliwack, BC.

Charters, Isadore. Interviewed by Anastasia Tataryn. Chilliwack, BC. 19 May 2005. Tape.

Douglas, Amelia. Interview with Sonny McHalsie, Randel Paul, Richard Daly, and Peter John. 16 August 1988. Stó:lō Archives, Stó:lō Research and Resource Management Centre, Chilliwack, BC.

Douglas, Chester. Interviewed by Chris Marsh and John Lutz. Cheam, BC. 20 May 2015.

———. Interviewed by Davis Rogers and Colin Osmond. Cheam, BC. 22 May 2015. Copies available at Stó:lō Research and Resource Management Centre, Chilliwack, BC.

Douglas, Sid. Interviewed by Keith Carlson, Katya MacDonald, and Sarah Nickel. Chilliwack, BC. 22 June 2007. Recording available at Stó:lō Archives, Stó:lō Research and Resource Management Centre, Chilliwack, BC.

Duff, Wilson. Fieldnotes. Notebooks 1–7, 1950. Wilson Duff Papers, BC Archives, Royal British Columbia Museum, Victoria, BC. Copies at Stó:lō Archives, Stó:lō Research and Resource Management Centre, Chilliwack, BC.

Ewen, Fred, and Marian Smith. Fieldnotes. Summer 1945. 268:2:1 (13). Marian Wesley Smith Collection. BC Archives, Royal British Columbia Museum, Victoria, BC.

Fediuk, Karen, and Brian Thom. "Contemporary and Desired Use of Traditional Resources in a Coast Salish Community: Implications for Food Security and Aboriginal Rights in British Columbia." Paper presented at the 26th Annual Meeting for the Society of Ethnobotany, Seattle, Washington. 27 March 2003.

Francis, Chris, and Danny Francis. Interviewed by Colin Osmond. Chehalis, BC. 22 May 2015. Copies at The Stó:lō Research and Resource Management Centre, Chilliwack, BC.

George, Rosaleen, and Elizabeth Herrling. Interview. Chilliwack, BC. 30 May 2000. Tape and Transcript. Stó:lō Archives, Stó:lō Research and Resource Management Centre, Chilliwack, BC.

Gutierrez, Al. Interviewed by Roy Point. Chawathil, BC. 2 February 1972. Transcript. Skulkayn Heritage Project, Box 2. Coqualeetza Training and Education Centre Archives, Chilliwack, BC.

Gutierrez, Matilda "Tillie." Interviewed by Amanda Fehr and Amber Kostuchenko. Chawathil, BC. 26 June 2007. Digitally Recorded. Copies at Stó:lō Archives, Stó:lō Research and Resource Management Centre, Chilliwack, BC.

———. Interviewed by Sonny McHalsie, Randel Paul, and Richard Daly. Chawathil, BC. 20 September 1988. Tape, Stó:lō Archives, Stó:lō Research and Resource Management Centre, Chilliwack, BC.

Hall, Bob. Interviewed by Ella Bedard. Sardis, BC. 31 May 2013.

Hope, Lawrence. Interviewed by Sonnie McHalsie, Randel Paul, and Richard Daly. Albert Flat's Reserve. 25 November 1988. Oral History Collection, 88SR46-49, Stó:lō Archives, Stó:lō Research and Resource Management Centre, Chilliwack, BC.

Jim, Mrs. August. Interviewed by Oliver Wells. In *The Chilliwacks and Their Neighbours*, edited by Ralph Maud, Brent Galloway, and Marie Weeden. Vancouver: Talonbooks, 1987.

Joe, Bob. Interviewed by Oliver Wells. In *The Chilliwacks and Their Neighbours*, edited by Ralph Maud, Brent Galloway, and Marie Weeden. Vancouver: Talonbooks, 1987.

———. Interviewed by Wilson Duff. Summer 1950. Wilson Duff, Fieldnotes, Notebook No. 3. Wilson Duff Papers, BC Archives, Royal British Columbia Museum, Victoria, BC. Copies at Stó:lō Archives, Stó:lō Research and Resource Management Centre, Chilliwack, BC.

Joe, Helen. Interviewed by Lesley Wiebe. Chilliwack, BC. 27 June 2007. Compact Disc Audio Copy, Stó:lō Archives, Stó:lō Research and Resource Management Centre, Chilliwack, BC.

———. Chilliwack, BC. 1 June 2000. Tape and Transcript. Stó:lō Archives, Stó:lō Research and Resource Management Centre, Chilliwack, BC.

Joe, Herb. Interviewed by Liam Haggerty, Heather Watson, and MacKinley Darlington. Chilliwack, BC. 20 May 2005.

John, Ron, and Patricia. Interviewed by Keith Carlson, Michelle Brandsma, and Colin Osmond. Chawalthil, BC. 21 May 2015. Copies at The Stó:lō Research and Resource Management Centre, Chilliwack, BC.

Johnny, Dave. Interviewed by Matilda Gutierrez. Chilliwack, BC. 23 June 1972. Stó:lō Heritage Project. Tape No. 35.

Julien, Louis. Interviewed by Chris Marsh and Daniel Palmer. Matsqui, BC. 19 May 2015. Copies at The Stó:lō Research and Resource Management Centre, Chilliwack, BC.

Kelly, Agnes. Interviewed by Sonny McHalsie, Randel Paul, Leona Kelly and Peter John. Ohamil First Nation, Hope, BC. 10 June 1988. Stó:lō Archives, Stó:lō Research and Resource Management Centre, Chilliwack, BC.

Kelly, Albert. Interviewed by Colin Osmond. Soowahlie, BC. 2 June 2015. Copies at the Stó:lō Research and Resource Management Centre, Chilliwack, BC.

Kelly, Leona. Interviewed by Lesley Wiebe. Shxw'ow'hamel, BC. 26 June 2007. Compact Disc Audio. Copy at Stó:lō Archives, Stó:lō Research and Resource Management Centre, Chilliwack, BC.

Malloway, Frank. Interviewed by Noah E. Miller. Matsqui, BC. 19 May 2015. Stó:lō Archives, Stó:lō Research and Resource Management Centre, Chilliwack, BC.

———. Interviewed by Noah E. Miller. Sardis, BC. 25 May 2015. Stó:lō Archives, Stó:lō Research and Resource Management Centre, Chilliwack, BC.

———. Interviewed by Heather Myles. In *You Are Asked to Witness: The Stó:lō in Canada's Pacific Coast History*, edited by Keith Thor Carlson. Chilliwack, BC: Stó:lō Heritage Trust, 1996.

Malloway, Ken. Interviewed by Katya MacDonald and Sarah Nickel. Hope, BC. 24 June 2007. Digitally Recorded. Copies at Stó:lō Archives, Stó:lō Research and Resource Management Centre, Chilliwack, BC.

———. Interviewed by Katya MacDonald and Sarah Nickel. Chilliwack, BC. 22 June 2007. Copies available at the Stó:lō Archives, Stó:lō Research and Resource Management Centre, Chilliwack, BC.

Malloway, Tony. Interviewed by Katya MacDonald, Chilliwack, BC. 28 June 2007. Recording available at Stó:lō Archives, Stó:lō Research and Resource Management Centre, Chilliwack, BC.

Matthews, Major James Skitt. Interviews with Coast Salish People. Digitized Records. City of Vancouver Archives. http://former.vancouver.ca/ctyclerk/archives/digitized/EarlyVan/index.htm.

McHalsie, Albert "Sonny." Informal discussion with Kathryn McKay. 31 May 2000. Notes in the possession of Kathryn McKay.

———. Interviewed by Adar Charlton. Chilliwack, BC. 28 May 2013.

———. Interviewed by Amanda Fehr. Hope, BC. 24 June 2007. Digitally Recorded. Copies at Stó:lō Archives, Stó:lō Research and Resource Management Centre, Chilliwack, BC.

———. Interviewed by Lesley Wiebe. Chilliwack, BC. 25 June 2007. Compact Disc Audio. Copy at Stó:lō Archives, Stó:lō Research and Resource Management Centre, Chilliwack, BC.

———. "Stó:lō Deceased: Cemeteries, Funerals and Burnings." Unpublished report— paper presentation, LYS Meeting, Chilliwack, BC. Stó:lō Research and Resource Management Centre, April, 2002.

McKay, Stan. Interviewed by Chris Marsh. Matsqui, BC. 19 May 2015.

———. Interviewed by Noah E. Miller and Colin Osmond. Matsqui, BC. 19 May 2015. Stó:lō Archives, Stó:lō Research and Resource Management Centre, Chilliwack, BC.

Oakes, Nicole. "Preliminary Report on the 1997 Archaeological Reconnaissance near Harrison Mills, Southwestern British Columbia." Chilliwack, BC. May 1998. Stó:lō Archives, Stó:lō Research and Resource Management Centre, Chilliwack, BC.

Pennier, Clarence. Interviewed by Colin Osmond. Sardis, BC. 20 May 2015. Copies at The Stó:lō Research and Resource Management Centre, Chilliwack, BC.

Pete, Rita. Interviewed by Amanda Fehr and Katya MacDonald. Skam, BC. 29 June 2007. Digitally Recorded. Copies at Stó:lō Archives, Stó:lō Research and Resource Management Centre, Chilliwack, BC.

Peters, Chief P.D. Interviewed by Larry Commodore. 21 July 1985. Stó:lō Oral History Project, 20 85-SR4, Stó:lō Archives, Stó:lō Research and Resource Management Centre, Chilliwack, BC.

Peters, Paris. Interviewed by Colin Osmond. Seabird Island, BC. 2 June 2015. Copies at Stó:lō Archives, Stó:lō Research and Resource Management Centre, Chilliwack, BC.

Peters, Susan. Interviewed by Roy Point. Chillliwack, BC. 29 February 1972. Stó:lō Heritage Project. Tape No. 10. Copies at The Stó:lō Research and Resource Management Centre, Chilliwack, BC.

Pierre, Theresa. Interview Transcript. Stó:lō Archives, Stó:lō Research and Resource Management Centre, Chilliwack, BC.

Point, Gwen. Interviewed by Lesley Wiebe. Chilliwack, BC. 20 June 2007. Compact Disc Audio. Copy at Stó:lō Archives, Stó:lō Research and Resource Management Centre, Chilliwack, BC.

———. Interviewed by Patricia Kelly. 2004. Audiotape. Copy at Stó:lō Archives, Stó:lō Research and Resource Management Centre, Chilliwack, BC.

Point, Jeff. Interviewed by Kathy McKay. Chilliwack, BC. 31 May 2000. Tape and Transcript. Stó:lō Archives, Stó:lō Research and Resource Management Centre, Chilliwack, BC.

Point, Mark. Interviewed by Melissa McDowell. Skowkale Reserve, BC. 30 May 2002. Transcript. Stó:lō Archives, Stó:lō Research and Resource Management Centre, Chilliwack, BC.

Point, Steven. Interviewed by Andrée Boisselle and Amanda Fehr. Chilliwack, BC. 29 June 2007. Digitally Recorded. Copies at Stó:lō Archives, Stó:lō Research and Resource Management Centre, Chilliwack, BC.

———. Interviewed by Ella Bedard. Sardis, BC. 31 May 2013.

———. Interviewed by Lesley Wiebe. Chilliwack, BC. 20 June 2007. Compact Disc Audio. Copy at Stó:lō Archives, Stó:lō Research and Resource Management Centre, Chilliwack, BC.

Schaepe, David, Marianne Berkey, Jonathon Stamp, and Tia Halstad. "Sumas Energy Two, Inc. Traditional Use Study–Phase Two: Stó:lō Cultural Relations to Air and Water." Unpublished report. 2004. Stó:lō Archives, Stó:lō Research and Resource Management Centre, Chilliwack, BC.

Schaepe, David, Susan Rowley, Stó:lō House of Respect Committee Members, Darlene Weston, Mike Richards. "The Journey Home—Guiding Intangible Knowledge Production in the Analysis of Ancestral Remains." Unpublished report. 2015. Stó:lō Archives, Stó:lō Research and Resource Management Centre, Chilliwack, BC. www.sfu.ca/ipinch/sites/default/files/resources/reports/the_journey_home_ver2_may2016.pdf.

Seymour, Clem. Interviewed by Adar Charlton. Seabird Island, BC. 28 May 2013.

Silver Sr., Ray. Interviewed by Chris Marsh and Daniel Palmer. Abbotsford, BC. 26 May 2015.

———. Interview with Emily Campbell, Katya MacDonald, and Lesley Wiebe. Sumas, BC. 27 June 2007. Copies at Stó:lō Archives, Stó:lō Research and Resource Management Centre, Chilliwack, BC.

———. Interviewed by Lesley Wiebe. 27 June 2007. Compact Disc Audio. Copy at Stó:lō Archives, Stó:lō Research and Resource Management Centre, Chilliwack, BC.

Smith, Marian. Unpublished Fieldnotes. Summer 1945. Royal Anthropological Institute, London, Great Britain. Copies at British Columbia Archives.

Stó:lō Nation Archives Oral History Collection. Stó:lō Archives, Stó:lō Research and Resource Management Centre, Chilliwack, BC.

Stó:lō Nation. "Chief Alexis Srouchelaleou." Genealogical Database. Chilliwack, BC: Stó:lō Research and Resource Management Centre, 2005.

———. "Joe Aleck." Genealogical Database. Chilliwack, BC: Stó:lō Research and Resource Management Centre, 2005.

Stó:lō Tribal Council. "Fisheries Co-Management Proposal for the Lower Fraser River Watershed." 1988.

Taillon, Joan. "Summary." Environmental Contaminants and Traditional Foods Workshop, Kamloops, BC, September 23–24, 2003.

Uslick, Mary. Interviewed by Nicola Campbell. 4 March 1994. UM-i-l, Stó:lō Nation Traditional Use Study. Transcript. Stó:lō Archives, Stó:lō Research and Resource Management Centre, Chilliwack, BC.

Wells, Oliver. Interview Collection (1961–1968). Stó:lō Archives, Stó:lō Research and Resource Management Centre, Chilliwack, BC.

Wheeler, Winona. "Historical Scholarship and Teaching in Canada After the TRC." Round table discussion, Annual Meeting of the Canadian Historical Association, Calgary, June 2016.

Wilson, Richard. Interviewed by Anastasia Tataryn. Chilliwack, BC. 19 May 2005. Tape.

Unpublished Theses and Dissertations

Amoss, Pamela T. "The Persistence of Aboriginal Beliefs and Practices among the Nooksack Coast Salish." PhD diss., University of Washington, 1972.

Clapperton, Jonathan. "Presenting and Representing Culture: A History of Stó:lō Interpretive Centres, Museums, and Cross-Cultural Relationships 1949–2006." MA thesis, University of Victoria, 2006.

Curtin, Joanne A. "Prehistoric Mortuary Variability on Gabriola Island, B.C." PhD diss., Ohio State University, 1998.

Downey, Allan. "The Creator's Game: Aboriginal Racialized Identities in Canada's Colonial Age, 1867–1990." PhD diss., Wilfrid Laurier University, 2014.

Fehr, Amanda. "The Relationships of Place: A Study of Change and Continuity in Stó:lō Understandings of I:yem." MA thesis, University of Saskatchewan, 2008.

Haagen, Claudia. "Strategies for Cultural Maintenance: Aboriginal Cultural Education Programs and Centres in Canada." MA thesis, University of British Columbia, 1990.

Haggarty, Liam. "A Cultural History of Social Welfare Among the Stó:lō." MA thesis, University of Saskatchewan, 2007.

Hiwasaki, Lisa. "Presenting Unity, Performing Diversity: Stó:lō Identity Negotiations in Venues of Cultural Representation." MA thesis, University of British Columbia, 1998.

Joseph, Susan. "Coast Salish Perceptions of Death and Dying." MA thesis, University of Victoria, 1994.

Klassen, Michael A. "Indigenous Heritage Stewardship and Transformation of Archaeological Practice: Two Case Studies from the Mid-Fraser Region of British Columbia." PhD diss., Simon Fraser University, 2013.

Laforet, Andrea. "Folk History in a Small Canadian Community." PhD diss., University of British Columbia, 1974.

Lerman, Norman. "An Analysis of Folktales of Lower Fraser Indians, British Columbia." MA thesis, University of Washington, 1952.

Linkous Brown, Kimberly. "To Fish for Themselves: A Study of Accommodation and Resistance in the Stó:lō Fishery." PhD diss., University of British Columbia, 2005.

Mathews, Darcy Lane. "Funerary Ritual, Ancestral Presence, and the Rocky Point Ways of Death." PhD diss., University of Victoria, 2014.

O'Neill, Amy. "Identity, Culture and the Forest: The Stó:lō." MA thesis, University of British Columbia, 1999.

Schaepe, David. "Pre-colonial Sto:lo-Coast Salish Community Organization: An Archaeological Study." PhD diss., University of British Columbia, 2009.

Thom, Brian. "The Living and the Dead." MA thesis, University of British Columbia, 1995.

Walls, Robert E. "The Making of the American Logger: Traditional Culture and Public Imagery in the Realm of the Bunyanesque." PhD diss., Indiana University, 1997.

Wike, Joyce A. "The Effect of the Maritime Fur Trade on Northwest Coast Indian Society." PhD diss., Columbia University, 1951.

Archival Sources

"Coqualeetza Land Claims: Army Drops Charges, Still No Answer from Ottawa on the Return of Coqualeetza." *Stalo Nation News* 10 (May 1976). Stó:lō Archives, Stó:lō Research and Resource Management Centre, Chilliwack, BC.

Coqualeetza Residential School Commencement Annuals, 1931–1935. Peter Czink Collection. Chilliwack Museum and Archives.

Edmeston, H, ed. *Coqualeetza Story.* Sardis: n.p., 1956. Copy available at Stó:lō Archives, Stó:lō Research and Resource Management Centre, Chilliwack, BC.

Elders' Gathering Memory Book. 1978. Coqualeetza Training and Education Centre. Copy at The Stó:lō Research and Resource Management Centre, Chilliwack, BC.

George Williams Fonds. Chilliwack Museum and Archives.

Indian Affairs Records. RG10. Library and Archives Canada. Ottawa, Canada.

"Introduction to the Skulkayn Heritage Project." 1972. Skulkayn Heritage Project, Box 2, Skulkayn Heritage Project Administrative File. Coqualeetza Training and Education Centre Archives.

King, Bruce. "White Conceptualization and Industrial Canning: The Disruption of Sto:lo Culture." 8 May 1991. Document 000503. Stó:lō Archives, Stó:lō Research and Resource Management Centre, Chilliwack, BC.

McDowell, Melissa. "'This is Stó:lō Indian Land': The Struggle for Control of Coqualeetza, 1968–1976." 2002. Stó:lō Archives, Stó:lō Research and Resource Management Centre, Chilliwack, BC.

Midtdal, Bronwen. "Models of Health: An Examination of Aboriginal Wellness at the Coqualeetza Indian Hospital." Unpublished Paper. Simon Fraser University, 2002. Document 1250. Stó:lō Archives, Stó:lō Research and Resource Management Centre, Chilliwack, BC.

The Native Voice iv, no. 1. (January 1950). Document 01679. Stó:lō Archives, Stó:lō Research and Resource Management Centre, Chilliwack, BC.

"Project Submission: Skulkayn Stalo Heritage Project." 12 May 1972. Skulkayn Heritage Project, Box 2, Skulkayn Heritage Project Administrative File. Coqualeetza Training and Education Centre Archives.

"Proposal: Coqualeetza Indian Centre of B.C., 'Stalo Center.'" 1973. Skulkayn Heritage Project, Box 3. Coqualeetza Training and Education Centre Archives.

Ralry, J.H. "Foreword." *Coqualeetza Yearbook, 1931.* 2009.047.003. Chilliwack Archives.

"The Skulkayn Indian Heritage Project: Progress Report." 2 May 1972. Skulkayn Heritage Project, Box 2, Skulkayn Heritage Project Administrative File. Coqualeetza Training and Education Centre Archives.

"Skulkayn Stalo Heritage Project." 22 February 1972. Skulkayn Heritage Project, Box 2, Skulkayn Heritage Project Administrative File. Coqualeetza Training and Education Centre Archives.

Stó:lō Nation Site Tour Source Book. Stó:lō Archives, Stó:lō Research and Resource Management Centre, Chilliwack, BC.

"Tillie Gutierrez's Work Schedule." 7–19 April 1972. CTECA, SHP Box 2. Tillie Gutierrez File.

Tommy, Wilfred, Tim Point, Amelia Douglas, and Tillie Gutierrez. "Skulkayn Heritage Project." 9 May 1972. Skulkayan Heritage Project, Box 2, Tillie Gutierrez File. Coqualeetza Training and Education Centre Archives.

Vancouver Sun. University of Calgary Microfilm Collection, AN5.V28. University of Calgary Libraries.

Washbrook, Kevin. "An Introduction to the Ethnobotany of the Stó:lō People in the Area Between New Westminster and Chilliwack on the Fraser River." November, 1995. Document 000625. Stó:lō Archives, Stó:lō Research and Resource Management Centre, Chilliwack, BC.

———. "Plants and Medicine: Talking about Power in Stó:lō Society." 10 June 1994. Document 000390. Stó:lō Archives, Stó:lō Research and Resource Management Centre, Chilliwack, BC.

Williams, George. "Coqualeetza Residential School Sports." 1931. AM 456. Chilliwack Archives.

Court Proceedings

Chief Robert Hope v. Lower Fraser Fishing Authority and others. BC Supreme Court Vancouver Registry. File No. c92-4333. Signed 8 July 1992.

Gutierrez, Tillie, witness for the Defence. *Regina v. Dorothy Van der Peet*. Proceedings at Trial. Provincial Court of British Columbia. 31 May 1989.

Regina v. Dorothy Van der Peet. Proceedings at Trial. Provincial Court of British Columbia. File No. 43322T. Copies at Stó:lō Archives, Stó:lō Research and Resource Management Centre, Chilliwack, BC.

Yale First Nation v. Her Majesty the Queen in Right of Canada et al. BC Supreme Court Victoria Registry. File No. 746.

Yale Indian Band v. Aitchelitz Indian Band et al. Federal Court. Vancouver, BC. File No. T-776-98.

Websites/Multimedia

Adichie, Chimamanda Ngozi. "The Danger of a Single Story." Filmed July 2009. *TED Global*.

BC Ministry of Aboriginal Relations and Reconciliation. *Yale First Nation Agreement-in-Principle Brochure*. http://www.gov.bc.ca/arr/firstnation/yale/down/yale_aip_brochure_01.pdf.

Bjerky, Irene. "First Peoples of Yale and Spuzzum." *Colourful Characters in Historic Yale*. http://www.virtualmuseum.ca/pm.php?id=story_line&fl=0&lg=English&ex=00 000150&sl=5044&pos=15.

c̓əsnaʔəm, the city before the city. University of British Columbia Museum of Anthropology, Vancouver, 25 January 2015–24 January 2016. http://www.thec-itybeforethecity.com; http://moa.ubc.ca/portfolio_page/citybeforecity/.

The Chilliwack Progress. Accessed through http://theprogress.newspapers.com/.

The Chilliwack Progress. 17 March 2006. As quoted in Fraser Valley Treaty Advisory. *Committee Local Media Excerpts to March 31st, 2006.* http://www.fvrd. bc.ca/NR/rdonlyres/37719ADD-6E99-4634-D00B53E396C7D86/928/ LocalMediaReporttoMarch3106.pdf.

"Declaration on the Safeguarding of Indigenous Ancestral Burial Grounds as Sacred Sites and Cultural Landscapes." 2014. https://www.sfu.ca/ipinch/resources/declarations/ancestral-burial-grounds/.

Feinberg, Jennifer. "Sto:lo Head to BC Supreme Court Over Yale Treaty." *Chilliwack Progress,* 20 June 2013. http://www.theprogress.com/news/212403421.html.

"Grace Islet Home on Sacred Aboriginal Cemetery to Be Demolished." CBC News. 10 August 2015. http://www.cbc.ca/news/canada/british-columbia/grace-islet-home-on-sacred-aboriginal-cemetery-to-be-demolished-1.3186534.

Hill-Tout, Charles. "Ethnological Studies of the Mainland Halkōmë'lem, a Division of the Salish of British Columbia." In "Report on the Ethnological Survey of Canada," 3–97. British Association for the Advancement of Science. 1902. Early Canadiana Online. http://eco.canadiana.ca/view/oocihm.14331. Also available in *The Salish People, Volume III: The Mainland Halkomelem,* edited by Ralph Maud. Vancouver: Talonbooks, 1978.

A Journey into Time Immemorial. Simon Fraser University Museum, Vancouver, 2009. http://www.sfu.museum/time/en/enter/.

Kines, Lindsay. "Province Buys Disputed Grace Islet for $5.45 million." *Times Colonist.* 16 February 2016. http://www.timescolonist.com/news/local/province-buys-disputed-grace-islet-for-5-45-million-1.1764939.

"Luxury Home on B.C. Burial Ground to be Torn Down." CTV News, 11 August 2015. http://bc.ctvnews.ca/luxury-home-on-b-c-burial-ground-to-be-torn-down-1.2511948.

Matas, Robert. "Taking It to Their Graves." *Globe and Mail,* 5 November 2008 and 13 March 2009. http://www.theglobeandmail.com/news/national/taking-it-to-their-graves/article662715/.

Reciprocal Research Network. https://www.rrncommunity.org/.

Sayers, Judith, Maureen Grant, Dave Schaepe, Robert Phillips, and Murray Brown. "When First Nations Burial Sites and Development Collide." *The Tyee,* 18 August 2014. https://www.thetyee.ca/Opinion/2014/08/18/First-Nations-Burial-Developments/.

Schaepe, David M., Natasha Lyons, Kate Kennessy, Kyle McIntosh, Michael Blake, Colin Pennier, Clarence Pennier, Andy Phillips and Project Members. *Sq'éwlets: A Stó:lō-Coast Salish Community in the Fraser Valley.* Virtual Museum of Canada. 2016. www.digitalsqewlets.ca.

Truth and Reconciliation Commission of Canada. "Honouring the Truth, Reconciling for the Future: Summary of the Final Report of the Truth and Reconciliation Commission of Canada. 2015. http://www.trc.ca/websites/trcinstitution/File/2015/Exec_Summary_2015_06_25_web_o.pdf.

———. "What We Have Learned: Principles of Truth and Reconciliation." (2015). http://www.trc.ca/websites/trcinstitution/File/2015/Findings/Principles_2015_05_31_web_o.pdf.

Wickwire, Wendy. "Teit, James Alexander." *Dictionary of Canadian Biography*. http://www.biographi.ca/en/bio/teit_james_alexander_1884_15E.html.

Wild Zone Productions. *The Lynching of Louis Sam*. Director David McIlwraith, 2005. Based on Keith Thor Carlson, "The Lynching of Louis Sam," *BC Studies* 109 (Spring 1999): 63–79.

Yale First Nation Final Agreement. http://www.aadnc-aandc.gc.ca/eng/1336657835560/1336658472497.

Yale First Nation Treaty Negotiations Agreement in Principle. 9 March 2006. http://www.ainc-inac.gc.ca/bc/treapro/ston/aip/yalaip/yalfin_e.pdf.

Zeng, X.Y. "Desecrated Monument Restored." *Hope Standard*, 14 April 2016. http://www.bclocalnews.com/news/375628511.

Newspapers and Magazines

". . . all that remains." *Chilliwack Progress*, 24 November 1948.

"Barclay Outlines Work Done by Coqualeetza." *Chilliwack Progress*, 4 August 1943.

Barclay, W.S. "Rights and Privileges." *Coqualeetza Courier*, July 1952.

"Battle on for Coqualeetza." *Chilliwack Progress*, 16 February 1949.

"Before Talk of Alcatraz Type Takeover Decide Hospital Use, Indians Told." *Vancouver Sun*, 13 February 1970.

"Big Occupational Program at Coqualeetza Hospital." *Chilliwack Progress*, 6 November 1946.

"Chilliwack Progressive Conservatives: Claim Federal Bungling Concerning Coqualeetza." *Chilliwack Progress*, 18 December 1968.

"Community Portrait: Anne Robertson . . . hospital teacher." *Chilliwack Progress*, 23 April 1952.

"Conversion of Coqualeetza to Sanitarium Half Completed." *Chilliwack Progress*, 5 February 1941.

"Coqualeetza Hospital Accredited." *Chilliwack Progress*, 8 August 1957.

"Coqualeetza Hospital Will be Closing September 30." *Chilliwack Progress*, 10 September 1969.

"Coqualeetza Hospital: Win Accreditation for 6th Time." *Chilliwack Progress*, 27 November 1963.

"Coqualeetza Important in TB Fight." *Chilliwack Progress*, 17 November 1943.

"Coqualeetza Storm." *Chilliwack Progress*, 23 December 1968.

"Coqualeetza teacher wins Letham Poster Prize." *Chilliwack Progress*, 26 May 1947.

"Dr. J.D. Galbraith Speaks to Kin: Coqualeetza Important in Tuberculosis Fight." *Chilliwack Progress*, 17 November 1943.

Falkenberg, Mark. "Family Feud: Stó:lō Say Fight Over Fishing Rights with Yale Band Comes Down to Respect for Traditional Fishing Patterns." *Chilliwack Progress*, 17 April 1998.

"Fate of Coqualeetza Discussed." *Chilliwack Progress*, 22 January 1969.

Freeman, Robert. "Bands Feud Over Canyon Cleaning." *Chilliwack Progress*, 18 May 1999.

"Health Workshop at Coqualeetza." *Chilliwack Progress*, 18 March 1964.

Henderson, Paul. "Sto:lo Lawsuit Names Feds and Province in Treaty Fight." *Chilliwack Times*, 25 June 2013. http://www.chilliwacktimes.com/news/ 245072611.html.

"Hospital to be Indian Centre?" *Vancouver Province*, 22 December 1969.

"Liet.-Gov. Inspects Institution: His Honor Pays Neighborly Call to Coqualeetza Hospital." *Chilliwack Progress*, 20 June 1951.

MacKinnon, A.G. "Hail and Farewell." *Coqualeetza Courier*, January 1959.

"New Head of Fisheries Meets Canyon Band." *The Hope Standard*, 13 July 2000.

"November 29 Letter from Mrs. Rose Abbot." *Indian Time*, September–December, 1953.

"Proposed Coqualeetza Multi-Centre Waiting for 'go' Signals." *Nesika: The Voice of B.C. Indians* 2, no. 5 (1973).

"Six Hospitals Follow Coqualeetza System." *Chilliwack Progress*, 28 January 1948.

"Skulkayn Hold the Fort: Indians call Mounties." *Vancouver Sun*, 29 April 1971.

Stanbrook, Barn, and Mike Doyle. "17 Natives Charged in Coqualeetza Clash: Stalo Band Lays Claim to Former Hospital." *Chilliwack Progress*, 5 May 1976.

"Sto:lo Ceremony Delayed After Grave-Site Pedestal Destroyed." *The Vancouver Province*, 3 November 2008.

"To Change Coqualeetza into 'San.'" *Chilliwack Progress*, 28 August 1940.

"Township Fire Protection." *Chilliwack Progress*, 24 November 1947.

"Will Not Fight Fires At Indian Hospital." *Chilliwack Progress*, 9 December 1942.

"Will Send Fire Trucks to Sardis." *Chilliwack Progress*, 3 June 1942.

"Wreckers Find Buried Documents." *Chilliwack Progress*, 2 February 1949.

Secondary Sources

Adams, David Wallace. "More Than a Game: The Carlisle Indians Take to the Gridiron, 1893–1917." *Western Historical Quarterly* 32, no. 1 (2001): 25–53.

Alfred, Taiaiake. *Wasase: Indigenous Pathways of Action and Freedom*. Peterborough, ON: Broadview Press, 2005.

Ames, Kenneth, and Herbert Maschner. *The Peoples of the Northwest Coast*. London: Thames and Hudson, 1999.

Ames, Michael. "Cultural Empowerment and Museums: Opening up Anthropology through Collaboration." In *Objects of Knowledge*, ed. S. Pearce. London: Athlone Press, 1990.

Amoss, Pamela T. "The Fish God Gave Us: The First Salmon Ceremony Revived." *Arctic Anthropology* 24, no. 1 (1987): 56–66.

Arcas Consulting. *Archaeological Investigations at Tsawwassen, B.C. Volume 3*. Prepared for Construction Branch, South Coast Region, Ministry of Transportation and Highways, Burnaby, BC, and the BC Archaeology Branch. Permits 1984–41, 1990–2. Coquitlam, BC, 1991.

———. *Archaeological Investigations at Tsawwassen, B.C. Volume 4*. Prepared for Construction Branch, South Coast Region, Ministry of Transportation and Highways, Burnaby, BC, and the BC Archaeology Branch. Permits 1984–41, 1990–2. Coquitlam, BC, 1999.

Archibald, Jo-Ann. "An Indigenous Storywork Methodology." In *Handbook of the Arts in Qualitative Research*, edited by J. Gary Knowles and Ardra L. Cole, 371–85. Thousand Oaks, CA: Sage, 2008.

———. *Indigenous Storywork: Educating the Heart, Mind, Body and Spirit*. Vancouver: University of British Columbia Press, 2008.

Ashcroft, Bill, Gareth Griffiths, and Helen Tiffin, eds. *Post Colonial Studies: The Key Concepts*. New York: Routledge, 2000.

Axtell, James. "Ethnohistory: An Historian's Viewpoint." *Ethnohistory* 26, no. 1 (1979): 2.

Bakhtin, Mikhail. *Questions of Literature and Aesthetics*. Moscow: Russian Progress, 1975.

Barker, Adam. "Locating Settler Colonialism." *The Journal of Colonialism and Colonial History* 13, no. 3 (Winter 2012): doi: 10.1353/cch.2012.0035.

Barnett, Homer. *The Coast Salish Indians of British Columbia*. Eugene: University of Oregon, 1995.

———. *Indian Shakers: A Messianic Cult of the Pacific Northwest*. Carbondale: Southern Illinois University Press, 1957.

Basso, Keith H. *Wisdom Sits in Places: Landscape and Language among the Western Apache*. Albuquerque: University of New Mexico Press, 1996.

Bernard, H. Russell. *Research Methods in Anthropology: Qualitative and Quantitative Approaches*, 4th ed. Lanham, MD: AltaMira Press, 2006.

———. *Research Methods in Anthropology: Qualitative and Quantitative Approaches*, 5th ed. Lanham, MD: AltaMira Press, 2011.

Bhabha, Homi. *The Location of Culture*. New York: Routledge, 1994.

Biersack, Aletta. "Introduction." In *Clio In Oceania: Toward a Historical Anthropology*, edited by Aletta Biersack. Washington, DC: Smithsonian Institution Press, 1990.

———, ed. *Clio In Oceania: Toward a Historical Anthropology*. Washington, DC: Smithsonian Institution Press, 1990.

Bierwert, Crisca. *Brushed by Cedar, Living by the River: Coast Salish Figures of Power*. Tucson: University of Arizona Press, 1999.

Blackhawk, Ned. "Currents in North American Indian Historiography." *Western Historical Quarterly* 42, no. 3 (Autumn 2011): 319–24.

Boas, Franz. *Indian Myths & Legends from the North Pacific Coast of North America*. Edited by Randy Bouchard and Dorothy Kennedy. Translated by Dietrich Bertz. Vancouver: Talonbooks, 2002.

———. *Indian Tribes of the Lower Fraser River*. London: Spottiswoode. British Association for the Advancement of Science, 1894.

———. "The Indian Tribes of the Lower Fraser River." In *The 64th Report of the British Association for the Advancement of Science for 1890*. London: British Association for the Advancement of Science, 1894, 454–63.

Boddy, Kasia. *Boxing: A Cultural History*. London: Reaktion Books, 2008.

Borden, Charles E. *Origins and Development of Early Northwest Coast Culture to About 3000 BC*. Ottawa: National Museums of Canada, 1975.

Borré, Kristen. "Seal Blood, Inuit Blood, and Diet: A Biocultural Model of Physiology and Cultural Identity." *Medical Anthropology Quarterly* 5, no. 1 (1991): 48–62.

272   TOWARDS A NEW ETHNOHISTORY

Borrows, John. *Freedom and Indigenous Constitutionalism.* Toronto: University of Toronto Press, 2016.

Boyd, Robert, ed. *Indians, Fire, and the Land in the Pacific Northwest.* Corvallis: Oregon State University Press, 1999.

Boyer, Ernest L. "The Scholarship of Engagement." *Journal of Public Service & Outreach* 1, no. 1 (1996): 11–20.

———. *Scholarship Reconsidered: Priorities of the Professoriate.* New York: Carnegie Foundation for the Advancement of Teaching, 1990.

Braun, Sebastian Felix, ed. *Transforming Ethnohistories: Narrative, Meaning, and Community.* Norman: University of Oklahoma Press, 2013.

Bringhurst, Robert. *A Story as Sharp as a Knife: The Classical Haida Mythtellers and Their World.* 2nd ed. Vancouver: Douglas and McIntyre, 2011.

Burchell, Graham, Colin Gordon, and Peter Miller, eds. *The Foucault Effect: Studies in Governmentality.* Chicago: University of Chicago Press, 1991.

Burley, David. *Senewelets: The Cultural History of Nanaimo Coast Salish and False Narrows Midden.* Victoria, BC: Royal British Columbia Museum, 1989.

Buscombe, Edward. *"Injuns!" Native Americans in the Movies.* London: Reaktion Books, 2006.

Butler, Caroline F. "Historicizing Indigenous Knowledge: Practical and Political Issues." In *Traditional Ecological Knowledge and Natural Resource Management*, edited by Charles R. Menzies. Lincoln, NE: University of Nebraska Press, 2006.

Cardinal, Harold. *The Rebirth of Canada's Indians.* Edmonton: Hurtig Press, 1979.

Carlson, Keith Thor. "Dialogue and History: The King's Promise and the 1906 Aboriginal Delegation to London." *Native Studies Review* 16, no. 2 (2005): 1–38.

———. "Expressions of Collective Identity." In *A Stó:lō-Coast Salish Historical Atlas*, edited by Keith Thor Carlson, David Schaepe, Albert "Sonny" McHalsie, et al., 24–29. Vancouver: Douglas and McIntyre/Chilliwack: Stó:lō Heritage Trust, 2001.

———. "History Wars: Considering Contemporary Fishing Site Disputes." In *A Stó:lō-Coast Salish Historical Atlas*, edited by Keith Thor Carlson, David Schaepe, Albert "Sonny" McHalsie, et al., 58–59. Vancouver: Douglas and McIntyre/Chilliwack: Stó:lō Heritage Trust, 2001.

———. "Innovation, Tradition, Colonialism and Aboriginal Fishing Conflicts in the Lower Fraser Canyon." In *New Histories for Old: Changing Perspectives on Canada's Native Pasts*, edited by Ted Binnema and Susan Neylan, 145–74. Vancouver: University of British Columbia Press, 2007.

———. "Introduction." In *A Stó:lō-Coast Salish Historical Atlas*, edited by Keith Thor Carlson, David Schaepe, Albert "Sonny" McHalsie, et al., 1–5. Vancouver: Douglas and McIntyre/Chilliwack: Stó:lō Heritage Trust, 2001.

———. "Orality About Literacy: The 'Black and White' of Salish History." In *Orality and Literacy: Reflections Across Disciplines*, edited by Keith Thor Carlson, Kristina Fagan, and Natalia Khanenko-Friesen, 43–69. Toronto: University of Toronto Press, 2011.

———. *The Power of Place, the Problem of Time: Aboriginal Identity and Historical Consciousness in the Cauldron of Colonialism.* Toronto: University of Toronto Press, 2010.

———. "Reflections on Indigenous History and Memory: Reconstructing and Reconsidering Contact." In *Myth and Memory: Stories of Indigenous-European Contact*, edited by John Sutton Lutz, 46–68. Vancouver: University of British Columbia Press, 2007.

———. "Stó:lō Migrations and Shifting Identities." In *A Stó:lō-Coast Salish Historical Atlas*, edited by Keith Thor Carlson, David Schaepe, Albert "Sonny" McHalsie, et al., 30–31. Vancouver: Douglas and McIntyre/Chilliwack: Stó:lō Heritage Trust, 2001.

———. "Stó:lō Soldiers, Stó:lō Veterans." In *You Are Asked to Witness: The Stó:lō in Canada's Pacific Coast History*, 125–38. Chilliwack, BC: Stó:lō Heritage Trust, 1996.

———. "Toward an Indigenous Historiography: Events, Migrations, and the Formation of 'Post-Contact' Coast Salish Collective Identities." In *Be of Good Mind: Essays on the Coast Salish*, edited by Bruce G. Miller, 138–81. Vancouver: University of British Columbia Press, 2007.

———, ed. *You Are Asked to Witness: The Stó:lō in Canada's Pacific Coast History*. Chilliwack, BC: Stó:lō Heritage Trust, 1997.

———, Melinda Marie Jetté, and Kenichi Matsui. "An Annotated Bibliography of Major Writings in Aboriginal History, 1990–99." *Canadian Historical Review* 82, no. 1 (2001): 122–171.

———, John Lutz, and David Schaepe. eds. "Turning the Page: Ethnohistory from a New Generation." *University of the Fraser Valley Research Review* 2, no. 2 (Spring 2009): 1–8.

———, with Albert "Sonny" McHalsie. "*I am Stó:lō!*": *Katherine Explores Her Heritage*. Vancouver: Douglas and McIntyre, 1998.

———, Sonny McHalsie, and Frank Malloway. 加拿大太平洋海岸第一民族的历史与文化 [*Canadian Pacific Coast First Nations History and Culture*]. Translated by Xing Chihong and Zhang Haixia. Saskatoon: Confucius Institute, University of Saskatchewan; Chilliwack, BC: Stó:lō Research and Resource Management Centre, 2015.

———, David Schaepe, Albert "Sonny" McHalsie, et al., eds. *A Stó:lō-Coast Salish Historical Atlas*, Vancouver: Douglas and McIntyre/Chilliwack: Stó:lō Heritage Trust, 2001.

Carlson, Roy, and Philip Hobler. "The Pender Canal Excavations and the Development of Coast Salish Culture." *BC Studies* 99 (Autumn 1993): 25–53.

Carter, Sarah. *The Importance of Being Monogamous: Marriage and Nation Building to 1915*. Edmonton: University of Alberta Press, 2008.

Codere, Helen. "The Amiable Side of Kwakiutl Life: The Potlach and the Play Potlach." *American Anthropologist*, New Series 58, no. 2 (1956): 334–51.

———. *Fighting with Property: A Study of Kwakiutl Potlatching and Warfare, 1792–1930*. Seattle: University of Washington Press, 1966. First published 1950 by J.J. Augustin.

Consentio, Frank. *Afros, Aboriginals, and Amateur Sport in Pre-World War One Canada*. Canada's Ethnic Groups Series Booklet No. 26. Toronto: Canadian Historical Association, 1998.

Cronon, William. "A Place For Stories: Nature, History, and Narrative." *The Journal of American History* 78, no. 4 (1992): 1347–76.

Cruikshank, Julie. *Do Glaciers Listen? Local Knowledge, Colonial Encounters, and Social Imagination*. Vancouver: University of British Columbia Press, 2005.

———. *The Social Life of Stories: Narrative and Knowledge in the Yukon Territory*. Vancouver: University of British Columbia Press, 1998.

———. "The Social Life of Texts: Editing on the Page and in Performance." In *Talking on the Page: Editing Aboriginal Oral Texts*, edited by Laura J. Murray and Keren Rice, 97–119. Toronto: University of Toronto Press, 1999.

Curtin, Joanne A. "The Evidence from Gabriola." *The Midden* 31, no. 2 (1999): 3–4.

Daly, Richard. *Our Box Was Full: An Ethnography for the Delgamuukw Plaintiffs*. Vancouver: University of British Columbia Press, 2005.

Darnell, Regna. "2009 Presidential Address: What is 'History'? An Anthropologist's Eye View." *Ethnohistory* 58, no. 2 (Spring 2011): 213–27.

Deloria, Philip J. *Indians in Unexpected Places*. Lawrence, KS: University of Kansas Press, 2004.

Deloria, Vince. *Dr. Custer Died for Your Sins; an Indian Manifesto*. London: Macmillan, 1969.

DeMallie, Raymond J. "'These Have No Ears': Narrative and Ethnohistorical Method." *Ethnohistory* 40, no.4 (1993): 515–38.

Dewhirst, John. "Coast Salish Summer Festivals: Rituals for Upgrading Social Identity." *Anthropologica*, New Series, 18, no. 2 (1976): 231–73.

Dippie, Brian W. *The Vanishing American: White Attitudes and U.S. Indian Policy*. Lawrence, KS: University of Kansas Press, 1982.

Doerfler, Jill. "Recent Works in North American Biography and Ethnography." *Ethnohistory* 55, no. 2 (2008): 331–4.

Downey, Allan, and Susan Neylan. "Raven Plays Ball: Situating 'Indian Sports Days' within Indigenous and Colonial Spaces in Twentieth-Century Coastal British Columbia." *Canadian Journal of History* 50, no. 3 (2015): 442–68.

Drees, Laurie Meijer. *Healing Histories: Stories from Canada's Indian Hospitals*. Edmonton: University of Alberta Press, 2013.

Dréze, Jean, and Amartya Sen. *Hunger and Public Action*. New York: Oxford University Press, 1989.

Duff, Wilson. *The Indian History of British Columbia: The Impact of the White Man*. Anthropology in British Columbia Memoir No. 5. Victoria: Royal British Columbia Museum, 1964.

———. *The Upper Stalo Indians of the Fraser Valley British Columbia*. Anthropology in British Columbia Memoir No. 1. Victoria: British Columbia Provincial Museum, 1952.

Edmonds, Penelope. *Urbanizing Frontiers: Indigenous Peoples and Settlers in 19th-century Pacific Rim Cities*. Vancouver: University of British Columbia Press, 2010.

Eells, Myron. *The Indians of Puget Sound, the Notebooks of Myron Eells*. Edited by George Castille. Seattle: University of Washington Press, 1985.

Escobar, Arturo. "Worlds and Knowledges Otherwise." In *Globalization and the Decolonial Option*, edited by Walter Mignolo and Arturo Escobar. Abingdon: Routledge, 2010.

España-Maram, Linda. *Creating Masculinity in Los Angeles's Little Manila: Working-Class Filipinos and Popular Culture, 1920–1950s.* New York: Columbia University Press, 2006.

Fehr, Amanda. "Relationships: A Study of Memory, Change, and Identity at a Place Called I:yem." *University of the Fraser Valley Research Review* 2, no. 2 (April 2009): 9–35.

———. "A Subversive Sincerity: Christian Gatherings and Political Opportunities in S'ólh Téméxw." In *Mixed Blessings: Indigenous Encounters with Christianity in Canada*, edited by Tolly Bradford and Chelsea Horton, 61–82. Vancouver: University of British Columbia Press, 2016.

Fisher, Robin. *Contact and Conflict: Indian-European Relations in British Columbia, 1774–1890.* Vancouver: University of British Columbia Press, 1977.

Fixio, Donald. "Methodologies in Reconstructing Native American History." In *Rethinking American Indian History*, edited by Donald Fixio, 117–30. Albuquerque: University of New Mexico Press, 1997.

Fogelson, Raymond. "Epilogue." In *Transforming Ethnohistories: Narrative, Meaning, and Community*, edited by Sebastian Felix Braun, 222–32. Norman: University of Oklahoma Press, 2013.

———. "The Ethnohistory of Events and Non-events." *Ethnohistory* 36, no. 2 (1989): 133–48.

Forsyth, Janice. "Bodies of Meaning: Sports and Games at Canadian Residential Schools." In *Aboriginal Peoples and Sport in Canada: Historical Foundations and Contemporary Issues*, edited by Janice Forsyth and Audrey R. Giles, 15–34. Vancouver: University of British Columbia Press, 2013.

———, and Audrey R. Giles, eds. *Aboriginal Peoples and Sport in Canada: Historical Foundations and Contemporary Issues.* Vancouver: University of British Columbia Press, 2013.

Foucault, Michel. *Power/Knowledge: Selected Interviews and Other Writings, 1972–1977.* Edited by Colin Gordon. New York: Pantheon Books, 1981.

Frank, Gloria Jean. "'That's My Dinner on Display': A First Nations Reflection on Museum Culture." *BC Studies* 125/126 (Spring/Summer 2000): 163–78.

Galloway, Brent. *Dictionary of Upriver Halkomelem*, Berkley: University of California Press, 2009. Available online at http://escholarship.org/uc/item/65r158r4.

———. "The Upriver Language Program at Coqualeetza." *Human Organization* 47, no. 4 (Winter 1988): 291–7.

Gaudry, Adam. "Insurgent Research." *Wicazo Sa Review* 26 (2011): 113–36.

———. "Researching the Resurgence: Insurgent Research and Community-engaged Methodologies in Twenty-First Century Academic Inquiry." In *Research as Resistance: Critical, Indigenous, and Anti-Oppressive Approaches*, 2nd ed., edited by Leslie Brown and Susan Strega, 243–65. Toronto: Canadian Scholars Press, 2015.

Gavigan, Shelley A. *Hunger, Horses, and Government Men: Criminal Law on the Aboriginal Plains, 1870–1905.* Vancouver: University of British Columbia Press, 2012.

Geertz, Clifford. "Deep Play: Notes on the Balinese Cockfight." *Daedalus* 134 (Fall 2005): 56–86. Accessed 9 October 2013. http://www.jstor.org/stable/20028014.

————. "Thick Description: Toward an Interpretive Theory of Culture." In *Interpretation of Cultures, Selected Essays*, 3–30. New York: Basic Books, 1973.

Glavin, Terry, and the Students of St. Mary's. *Amongst God's Own: The Enduring Legacies of St. Mary's Mission*. Mission, BC: Longhouse Publishing, 2002.

Goodyear, Frank H. Jr. Foreword to *Away From Home: American Indian Boarding School Experiences, 1879–2000*. Edited by Margaret Archuleta, Brenda J. Child, and K. Tsianina Lomawaima. Phoenix: Heard Museum, 2000.

Green, Lesley Fordred, and David R. Green. "From Chronological to Spatio-Temporal Histories: Mapping Heritage in Arukwa, Area Indigena Do Uaca Brazil." *History and Anthropology* 14, no. 3 (2003): 289–95.

Gupta, Akhil, and James Ferguson. "Culture, Power, Place: Ethnography at the End of an Era." In *Culture, Power, Place: Explorations in Critical Anthropology*, edited by Akhil Gupta and James Ferguson, 1–29. Durham, NC: Duke University Press, 1997.

Harkin, Michael. *Dialogues of History: Transformations and Change in Heiltsuk Culture, 1790–1920*. Chicago: University of Chicago, 1988.

————. "Ethnohistory's Ethnohistory: Creating a Discipline from the Ground Up." *Social Science History* 34, no. 2 (Summer 2010): 113–28.

————. *The Heiltsuks: Dialogues of Culture and History on the Northwest Coast*. Lincoln, NE: University of Nebraska Press, 1997.

Harmon, Alexandra. "Coast Salish History." In *Be of Good Mind: Essays on the Coast Salish*, edited by Bruce G. Miller, 30–54. Vancouver: University of British Columbia Press, 2007.

————. *Indians in the Making: Ethnic Relations and Indian Identities around Puget Sound*. Berkeley: University of California Press, 1998.

Harris, Cole. *Making Native Space: Colonialism, Resistance and Reserves in British Columbia*. Vancouver: University of British Columbia Press, 2002.

Harris, Douglas C. *Fish, Law, and Colonialism: The Legal Capture of Salmon in British Columbia*. Toronto: University of Toronto Press, 2001.

————. *Landing Native Fisheries: Indian Reserves and Fishing Rights in British Columbia, 1849–1925*. Vancouver: University of British Columbia Press, 2008.

Haubsbaum, Eric, and Terence Ranger, eds. *The Invention of Tradition*. Cambridge: Cambridge University Press, 1984.

Hill-Tout, Charles. "Prehistoric Mounds of British Columbia." *Museum and Art Notes* 4 (December 1930): 120–6.

————. *The Salish People: The Local Contribution of Charles Hill-Tout, Vol. II: The Squamish and the Lilloet*, edited by Ralph Maud. Vancouver: Talonbooks, 1978.

Hodgson, Corinne. "The Social and Political Implications of Tuberculosis Among Native Canadians." *Canadian Review of Sociology* 30, no. 4 (1993): 502–12.

Hoffman, Alice M., and Howard S. Hoffman. "Reliability and Validity in Oral History: The Case for Memory." In *Memory and History: Essays on Recalling and Interpreting Experience*, edited by Jaclyn Jeffrey and Glenace Edwall, 107–30. Lanham, MD: University Press of America, 1994.

Hoover, Alan. "A Response to Gloria Jean Frank." *BC Studies* 125/126 (Spring/Summer 2000): 65–69.

Howay, F.W. "The Dog's Hair Blankets of the Coast Salish." *Western Historical Quarterly* 9 (April 1918): 83–92.

———. "The First Use of Sail by the Indians of the Northwest Coast." *American Neptune* 1 (October 1941): 374–80.

———. "Indian Attacks Upon Maritime Traders of the North-west Coast, 1785–1805." *Canadian Historical Review* 6, no. 4 (1925): 287–309.

Hymes, Dell H. *Now I Know Only So Far: Essays in Ethnopoetics.* Lincoln, NE: University of Nebraska Press, 2003.

Iacovetta, Franca, Valerie J. Korinek, and Marlene Epp, eds. *Edible Histories, Cultural Politics: Towards a Canadian Food History.* Toronto: University of Toronto Press, 2012.

Ishioka, Tomonori. "Boxing, Poverty, Foreseeability–An Ethnographic Account of Local Boxers in Metro Manila, Philippines." *Asia Pacific Journal of Sport and Social Science* 1, no. 2 (2013): 143–55.

Jenness, Diamond. *Faith of a Coast Salish Indian.* Anthropology in British Columbia Memoir No. 3. Victoria, BC: British Columbia Provincial Museum, 1955.

Johnson, Leslie Main. "Aboriginal Burning for Vegetation Management in Northwest British Columbia." In *Indians, Fire, and the Land in the Pacific Northwest*, edited by Robert Boyd, 238–54. Corvallis: Oregon State University Press, 1999.

Justice, Daniel Heath. "'Go Away Water!': Kinship Criticism and the Decolonization Imperative." In *Reasoning Together: The Native Critics Collective*, edited by Craig S. Womack, Daniel Heath Justice, and Christopher B. Teuton, 147–68. Norman: University of Oklahoma Press, 2008.

Kan, Sergei, and Pauline Turner Strong. *New Perspectives on Native North America.* Lincoln, NE: University of Nebraska Press, 2006.

Kelm, Mary-Ellen. *Colonizing Bodies: Aboriginal Health and Healing in British Columbia, 1900–50.* Vancouver: University of British Columbia Press, 1998.

Kew, Michael J., and Bruce G. Miller. "Locating Aboriginal Governments in the Political Landscape." In *Seeking Sustainability in the Lower Fraser Basin: Issues and Choices*, edited by Michael Healey, 47–63. Vancouver: Institute for Resource and the Environment/Westwater Research 1999.

King, Thomas. *The Truth About Stories: A Native Narrative.* Toronto: House of Anansi Press, 2003.

Knickerbocker, Madeline Rose. "'What We've Said Can be Proven in the Ground': Stó:lō Sovereignty and Historical Narratives at XA:YTEM, 1990–2006." *Journal of the Canadian Historical Association* 24, no. 1 (2013): 297–342.

Knight, Rolf. *Indians at Work: An Informal History of Native Indian Labour in British Columbia, 1858–1930.* Vancouver: New Star, 1972.

Kovach, Margaret. *Indigenous Methodologies: Characteristics, Conversations, and Context.* Toronto: University of Toronto Press, 2009.

Laclau, Ernesto, and Chantal Mouffe. *Hegemony and Socialist Strategy: Towards a Radical Democratic Politics.* London: Verso, 2001.

Laforet, Andrea, and Annie York. *Spuzzum: Fraser Canyon Histories, 1808–1939.* Vancouver: University of British Columbia Press, 1998.

Laliberte, David J. "Natives, Neighbors, and the National Game: Baseball at the Pipestone Indian Training School." *Minnesota History* 62, no. 2 (2010): 60–9.

Langbein, John H. "Albion's Fatal Flaws." *Past & Present* 98 (1983): 96–120.

Lepofsky, Dana, Michael Blake, Douglas Brown, et al. "The Archaeology of the Scowlitz Site, SW British Columbia." *Journal of Field Archaeology* 27, no. 4 (2000): 391–416.

———, David Schaepe, Anthony Graesch, et al. "Exploring Stó:lō-Coast Salish Interaction and Identity in Ancient Houses and Settlements in the Fraser Valley, British Columbia." *American Antiquity* 74, no. 4 (2009): 595–626.

Lomawaima, K. Tsianina, and Teresa L. McCarty. "When Tribal Sovereignty Challenges Democracy: American Indian Education and the Democratic Ideal." *American Educational Research Journal* 39, no. 2 (2002): 279–305.

Louis, Emery. "B.C. Indians Top Boxers." *Indian World* 3, no.1 (1980): 46.

Lutz, John Sutton. "Making 'Indians' in British Columbia: Power, Race and the Importance of Place." In *Power and Place in the North American West*, edited by John Finlay and Richard White, 61–86. Seattle: University of Washington Press, 1999.

———. *Makúk: A New History of Aboriginal-White Relations*. Vancouver: University of British Columbia Press, 2008.

———, ed. *Myth and Memory: Stories of Indigenous-European Contact*. Vancouver: University of British Columbia Press, 2007.

Lux, Maureen K. "Care for the 'Racially Careless': Indian Hospitals in the Canadian West, 1920–1950s." *Canadian Historical Review* 91, no. 3 (September 2010): 407–34.

———. *Medicine That Walks: Disease, Medicine, and Canadian Plains Native People, 1880–1940*. Toronto: University of Toronto Press, 2001.

———. *Separate Beds: A History of Indian Hospitals in Canada, 1920s–1980s*. Toronto: University of Toronto Press, 2016.

MacDonald, Katya C. "Crossing Paths: Knowing and Navigating Paths of Access to Stó:lō Fishing Sites." *University of the Fraser Valley Research Review* 2, no. 2 (2009): 36–53.

Macdonald, Sharon, and Katja Fausser. "Towards European Historical Consciousness." In *Approaches to European Historical Consciousness*, edited by Sharon Macdonald, 9–30. Hamburg: Koerber Stiftung, 2000.

Madison, D. Soyini. *Critical Ethnography: Method, Ethics, and Performance*. Thousand Oaks, CA: Sage, 2005.

———. *Critical Ethnography: Method, Ethics, and Performance* 2nd ed. Thousand Oaks, CA: Sage, 2012.

Maracle, Lee. *Bobbi Lee: Indian Rebel. Struggles of a Native Canadian Woman*. Richmond, BC: LSM Press, 1975.

———. "Towards a National Literature: 'A Body of Writing.'" In *Across Cultures/Across Borders: Canadian Aboriginal and Native American Literatures*, edited by Paul DePasquale, Renate Eigenbrod, and Emma LaRocque, 77–96. Peterborough: Broadview, 2010.

Matson, Richard G. and Gary Coupland. *Prehistory of the Northwest Coast*. San Diego: Academic Press, 1995.

Mauzé, Marie, Michael E. Harkin, and Sergei Kan, eds. *Coming to Shore: Northwest Coast Ethnology, Traditions, and Visions*. Lincoln, NE: University of Nebraska Press, 2004.

Mawani, Renisa. *Colonial Proximities: Crossracial Encounters and Juridicial Truths in British Columbia, 1871–1921*. Vancouver: University of British Columbia Press, 2009.

McHalsie, Albert "Sonny." "Are the Spirits Addicted?" *Sqwelqwel: Stó:lō Tribal Council Newsletter* (May/June, 1993): Section T.

———. "Halq'emélem Place Names in Stó:lō Territory." In *A Stó:lō-Coast Salish Historical Atlas*, edited by Keith Thor Carlson, David Schaepe, Albert "Sonny" McHalsie, et al., 134–53. Vancouver: Douglas and McIntyre/Chilliwack: Stó:lō Heritage Trust, 2001.

———. "We Have to Take Care of Everything that Belongs to Us." In *Be of Good Mind: Essays on the Coast Salish*, edited by Bruce G. Miller, 82–130. Vancouver: University of British Columbia Press, 2007.

McIlwraith, Thomas. "The Problem of Imported Culture: The Construction of Contemporary Stó:lō Identity." *American Indian Culture and Research Journal* 20, no. 4 (1996): 41–70.

McIvor, Dorothy Matheson. *Coqualeetza: "Vestiga Nulla Retorsum (No Backward Step)."* William's Lake, BC: Blue Door Publishing, 2001.

Menzies, Charles R., and Caroline F. Butler. "Working in the Woods: Tsimshian Resource Workers and the Forest Industry of British Columbia." *American Indian Quarterly* 25, no. 3 (2001): 409–30.

Meuli, Jonathan. *Shadowhouse*. Amsterdam: Harwood Academic Publishers, 2001.

Meyers, Fred R. "Ways of Placemaking." In *Cultural Landscapes and the Environment*, edited by Kate Flint and Howard Morphy. Oxford: Oxford University Press, 2000.

Mignolo, Walter. "Delinking." *Cultural Studies* 21, no. 2 (2007): 449–514.

Miller, Bruce G., ed. *Be of Good Mind: Essays on the Coast Salish*. Vancouver: University of British Columbia Press, 2007.

———. *The Problem of Justice: Tradition and Law in the Coast Salish World*. Lincoln, NE: University of Nebraska Press, 2002.

———. "The 'Really Real' Border and the Divided Salish Community." *BC Studies* 112 (1996–1997): 63–79.

Miller, Christopher, and George Hammell. "A New Perspective on Indian-White Contact: Cultural Symbols and Colonial Trade." *Journal of American History* 73, no. 2 (1986): 311–28.

Miller, Jay. *Lushootseed Culture and the Shamanic Odyssey: An Anchored Radiance*. Lincoln, NE: University of Nebraska Press, 1999.

———. "Tsimshian Ethno-Ethnohistory: A 'Real' Indigenous Chronology." *Ethnohistory* 45, no. 4 (1998): 657–74.

Miller, J.R. *Shingwauk's Vision: A History of Native Residential Schools*. Toronto: University of Toronto Press, 1996.

———. *Skyscrapers Hide the Heavens: A History of Indian-White Relations in Canada*, 3rd ed. Toronto: University of Toronto Press, 2000.

Nadasdy, Paul. *Hunters and Bureaucrats: Power, Knowledge, and Aboriginal-State Relations in the Southwest Yukon*. Vancouver: University of British Columbia Press, 2003.

Narayan, Kirin. "How Native Is a 'Native' Anthropologist?" *American Anthropologist* 95, no. 3 (1993): 671–86.

Newell, Dianne. *Tangled Webs of History: Indians and the Law in Canada's Pacific Coast Fisheries*. Toronto: University of Toronto Press, 1993.

Nicholas, George P. "Decolonizing the Archaeological Landscape: The practice and politics of archaeology in British Columbia." *The American Indian Quarterly* 30 no.3/4 (2006): 350–80.

———, and Thomas D. Andrews. "Indigenous Archaeology in a Postmodern World." In *At a Crossroads: Archaeology and First Peoples in Canada*, edited by George P. Nicholas and Thomas D. Andrews, 1–18. Burnaby, BC: Archaeology Press, 1997.

Norman, Alison. "'Fit for the Table of the Most Fastidious Epicure': Culinary Colonialism in the Upper Canadian Contact Zone." In *Edible Histories, Cultural Politics: Towards a Canadian Food History*, edited by Franca Iacovetta, Valerie J. Korinek, and Marlene Epp, 31–51. Toronto: University of Toronto Press, 2012.

Obeyesekere, Gananath. *The Apotheosis of Captain Cook: European Myth-making in the Pacific*. Princeton: Princeton University Press, 1992.

Parnaby, Andrew. "'The best men that ever worked the lumber': Aboriginal Longshoremen on Burrard Inlet, BC, 1863–1939." *The Canadian Historical Review* 87, no. 1 (2006): 53–78.

Peavy, Linda, and Ursula Smith. "World Champions: The 1904 Girls' Basketball Team from Fort Shaw Indian Boarding School." *Montana: The Magazine of Western History* 51, no. 4 (2001): 2–25.

Pennier, Henry. *Call me Hank: A Stó:lō Man's Reflections on Logging, Living, and Growing Old*, edited by Keith Carlson and Kristina Fagan. Toronto: University of Toronto Press, 2006.

Pettipas, Katherine. *Severing the Ties That Bind: Government Repression of Indigenous Religious Ceremonies on the Prairies*. Winnipeg: University of Manitoba Press, 1994.

Phillips, Mark Salber, and Gordon Schochet, eds. *Questions of Tradition*. Toronto: University of Toronto Press, 2004.

Purvis, Ron. *T'Shama, is an Indian Word Loosely Meaning "White Man, Staff, or Authority."* Surrey, BC: Heritage House Publishing Company Ltd., 1994.

Raibmon, Paige. *Authentic Indians*. Durham, NC: Duke University Press, 2005.

Ray, Arthur. *Telling It to the Judge: Taking Native History to Court*. Montreal: McGill-Queen's University Press, 2012.

Rice, Eugene. "Ernest Boyer's 'Scholarship of Engagement' in Retrospect." *Journal of Higher Education Outreach and Engagement* 20, no. 1 (2016): 29–33.

Roth, Christopher. "'The Names Spread in All Directions': Hereditary Titles in Tsimshian Social and Political Life." *BC Studies* 130 (2001): 69–92.

Rozin, Paul. "Why We Eat What We Eat, and Why We Worry About It." *Bulletin of the American Academy of Arts and Sciences* 50, no. 5 (1997): 26–48.

Sahlins, Marshall. "Comments." In Robert Borofsky's "Cook, Lono, Obeyeskere, and Sahlins: Forum on Theory in Anthropology." *Current Anthropology* 38, no. 2 (April 1997): 271.

———. *Historical Metaphors and Mythical Realities: Structure in the Early History of the Sandwich Island Kingdom*. Ann Arbor: University of Michigan Press, 1981.

———. *How "Natives" Think: About Captain Cook, for Example*. Chicago: University of Chicago Press, 1995.

———. *Islands of History*. Chicago: University of Chicago Press, 1985.

Santos-Granero, Fernando. "Writing History into the Landscape: Space, Myth, and Ritual in Contemporary Amazonia." *American Ethnologist* 25, no. 2 (1998): 128–48.

Saywell, John. *Canadian Annual Review of Politics and Public Affairs 1969*. Toronto: University of Toronto Press, 1970.

Schaepe, David M. "Rock Fortifications: Archaeological Insights Into Pre-contact Warfare and Sociopolitical Organization Among the Stó:lō of the Lower Fraser River Canyon, B.C." *American Antiquity* 71, no. 4 (October 2006): 671–705.

———. "Rock Wall Fortifications: Reconstructing a Fraser Canyon Defensive Network." In *A Stó:lō-Coast Salish Historical Atlas*, edited by Keith Thor Carlson, David Schaepe, Albert "Sonny" McHalsie, et al., 52–53. Vancouver: Douglas and McIntyre/Chilliwack: Stó:lō Heritage Trust, 2001.

———. "Stó:lō Identity and the Cultural Landscape of S'ólh Téméxw." In *Be of Good Mind: Essays on the Coast Salish*, edited by Bruce G. Miller, 234–59. Vancouver: University of British Columbia Press, 2007.

Scott, James C. *Seeing Like a State: How Certain Schemes to Improve the Human Condition Have Failed*. New Haven: Yale University Press, 1999.

Seixas, Peter. "Introduction." In *Theorizing Historical Consciousness*, edited by Peter Seixas. Toronto: University of Toronto Press, 2004.

———, ed. *Theorizing Historical Consciousness*. Toronto: University of Toronto Press, 2004.

Sellars, Bev. *They Called Me Number One: Secrets and Survival at an Indian Residential School*. Vancouver: Talonbooks, 2013.

Sheehan, Rebecca. "'Little Giants of the Ring': Fighting Race and Making Men on the Australia-Philippines Boxing Circuit, 1919–1923." *Sport in Society* 15, no. 4 (2012): 447–61.

Sider, Gerald, and Gavin Smith. "Introduction." In *Between History and Histories: The Making of Silences and Commemorations*, edited by Gerald Sider and Gavin Smith, 3–28. Toronto: University of Toronto Press, 1997.

Sioui, Georges. *For an Amerindian Autohistory: An Essay on the Foundations of a Social Ethic*. Montreal: McGill-Queen's University Press, 1992.

Sleigh, Daphne. *The Man Who Saved Vancouver: Major James Skitt Matthews*. Vancouver: Heritage House, 2008.

Smith, Harlan, and Gerald Fowke. *Cairns of British Columbia and Washington*. Memoir of the American Museum of Natural History, Vol. II, Part II. New York: American Museum of Natural History: 1901.

Smith, Keith D. *Liberalism, Surveillance, and Resistance: Indigenous Communities in Western Canada, 1877–1927*. Edmonton: Athabasca University Press, 2009.

Smith, Linda Tuhiwai. "Culture Matters in the Knowledge Economy." In *Interrogating Development: Insights from the Margins*, edited by Frédérique Apffel-Marglin,

Sanjay Kumar, and Arvind Mishra, 217–33. New Delhi: Oxford University Press, 2010.

———. *Decolonizing Methodologies: Research and Indigenous Peoples*. London: Zed Books/Dunedin: University of Otago Press, 1999.

Soucy, Alexander. "The Problem with Key Informants." *Anthropological Forum* 10, no. 2 (2000): 179–99.

Stewart, Hilary. *Cedar: Tree of Life to the Northwest Coast Indians*. Vancouver: Douglas and McIntyre, 1984.

Stogan, Vince. "When I came home my Elders taught us that all the people who have passed on are still around us." In *In the Words of Elders: Aboriginal Cultures in Transition*, edited by Peter Kulchyski, Don McCaskill, and David Newhouse, 443–58. Toronto: University of Toronto Press, 1999.

Suttles, Wayne. "Affinal Ties, Subsistence and Prestige among the Coast Salish." In *Coast Salish Essays*, edited by Wayne Suttles, 15–25. 1972. Reprint, Vancouver: Talonbooks, 1987.

———. "Central Coast Salish." In *Handbook of North American Indians*, edited by William Sturtevant, 453–75. Washington: Smithsonian Institute, 1990.

———. "The Early Diffusion of the Potato among the Coast Salish." *Southwestern Journal of Anthropology* 7, no. 3 (Autumn 1951): 272–88.

———. "Katzie Ethnographic Notes." In Anthropology in British Columbia, Memoir No. 2, edited by W. Duff. Victoria: British Columbia Provincial Museum, 1955.

———. "The Persistence of Intervillage Ties." In *Coast Salish Essays*, edited by Wayne Suttles, 209–30. 1972. Reprint, Vancouver: Talonbooks, 1987.

———. "Post-contact Change Among the Lummi Indians." *British Columbia Historical Quarterly* 18, no. 1–2 (January–April 1954): 29–102.

———. "Private Knowledge, Morality, and Social Classes among the Coast Salish." In *Coast Salish Essays*, edited by Wayne Suttles, 3–14. 1972. Reprint, Vancouver: Talonbooks, 1987.

Tanner, Helen Hornbeck. "In the Arena: An Expert Witness View of the Indian Claims Commission." In *Beyond Red Power: American Indian Politics and Activism since 1900*, edited by Daniel M. Cobb and Loretta Fowler, 178–200. Santa Fe: SAR Press, 2007.

Tapp, Anne R. "'Mecca of Oriental Pugdom': Philippine Boxing 1898–1921." *Pilipinas: A Journal of Philippine Studies* 27 (1996): 21, 26–7.

———. "Under Flickering Shadows: The Boxing Career of Gaudencio Cabanela." *Pilipinas: A Journal of Philippine Studies* 31 (1998): 97–113.

Tedlock, Denis. *The Spoken Word and the Work of Interpretation*. Philadelphia: University of Pennsylvania Press, 1983.

Teit, James A. "Tales from the Lower Fraser River." In *Memoirs of the American Folklore Society*, XI (1917): 129–34.

Tennant, Paul. *Aboriginal People and Politics: The Indian Land Question in British Columbia, 1849–1989*. Vancouver: University of British Columbia Press, 1990.

Theodoratus, Robert J. "Loss, Transfer, and Reintroduction in the Use of Wild Plant Foods in the Upper Skagit Valley." *Northwest Anthropological Research Notes* 23, no. 1 (1988): 35–52.

Thom, Brian. "The Marpole-Late Transition in the Gulf of Georgia Region." *The Midden* 30, no. 2 (1998): 2–7.

———. *Stó:lō Traditional Culture: A Short Ethnography of the Stó:lō People*. Chilliwack, BC: Stó:lō Curriculum Consortium, 1996.

Turkel, William. *The Archive of Place: Unearthing the Pasts of Chilcotin Plateau*. Vancouver: University of British Columbia Press, 2007.

Turner, Nancy J. "'Time to Burn': Traditional Use of Fire to Enhance Resource Production by Aboriginal Peoples in British Columbia." In *Indians, Fire, and the Land in the Pacific Northwest*, edited by Robert Boyd, 185–218. Corvallis: Oregon State University Press, 1999.

Varacini, Lorenzo. *Settler Colonialism: A Theoretical Overview*. New York: Palgrave Macmillan, 2010.

Wagner, Henry R. *Spanish Explorations in the Strait of Juan de Fuca*. New York: AMS Press, 1971.

Waldram, James B. *Revenge of the Windigo: The Construction of the Mind and Mental Health of North American Aboriginal Peoples*. Toronto: University of Toronto Press, 2004.

Walters, Kristina. "'A National Priority': Nutrition Canada's *Survey* and the Disciplining of Aboriginal Bodies, 1964–1975." In *Edible Histories, Cultural Politics: Towards a Canadian Food History*, edited by Franca Iacovetta, Valerie J. Korinek, and Marlene Epp, 433–52. Toronto: University of Toronto Press, 2012.

Ware, Reuben M. *Five Issues, Five Battlegrounds: An Introduction to the History of Indian Fishing in British Columbia, 1850–1930*. Sardis, BC: Coqualeetza Education Training Centre, for the Stó:lō Nation, 1983.

Webber, Ellen. "An Old Kwanthum Village—Its People and Its Fall." *American Antiquarian and Oriental Journal* 21 (1999): 309–14.

Wells, Oliver N. *The Chilliwacks and Their Neighbours*. Edited by Ralph Maud, Brent Galloway and Marie Weeden. Vancouver: Talonbooks, 1987.

Wherrett, George Jasper. *The Miracle of Empty Beds: A History of Tuberculosis in Canada*. Toronto: University of Toronto Press, 1977.

White, Richard. *The Middle Ground: Indians, Empires, and Republics in the Great Lakes Region 1650–1815*. Cambridge: Cambridge University Press, 1991.

———. *The Organic Machine*. New York: Hill and Wang, 1995.

Wickwire, Wendy. "A Response to Alan Hoover." *BC Studies* 128 (Winter 2000/2001): 71–4.

Wiebe, Lesley. "Stó:lō Traditional Food 'Talk' as Metaphor for Cross-cultural Relations." *University of the Fraser Valley Research Review* 2, no. 2 (Spring 2009): 137–51.

Wike, Joyce A. "Problems in the Fur Trade Analysis: The Northwest Coast." *American Anthropologist* 60 (1958): 86–101.

Williams, Robert A. *Linking Arms Together: American Indian Treaty Visions of Law and Peace, 1600–1800*. New York: Oxford University Press, 1997.

Wilson, Angela Cavender. "Power of the Spoken Word: Native Oral Traditions in American Indian History." In *Rethinking American Indian History*, edited by Donald Fixio, 101–16. Albuquerque: University of New Mexico Press, 1997.

Wilson, Sean. *Research is Ceremony: Indigenous Research Methods*. Black Point, NS: Fernwood, 2008.

Wineburg, Sam. *Historical Thinking and Other Unnatural Acts*. Philadelphia: Temple University Press, 2001.

Wolfe, Patrick. "Settler Colonialism and the Elimination of the Native." *Journal of Genocidal Research* 8, no. 4 (December 2006): 387–409.

———. *Settler Colonialism and the Transformation of Anthropology: The Politics and Poetics of an Ethnographic Event*. New York: Cassell, 1999.

Wood, Jody. "Coqualeetza Legacy of Land Use." In *A Stó:lō-Coast Salish Historical Atlas*, edited by Keith Thor Carlson, David Schaepe, Albert "Sonny" McHalsie, et al., 74–75. Vancouver: Douglas and McIntyre/Chilliwack: Stó:lō Heritage Trust, 2001.

Wunder, John R. "Native American History, Ethnohistory, and Context." *Ethnohistory* 55, no. 2 (2008): 331–4.

CONTRIBUTORS

Ella Bedard is a historian-turned-law student committed to social justice and reconciliation. She came to the Ethnohistory Field School while completing a Master's in History at the University of Victoria. Ella's field school research was a life history of Stó:lō elder Matilda Gutierrez. That research inspired the essay included in this collection. What she appreciates most about the Field School and her time working for the Stó:lō is that it taught her to see natural landscapes as storied places full of social as well as natural history. She is currently studying law at Osgoode Hall University in her hometown, Toronto.

Keith Thor Carlson is Professor of History at the University of Saskatchewan where he holds the Research Chair in Indigenous and Community-Engaged History. He is the author of five books, including *The Power of Place, the Problem of Time: Aboriginal Collective Identity and Historical Consciousness in the Cauldron of Colonialism* (2010), the editor or co-editor of four additional books, including *The Stó:lō-Coast Salish Historical Atlas* (2001) and *Orality and Literacy: Reflections Across Disciplines* (2011), and with John Lutz and the Stó:lō Nation he oversees the only graduate-level humanities-based ethnohistory field school in North America. Keith is also the director of the Community-Engaged History Collaboratorium which provides paid summer internships to students interested in working in partnership with Indigenous and heritage organizations on original research projects the communities have identified and designed themselves.

Adar Charlton is a PhD student at the University of Saskatchewan in the Department of English under the supervision of Dr. Kristina Bidwell. She specializes in Indigenous literature and is preparing a dissertation on place-based identity in northwestern Ontario Anishinaabe literature. She came to the field school because of an interest in community-based scholarship and a decided lack of previous exposure in her humanities-based education. As a non-Indigenous scholar, she hopes that her work promotes respect, acknowledgement, and understanding of Indigenous presence on and rights to land.

Amanda Fehr is a settler Canadian from Saskatoon, Saskatchewan. She recently completed her PhD through the Department of History at the University of Saskatchewan. Her dissertation explores the intersections of religious and political expression during the twentieth century in Île-à-la-Crosse and the English River First Nation in Saskatchewan. She attended the Ethnohistory Field School in 2007 as a master's student interested in learning about oral history methodologies. Her field school paper became the basis for her master's thesis about the I:yem Memorial.

Adam Gaudry is a Metis Assistant Professor in the Faculty of Native Studies and Department of Political Science at the University of Alberta. His research is primarily concerned with nineteenth-century Metis political thought, the formation of a Metis–Canada treaty relationship in 1870, and the subsequent non-implementation of that agreement. This project argues for the ongoing existence a "Manitoba treaty" between the Metis people and Canada that necessitates the maintenance of a respectful and bilateral political relationship between treaty partners. This work is being revised into a book for publication. Adam also writes on matters of Metis identity, particularly the role of nationalism and peoplehood in informing Metis citizenship.

John Sutton Lutz is the chair and a professor in the Department of History at the University of Victoria with a research focus on the relations between Indigenous people and Europeans in the Pacific Northwest. He is the author of *Makúk: A New History of Native-White Relations* (2008) and editor of several volumes, including *Myth and Memory: Stories of Indigenous-European Contact* (2007) and *Making and Moving Knowledge: Interdisciplinary and Community-Based Research in a World on the Edge* (2008), co-director of the award-winning Great Unsolved Mysteries in Canadian History Internet project, and founding co-director of the Ethnohistory Field School with the Stó:lō.

A settler scholar from Saskatoon, **Katya C. MacDonald** defended her PhD dissertation in history at the University of Saskatchewan in the summer of 2017. Her dissertation research explores processes of making handmade items and their socioeconomic histories in Île-à-la-Crosse, Saskatchewan, and Sliammon, British Columbia. She attended the field school in 2007. The experience was one of her first introductions to community-engaged scholarship and oral histories, and her field school project informed her MA thesis, which focused, in part, on community histories of the politically Stó:lō community of Seabird Island.

Kathryn McKay is currently working on her PhD, "Unsettled Minds: Race and Rural Madness in British Columbia, 1900–50." She attended the Stó:lō Ethnohistory Field School in 2000 as part of her MA coursework and expanded her work on burial traditions into her master's thesis, "Recycling the Soul: Death and the Continuity of Life in the Coast Salish Burial Practices" in 2002.

A Calgarian temporarily residing in Saskatoon, **Chris Marsh** is a PhD candidate at the University of Saskatchewan presently writing his dissertation on North West Mounted Police-Niitsitapi (Blackfoot) community relations from 1886 to 1920. It also examines the development, structure, and function of the Indian Police Scout system in southern Alberta. Overall, Chris is interested in Native-newcomer history and police history across the Canadian and American Wests. He participated in the 2015 Ethnohistory Field School to gain experience in working with First Nations communities and to acquire practical experience in the methodology of oral history.

A former resident of Chilliwack, **Noah E. Miller** attended the 2015 Ethnohistory Field School as an MA candidate at the University of Victoria. His primary research programme examines the nature of the relationship between judge and jury in the 1889 trial of Florence Maybrick. He completed his BA (Hons.) in Law and Society at the University of Calgary in 2011 and holds certificates in Teaching and Learning in Higher Education (University of Victoria) as well as Teaching English as a Foreign Language (University of Toronto).

Naxaxalhts'i, also known as Dr. **Albert "Sonny" McHalsie**, is a historical researcher and cultural interpreter who is employed as Sx̱weyx̱weyá:m (Historian)/Cultural Advisor for the Stó:lō Research and Resource Management Centre in Chilliwack, British Columbia. Sonny has a strong publication record, including the foreword to Keith Carlson's *The Power of Place, the Problem of Time* (2010) and a chapter in Bruce G. Miller's *Be of Good Mind* (2008). Earlier, he served as co-editor and contributing author to *A Stó:lō-Coast Salish Historical Atlas* (2001), and contributor to *You Are Asked To Witness: The Stó:lō in Canada's Pacific Coast History* (1996). Sonny is also co-author of the book *"I am Stó:lō!": Katherine Explores Her Heritage* (1997). Sonny offers interpretive narrated tours of Stó:lō territory where he discusses how Halq'eméylem place names define Stó:lō rights and title and the unique relationship the Stó:lō maintain to their land and resources. He is a member of the Shxw'ōwhámél First Nation, and is a proud father and grandfather. He continues to fish at his ancestral fishing ground at Aseláw, located within the Stó:lō Fishery in the lower Fraser Canyon.

Colin Osmond is a PhD student at the University of Saskatchewan. He examines the changing social and racial conceptions of identity that developed between Coast Salish people and settler societies in the twentieth century. Using ethnohistorical methodology and oral history, he works closely with Coast Salish communities to listen and learn their history, and aims to design projects that meet community needs and interests. Colin attended the Stó:lō field school after learning the importance of community-based fieldwork at a previous field school (in Sliammon, British Columbia). Born and raised in Nova Scotia, Colin lives with his wife and son in Saskatoon, Saskatchewan.

David Schaepe is the Director and Senior Archaeologist of the Stó:lō Research and Resource Management Centre at Stó:lō Nation. He has worked for over fifteen years as a community-based researcher addressing issues of Aboriginal rights and title, heritage management policy and practice, repatriation, land-use planning, archaeological research, and education and outreach. He earned his PhD in anthropology from the University of British Columbia in 2009. In addition to working at Stó:lō Nation, he is an adjunct professor in Simon Fraser University's School of Resource and Environmental Management, and an instructor of Indigenous Studies at the University of the Fraser Valley. His research interests are multidisciplinary in nature and include household archaeology, oral history, Stó:lō-Coast Salish settlement patterning and community organization, cultural landscape management, and issues of Aboriginal rights and title. Schaepe has over twenty-five years of experience in archaeology/anthropology and cultural heritage research and resource management.

Anastasia Tataryn is currently a Lecturer in Law, University of Liverpool, UK. The unpredictable journey that brought her here was greatly influenced by an offer that came in her final year of an Honours BA at the University of Saskatchewan—the opportunity to participate in the Ethnohistory Field School. The spark of exploring living identity, with all its messy complexities, was ignited. What followed included a stint in professional training in contemporary dance, an MA in History at York University, an LLM at Osgoode Hall, and a PhD in Law at Birkbeck, University of London. Anastasia's current research bridges poststructuralism and decolonizing theory with analyses of social transformation in post-revolution Ukraine, and she is currently working on a monograph with Routledge, *Law, Migration and Labour: Ecotechnics and the Limits of Legal Subjectivity.*

Lesley Wiebe is a grade four teacher and fine-art photographer originally from Lashburn, Saskatchewan. She completed her Bachelor of Education

(2004) and Bachelor of Arts (2006) degrees at the University of Alberta, and received a Master's of Arts in History (2014) from the University of Saskatchewan. In 2007, she attended the joint University of Victoria and University of Saskatchewan Ethnohistory Field School as a part of her master's coursework. She currently lives with her husband, Adam Wiebe, and Labrador retriever, Cinder.